GREEN WEALTH

CONTEMPORARY STUDIES IN ECONOMIC AND FINANCIAL ANALYSIS

Series Editor: Simon Grima

Volume 109A:	The New Digital Era: Digitalisation and Emerging Risks and Opportunities
	Edited by Simon Grima, Ercan Ozen, and Hakan Boz
Volume 109B:	The New Digital Era: Digitalisation and Emerging Risks and Opportunities
	Edited by Simon Grima, Ercan Ozen, and Hakan Boz
Volume 110A:	Smart Analytics, Artificial Intelligence and Sustainable Performance Management in a Global Digitalised Economy
	Edited by Pallavi Tyagi, Simon Grima, Kiran Sood, B. Balamurugan, Ercan Ozen, and Thalassinos Eleftherios
Volume 110B:	Smart Analytics, Artificial Intelligence and Sustainable Performance Management in a Global Digitalised Economy
	Edited by Pallavi Tyagi, Simon Grima, Kiran Sood, B. Balamurugan, Ercan Ozen, and Thalassinos Eleftherios
Volume 111A:	Smart Analytics, Artificial Intelligence and Sustainable Performance Management in a Global Digitalised Economy
	Edited by Pallavi Tyagi, Simon Grima, Kiran Sood, B. Balamurugan, Ercan Ozen and Thalassinos Eleftherios
Volume 111B:	Digital Transformation, Strategic Resilience, Cyber Security and Risk Management
	Edited by Simon Grima, Eleftherios Thalassinos, Grațiela-Georgiana Noja, Theodore V. Stamataopoulos, Tatjana Vasiljeva, and Tatjana Volkova
Volume 111C:	Digital Transformation, Strategic Resilience, Cyber Security and Risk Management
	Edited by Kiran Sood, B. Balamurugan, and Simon Grima
Volume 112A:	Contemporary Challenges in Social Science Management: Skills Gaps and Shortages in the Labour Market, Part A
	Edited by Anne Marie Thake, Kiran Sood, Ercan Özen, and Simon Grima
Volume 112B:	Contemporary Challenges in Social Science Management: Skills Gaps and Shortages in the Labour Market, Part B
	Edited by Anne Marie Thake, Simon Grima, Ercan Özen, and Kiran Sood
Volume 113A:	Sustainable Development Goals: The Impact of Sustainability Measures on Wellbeing, Part A
	Edited by Ridhima Sharma, Indira Bhardwaj, Simon Grima, Timcy Sachdeva, Kiran Sood, and Ercan Özen
Volume 113B:	Sustainable Development Goals: The Impact of Sustainability Measures on Wellbeing, Part B
	Edited by Ridhima Sharma, Indira Bhardwaj, Simon Grima, Timcy Sachdeva, Kiran Sood, and Ercan Özen
Volume 114:	Sustainability Development through Green Economics
	Edited by Sanjay Taneja, Pawan Kumar, Reepu, Balamurugan Balusamy, Kiran Sood, and Simon Grima.
Volume 115:	Economic Development and Resilience by EU Member States
	Edited by Simon Grima, Inna Romānova, Grațiela-Georgiana Noja, and Tomasz Dorożyński
Volume 116:	Exploring ESG Challenges and Opportunities: Navigating Towards a Better Future
	Edited by Simon Grima, Dimitrios Maditinos, Grațiela-Georgiana Noja, Jelena Stankevičienė, Malgorzata Tarczynska-Luniewska, and Eleftherios Thalassinos

CONTEMPORARY STUDIES IN ECONOMIC AND
FINANCIAL ANALYSIS   VOLUME 117

GREEN WEALTH: NAVIGATING TOWARDS A SUSTAINABLE FUTURE

EDITED BY

SIMON GRIMA
University of Malta, Malta

DIMITRIOS MADITINOS
Democritus University of Thrace, Greece

GRAȚIELA-GEORGIANA NOJA
West University of Timișoara, Romania

JELENA STANKEVIČIENĖ
Vilnius University, Lithuania

MALGORZATA TARCZYNSKA-LUNIEWSKA
University of Szczecin, Poland

ELEFTHERIOS I. THALASSINOS
University of Piraeus, Greece

and

KESRA NERMEND
University of Szczecin, Poland

United Kingdom – North America – Japan
India – Malaysia – China

Emerald Publishing Limited
Emerald Publishing, Floor 5, Northspring, 21–23 Wellington Street, Leeds LS1 4DL

First edition 2025

Editorial matter and selection © 2025 Simon Grima, Dimitrios Maditinos, Grațiela-Georgiana Noja, Jelena Stankevičienė, Malgorzata Tarczynska-Luniewska, Eleftherios I. Thalassinos and Kesra Nermend.
Individual chapters © 2025 The authors.
Published under exclusive licence by Emerald Publishing Limited.
Printed and bound by CPI Group (UK) Ltd, Croydon, CR0 4YY

Reprints and permissions service
Contact: www.copyright.com

No part of this book may be reproduced, stored in a retrieval system, transmitted in any form or by any means electronic, mechanical, photocopying, recording or otherwise without either the prior written permission of the publisher or a licence permitting restricted copying issued in the UK by The Copyright Licensing Agency and in the USA by The Copyright Clearance Center. Any opinions expressed in the chapters are those of the authors. Whilst Emerald makes every effort to ensure the quality and accuracy of its content, Emerald makes no representation implied or otherwise, as to the chapters' suitability and application and disclaims any warranties, express or implied, to their use.

British Library Cataloguing in Publication Data
A catalogue record for this book is available from the British Library

ISBN: 978-1-83662-219-2 (Print)
ISBN: 978-1-83662-218-5 (Online)
ISBN: 978-1-83662-220-8 (Epub)

ISSN: 1569-3759 (Series)

INVESTOR IN PEOPLE

CONTENTS

About the Editors ix

About the Contributors xiii

Acknowledgement xxv

Introduction
Grațiela-Georgiana Noja 1

Chapter 1 Sustainable Finance for a Blue Economy
Anna Spoz and Magdalena Zioło 5

Chapter 2 Sustainable Futures: Navigating Environmental Challenges Through Local Governance in the Tirreno-Eolie Area
Carlotta D'Alessandro, Giuseppe Ioppolo, Alberto Bongiorno, Giuseppe Caristi and Katarzyna Szopik-Depczyńska 23

Chapter 3 Technological Innovation and Sustainable Development: Attracting Environmentally-friendly and Socially Responsible Investors
Grațiela-Georgiana Noja, Petru Ștefea, Andrea Gînguță, Alexandra-Mădălina Țăran, Irina-Maria Grecu and Andrei Cristian Spulbăr 45

Chapter 4 Environmental Challenges and Effects Induced by the Shadow Economy
Sorana Vătavu, Cristian Tudorescu, Oana-Ramona Lobonț, Nicoleta-Claudia Moldovan and Florin Costea 65

Chapter 5 Sustainable Economic Stake and Coproduction in Competition: A Dynamic Analysis
Alexandru Jivan, Miruna Lucia Năchescu and Mihaela Neamțu 91

Chapter 6 Less Is More, More Is Less (Cleopas Mlilo): Exploring the Elusive Sustainability in the Fashion Industry
Alexandra-Codruța Bîzoi and Cristian-Gabriel Bîzoi   109

Chapter 7 Bioeconomy Development in the European Union: Social and Economic Influencing Factors
Emilia Mary Bălan, Cristina Georgiana Zeldea and Laura Mariana Cismaș   131

Chapter 8 Challenges in Applying Principal Adverse Impact Indicators to Sovereign Debt Portfolios
Bentje Böer, Anna Broughel and Mark Kantšukov   157

Chapter 9 The Role of Financial Innovations in Sustainable Development
Agnieszka Majewska and Sebastian Majewski   181

Chapter 10 Transition to a Circular Economy in ASEAN-5: Inferences on Sustainable Development in a Globalised World
Grațiela-Georgiana Noja, Monica Boldea, Maria-Izabela Purdescu and Alina Ionașcu   195

Chapter 11 Essence and Appearance: A Critical Exploration of Corporate Greenwashing Through Ethical Dilemmas in Global Supply Chains
Alexandra-Codruța Bîzoi and Cristian-Gabriel Bîzoi   211

Chapter 12 Technologies Promoting the Digital Tourism Economy and Student Attitudes Towards Artificial Intelligence in Tourism
Simona Biriescu and Laura Olteanu   239

Chapter 13 Role of Pro Bono Legal Services in the Sector of ESG
Aleksandra Klich and Qerkin Berisha   257

Chapter 14 Comparative Analysis of CSR and ESG Actions in Greece: A Study Using Artificial Neural Networks and Machine-Learning Techniques
Foteini I. Pagkalou, Eleftherios I. Thalassinos and Konstantinos I. Liapis   273

Chapter 15 Willingness to Pay Extra for Eco-friendly Products: A Sequential Mediation Analysis of Behavioural Antecedents and Attitude Towards Behavioural Sustainability
Cuc Lavinia Denisia, Rad Dana, Hategan Camelia-Daniela, Pelau Corina and Szentesi Silviu Gabriel 295

Chapter 16 Green Wealth in Motion: Leveraging the Sharing Economy for a Circular Future
Virginija Grybaitė 307

Index 323

ABOUT THE EDITORS

Simon Grima is the Deputy Dean of the Faculty of Economics, Management and Accountancy, Associate Professor and the Head of the Department of Insurance and Risk Management. Simon is also a Professor at the University of Latvia, Faculty of Business, Management and Economics a visiting Professor at UNICATT Milan and an affiliate professor at Haxhi Zeka University, Kosovo.. He served as the President of the Malta Association of Risk Management (MARM) and was President of the Malta Association of Compliance Officers (MACO) between 2013 and 2015, and between 2016 and 2018 respectively. He is again the current president of MARM since 2023. Moreover, he is the co-chair of the Scientific Education Committee of the Federation of European Risk Managers (FERMA) and is a member of the Strategic Risk Leaders Association (SRLA) previously the Public Risk Management Association (PRIMO). His research focus is on Governance, Regulations and Internal Controls and has over 30 years of experience varied between Financial Services, academia and public entities. He has acted as co-chair and is a member of the scientific program committee on some international conferences and is a chief editor, editor and review editor of some Journals and Book Series. He has been awarded outstanding reviewer for Journal of Financial Regulation and Compliance in the 2017 and 2022 and the outstanding author contribution for the Book Series Contemporary Studies in Economic and Financial Analysis Emerald Literati Awards in 2024. Moreover, Simon acts as an Independent Director for Financial Services Firms, sits on Risk, Compliance, Procurement, Investment and Audit Committees and carries out duties as a Compliance Officer, Internal Auditor and Risk Manager.

Dimitrios Maditinos holds a degree with specialisation in Business Administration and Informatics from Lund University in Sweden and a PhD degree in Finance and Financial Modelling from Greenwich University in London, UK. Currently, he is Professor in Business Administration and Informatics at International Hellenic University. Formerly, starting in 1985, he went through all the academic levels (from lecturer till full professor) working at Technological Educational Institute of Kavala and then at Eastern Macedonia and Thrace Institute of Technology. He has been teaching courses related to business, informatics, and e-business in both undergraduate and postgraduate levels. His research interests are in financial modelling, performance measurement, investors behaviour, e-business and e-commerce, applications and internet use, digital business, innovation, management information systems, SCM, and business digitalisation, with 4 volumes, 65 papers published in International Scientific Journals, and more than 90 papers presented in international conferences. Moreover, he serves as Scientific Board Member in many International Scientific Journals like *Qualitative Research in*

Finance Markets, and *European Research Studies Journal*, among others, and as a Reviewer in International Journals like *Industrial Management & Data System*, *Management Research Review* (MRR), *Cyberpsychology, Behavior, and Social Networking, Journal of Enterprise Information Management, Journal of Accounting, Auditing and Performance Evaluation, Baltic Journal of Management*.

Grațiela-Georgiana Noja, PhD Habil., is the *Vice-Dean* of the Faculty of Economics and Business Administration, West University of Timisoara, Romania, in charge of scientific research activities, and a *Professor* at the same faculty, Department of Marketing and International Economic Relations. She is also a Doctoral Adviser in the field of Economics within the Doctoral School of Economics and Business Administration. She completed her studies with the highest honours at the West University of Timisoara and developed over 15 national and international projects throughout the years as a manager, project assistant, expert, researcher, task responsible, and trainer. She has around 40 publications indexed in the Web of Science Core Collection and a couple dozen other publications in relevant international journals/books/collective volumes. She is an Active Member of the International Strategic Management Association and has a wide membership in various educational organisations, research networks, scientific and review committees of top-tier journals, and international conferences. Her main research and teaching activities are developed within the economics and international business framework, with a keen focus on European economic integration, international migration, digital transformation, and sustainable economic development.

Jelena Stankevičienė is a Professor at the Department of Finance at Vilnius University (Lithuania). Her main research topics include sustainable green finance, green economy, circular economy, financial management for value creation, risk management, knowledge transfer, higher education management, multi-criteria decision methods. She is an Author of more than 100 scientific publications, most of them indexed in Web of Science, Scopus, EBSCO, Emerald, and other databases. She is a Co-author of three monographs. Throughout her career, she has been involved in EU development and Lithuanian projects and gained solid knowledge and experience in developing international activities. From her positions as a dean of the Faculty of Business Management, she shows both academic and practical experiences within the field of management and social responsibilities. Since 2008, she has been Editor-in-Chief of periodical peer-reviewed scientific journals, abstracted by international databases (including CA WoS Q2 and Scopus) and a Chairwoman and a Member of scientific and organising committees of different international conferences. Currently, she is an Editor-in-Chief of journal *Ekonomika*. https://www.journals.vu.lt/ekonomika

Malgorzata Tarczynska-Luniewska works at the Department of Econometrics and Statistics at the Institute of Economics and Finance, University of Szczecin. She specialises in quantitative methods, capital markets, finance, and economic and financial analysis. Her scientific interests include issues related to sustainable development and ESG problems. She has participated in many scientific and educational projects for over 20 years. She has also been a Member of research or expert teams for the economic environment. She is the author of numerous publications, including articles and chapters in monographs of a scientific and didactic nature. She is on behalf of the Ministry and a Member of the evaluation team of scientific units. She is the Subject Editor of the journal *Wiadomości Statystyczne. The Polish Statistician*. She is a Member of many professional associations and organisations of national and international scope. https://orcid.org/0000-0002-7338-1989

Eleftherios I. Thalassinos, PhD (UIC, Chicago, USA, 1983), DHC Degrees in Economics (Danubius University of Galati, Romania, 2013; University of Craiova, Romania, 2015; and Rostov State University of Economics, Russia, 2018), MBA, (De-Paul U Chicago, USA, 1979), BA, (U of Athens, Greece, 1976), is a Jean Monnet Chair Professor experienced in European Economic Integration and International Finance. He is the Editor-in-Chief of ERSJ, IJEBA, and IJFIRM and Chair of ICABE. He is Guest Editor in the Book Series Contemporary Studies in Economic and Financial Analysis published by Emerald, Contributions to Management Sciences by Springer, Business, Technology, and Finance by Nova, JRFM, RESOURCES, RISKS, and SUSTAINABILITY by MDPI. He is a Member of the Editorial Boards of several journals. His professional experience includes quantitative analysis, technical and financial analysis, banking, business consulting, project evaluations, international business, international finance, and maritime economics. He has a long track of publications in several journals, collective volumes, and chapter books. Among them a publication as a chapter book in the World Scientific Handbook in Financial Economics Series Vol. 5 dedicated to the memory of Late Milton Miller, Nobel prize winner in Economics in 1990. Parallel to his academic career, he has performed as Bank Director for 12 years, Ministerial Advisor for 6 years, Public Servant for 4 years, and independent consultant for a long time.

Kesra Nermend is a Professor at the University of Szczecin along with the Head of the Department of Decision Support Methods and Cognitive Neuroscience; the Director of the Institute of Management, University of Szczecin; the Director of the Center for Transfer and Technology at the University of Szczecin; and the President of the Center for Research and Development for the University of Szczecin. His research interests are primarily shaped by issues surrounding the application of quantitative methods and IT tools in the analysis of the socio-economic processes, with particular emphasis on multi-criteria methods, multi-dimensional data analysis, cognitive neuroscience techniques in the study of social behaviour, and consumer preferences modelling in business decision-making process in management. Additionally, he has published more than 130 publications (including many monographs published in SPRINGER and articles in journals from the Philadelphia list), mainly using quantitative methods and tools to analyse economic problems and decision support.

ABOUT THE CONTRIBUTORS

Emilia Mary Bălan is a Scientific Researcher at the Institute for Advanced Environmental Research (ICAM) and the Institute for World Economy (IEM). She holds a PhD in Economics from the West University of Timisoara and is a graduate of Politehnica University of Bucharest, where she earned a bachelor's degree from the Faculty of Engineering and Management of Technological Systems (now the Faculty of Industrial Engineering and Robotics). Since 2005, she has also developed expertise in the agriculture market. From 2019 onwards, her main areas of specialisation have been bioeconomy, circular economy, renewable energy, and environmental protection.

Qerkin Berisha is a Professor at the University of Prishtina Faculty of Law, teaching Civil Law, Civil Law Clinics, and EU Commercial Law. He has over 20 years of experience in academic institutions, public administration, civil society, and legal consultancy. He has held senior positions in the Civil Service, including roles in the Strategic Planning Office of the Office of the Prime Minister of Kosovo and leading the Legal Department in the Ministry of Finance. He has extensive experience supporting Kosovo's central government institutions and ministries in drafting legislation, developing policies, and strategic planning, including harmonising Kosovo legislation with the EU Acquis. He has authored and co-authored several publications in the legal field.

Simona Biriescu, PhD, is an Associate Professor at the West University of Timişoara (Romania), Faculty of Economics and Business Administration, Department of Business Information Systems. In 2002, she obtained a Doctorate in Management. She received a diploma and a prestigious certificate in France, Diplome d'Etudes Superieures Specialisees and Certificat d'aptitude a l'Administration des Entreprises, at the Universite de Nice – Sophia Antipolis, Institut d'Administration des Entreprises, 1996. She also obtained a Trainer's Diploma and Trainer's Certificate in Education at Babeş-Bolyai University, Teaching, Cluj Napoca, 2007. She is a Member of the undergraduate and master's commissions, doctoral theses and Member of the final commission of the National Olympiad of Informatics for students held at 'Dănărea de Jos' University in Galati, 2013. She is currently a Member of the Regional Science Association (ARSR) of A.S.E. Bucharest since 2002, a Member of RSAI International since 2003, and a Member of ERECO P.G.V. Grenoble, France, since 2005.

Alexandra-Codruţa Bîzoi is a Lecturer at the West University of Timisoara (Romania), Faculty of Economics and Business Administration, Management Department. She defended her doctoral thesis in the Finance Department and received the Magna Cum Laude appreciation for her thesis. Her research interests are behavioural tax compliance, business ethics, and supply chain management. She holds courses for both bachelor and master students in the Romanian and French lines of study. She also worked in Project Management, and thanks to the fact she is fluent in English, French, German, Italian, and Spanish, she coordinated the Faculty's International Relations Office.

Cristian-Gabriel Bîzoi is an Associate Professor at the West University of Timisoara (Romania), Faculty of Economics and Business Administration, Management Department. He also coordinates the Center of Long-Life-Learning and Distance Learning and participated in implementing and developing the Moodle e-learning platform at the university level for several years, which helped a smooth transition towards online learning during the pandemic. His research interests lie in supply chain management, risk management, business ethics, project management, and innovation management. He holds courses for both bachelor's and master's students. He has worked for the local Regional Development Agency, evaluating European-funded projects.

Bentje Böer currently works as a Consultant for the OECD and World Bank, where she focuses on real economy impacts of climate-related financial policies and effects on emerging economies. She is also a Research Analyst for AidData at William and Mary, contributing to development policy analysis for UN and governmental agencies. Previously, she worked with the German Finance Agency on Green Finance on sustainability reporting by sovereign issuers. She holds a BSc in Economics from Bonn University and an MA in International Relations from Johns Hopkins School of Advanced International Studies.

Monica Boldea, PhD, is a Lecturer at the Faculty of Economics and Business Administration, West University of Timisoara, Romania. She is a highly experienced professional specialising in both modern languages and economics. After graduating from the West University of Timisoara, she pursued a 3-year postgraduate specialisation in Diplomacy and Foreign Relations. Being committed to continuous professional development, she furthered her academic endeavour by undergoing continuous training in the field of economics with doctoral studies, followed by a post-doctoral programme with the Romanian Academy in Bucharest. Thus, her main research focuses on regional development issues, the influence of culture and institutions on economic development, as well as issues of globalisation, human capital, and international migration. Currently, she conducts tailored training sessions for students in Economics, catering to their need for foreign language skills while debating case studies in the field of their immediate interest. Her engagement as a Lecturer, being detail-oriented and passionate about her work, as well as her involvement and participation at countless national and international conferences, highlights her dedication to advancing in the field through commitment and collaboration.

About the Contributors xv

Alberto Bongiorno is a Master of Science (MSc) student in the field of Business & Consulting at the Department of Economics, University of Messina. His focus is dedicated to the study of environmental sustainability and environmental management at the local level, with the aim of identifying potential solutions for a sustainable future.

Anna Broughel is a Lecturer in Sustainable Energy Transition Policy and a Faculty Co-lead of the Technology and Innovations focus area at Johns Hopkins University School of Advanced International Studies (SAIS). Prior to her current position, she served as the Director at the Clean Energy Leadership Institute, an Energy Economist and Statistician at Tetra Tech, and an ORISE Fellow at the Solar Energy Technologies Office within the US Department of Energy. Since 2020, she has been elected as the VP of communications and has been serving on the executive council of the United States Association for Energy Economics. She holds an MA in International Economics from the University of Konstanz and a PhD in Economics and Policy, conferred by the State University of New York in association with Syracuse University, where she was a Fulbright Scholar. She completed her post-doctoral training at the University of St. Gallen in Switzerland and the University of Maryland, College Park.

Hategan Camelia-Daniela is a Doctor in Accounting, with over 30 years of experience in the field of accounting and auditing, being a Teacher, and now a Full Professor at the West University of Timisoara, Romania. She is also PhD Supervisor in the field of Accounting. She has a deep knowledge of accounting information and the analysis of financial indicators reported by companies and has extensive experience as a researcher in publishing articles and participating in academic international conferences. The written articles were published in international journals indexed in several databases, namely, Clarivate Web of Science and Scopus. Also professionally, she is a financial auditor with over 20 years of experience and was a trainer within the professional body of auditors in Romania.

Giuseppe Caristi is a Full Professor on Mathematical Methods of Economy, Finance, and Actuarial Science. He is a Member of the Doctoral School in Public Administration Science. He is Editor-in-Chief of International Journal Mathematical Analysis and International Journal of Contemporary Mathematical Sciences. He is Author of over 180 scientific publications in international journals and 5 monographs on Mathematics for Economics, Optimisation Theory, Nonlinear Analysis, and Mathematical Models for Applied Sciences.

Laura Mariana Cismaş is a Professor of Economics at the Department of Marketing, International Business and Economics, Faculty of Economics and Business Administration, from the West University of Timisoara. Her teaching experience with the West University of Timisoara and in the field of scientific research regarding macroeconomics, microeconomics, regional economics,

European macroeconomics, and European economic policies goes back more than 32 years. She is a Member of prestigious professional and scientific associations and international journals' editorial staff. She was also a Member of RSAI, ERSA, and PGV research projects.

Pelau Corina, PhD, is Professor and Coordinator at the Bucharest University of Economic Studies, UNESCO Department for Business Administration. She holds a PhD degree in Marketing (2008) from the Bucharest University of Economic Studies, Romania; a master degree in 'International Business' (2006) from the Friedrich Alexander University Erlangen Nürnberg, Germany; a bachelor degree in Business Administration (2004) from the Bucharest University of Economic Studies; and a bachelor degree in Mathematics (2009) from the Western University of Timisoara, Romania. Her main research field is consumer research, with focus on the relation between consumers and artificial intelligence, neuroscientific approaches of consumer behaviour and sustainable consumption. Her research has been published by several indexed journals. Her research work has been rewarded with the Best Paper in an Economic Journal Award by AFER (Association of Economic Faculties in Romania) in 2018, the Opera Omnia Award for Excellence in Scientific Research by the Bucharest University of Economic Studies (2019). She is Member of the Association for Consumer Research (since 2015) and Member of the European Marketing Academy (since 2018). Starting with 2021, she is part of the Executive Committee of the European Marketing Academy as National Representative for Romania and Co-coordinator of the Climber Community Interest Group at EMAC.

Florin Costea is currently a Postdoctoral researcher at the West University of Timisoara and a Member of the research team of a Research project funded by Romania's National Recovery and Resilience Plan (PNRR) – Pillar III, Component C9, Investment I8. His doctoral research focused on the relationship between public sector governance and entrepreneurship. His research results were disseminated at international conferences, and he published articles in journals indexed in international databases, including three papers in journals indexed Clarivate – Web of Science, with an impact factor. He is also the head of Finance in the Romanian corporate headquarters of a multinational company.

Carlotta D'Alessandro is a PhD Candidate specialising in Sustainability and Circular Economy at the Department of Economics, University of Messina. Her research is dedicated to addressing critical issues in sustainability and promoting circular economy practices, working towards a more sustainable and circular future.

Rad Dana, PhD, is Associate Professor in the Faculty of Educational Sciences, Psychology, and Social Sciences at Aurel Vlaicu University of Arad, Romania. She is Head of Center of Research Development and Innovation in Psychology. She holds a double specialisation in Psychology (PhD in Applied Cognitive

Psychology) and Systems Engineering (PhD student in Systems Engineering). She was Research Scientist in more than 20 European Union funded projects. Her research interests include applied cognitive sciences, cognitive systems engineering, organisational psychology, and psychoinformatics. She is Coauthor of 20 books and more than 175 international conferences and journal papers. She is registered as Autonomous Psychologist with the right to practice freely in the specialisations: clinical psychology, educational psychology, school and vocational counselling, and work and organisational psychology.

Cuc Lavinia Denisia, PhD, is Full Professor at Department of Economic Disciplines, Faculty of Economics at Aurel Vlaicu University of Arad, Romania. She is the Author or Co-author of 3 books and has published over 35 articles in scientific journals indexed in international databases or at international conferences. Her main research interests are management, financial accounting, managerial accounting, controlling, and financial analysis. She is qualified in coordinating PhD students in Management since 2023 when she was accepted into the Interdisciplinary Doctoral School of Aurel Vlaicu University of Arad. She holds several administrative positions in the department council, the Faculty council, various commissions at the Faculty or University level.

Szentesi Silviu Gabriel, PhD, is a Full Professor at the Department of Economic Disciplines, School of Economic Studies at Aurel Vlaicu University of Arad, Romania. He is the Author or Co-author of 21 books and has published over 40 articles in scientific journals indexed in international databases or at international conferences. Since 2018 habilitated in Communication Sciences at the University of Paul Valery Montpellier 3 France and since 2022 habilitated in Management at the West University of Timişoara where is active in teaching German language Marketing, Econometrics, and Business Communication and Negotiation. His main research interests are management, environmental management, marketing research, and communication. He has been qualified in coordinating PhD students in Management since 2023 when he joined the Interdisciplinary Doctoral School of Aurel Vlaicu University of Arad. Also professionally, he is a Trainer for Entrepreneurship and Marketing from the German Forum in Romania.

Andrea Gînguță is a Teaching Assistant at the Faculty of Economics and Business Administration, West University of Timisoara, Romania, Department of Management and Entrepreneurship, and a PhD student in the accounting field at the same faculty. Having a bachelor's degree in finance and a master's degree in management (diagnosis, assessment, and business consulting) at the Faculty of Economics and Business Administration, her research is currently focused on artificial intelligence and technological innovation, business performance, ethics, and sustainable business development.

Irina-Maria Grecu is a Teaching Assistant and PhD student in Economics at the West University of Timisoara, Romania, Faculty of Economics and Business

Administration. She holds a master's in Management and European Integration and a BA in Economics and International Business at the West University of Timisoara, where she graduated with the highest honours. Her main research activities are focused on the process of international labour migration in EU-27, especially in Romania, on the values of the employee of the future and on the digitalised and globalised era labour market outcomes.

Virginija Grybaitė, is an associate professor at the Department of Business Technologies and Entrepreneurship at Vilnius Gediminas Technical University. She has authored or co-authored over 30 publications in scientific journals, alongside contributing to six educational and methodological books. Her research interests are entrepreneurship, sharing economy, digital economy, green economy, and sustainable development.

Alina Ionașcu is a Doctoral Candidate at the West University of Timisoara, Romania, researching the nexus of globalisation and European economic integration. Her academic journey, enriched by a master's in European studies and an ongoing master's in business law, equips her with diverse perspectives on these themes. Her experience extends to an Erasmus exchange in Lille, France, and a Student Evaluator in an Economic Studies role at the Romanian Agency for Quality Assurance in Higher Education. This blend of education and experience underpins her commitment to exploring the theoretical underpinnings of globalisation and integration, as evidenced in the systematic and bibliometric analysis of relevant scientific literature.

Giuseppe Ioppolo, PhD, is Civil Engineer and is a Full Professor in Environmental Management and Sustainability at the University of Messina, Department of Economics. He is the Scientific Coordinator of Lean & Quality Solutions LAB. He is Author of about 150 publications, with *Scopus H-Index 35*; his main research topics are urban metabolism and sustainable urban development, circular economy assessment, decision support system models, sustainability indicators development. He is Chair and Board Member on International Conferences on Sustainability and Industrial Ecology as ISIE, ISDRS, and WSF Conferences; he is Section Editor-in-Chief of Sustainability MDPI. He was Visiting Professor at Tsinghua University (China), UCSB (USA), Tokyo University (Japan), Aachen University (German), Szczecin University (Poland), CML-IE Leiden University (Netherlands). PI and Co-PI in PRIN and PRIN-PNRR currently running scientific projects.

Alexandru Jivan performed as an Economist, Chief Economist, and Head of Office, in economic and administrative units and also in the research field (e.g. as a Researcher within the Institute of Economic Forecasting, Bucharest). As a Teacher – focused mainly on the issues of productivity, efficiency and especially on *service economy* – since 1999 he was *full professor* in the West University of Timișoara. He is also a PhD Coordinator within the Doctoral School of

Economics and Business Administration (Economics field) and Former Director of this Doctoral School. He was Member in diverse scientific organisations – exemplifying just the former membership of the Commission for Titles Certifying in the Romanian Education Ministry, and the former honorary membership of the Services World Forum (1994). He also was a Member of the editorial teams, or scientific committees, of several journals and scientific events, organiser, reviewer for scientific journals and events. He published more than 10 books, 10 university courses, more than 150 articles and papers in reviews and volumes, having more than 25 researching participations in scientific contracts (director/coordinator in 5 contracts).

Mark Kantšukov is a Lecturer in Finance at the School of Economics and Business Administration, University of Tartu, where he teaches a range of finance-related courses in both bachelor's and master's programmes. He is also a Guest Lecturer at the Estonian Business School in Tallinn. His academic interests include business valuation, corporate finance, financial markets, behavioural finance, and green finance. He serves as a Member of the Nasdaq Tallinn Listing and Surveillance Committee and the evaluation committee of the Estonian Association of Appraisers. He holds a PhD in Economics from the University of Tartu.

Aleksandra Klich, PhD, is Legal Advisor; Graduate of the Faculty of Law and Administration, University of Szczecin and l'Université d'été du droit continental, Paris – Sorbonne. She is Member of the Regional Chamber of Legal Advisors in Szczecin. She serves as the Head of the Law Clinic of the Faculty of Law of the Faculties of Law of the USA and is a Board Member of the European Network for Clinical Legal Education (ENCLE). As a Trainer, she conducts trainings and workshops on civil procedure, consumer rights, medical law, patients' rights, data protection, and RODO. She is Member of the Council of the University Legal Clinics Foundation. As a Legal Advisor, she specialises in medical law, with a particular focus on patients' rights and the pursuit of civil law claims by patients and medical professionals. She serves as Vice Chair of the Provincial Commission for Adjudication of Medical Events in Szczecin for the second term for 2018–2023.

Konstantinos I. Liapis is a Professor of Accounting & Business Administration at the Panteion University of Social and Political Sciences, Department of Economic and Regional Development. His areas of interest in science include accounting, managerial accounting, mergers & acquisitions, banking and finance, business economics, and operation research. He has more than 100 contributions to international academic conferences and other publications; he has written several books and papers in scientific journals. His work has received more than 500 citations. He held high-ranking positions in the business and banking sectors, worked as an accountant and business consultant for more than 30 years, also taught undergraduate and graduate courses at several other universities. He is a Member of the Advisory Council and Editorial Board of the European

Research Studies Journal and International Journal of Economics and Business Administration.

Oana-Ramona Lobonţ, PhD habil., is a Professor at the Finance Department from the Faculty of Economics and Business Administration, West University of Timisoara, with over 21 years of experience in socio-economic research. The main areas of interest include, among others, public economics, energy economics, institutional economics, political economics, governance, health economics, environmental and climate change, and societal impact and policy on the other. Her research in these fields has been published in 10 books and over 70 papers indexed in Web of Science academic journals, from which 10 Highly Cited Papers.

Agnieszka Majewska is Associate Professor in the Institute of Economics and Finance (Department of Sustainable Finance and Capital Markets) at the University of Szczecin. Her research interest includes the use of quantitative methods on the financial market, quantitative analysis of companies, sustainable finance, financial inclusion, risk management, capital market analysis, derivatives and financial engineering, and investing in the capital market. She is the Author of several books and more than 100 scientific articles. She has carried out a number of research projects and expertise. She is the Reviewer of many scientific articles, bachelor's and master's theses, and dissertations.

Sebastian Majewski is Associate Professor of Economics at the University of Szczecin, Deputy Director of the Institute of Economics and Finance at the University of Szczecin, and Vice President of the Polish Association of Neurology Program (PSPN). His economics interests of are focused on financial markets, quantitative methods for supporting stock exchange investment (especially portfolio analysis), financial engineering, behavioural finance, and sports finance. He is the Author of more than 100 scientific articles, books, and chapters. He is an External Expert for courts, investment funds, and financial companies in cases concerning financial instruments, strategies, and financial assets valuations.

Nicoleta-Claudia Moldovan, PhD habil., is a Professor at the Finance Department from the Faculty of Economics and Business Administration, West University of Timisoara. She is a PhD Advisor in Economics, Finance specialisation, and also holds a postdoctoral degree in Economics. She has 29 years of experience in research and teaching in higher education. Her research mainly addresses public policies, good governance, fiscal policies, entrepreneurship, and economic competitiveness, with more than 20 papers in journals indexed by Clarivate – Web of Science, with an impact factor, including one highly cited paper. She is an Evaluator in the Finance domain in the Romanian Agency for Quality Assurance in Higher Education and is the Director of the Accreditation Department.

Miruna Lucia Năchescu, PhD, is the Chief of Staff for the Rector Office and Associate Professor at the West University of Timisoara, the Economics and Business Administration Faculty, Department of Finance, where she has

About the Contributors xxi

also completed her studies (an undergraduate programme in Accounting and Informational Management Systems, a master's programme in Capital Markets, a PhD in Finance, and a post-doctoral programme in Corporate Governance). She is teaching and doing research in the field of economics, focused on the financial international markets and financial management of entities but also the proper development of various sectors and public policies for sustainable economic development. She has worked as CFO of several small companies and in fiscal consultancy, is a Member of CECCAR, and has published papers in journals indexed in the Web of Science Collection and other relevant international journals, books, or conference volumes. She was involved in more than 15 projects as a manager, trainer, expert coordinator, researcher, etc. She provides the management of all support activities related to the Rector's Office events and public relations, therefore, has specialised in diplomacy and protocol, and has gained lots of experience in organising academic and cultural events for the last 10 years.

Mihaela Neamțu, PhD habil., is Professor of Mathematics at the Faculty of Economics and Business Administration, West University of Timisoara, Romania. The main direction of the research field is related to the study of dynamical systems from economy, computer science, biology, and medicine described by nonlinear differential equations with time delay. The ability to manage research teams is proved by the tenure as Director in two national research projects and the Management Committee Membership in COST Action 2016–2020. Throughout the students' academic journey, she assisted and guided them enabling real access to the labour market. In this way, she participated as subject matter expert in 10 projects. Alongside the above listed grants, I would like to highlight my membership in 11 multi-annual CNCSIS/UEFSCDI research projects, in 1 international Brancusi research project and in 3 ERASMUS+ projects as researcher. The autonomy of the research activity is reflected by the outcome materialised in 6 books, over 110 articles in ISI and BDI journals. She reviewed articles submitted to BDI and ISI journals. It is worth mentioning the amount of 670 citations in ISI and BDI journals. Also, she is Editor-in-Chief at Timișoara Journal of Economics and Business.

Laura Olteanu, PhD, is a Lecturer at the Babeș Bolyai University Cluj Napoca (Romania), Faculty of Economic Sciences and Business Administration, Department of Business Administration. Her main areas of research and teaching activities are marketing, consumer behaviour, and marketing research. She obtained the scientific title of Doctor of Economics at the Academy of Economic Studies Bucharest (ASE). She was part of the university senate for two terms, during which she was a Member of the Commission for academic development projects, relations with the business environment and forecasts of the UBB Senate, and a Member of the Commission for Intercultural Dialogue of the UBB Senate. Within the research activity, she stands out with three specialised books as the sole author, in the field in which he works, as well as numerous specialised articles.

Being concerned with social rights, she is part of the Commission for Equal Opportunities between women and men, as a Titular Member within the National Agency for Equal Opportunities between women and men.

Foteini I. Pagkalou She is a PhD candidate at the Panteion University of Social and Political Sciences in the field of Corporate Governance, Corporate Social Responsibility, and Corporate Information. She is a full-time Teacher in secondary education and holds two postgraduate titles – in Applied Economics and Management and in Leadership and Management in Education, and two undergraduate titles – in Public Administration and a degree in Mechanical Engineering. She is seconded to the Panteion University and provides tutorials in business economics and accounting. Her scientific interests include corporate responsibility, operations research, strategic marketing, total quality management, and management accounting. Part of her research work has been published in the Journal of Risk and Financial Management and Springer.

Maria-Izabela Purdescu is a dedicated and passionate undergraduate student who is currently studying at the Faculty of Economics and Business Administration, West University of Timisoara, Romania. She has chosen to major in Economics and International Business and has shown a great interest in various topics related to these fields. She is particularly interested in the world economy and is always eager to learn more about the latest trends and developments in this area. She has also developed a keen interest in sustainable economic development, international trade, data analysis, and international investment, which she believes are essential aspects of the modern global economy.

Anna Spoz, PhD, is Assistant Professor at the Department of Finance and Accountancy at the John Paul II Catholic University of Lublin, Poland. Her research and teaching scope focus on finance, particularly corporate finance, accounting, and tax and sustainable finance. She is Author and Co-author of numerous publications on finance, accounting, reporting, and management. She is Reviewer of international publications. She combines teaching and scholarly activities with work in the business.

Andrei Cristian Spulbăr is an accomplished Romanian professional specialising in economic sciences and regional development. Born on 31 March 1998, in Craiova, Romania, he has made significant strides in both his academic and professional journey. He holds a master's degree in Economic Sciences from the University of Craiova, focusing on Finance and Business Administration, and is currently pursuing a doctoral degree in Finance. His professional experience includes roles at Hewlett Packard Enterprise, Ernst & Young, and currently, the South-West Oltenia Regional Development Agency. His research endeavours are extensive, with contributions to economic journals on topics like cybercrime's global effects, financial education, and market volatility, particularly in the context of emerging markets and economic crises. He is fluent in English and possesses basic French skills, enhancing his ability to contribute to and collaborate on international economic discussions.

Petru Ștefea is a *Professor* at the Faculty of Economics and Business Administration, West University of Timisoara, Romania. He pursues research and teaching activities on topics related to financial analysis, economic analysis, financial output analysis, structural funding, investment finance, and efficiency. During his academic career, he was also the Vice-Rector of the West University of Timisoara (between 2008 and 2016), Dean of the Faculty of Economics and Business Administration at the West University of Timisoara, a Member of CECCAR as an expert accountant since 2001, and a Member of ANEVAR as a company assessor since 1997. He has a wide expertise in national and international projects and comprehensive membership in various educational and professional organisations and research centres.

Katarzyna Szopik-Depczyńska, PhD, DSc, is Associate Professor in Management and Quality Sciences in the University of Szczecin, Institute of Management. She is the Author of about 170 publications, including Q1 and Q2 journals such as journal of cleaner production, business strategy and the environment, sustainable cities and society, land use policy, ecological indicators, sustainability. Her Scopus **H-Index is 15**. Her main research topics are innovation management, R&D, sustainability, CSR, logistics, and transportation issues. She is Section Co-Editor of Sustainability journal (MDPI). She was a Visiting Professor at the University of Messina (Italy). She attended various national and international congresses (also as invited speaker), and she was involved as Member of the scientific committees of several international conferences. She has also an experience in the field of cooperation with local government institutions. She was also a Guest Editor of Special Issues in Sustainability journal. She is a Reviewer for Q1 journals such as *Environmental Innovation and Societal Transition* (IF 8.41), *Journal of Cleaner Production* (IF: 7.246), *Science of the Total Environment* (IF: 6.551), *Environmental Science and Policy* (IF: 4.767), *Land Use Policy* (IF: 3.682), *Transportation Research. Part A: Policy and Practice* (IF: 3.992), *Sustainability* (IF: 2.576), *JCMS: Journal of Common Market Studies* (IF: 2.089), and many more.

Alexandra-Mădălina Țăran is a Teaching Assistant Ph.D. at the Faculty of Economics and Business Administration, West University of Timisoara, Romania, in the finance field, studying different aspects related to the relationship between public governance, climate change, and health systems. She has around 12 publications indexed in the Web of Science Core Collection and other publications in relevant international journals/books/collective volumes. Her research mainly addresses the public economic field, namely public policies, welfare, climate change and good governance, with interdisciplinary research directions that focus on health economics, digitalization, wellbeing, sustainability, and economic growth.

Cristian Tudorescu is a Graduate of the Bachelor in Finance and Banking programme, which is organised within the Finance Department at the Faculty of Economics and Business Administration, West University of Timisoara. His bachelor thesis research focused on understanding the intricate dynamics between the environment and the economy to develop more informed policies to promote sustainable development.

Sorana Vătavu, PhD, is Associate Professor within the Finance Department at the Faculty of Economics and Business Administration from the West University of Timisoara. She has extensively developed numerous research studies, attested by more than 20 publications indexed in the Clarivate – Web of Science Core Collection and more than 20 articles and papers in international journals and books or conference proceedings. Her main research and teaching activities are developed within the finance field, with a focus on corporate finance and corporate social responsibility strategies, better public governance, but also on welfare and sustainable development in terms of the economic and social areas.

Cristina Georgiana Zeldea is a Scientific Researcher at the Institute for Economic Forecasting – Romanian Academy since August 2022. Between January 2018 and August 2022, she was Assistant Researcher at the Institute for World Economy. She graduated from the Faculty of International Business and Economics in 2017, within Bucharest University of Economic Studies, and holds an MSc degree in International Financial Risk Management. She holds a PhD degree in the field of risk in financial markets.

Magdalena Zioło is Professor at the University of Szczecin, Poland. Her research and teaching scope focus on finance, banking, and sustainability. She has extensive experience gained in financial institutions. She has received scholarships from the Dekaban-Liddle Foundation (University of Glasgow, Scotland) and Impakt Asia Erasmus + (Ulan Bator, Mongolia). She is a Member of Polish Accreditation Commission, Member of the Financial Sciences Committee of PAS (the Polish Academy of Sciences), Member of the Advisory Scientific Committee of the Financial Ombudsman, Expert of the National Centre for Research and Development, Expert of the National Science Centre and the National Agency for Academic Exchange, Expert of the Accreditation Agency of Curacao. She was a Member of State Quality Council, Kosovo Accreditation Agency and Visiting Professor of the University of Prishtina (Kosovo). She is Principal Investigator in the research projects funded by National Science Center, Poland, in the field sustainable finance. She is the author and editor of numerous books, mostly about financing sustainable development.

ACKNOWLEDGEMENT

Part of this work was supported by a grant from the Romanian Ministry of Research, Innovation, and Digitalisation, the project with the title 'Economics and Policy Options for Climate Change Risk and Global Environmental Governance' (CF 193/28.11.2022, Funding Contract no. 760078/23.05.2023), within Romania's National Recovery and Resilience Plan (PNRR) – Pillar III, Component C9, Investment I8 (PNRR/2022/C9/MCID/I8) – Development of a programme to attract highly specialised human resources from abroad in research, development and innovation activities.

INTRODUCTION

Grațiela-Georgiana Noja

West University of Timișoara, Romania

In contemporary times, humanity is faced with environmental challenges of an unprecedented magnitude. These challenges require a thoughtful and proactive approach to identify meaningful and sustainable solutions. Consequently, sustainable economic development has emerged as a potential solution to balance economic growth with environmental preservation. This has prompted scholars, policymakers, and activists to explore innovative approaches prioritising the welfare of both people and the planet.

In this context, the book *Green Wealth: Navigating Towards a Sustainable Future* innovatively addresses the topical subject of sustainable development and green innovation. It aims to contribute to this emerging field by helping readers interested in interdisciplinary methods, tailored strategies, and policies to manage environmental risks and enhance economic welfare. Moreover, the book ambitiously addresses environmental challenges and provides accurate research for a resilient, eco-friendly future through a comprehensive and integrated approach. Through its 16 chapters, the book undertakes a multidisciplinary approach that embeds principles of economics, ecology, sociology, mathematics, and political science, providing a comprehensive understanding of this emerging field of study.

At the core of this exploration lies the concept of green wealth, which surpasses traditional notions of prosperity by incorporating ecological integrity and social well-being into the fabric of economic progress. Pressing issues like climate change, biodiversity loss, and resource shrinkage have brought to the fore the critical need to ensure sustainable development.

Green Wealth: Navigating Towards a Sustainable Future serves as a manifesto for this transformative journey towards a more resilient and inclusive future. It embeds theoretical underpinning, advanced econometric studies, and mathematical models that shed light on the numerous ways in which sustainable economic development can be achieved. More specifically, the book starts with a detailed description of the role of sustainable finance for a blue economy and the role of local governance in coping with environmental challenges, including those induced by the shadow economy, and ensuring a sustainable future. It further presents the inferences between technological and financial innovations and sustainable development and outlines the importance of attracting environment-friendly and socially responsible investors. The following section provides a dynamic analysis of sustainable economic stake and coproduction in competition and explores the elusive sustainability in the fashion industry and tourism sectors. Finally, the book captures the social and economic factors of bioeconomy development at the level of the European Union and assesses the effectiveness of policy pathways to sustainability, while also addressing the role of artificial neural networks and machine-learning techniques for comparative CSR and ESG actions.

On these lines, the book fundamentally explores the innovative initiatives governments, businesses, and communities undertake to drive positive change in societies worldwide. From renewable energy projects that mitigate carbon emissions to inclusive economic policies that empower marginalised populations, each chapter offers insights into practical strategies for establishing a greener and more prosperous world.

To mitigate the environmental impacts of energy production and consumption, researchers are exploring efficient and economically viable technical solutions. Environmental protection can be enhanced by intensifying the environmental innovation process, which can be facilitated by research and development support from governing authorities. Furthermore, energy innovation is crucial in reducing energy intensity and environmental pollution. Technological innovations help reduce carbon emissions, making them essential for achieving environmental sustainability.

In this complex frame of facts and challenges, the current book transcends the realm of theory, providing readers with actionable steps to catalyse sustainable development in their respective spheres of influence. Whether one is a researcher interested in this theme, a policymaker crafting environmental regulations, a business leader seeking to integrate sustainability into corporate strategy, or an individual committed to making a difference in their community, *Green Wealth: Navigating Towards a Sustainable Future* equips them with the knowledge and inspiration to effect meaningful change.

Green Wealth: Navigating Towards a Sustainable Future is a book that urges a fresh perspective on sustainable economic development. It advocates for an approach that equally regards the welfare of our ecosystems and economic development.

The book demonstrates cutting-edge solutions that have been developed to combat some of the most significant environmental challenges of our time, including, but not limited to, environmental challenges/climate change, bioeconomy development, technological innovations, sustainable finance, and the blue economy. The strategies discussed in the book are drawn from global initiatives and best practices and can be applied in diverse contexts.

The book's focus on innovative solutions underscores the need for transformative actions to catalyse progress towards achieving sustainable development goals. The book highlights that sustainability is an issue that goes beyond the environmental domain and extends into the social and economic spheres. It also examines sustainability's social and ethical dimensions, such as greenwashing in global supply chains.

In conclusion, *Green Wealth: Navigating Towards a Sustainable Future* proffers an inspiring guidebook on the roadmap towards a sustainable world. The originality of the book resides in the topical subject it approaches, as well as in the innovative way in which it is designed and structured to provide a basic overview and a nuanced understanding of sustainable development and green wealth. The interdisciplinary approach adopted in this book bridges gaps between various fields, fostering a holistic perspective essential for effective problem-solving and offering a multifaceted framework capable of navigating the intricacies of sustainable development.

CHAPTER 1

SUSTAINABLE FINANCE FOR A BLUE ECONOMY

Anna Spoz[a] and Magdalena Zioło[b]

[a]The John Paul II Catholic University of Lublin, Poland
[b]University of Szczecin, Poland

ABSTRACT

Purpose: *The concept of a blue economy is gaining importance. 40% of the world's population lives near coastal areas, and 80% of world trade is achieved using the seas. Sustainable financing for the blue economy is an emerging scope in climate finance. To date, little research has been published on this topic. Shiiba et al. (2022) proposed a conceptual framework for a blue finance mechanism; however, this approach was incomplete as it referred only to ocean sustainability and overlooked financial instruments and various financial models and schemes determined by a financial system, such as those in the United States, Germany, and Japan.*

Methodology: *The chapter aims to show the state of the art in sustainable financing in a blue economy and provide recommendations to improve the existing financial model.*

A critical literature review, network approach, and case study.

Findings: *The diversity and often uniqueness of blue economy projects underline the necessity for their financing system to be based on established regulatory frameworks in this area. However, specific solutions (e.g. the structure of acquired capital) should be considered on a case-by-case basis.*

Limitations: *Challenges include competition with government-owned sectors, infrastructure limitations, and limited public awareness of sustainable blue economy opportunities. Additionally, constraints like risk-averse local financial institutions and a lack of innovative business models hinder financing and entrepreneurship.*

Keywords: Climate change; sustainability; global finance; strategy; responsible finance

JEL Codes: Q01; G10; Q56; Q25

1. INTRODUCTION

The dissemination of the concept of sustainable development, along with the growing awareness of the impact of current generations' actions on the availability of resources for future generations, has led, among other things, to the emergence of the concept of the blue economy. Protecting and maintaining the biodiversity of seas and oceans, as well as building a resilient and environmentally sustainable maritime economy, are the main goals of the blue economy (Knodt et al., 2023), which can serve as a framework integrating policies for sustainable development and the sustainable development of seas and oceans.

The blue economy, due to the context of climate change and its impact on aquatic ecosystems, remains an important area of research interest, but it is also a challenge from the perspective of the progressive degradation of water and water resources. The negative impact of human activity on the blue economy is observable both in the context of its pollution and excessive and destructive exploitation of resources, for example illegal fishing, the destruction of coral reefs and coastlines, and eutrophication as a result of global warming. The indicated examples of the negative impact of man on the blue economy threaten its stability, and at this point, it is worth recalling the economic, environmental, and social functions of the blue economy, pointing to its importance, inter alia, for quality of life, well-being, and sustainable development. One of the factors of the progressive degradation and destruction of the blue economy is its unsustainable financing, that is financing activities based on one decision criterion, namely, the profit criterion, not taking into account the negative social and environmental consequences. Redirecting funding streams to projects supporting the development of the blue economy requires redefining the decision-making criteria and building a sustainable financial mechanism for the blue economy with the participation of all stakeholders.

The importance of oceans is well-documented in scientific research. They are home to over 80% of all life on Earth, are a crucial source of food and economic security for millions of people, play a significant role in climate regulation processes, and are the world's largest carbon dioxide sink (Chen & Huang, 2023). Sustainable blue economy faces various challenges, including global warming, ocean acidification, and still limited knowledge about the oceans, as about 95% of their waters remain unexplored. Understanding the blue economy, implementing it on a global scale, and effectively managing it are crucial in ensuring the sustainable development of seas and oceans (Howard et al., 2017).

Some actions have already been taken, including noting the need for intervention, including the protection of the blue economy, SDGs14 Life below water was included among the SDGs, but it is not the only objective having an impact on restoring stability and balance to the blue economy. SDGs and their implementation will require not only public financing but above all the inclusion of private capital, and here, there are questions on how to build a financial mechanism for the blue economy with the participation of stakeholders and types of capital and financial instruments.

The financial system plays a key role in the process of achieving the Sustainable Development Goals. With increasing demand for ocean resources and increasing pollution and acidification, sustainable blue finance aims to protect and ensure the sustainability of oceans and water resources while supporting economic growth and development. The Paulson Institute has estimated that biodiversity financing faces an average annual shortfall of approximately $711 billion (Sumaila et al., 2022). With the emergence of the so-called blue economy various financing mechanisms and financial structures are proposed to simultaneously protect marine biodiversity and generate profits (Christiansen, 2021). Sustainable blue financing mechanisms should be coordinated with conventional financing sources to effectively implement the designated tasks. The aim of the chapter is to present the current state of knowledge in the field of sustainable financing in the blue economy and to present recommendations for improvements to the existing financial model.

In particular, the following research questions were asked:

1. What is the current state of research on sustainable finance for a blue economy?
2. What keywords do the authors use to describe sustainable finance for a blue economy?
3. What actions are taken in the European Union and at the level of individual countries in terms of financing the blue economy?

The chapter is organised as follows: Section 2 presents a critical literature review; Section 3 presents mechanisms of financing the blue economy; Section 4 case study and Section 5 outlines our conclusion and recommendations.

2. LITERATURE REVIEW OF SUSTAINABLE FINANCE FOR A BLUE ECONOMY STATE OF THE ART

While the concept of the blue economy emerged in 2010, there is still no universal definition. According to the European Commission, the blue economy encompasses 'activities related to the ocean, seas, and coasts and covers a wide range of interlinked established and emerging sectors, including coastal tourism, aquaculture, ocean energy, marine biotechnology, shipbuilding, maritime transport, and fisheries' (European Commission, 2024a). The World Bank (2024) describes it as the 'sustainable use of ocean resources for economic growth, improved livelihoods, and jobs while preserving the health of ocean ecosystems'. A United Nations representative recently defined the blue economy as an economy that

> comprises a range of economic sectors and related policies that together determine whether the use of ocean resources is sustainable. An important challenge of the blue economy is to understand and better manage the many aspects of oceanic sustainability, ranging from sustainable fisheries to ecosystem health to preventing pollution. Secondly, the blue economy challenges us to realize that the sustainable management of ocean resources will require collaboration across borders and sectors through a variety of partnerships, and on a scale that has not been previously achieved. This is a tall order, particularly for Small Island Developing States (SIDS) and Least Developed Countries (LDCs) who face significant limitations.

The UN notes that the blue economy will aid in achieving the UN Sustainable Development Goals, of which one goal, 14, is 'Life Below Water' (The United Nations, 2024). Meanwhile, the World Wild Fund describes the blue economy in two senses: 'For some blue economy means the use of the sea and its resources for sustainable economic development. For others, it simply refers to any economic activity in the maritime sector whether sustainable or not' (Principles for a Sustainable Blue Economy, 2024).

The Web of Science (WoS) database was used to search for publications in the area of sustainable finance for the blue economy. A total number of 128 publications from years 2013 to 2024 were found which contained the search terms in the title, keywords, or abstract – 106 publications referring to 'sustainable blue economy' and 22 publications referring to 'blue economy financ*'.

The sample summary shows that the majority of publications are journal articles, with the number of publications increasing significantly since 2019, except for a small decline in 2020 (Table 1.1; Fig. 1.1).

Table 1.1. Description of the Sample.

Sample size	128
Publication type	
Journal	117
Book	2
Conference paper	9
Publication year	
2024 (Q1)	11
2023	47
2022	30
2021	14
2020	7
2019	10
2018	3
2017	2
2016	2
2015	0
2014	1
2013	1

Source: Own compilation based on WoS database.

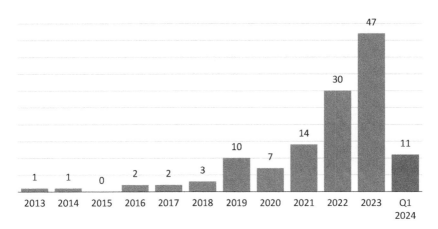

Fig. 1.1. Number of Publications from 2013 to Q1 2024.
Source: Own compilation based on WoS database.

The analyses of co-occurrence of keywords in publications allowed us to divide the keywords into clusters containing terms commonly used by the authors to describe the analysed phenomenon. Using VOSviewer software (version 1.6.20), five clusters containing the following terms were extracted:

1. biodiversity, communities, conservation, ecosystem services, impacts, Mediterranean Sea, populations, resilience;
2. climate change, climate-change, coral reefs, management, marine, ocean governance;
3. coastal, fisheries, ocean, sustainability, Sustainable Development Goals;
4. blue economy, China, European countries, growth;
5. blue growth, sustainable blue economy, sustainable development.

The network showing links between keywords identified in the analysed publications is present in Fig. 1.2.

The literature contains research on financing projects related to the blue economy and the use of individual financial instruments in this process. Tirumala and Tiwari (2022) note that the financial needs related to the implementation of the goals of the blue economy are much greater than monetary resources obtained from conventional sources of financing; therefore, the capital market may be a source of additional financial resources.

The most extensively described capital market instruments are blue bonds. This type of debt security is used to raise funds for the implementation of sustainable blue economy projects related to oceans and fresh waters that are consistent with the implementation of Sustainable Development Goal 14 'Life below water' (Adam & Olayele, 2022). Investors' decisions to purchase blue bonds often result from the belief in the appropriateness of implementing this

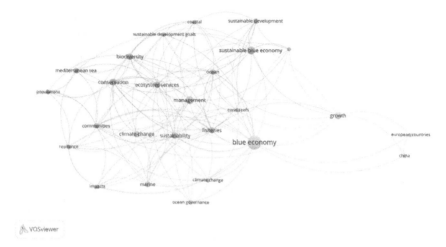

Fig. 1.2. Map of Keyword Combinations with the Most Frequent Co-occurrences.
Source: Own compilation based on WoS database.

type of project while assuming a financial return on the investment (Thompson, 2022). The blue bonds market is gaining support from policymakers, philanthropic and international organisations, and investors looking to align their investments with global goals. It is also a source of additional capital for countries with large ocean areas seeking financing for projects related to the blue economy (Benzaken et al., 2024).

Blue bonds are intended to fill the financial gap in obtaining funds for the implementation of projects related to the sustainable development of seas and oceans, mainly from private entities. And although almost 6 years have passed since the first blue bonds were issued in the Seychelles in 2018, the importance of the blue bonds market is still small. Currently, they constitute less than 0.5% of the sustainable debt market (Bosmans & de Mariz, 2023). Tirumala and Tiwari (2022) add that accelerating investment requires access to additional financial instruments and transformational change among stakeholders.

Kılıç (2024) characterised the process of financing activities related to climate change by small island states (Seychelles) at the expense of issuing sustainable debt, that is through blue bonds. A similar study, but for the Bahamas, was conducted by March et al. (2023). Their article presents the development of the blue economy along with an analysis of the conditions for using blue bonds as a financing mechanism.

The banking system is one of the key elements of the financial system and is responsible for providing capital to various entities for the implementation of specific projects. Mirza et al. (2024) conducted a study to assess whether blue and green loans help optimise interest rate spreads and default probabilities. The obtained results confirmed that the blue-green exposure positively supports the loan portfolio in terms of both profitability and risk management.

Another study on credit in the context of the blue economy is that of Shan et al. (2023). Its aim was to analyse the impact of lending to blue and sustainable companies and increased digitalisation on the financial results of the banking sector. The study covered banks from 27 European Union member states. The results obtained confirmed a positive relationship between banks' performance and their blue lending activities, sustainable credit, and digitalisation. Increased bank financing for blue and other sustainable companies, along with greater investments in digitalisation, is contributing to an increase in net interest margins.

In turn, Christiansen (2021) focused on analysing blended finance as a guiding principle in implementing blue economy projects. The author noted that in this approach, blended finance is used to create new markets and can become a developer rent, which will be taken over by the financial sector, or a technical solution that enables the maintenance of the original belief in market-based environmental management.

Mallin et al. (2019) point out that financing projects related to the blue economy can take place outside the capital market and banking system on the basis of non-repayable donations offered by philanthropic organisations. The authors note that some of these organisations are now starting to implement innovative profit-oriented investment strategies. Special attention is paid to the protected area of the Phoenix Islands in Kiribati, where financing from US philanthropic foundations is intended to support the functioning and management of large-scale marine-protected areas, ultimately compensating the government for lost fishing licence revenues through the creation of a trust fund. Research has shown that by accepting funding from philanthropic foundations, the Kiribati government is gradually relinquishing decision-making authority over territory and resources. Additionally, achieving financial stability for the nature conservation trust fund is also challenging.

Watson et al. (2023) focused on the role of the insurance sector in implementing blue economy projects. According to the authors, the development of financial tools supporting risk management, such as insurance, to ensure fair resilience to marine climate shocks will provide coastal communities with access to financial resources necessary to reduce their vulnerability to such shocks and improve their long-term adaptive capacity. The implementation of new insurance products as risk management tools can potentially help incentivise sustainable use of marine resources and strengthen the economic resilience of coastal communities to climate change.

One direction of research in the field of the blue economy is the analysis of cash flows. Schutter et al. (2024) conducted research on identifying the sources and recipients of funds related to the blue economy from 2017 to 2021. Their analysis indicates that blue financing is mainly directed towards Europe and Central Asia. In turn, Maraseni et al. (2022) showed that initiatives related to obtaining financing for blue economy projects are rated higher in developing countries than in developed ones, and the reason for this may be the fact that developing countries are the main beneficiaries of these programmes and receive more funds and help in this regard.

Taking a different perspective on cash flows related to the blue economy, Booth et al. (2022) highlighted the maritime tourism industry as an untapped source of income that could be allocated to the protection of seas and oceans. Meanwhile, Islam and Sarker (2022) proposed conceptual frameworks combining blue financing and sustainable development by strengthening the emerging blue economy, particularly through promoting sustainable coastal and maritime tourism in the Asia-Pacific region.

Issues related to the blue economy, including the financing of its projects, are considered at both national and international levels. Chen and Huang (2023) described the initiative of the High Level Panel for a Sustainable Ocean Economy (Ocean Panel), which was established in September 2018 to present the latest leading solutions to key oceanic issues. Creating innovative solutions in the areas of technology, finance, and management can accelerate the transition to more sustainable ocean utilisation.

3. THE PRINCIPLES AND MECHANISMS OF SUSTAINABLE BLUE FINANCE

The principles for financing sustainable blue economy introduced in 2018 serve as the foundation for investing in the ocean economy. They were developed by the European Commission, WWF, World Resources Institute, and the European Investment Bank and were introduced by UNEP FI as a set of 14 principles providing global frameworks for the investment process in the blue economy. The target audience for the principles of financing sustainable blue economy includes banks, insurers, and investors.

A synthetic summary of the principles for financing sustainable blue economy is provided in Table 1.2.

Financing blue economy projects requires the implementation and coordination of financial instruments at local, national, and international levels. Individual financial instruments are provided by various types of stakeholders, including national and international institutions, financial entities, and enterprises operating in the public and private sectors. The financial instruments provided by these entities include traditional loans and grants, venture capital funds, private and public equity funds, pension funds, and investment funds. The use of individual instruments depends on the nature of the project and the expectations of stakeholders regarding the return on investment under blue economy projects. It is worth emphasising that investments in a sustainable blue economy can be profitable. According to the study of the High Level Panel for a Sustainable Ocean Economy (oceanpanel.org), investing EUR 2.54 trillion in four ocean solutions – the production of offshore wind energy, sustainable food production in the oceans, decarbonisation of international shipping, and the protection and restoration of mangroves – would allow for By 2050, net benefits of EUR 14.11 trillion will be achieved (The Blue Economy Report, 2022).

Table 1.2. Sustainable Blue Economy Finance Principles.

Principle	Description
Protective	Supporting investments, projects, and actions aimed at restoring, protecting, or maintaining the diversity, productivity, resilience, essential functions, values, and overall state of marine ecosystems as well as the livelihoods and dependent communities associated with them
Compliant	Supporting investments, projects, and actions aligned with legal frameworks and other relevant frameworks at the international, regional, and national levels, which serve as the basis for the health and sustainable development of oceans
Risk-aware	Striving to make investment decisions based on holistic and long-term assessments that take into account economic, social, and environmental factors as well as quantitative risks and systemic impacts. Striving for decision-making processes and actions to take into account new, up-to-date knowledge about potential threats, cumulative effects, and opportunities related to business activities
Systemic	Striving to identify systemic and cumulative effects of implemented investments, activities, and projects throughout the value chain
Inclusive	Supporting investments, projects, and activities that address, support, and improve local livelihoods and working effectively with stakeholders to identify, respond to, and mitigate emerging issues
Cooperative	Collaborating with financial institutions and other stakeholders to promote and implement sustainable blue economy finance principles by sharing knowledge about the oceans, best practices in sustainable blue economy, lessons learned, and future ideas
Transparent	Providing information about investment, banking, and insurance activities and projects, as well as their social, environmental, and economic impacts (both positive and negative) while maintaining confidentiality. Additionally, updates on the progress of implementing these principles will be provided
Purposeful	Making every effort to ensure that investment, banking, and insurance activities and projects are aimed at achieving Sustainable Development Goal No. 14 and other Sustainable Development Goals
Impactful	Supporting investments, actions, and projects that will contribute to providing social, environmental, and economic benefits from ocean resources to both current and future generations
Precautionary	Supporting ocean-related investments, activities, and projects that have assessed their environmental and social risks and impacts based on sound scientific evidence. The precautionary principle will prevail, especially when scientific data are not available
Diversified	Recognising the importance of small- and medium-sized enterprises (SMEs) in the blue economy, efforts should be made to diversify the range of investment, banking, and insurance instruments to facilitate various sustainable development projects. This includes projects in both traditional and non-traditional marine sectors, as well as small- and large-scale initiatives
Solution-driven	Striving to channel investments, banking, and insurance towards innovative commercial solutions to marine issues that positively impact marine ecosystems and livelihoods dependent on the oceans. Endeavouring to establish business cases for implementing such projects and encouraging the dissemination of best practices developed in this way
Partnering	Cooperating with entities from the public, private, and non-governmental sectors to accelerate progress towards a sustainable blue economy. Establishing and implementing approaches to spatial planning for coastal and marine areas
Science-led	Actively seeking to develop knowledge and data on potential risks and impacts associated with investment, banking, and insurance activities, as well as encouraging the creation of sustainable financing opportunities in the blue economy. Sharing scientific information and data on the marine environment

Source: Own elaboration based https://www.unepfi.org/blue-finance/the-principles/ (Accessed: 27 April 2024).

At the international level, the European Commission supports the transition to sustainable investments, including in the area of sustainable blue economy. To standardise the concept of sustainable activities, it started working on the development of the EU Taxonomy. This provided a common language and a clear definition of 'sustainable' financing for investors, businesses, and decision-makers. In July 2021, the Commission published its new 'strategy for financing the transition to a sustainable economy' (European Commission, 2024b). This strategy aims to support the European Green Deal by directing private investments towards transitioning to a climate-neutral economy.

The Recovery and Resilience Facility (RRF) provides loans and grants worth €723.8 billion to support reforms and investments focusing on country-specific recommendations, as well as the green and digital transitions. Although the implementation of blue economy projects is not directly mentioned in the legal basis of the RRF, many recovery and resilience plans of coastal states benefit from the support of this instrument. These countries include Belgium, Cyprus, Greece, France, Italy, Poland, Portugal, and Spain. Projects implemented with financial support from the RRF include greening and innovation in the fisheries and aquaculture sectors, monitoring marine and coastal biodiversity, wastewater treatment, flood protection, modernisation of port infrastructure, coastal tourism, investments in green shipping and support blue skills (The Blue Economy Report, 2022).

To support investments, innovation, and sustainable growth in the blue economy, the European Union launched the BlueInvest platform in April 2019. Its goal is to support innovative SMEs and startups implementing projects related to sustainable blue economy. BlueInvest operates on two fronts. On the one hand, it provides tailored support and investment readiness advice to SMEs and startups in the sector, and on the other hand, it facilitates access to investors and contributes to the creation of a dedicated financial ecosystem for Blue Tech SMEs.

Another financial instrument implemented at the international level is the European Maritime and Fisheries Fund (EMFF), aimed at improving access to financing and investment readiness for startups, early-stage enterprises, and SMEs. From 2016 to 2021, EMFF funds were allocated to 60 projects, including many supporting biodiversity and ecosystem regeneration through innovation.

In 2020, the European Commission partnered with the European Investment Fund (EIF) to launch BlueInvest fund to provide financing for core equity funds focused on supporting innovative blue economy businesses. Investments are made in 'intermediary' funds and not directly in companies. By 2022, the total amount of approved or signed commitments within the fund was EUR 100 million, and the total expected amount of mobilised capital (in the case of private investments) was up to EUR 300 million. The platform's operation has been extended until 2026.

Based on the BlueInvest model, the EIF, and the Portuguese national promotional institution, Banco Português de Fomento (BPF) have launched a EUR 50 million capital collaboration under the name Portugal Blue to support

Portuguese companies operating in the blue economy. The EIF and BPF have each contributed EUR 25 million to this joint programme, which is expected to catalyse investments of over EUR 75 million in blue economy funds and companies, such as startups, SMEs, and mid-cap companies (European Investment Fund, 2024).

The Blue Economy 2022 Report shows that government financing, venture capital, and private capital can play an important role in the coming years in supporting the development of sustainable innovations and technologies that will contribute to the protection of oceans and coastlines – the overall blue economy. Additionally, the Union, ensuring support for the implementation of blue growth in the long term under the Horizon 2020 programme, announced special calls for applications under the Blue Growth initiative for a total amount of EUR 448 million. A total of 66 projects were financed to unlock the potential of sea, ocean, and inland water resources for use in various maritime industries, while protecting biodiversity and increasing resilience to climate change.

The Blue Economy 2022 Report shows that government financing, venture capital, and private capital can play an important role in the coming years in supporting the development of sustainable innovations and technologies that will contribute to the protection of oceans and coastlines – the overall blue economy. Additionally, the European Union, ensuring support for the implementation of blue growth in the long term under the Horizon 2020 programme, announced special calls for applications under the Blue Growth initiative for a total amount of EUR 448 million. In total, 66 projects were financed, aimed at unlocking the potential of marine, ocean, and inland water resources for applications in various branches of the maritime industry while simultaneously preserving biodiversity and enhancing resilience to climate change.

The European Bank for Reconstruction and Development (EBRD) is also involved in financial support for projects related to the blue economy. By 2022, EBRD direct investments in blue economy sectors amounted to EUR 7.37 billion (total project value EUR 20.9 billion) and mainly concerned water and sewage systems (approx. EUR 3.85 billion); shipbuilding industry and water transport (approx. EUR 1.87 billion); ports and port activities (approx. EUR 870 million); solid waste management (approx. EUR 470 million); and investments in real estate and coastal tourism (approx. EUR 330 million). EBRD also has extensive experience in investing in effective wastewater treatment plants, which is essential for improving water quality and protecting the blue economy. Over the years 2020–2022, the Bank allocated EUR 70 million for investments worth EUR 938 million in modern wastewater treatment systems in Bulgaria, Croatia, and Romania.

4. BLUE ECONOMY FINANCING CASE STUDY

Benzaken et al. (2022) developed the case study of Seychelles, a representative of Small Island Developing States, and showed that sustainable blue economy financing is a combination of local and global factors including availability and affordability of global finance, attractiveness, local enabling environment, and implementation capability and private sector development.

Despite being a high-income country, Seychelles faces challenges in accessing public finance. While ineligible for Official Development Assistance (ODA) due to its income status, Seychelles utilises other sources of funding, including Multilateral Development Banks, bilateral financing, and philanthropic financing. Seychelles is the beneficiary of World Bank's Third South West Indian Ocean Fisheries Governance and Shared Growth Project (SWIOFISH3) for fisheries development. Concessional lending from IMF and World Bank is used for budget support, debt management, and taxation reforms. Another source of financing is the African Development Bank's Fund for Africa Private Sector Assistance grant for biotechnology. Bilateral finance from China, Japan, or United Arab Emirates is the source of financing infrastructure development and philanthropic grants available through international partnerships with non-government institutions are used for financing projects related to conservation, climate change, and marine research.

In case of Seychelles, the main barrier to access public financing is ineligibility for ODA due to high-income status. Other identified barriers include taxation that needs reforms to increase domestic revenue, limited awareness and expertise in acquiring new financing opportunities, and challenges in assigning a monetary value to natural assets and demonstrating the benefits of the blue economy.

Due to limited access to public funds, they are insufficient for blue economy investments. Therefore, it is necessary to also use financing from the private sector. Various factors affecting access to affordable private finance are examined, including global economic trends, investor expectations, and local fiscal constraints. Creating a conducive environment through good governance and regulatory measures is crucial to mitigate investment risks.

The main barrier to access private funding is high cost of credit. This cost is several times higher for African countries compared to OECD countries due to the lack of developed financial infrastructure and risk mitigation instruments. Capacity-building initiatives are identified as crucial to developing investable projects at scale and attracting international partners. While funding streams like blue bonds and debt swaps are welcomed, they are deemed insufficient to meet the substantial investment requirements for sustainable blue economy transitions. One of the challenges is the need for expertise in navigating the global financial landscape and exploring innovative risk-based models to facilitate private sector investments in nature-based solutions.

Local drivers of investing in the blue economy are considered in terms of attractiveness and local enabling environment. Seychelles' attractiveness to investment results from both global factors such as interest in the blue economy and favourable financial climates, as well as local drivers like valuable marine resources and investment opportunities. Success in negotiations for initiatives like the blue bond and debt swap is credited to factors such as timeliness, strong partnerships, and effective risk mitigation measures. However, barriers to sustainable blue economy development includes a decrease of dynamics in the blue economy implementation at national level, competition with other countries, and local constraints like infrastructure limitations and the need for sustainability approaches in fisheries and tourism.

The key role in creating local enabling environment plays good governance. The examples of effective governing include the blue bonds and debt swap, the Seychelles Blue Economy Roadmap (2018), and good financial management practices. Institutional arrangements like SeyCCAT are viewed as crucial for transparency and accountability. Challenges include the need for better coordination in decision-making processes, centralised resource mobilisation mechanisms, and expertise in developing bankable projects. There's also a call for methodologies to value natural assets and improve data collection systems for tracking financial flows. Despite successes, there's recognition of the need for additional capacity and expertise for long-term sustainable development initiatives.

Regarding the possibility of local implementations in the development of the blue economy, the key need is a conducive regulatory and fiscal environment to attract private investment and empower the local private sector. Examples such as approved aquaculture regulations unlocking World Bank investment and government support for value-adding activities in fisheries and tourism are cited as drivers of economic diversification. Challenges include competition with government-owned sectors, infrastructure limitations, and limited public awareness of sustainable blue economy opportunities. Additionally, constraints like risk-averse local financial institutions and a lack of innovative business models hinder financing and entrepreneurship. Capacity needs range from structural reforms to technical expertise and education support to further empower the local private sector.

The Covid-19 had negative impact on Seychelles economy, resulting mainly from the collapse of international tourism, which was the main source of government revenue, leading to a realisation of the unsustainability of over-dependence on tourism in the long term. The reallocation of public finance to health and income support, coupled with concerns about debt repayments, constrained investment in the sustainable blue economy, affecting seed capital for startups and access to local credit and government guarantees for SMEs. Access to private finance became challenging due to the temporary downgrading of Seychelles' credit rating and debt to gross domestic product ratio. However, opportunities for post-Covid-19 recovery include reconsidering the revenue mix with a focus on sustainability, research, and innovation, improving the governance and regulatory environment for local private sector development, and encouraging entrepreneurship. Investment priorities post-Covid-19 include enhancing the sustainability and resilience of fisheries and tourism, promoting emerging sectors such as research and innovation, renewable energy, waste management, and addressing food security concerns.

Table 1.3 presents a summary of features of Seychelles sustainable blue economy finance ecosystem.

Table 1.3. The Features of Seychelles Sustainable Blue Economy Finance Ecosystem.

Access to finance	• ODA eligibility • Innovation in finance • Credit cost • Blue bond and debt swap lessons • Impact of Covid-19
Attractiveness	• Blue economy concept • Sustainable Development Goals • Global investment climate • Natural assets
Local enabling environment	• Good governance • Accountability and transparency • Financial management • Blue bonds and debt swap lessons • Investment strategy • Impact of Covid-19
Local implementation	• Entrepreneurship/capacity • Ease of doing business • Private sector development (SMEs) • Local financial institutions • Blue bonds and debt swap lessons

Source: Own elaboration based on Benzaken et al. (2024).

5. CONCLUSION AND RECOMMENDATION

The blue economy plays a key role for the economy, society, and the environment. In particular, it provides employment and valuable resources for market participants, and it is a valuable public good. However, human activities create a significant degree of degradation of the blue economy's resources, destroying some that cannot be replenished or restored. Destructive activities include those with direct impact, such as overfishing, the destructive exploitation of coasts and coral reefs, water pollution (e.g. oceans, seas, rivers), the loss of biodiversity, and eutrophication; however, the indirect consequences of human actions and decisions can also result in significant damage including growing risks to the climate and, subsequently, climate change. The implementation of activities detrimental to the blue economy is often economically profitable but generates negative repercussions. Providing innovative sustainable blue financing requires the involvement of all stakeholders, and in order to do so, they must be defined along with the role they play in the financing mechanism if, in particular, it concerns public sector entities (i.e. governments), the enterprise sector, or NGOs. Some governments have implemented individual actions (Seychelles) to ensure sustainable financing and funding mechanisms for their blue economies; however, it is not enough to ensure the sustainability of a blue economy as it requires the involvement of all stakeholders and the cooperation of public and private capital with a crucial role for financial institutions in redirecting unsustainable cash flows in blue economy.

The economic and ecological importance of seas and oceans makes the concept of the blue economy a global concept related to sustainable development. Its goal is to protect and ensure environmentally sustainable development of seas and oceans. Achieving the goals of the blue economy in line with the Sustainable Development Goals requires a change in the financing paradigm. Traditional finance sought to maximise profits without considering negative externalities such as climate change, depletion of natural resources, and environmental degradation. Sustainable finance integrates financial issues and non-financial factors.

Implementation of projects related to the blue economy is capital-intensive. Depending on the size and complexity of the project, it often exceeds the financial capabilities of both private and public entities. Therefore, it is essential to build a framework of a financial system that combines private and public funds, assuming efficiency in their expenditure. In this chapter, examples of financial instruments through which the European Union supports the sustainable development of the blue economy are described. EU funds usually serve as support and complementation for the capital available to entities implementing such projects. To obtain capital, project contractors can use financial resources from the capital market (e.g. blue bonds) and blue loans offered by banks. The extent to which various sources of external financing are utilised depends on the development of the capital market and the model of the banking system. In countries with an Anglo-Saxon model, capital markets will be more significant, while in countries with a continental model, banks will play a leading role.

In the process of ensuring the effectiveness of the sustainable financing system for the blue economy, a clear regulatory framework for financing and implementing sustainable blue economy projects is extremely important. It would be expected and, in the authors' opinion, extremely useful to develop good practices in this area, including cooperation between entities at the national, local, and international levels.

The IFAC Guidance for financing the blue economy, building on the Green Bond Principles and the Green Loan Principles, deserves a positive assessment. The complexity and diversity of the implemented blue economy projects make it worth considering expanding the range of financial instruments dedicated to the blue economy. Additionally, it is crucial to establish a clear division of risk between parties, especially considering the long or uncertain returns on investment in certain projects.

Facilitating access to external sources of financing, especially in countries with a continental model of the banking system, requires cooperation between governments and representatives of the banking sector in order to develop an offer of blue loans granted on preferential terms and establish the rules for co-financing projects from public (EU) and private funds (loans).

The diversity and often uniqueness of blue economy projects underline the necessity for their financing system to be based on established regulatory frameworks in this area. However, specific solutions (e.g. the structure of acquired capital) should be considered on a case-by-case basis.

REFERENCES

Adam, J. P., & Olayele, F. (2022). Africa's Blue Economy as a development finance opportunity: Lessons for policy innovation. In F. Olayele & S. Yiagadeesenm (Eds.), *Sustainable development in post-pandemic Africa* (pp. 196–217). Routledge.
Benzaken, D., Adam, J. P., Virdin, J., & Voyer, M. (2024). From concept to practice: Financing sustainable blue economy in lessons learnt from the Seychelles experience. *Marine Policy*, *163*, 106072.
Benzaken, D., Voyer, M., Pouponneau, A., & Hanich, Q. (2022). Good governance for sustainable blue economy in small islands: Lessons learned from the Seychelles experience. *Frontiers in Political Science*, *4*, 1040318.
Booth, H., Mourato, S., & Milner-Gulland, E. J. (2022). Investigating acceptance of marine tourism levies, to cover the opportunity costs of conservation for coastal communities. *Ecological Economics*, *201*, 107578.
Bosmans, P., & de Mariz, F. (2023). The Blue Bond market: A catalyst for ocean and water financing. *Journal of Risk and Financial Management*, *16*(3), 184.
Chen, Z., & Huang, W. (2023). Evolutionary game analysis of governmental intervention in the sustainable mechanism of China's Blue finance. *Sustainability*, *15*(9), 7117.
Christiansen, J. (2021). Fixing fictions through blended finance: The entrepreneurial ensemble and risk interpretation in the Blue Economy. *Geoforum*, *120*, 93–102.
European Commission. (2024a). *Map of the week – Developing skills for the Blue Economy – Coastal tourism.* https://maritime-forum.ec.europa.eu/contents/map-week-developing-skills-blue-economy-coastal-tourism_en
European Commission. (2024b). *Strategy for financing the transition to a sustainable economy.* https://eur-lex.europa.eu/legal-content/EN/TXT/HTML/?uri=CELEX:52021DC0390&from=BG
European Investment Fund. (2024). https://www.eif.org/what_we_do/resources/portugal-blue/index.htm
Howard, J., McLeod, E., Thomas, S., Eastwood, E., Fox, M., Wenzel, L., & Pidgeon, E. (2017). The potential to integrate blue carbon into MPA design and management. *Aquatic Conservation: Marine and Freshwater Ecosystems*, *27*, 100–115.
Islam, M. W., & Sarker, T. (2022). Financing sustainable coastal and maritime tourism in the blue economy of the Asia-Pacific. In T. Cadman & T. Sarker (Eds.), *De Gruyter handbook of sustainable development and finance* (pp. 543–566). De Gruyter.
Kılıç, A. O. (2024). Seychelles blue bond: Indebting ecological restructuring of fisheries. *Marine Policy*, *163*, 106144.
Knodt, S., Visbeck, M., & Biber, A. (2023, June). Sustainable Blue Economy: Transformation, value and the potential of marine ecosystems. In *OCEANS 2023-Limerick* (pp. 1–5). IEEE. doi:10.1109/OCEANSLimerick52467.2023.10244621.
Mallin, M. A. F., Stolz, D. C., Thompson, B. S., & Barbesgaard, M. (2019). In oceans we trust: Conservation, philanthropy, and the political economy of the Phoenix Islands protected area. *Marine Policy*, *107*, 103421.
Maraseni, T., Karki, S., Koju, U., Shresta, A., & Cadman, T. (2022). Evaluating the governance of sustainable development: The quality and legitimacy of the blue economy. *De Gruyter handbook of sustainable development and finance*, 567.
March, A., Failler, P., & Bennett, M. (2023). Challenges when designing blue bond financing for small Island developing states. *ICES Journal of Marine Science*, *80*(8), 2244–2251.
Mirza, N., Umar, M., Sbia, R., & Jasmina, M. (2024). The impact of blue and green lending on credit portfolios: A commercial banking perspective. *Review of Accounting and Finance*, ahead-of-print, https://doi.org/10.1108/RAF-11-2023-0389
Ocean Solutions That Benefit People, Nature and the Economy. (2022). *High level panel for a sustainable ocean economy, ocean solutions report | high level panel for a sustainable ocean economy.* oceanpanel.org.
Principles for a Sustainable Blue Economy. (2024). http://wwf.panda.org/our_work/oceans/publications/sustainable_blue_economy_reports.cfm
Schutter, M. S., Cisneros-Montemayor, A., Voyer, M., Allison, E. H., Domarchuk-White, C., Benzaken, D., & Mohammed, E. Y. (2024). Mapping flows of blue economy finance: Ambitious narratives, opaque actions, and social equity risks. *One Earth.*

Shan, S., Mirza, N., Umar, M., & Hasnaoui, A. (2023). The nexus of sustainable development, blue financing, digitalization, and financial intermediation. *Technological Forecasting and Social Change, 195*, 122772.

Shiiba, N., Wu, H. H., Huang, M. C., & Tanaka, H. (2022). How blue financing can sustain ocean conservation and development: A proposed conceptual framework for blue financing mechanism. *Marine Policy, 139*, 104575.

Sumaila, R., Konar, M., Hart, B., & Walsh, M. (2022). *7 ways to bridge the blue finance gap*, 2020. https://www.wri.org/insights/7-ways-bridge-blue-finance-gap

The Blue Economy Report. (2024). https://oceans-and-fisheries.ec.europa.eu/system/files/2022-05/2022-blue-economy-report_en.pdf

The Nation Unies. (2024). *Diving into the blue economy*. https://www.un.org/fr/desa/diving-blue-economy

The World Bank. (2024). *What is the blue economy?* https://www.worldbank.org/en/news/infographic/2017/06/06/blue-economy

Thompson, B. S. (2022). Blue bonds for marine conservation and a sustainable ocean economy: Status, trends, and insights from green bonds. *Marine Policy, 144*, 105219.

Tirumala, R. D., & Tiwari, P. (2022). Innovative financing mechanism for blue economy projects. *Marine Policy, 139*, 104194.

United Nations. (2022). *Blue Economy: Oceans as the next great economic frontier*. https://unric.org/en/blue-economy-oceans-as-the-next-great-economic-frontier/

Watson, J. R., Spillman, C. M., Little, L. R., Hobday, A. J., & Levin, P. S. (2023). Enhancing the resilience of blue foods to climate shocks using insurance. *ICES Journal of Marine Science, 80*(10), 2457–2469.

CHAPTER 2

SUSTAINABLE FUTURES: NAVIGATING ENVIRONMENTAL CHALLENGES THROUGH LOCAL GOVERNANCE IN THE TIRRENO-EOLIE AREA

Carlotta D'Alessandro[a], Giuseppe Ioppolo[a], Alberto Bongiorno[a], Giuseppe Caristi[a] and Katarzyna Szopik-Depczyńska[b]

[a]*Department of Economics, University of Messina, Messina, Italy*
[b]*Department of Business Management, Institute of Management, University of Szczecin, Szczecin, Poland*

ABSTRACT

Purpose/Objective: *Recognising the urgency to safeguard the planet and foster resilience against climate-related health challenges, this study aligns with the 2030 Agenda and explores local initiatives, such as those by the local action group (LAG).*

Design/Methodology/Approach: *This analysis identified the strengths, weaknesses, opportunities, and threats faced by the Tirreno-Eolie LAG, providing a solid foundation for developing the Local Development Plan (LDP). Moreover, an analytic hierarchy process (AHP) analysis was employed to yield a prioritised ranking of the outlined LDP strategies based on the stakeholder input.*

Findings: *The analysis of the LDP for LAG revealed a comprehensive set of actions designed to promote sustainable development at the local level: 1. urban redevelopment projects, 2. preservation of historical buildings, 3. environmental awareness initiatives in Sicily, 4. biological diversity programmes and education, 5. promoting circular economy principles, 6. implementing sustainable corporate governance, 7. developing information systems for control and security, 8. establishing partnerships with local associations, 9. leveraging European initiatives, 10. deployment of newer and greener technologies, 11. redevelopment of infrastructure.*

Significance/Implications/Conclusions: *By strategically implementing the LDP's recommendations, LAG can contribute to building a more sustainable, resilient, and culturally vibrant Sicily.*

Limitations: *Firstly, the available information on the LAG Tirreno-Eolie may be limited. Secondly, the complex and ever-changing nature of social and environmental systems can constrain the objective of the research.*

Future Research: *Future research may investigate the effectiveness of formulated actions and outcomes over time, conduct comparative analyses with regions implementing similar sustainability initiatives, and investigate the scalability and adaptability of the LDP framework to diverse contexts.*

Keywords: Sustainable development; climate change; local action group; responsible governance; local development plan; socio-environmental systems

JEL Codes: Q01; Q50; R00

1. INTRODUCTION

Climate change presents a substantial risk to worldwide health in the 21st century. Its impacts extend to the alteration of the natural environment and various ecosystems, which, in turn, affects negatively human health (Zhao et al., 2022). Indeed, global warming has driven an increment in average temperatures, resulting in more frequent heat waves and droughts (Agovino et al., 2019). Precipitation patterns have also shifted, increasing the likelihood of storms and floods (Agovino et al., 2019).

All citizens worldwide, from low-lying areas to high altitudes and across income levels, are vulnerable independently of age, economic, or social state (Zhao et al., 2022).

Furthermore, climate change can act as a multiplier of present social and economic inequalities in urban areas, hindering efforts to root out hunger and poverty (Gasper et al., 2011). This leaves marginalised groups even more vulnerable to the impacts of a changing climate (Gasper et al., 2011). Along with these lines, climate change, being characterised also by the exploitation of natural resources, presents a significant obstacle to pursuing a sustainable future (Agovino et al., 2019).

As per the definition of UN's World Commission in the report 'Our Common Future', sustainable development is 'development that meets the needs of the present, without compromising the ability of future generations to meet their own needs' (WCED, 1987).

Moreover, nowadays, there has been a noticeable trend towards witnessing a surge in initiatives – events, policies, and manoeuvers – aimed at identifying solutions to minimise environmental impacts and achieving sustainability.

In the same vein, the United Nations embraced the 2030 Agenda for Sustainable Development, a worldwide blueprint delineating 17 Sustainable Development Goals (SDGs) aimed at fostering a more sustainable future for humanity (Nations, 2015). Moreover, the notion of sustainability has deeply influenced urban development since its inception, drawing from principles rooted in both economic and ecological ideologies (Zeng et al., 2022).

Among these, SDG 11, 'Make cities and human settlements inclusive, safe, resilient and sustainable' specifically addresses the challenges and opportunities of urban sustainability (du Plessis, 2022).

Indeed, the local and regional area presents a unique opportunity for advancing sustainable initiatives (Palm et al., 2019). This is due, in part, to the close vicinity of local governments to their inhabitants, allowing them to identify unsatisfied necessities and function as a catalyst for different and innovatory solutions that promote sustainability (Palm et al., 2019).

A sustainable urban ecosystem represents 'ecosystems which are ethical, effective (healthy and equitable), zero-waste, self-regulating, resilient, self-renewing, flexible, psychologically fulfilling and cooperative' (Dizdaroglu, 2015).

Urban sustainability prioritises the long-term viability of cityscapes; it encompasses factors like fairness between generations, equity within the current population, responsible use of natural resources, a diverse and robust economy, self-reliance of the community, societal wellness, and meeting basic person exigencies (Zeng et al., 2022). Additionally, urban sustainability encompasses various facets such as biodiversity, energy management, material usage, air quality control, mitigation of heat islands, noise reduction, and more (Verma & Raghubanshi, 2018).

Driven by the urgency of tackling unsustainable patterns and escalating environmental threats, the circular economy has evolved as a leading approach to achieving sustainable development (Dagilienė et al., 2021).

Circular economy offers a framework for promoting the conscientious and cyclical use of resources (Fig. 2.1); this approach prioritises minimising material input and waste production to reach the ultimate goal of separating economic expansion from dependence on finite natural resources (Moraga et al., 2019). This is particularly true for urban areas, where over half the global population resides, unlock significant potential for sustainability (Dagilienė et al., 2021).

In this connection, sustainable development is gaining ground in rural areas, where agriculture, local populations, and natural resources are intrinsically linked (Palmisano et al., 2016).

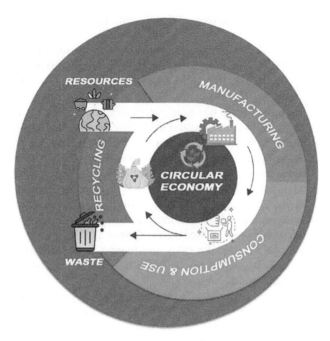

Fig. 2.1. A Circular Economy Framework for Resource Use. *Source*: Authors.

Furthermore, recognising the significant portion of Europe comprised of rural regions (approximately 57%), European policy has increasingly emphasised local community engagement in decision-making processes (Menconi et al., 2018). This shift reflects the understanding that local communities are best positioned to address the unique challenges and opportunities of their rural area. Particularly, to ensure the continued vitality and economic profitability of rural regions, the European Union has implemented the Common Agricultural Policy (CAP).

The CAP strives to accomplish threefold objectives: securing a sustainable future for European agriculture, providing more focused assistance for smaller farms, and granting increased adaptability for European Union states to tailor CAP sized to their specific local contexts (CAP 2023–27, 2023).

The policy offers the LEADER Programme as a key mechanism for promoting community-driven local development strategies (Menconi et al., 2018).

In particular, the LEADER programme, which stands for 'Liaisons entre Actions de Développement de L'Economie Rural' (French for 'Links Between Actions for the Development of the Rural Economy') follows a bottom-up approach, encouraging collaboration among diverse stakeholders such as farmers, rural businesses, local organisations, public authorities, and individuals. Through this process, LAGs (acronyms for the Italian Gruppo di Azione Locale or GAL) are formed (European Commission, 2006). These LAGs cover a fundamental position in driving rural development by formulating and handling their own local development strategies with dedicated budgets. Additionally,

LAGs promote the involvement of the local communities and the business actors (Esparcia et al., 2015).

Furthermore, the LEADER approach fosters stronger community bonds, cross-sectoral innovation, and knowledge exchange between LAGs at national and EU-wide levels (European Commission, 2006). What is more, entrusted with the development and execution of context-specific strategies, LAGs serve as a central pillar in promoting sustainable solutions and fostering community engagement. This aligns perfectly with the broader international push to tackle the critical issues outlined previously.

To delve deeper into the position of LAGs in favouring solutions at the local level, this study examines the case of the LAG Tirreno-Eolie in Italy. This specific LAG operates within a geographically unique area encompassing the Aeolian Islands, a volcanic archipelago facing environmental challenges.

To ensure the sustainable development of the LAG Tirreno-Eolie district, a comprehensive SWOT analysis was executed to recognise its strengths, weaknesses, opportunities, and threats. This analysis served as a valuable foundation for defining the LDP, ensuring that the plan is tailored to the specific needs and challenges of the region and promoting sustainable development principles within the territory.

2. METHODS

This study employed a combined methodology approach, employing both qualitative and quantitative information gathering and assessment methods across four phases. This comprehensive approach allowed for triangulation, where findings from different methods were used to strengthen and validate the overall results.

More specifically, this mixed methods study, began by presenting the LAG Tirreno-Eolie case, then delved into a SWOT analysis, deployed the LDP based on its findings, and concluded with AHP evaluation of the plan's strategies (Fig. 2.2).

In particular, researchers use case studies to explore programmes, events, activities, processes, or individuals in detail, uncovering their unique characteristics (Creswell, 2014).

From this perspective, this research employed a single-case study design, focusing on the LAG Tirreno-Eolie, a LAG operating in Sicily, Italy (Fig. 2.3).

LAGs, acting as a hybrid of public and private entities, are the driving force behind the LEADER programme. As a local development district, they are instrumental in promoting economic and social progress within their territories (GALTIRRENOEOLIE, 2014).

In particular, the LAG Tirreno-Eolie derives its nomenclature from its geographical demarcation, which includes the entirety of the eastern zone of Messina and extends across an area measuring 311 square kilometres, incorporating the Aeolian archipelago. The Tirreno-Eolie LAG district covers a portion of territory facing the sea, encompassing the Milazzo Plain and the Aeolian Islands. According to the ISTAT (2011) surveys, within this area, approximately 82,0426 people reside with a population density of 265 habitants per square kilometre.

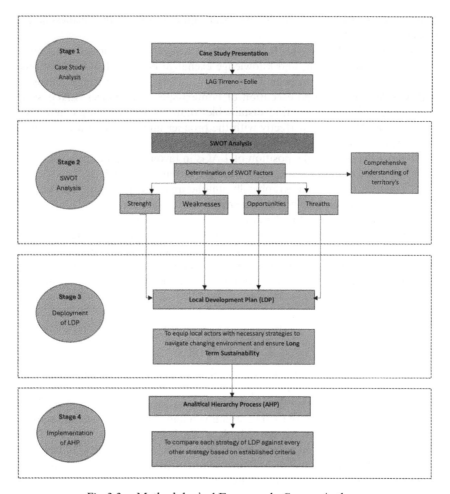

Fig. 2.2. Methodological Framework. *Source*: Authors.

More specifically, the demographic settlement structure of the municipalities displays the most populated areas in Milazzo (1.21439 ab./km^2) and Torregrotta (1.76854 ab./km^2). The following table (Table 2.1) shows the demographic information about the LAG district (ISTAT, 2017).

Similarly, demographic information is presented in Table 2.2 for the Aeolian Islands.

Settlement patterns in this district exhibit a positive correlation between social cohesion and the preservation of local traditions. However, economic and infrastructural limitations hinder development in these areas, motivating a shift in population distribution towards the coast. The coastal regions offer more favourable conditions for economic prosperity and improved quality of life due to superior infrastructure and environmental attributes.

Sustainable Futures 29

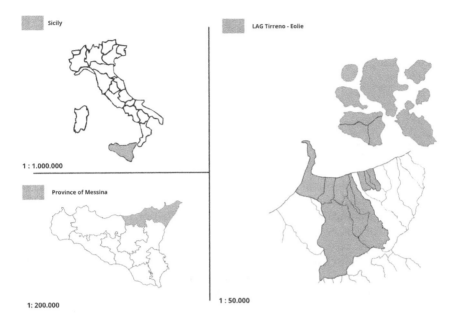

Fig. 2.3. LAG Tirreno-Eolie Municipalities. *Source*: Authors.

Table 2.1. Demographic Information of the Municipalities in the LAG Tirreno-Eolie District.

	Mainland	
Municipality	Resident Population	Population Density
Torregrotta	7.410	1.76854 ab./km²
Milazzo	31.473	1.21439 ab./km²
Venetico	3.979	87,868 ab./km²
San Filippo del Mela	7.048	66,576 ab./km²
Pace del Mela	6.246	48,917 ab./km²
Valdina	1.337	48,355 ab./km²
Gualtieri Sicaminò	1.758	10,811 ab./km²
Condrò	486	9,333 ab./km²
Santa Lucia del Mela	4,607	5,105 ab./km²
San Pier Niceto	2.791	7,042 ab./km²

Source: ISTAT (2017).

Turning attention to the Aeolian Islands, they constitute an integral component of the LAG district framework, showcasing a distinctive repository of artistic, archaeological, cultural, and historical heritage.

Indeed, each of the seven islands in the archipelago has a volcanic origin, resulting in distinctive rock formations and a rugged coastline. Over time, this has led to the development of unique ecological resources, including diverse plant and animal species, creating a rich ecological tapestry. These natural assets not only hold

Table 2.2. Demographic Information for the Aeolian Islands in the LAG Tirreno-Eolie District.

Municipality	Aeolian Island Resident Population	Population Density
Lipari	12.753	141,39 ab./km^2
Malfa	956	114,59 ab./km^2
Santa Maria di Salina	981	97,71 ab./km^2
Leni	698	77,02 ab./km^2

Source: ISTAT (2017).

intrinsic value but also contribute significantly to the ecological balance and overall health of the ecosystem. This, in turn, fuels tourism, a key driver of local prosperity. The islands' unparalleled landscapes, characterised by their uncontaminated beauty, further enhance their attractiveness as tourist destinations.

Furthermore, to enhance the district's resilience and tailored ability in the presence of climate change, sustainable practices can be implemented alongside collaborative partnerships. These partnerships can facilitate knowledge sharing and resource mobilisation to address climate risks. Specifically, sustainable practices can help mitigate greenhouse gas emissions, while collaborative partnerships can facilitate knowledge sharing and resource mobilisation to address economic downturns. Ultimately, this can help the generation of a more sustainable and climate-resilient district.

However, these areas often face economic and infrastructural limitations, including limited adoption of modern technologies. This lack of technological advancement can hinder development in crucial sectors like agriculture and waste management, making it challenging to embrace sustainable practices.

Moreover, these challenges have motivated a shift in population distribution towards the coast, where superior infrastructure and environmental attributes create more favourable conditions for economic prosperity and a better quality of life.

Having outlined the LAG Tirreno-Eolie's operational framework and geographical scope, this analysis now directs its focus towards the organisation's impact on local development within the district. The LAG's strategic positioning as a key stakeholder within the LEADER programme empowers it to facilitate the emergence and implementation of localised initiatives. This fosters socioeconomic and environmental well-being, an important goal of local development initiatives.

In this perspective, local development is considered a comprehensive approach that strives to enhance the economic, social, and environmental wellness of a specific territory. This is achieved by leveraging the area's own resources (endogenous resources) to bolster the living conditions of its residents (Milán-García et al., 2019).

Additionally, identity is fostered by local development, allowing places to stand out in a globalised world. However, overemphasising unique traits can simplify a territory's complexity, potentially misinterpreting its core function and neglecting its inherent diversity (Ioppolo, 2010). In this perspective, sustainability can act as an interpreter of these territorial variations, becoming a measure of balanced development across economic, social, and environmental aspects (Ioppolo, 2010).

Effective sustainable local development requires a built-in capacity for continuous adaptation and self-renewal; this ensures long-term success, while adhering to the limitations imposed by the local ecological context (Milán-García et al., 2019). A well-crafted LDP fosters this very principle of adaptability. By systematically analysing the territory's strengths, weaknesses, opportunities, and threats (SWOT analysis), LDP equips local actors with the necessary strategies to navigate a changing environment and ensure the region's long-term sustainability.

More specifically, the SWOT framework serves a dual purpose in strategic decision-making. It can be employed for initial assessments during the planning phase and acts as a foundational step for developing a comprehensive strategic management plan (Srivastava et al., 2005).

This framework will systematically examine the territory's:

- *Strengths*: Internal factors that contribute to the success of the LDP.
- *Weaknesses*: Internal factors that hinder the effectiveness of the LDP.
- *Opportunities*: External factors that present favourable conditions for the LDP's goals.
- *Threats*: External factors that pose challenges to the LDP's implementation.

Moreover, understanding the interplay between local development and sustainability proves particularly significant for LAG Tirreno-Eolie in the context of its ongoing LDP formulation.

More specifically, LDPs play an important role in enhancing rural revitalisation. They leverage strengths and establish a foundation for continuous renewal (Atkočiūnien et al., 2024).

LDPs should prioritise strategies that address the most pressing exigencies of rural communities. Furthermore, LDPs can foster collaboration among local stakeholders and receiving while promoting conscientious utilisation of local resources (Atkočiūnien et al., 2024).

The LDP formulated for the LAG Tirreno-Eolie will create a framework for utilising local resources, fostering collaboration, and implementing strategies that promote long-term economic, social, and environmental prosperity within the territory. However, with a multitude of potential strategies, prioritising them effectively becomes crucial. To address this, the next section will delve into the AHP, a decision-making tool that allowed to rank the various strategies based on their contribution to sustainable development in the LAG Tirreno-Eolie.

The AHP, developed by Saaty (1980), offers a structured method for navigating complex decision-making. It functions by decomposing the issue into a hierarchical structure, where the overarching object sits at the top. Below, it branches out various criteria and alternative solutions.

AHP is an analysis of measurement which facilitates the prioritisation of these alternatives through a multi-step process. Firstly, AHP, multi-criteria decision-making method that aids in resolving issues, was conducted through pairwise comparisons (Abdel-Basset et al., 2018; Saaty, 1980).

This involves systematically comparing each strategy (indicated numerically in Fig. 2.4) against every other strategy based on each established criteria (economic, social, and environmental sustainability), with equal weight given to each criterion.

Through these comparisons, subjective judgements were converted into quantifiable values. This is commonly made on a scale of 1 to 9, with 1 indicating equal significance and 9 standing for extreme importance. The resulting comparisons were then compiled into reciprocal matrices (one matrix for each set of strategies with a shared parent node).

Secondly, weights were assigned to each criterion. These weights reflected the relative significance of each criterion in achieving sustainable development for the LAG Tirreno-Eolie. This step involved personal interviews with experts who provided their insights concerning the relevance of diverse criteria. In particular, key stakeholders – local entrepreneurs and policymakers – who participated in face-to-face interviews were identified. During the interviews, participants were presented with a series of two-part questions. These questions compared the importance of different LDP strategies for the context' sustainability (e.g. 'Which is more important for LAG Tirreno-Eolie's sustainable development: Urban Redevelopment Projects or Promoting Circular Economy Principles?' followed by 'How much more important is it?').

Following the interviews, responses were turned into numerical values using Saaty's scale (1 = equal importance, 3 = a bit more important, 5 = much more important, 7 = very much more important, 9 = absolutely more important) (Saaty, 1990). Additionally, intermediates values (such as 2, 4, 8) were also used.

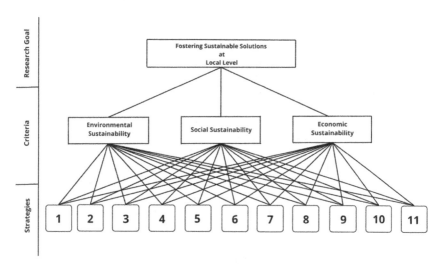

Fig. 2.4. Hierarchy AHP on Three Levels. *Source*: Authors.

These values were then compiled into comparison matrices using an Excel spreadsheet. Matrices were normalised (dividing each element by the column sum), and the weights for each strategy were calculated as the average of each row.

An important step involved assessing the consistency of the responses. Consistency ratios, a measure of deviation from perfect consistency within the matrices (Saaty, 1990), were calculated. If a ratio exceeded 0.10, indicating inconsistency, interviewees were contacted for clarification.

For each stakeholder were provided six individual comparison matrices, representing their judgements on the relative importance of LDP strategies. To arrive at a consensual weight for each strategy, reflecting the combined perspectives of all stakeholders, a two-step process was employed. Firstly, the geometric mean of all corresponding entries across individual matrices was calculated. These means were then used to create a new comparison matrix, from which final weights were derived.

To conclude, AHP utilised these comparisons and weights to calculate a score for each strategy. This score showed the overall effectiveness of each strategy in fostering sustainable development. By analysing these scores, it was possible to rank the different strategies and identify the ones that best align with the LAG's goals for sustainable development.

This application of AHP allowed to prioritise LDP strategies based on the combined insights of local stakeholders, ensuring a more comprehensive and representative understanding of their relative significance for achieving sustainable development in the Tirreno-Eolie context.

3. RESULTS AND DISCUSSION

Building upon the urgency of tackling climate change and fostering local sustainability, this study examined the LDP formulated for the LAG Tirreno-Eolie in Sicily, Italy. As highlighted in the introduction, this research aimed to highlight the function of LAGs in promoting sustainable solutions at the local level. This section offers the key outcomes from the elaboration of the LDP and discusses their significance in the context of local sustainable development efforts.

As a foundational step in formulating the LDP for the LAG Tirreno-Eolie was conducted a comprehensive SWOT analysis (Fig. 2.5) to gain a deeper understanding of the territory's internal strengths and weaknesses, as well as the external opportunities and threats that could affect the success of the development plan.

Analysing these factors through a SWOT framework was crucial for crafting a realistic and effective sustainable development process. In this direction, the LAG Tirreno-Eolie boasts a unique set of strengths that position it well for achieving sustainable development. The district comprehends significant environmental and natural values which can be translated into rich natural heritage.

Its crown jewel is the Aeolian archipelago, a volcanic wonderland with captivating scenery and the potential to tap into geothermal energy. This natural beauty is complemented by the region's rich cultural heritage, historical sites, and

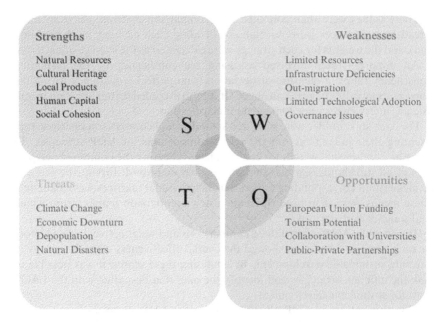

Fig. 2.5. Internal and External Factors Influencing Sustainable Development in LAG Tirreno-Eolie – A SWOT Analysis. *Source*: Authors.

traditional practices that hold immense potential to attract tourists and solidify cultural identity.

In this regard, consumer preferences are increasingly influenced by cultural identity, driving businesses to integrate cultural aspects into their products to stand out in the market (Sacco et al., 2009). Indeed, production is increasingly employing cultural branding strategies, appealing to consumers' sense of identity through their products (Sacco et al., 2009).

Furthermore, the area might possess strong agricultural production or specific local products that could fuel a circular economy and set the territory apart. The human capital – the skills, knowledge, and traditions of the local population – represents another significant strength, offering a valuable asset for sustainable development initiatives. Finally, a strong sense of community and collaboration among residents can serve as a powerful force in facilitating the implementation of the LDP.

However, the evaluation of territorial constraints was a critical process that involved assessing the effect of several elements on the strategic landscape of a given territory. This evaluation encompassed two primary considerations: the enduring impact of these factors on the territory and their significance within the broader strategic framework. Thus, the LAG Tirreno-Eolie weaknesses need to be addressed. Limited resources, both financial and in terms of specific expertise, could pose a hurdle to effective LDP implementation. Inadequate infrastructure, such as transportation networks or renewable energy systems, could further hinder progress. A decline in population, particularly among younger generations, could strain the workforce and stifle innovation. Limited adoption of modern technologies in agriculture, waste management, and other sectors could make it challenging to embrace sustainable practices. Finally, the LAG might be grappling with internal governance issues related to decision-making or transparency.

Fortunately, numerous opportunities exist to capitalise on the LAG's strengths and mitigate its weaknesses. EU funding programmes like the LEADER initiative offer a chance to leverage financial resources specifically allocated for rural development and sustainable projects. The territory's natural beauty and cultural heritage can be harnessed to develop sustainable tourism practices that attract eco-tourists. Partnerships with universities can provide access to research expertise and support the development of innovative solutions for local challenges. Collaboration between public entities and private businesses through public–private partnerships (PPPs) can foster investment in sustainable development projects. Furthermore, the LAG can learn valuable lessons from successful sustainable development initiatives implemented in other territories.

Looking ahead, some threats need to be considered. The aftermaths of climate change, among others drastic temperature events, increasing sea levels, and water deficiency, constitute a serious threat to the territory's agricultural production, infrastructure, and overall well-being. A global or regional economic downturn could reduce tourism activity and limit funding for sustainable development projects. Moreover, fluctuations in the prices of agricultural products or energy resources could affect the economic viability of local businesses. Furthermore, a continued decline in population could lead to a shortage of skilled labour and weaken the social fabric of the community. Finally, the volcanic nature of the Aeolian Islands necessitates considering the risk of eruptions or earthquakes that could cause significant damage.

To guide the LAG Tirreno-Eolie's efforts towards sustainable development, a comprehensive planning process had been defined. This process, with its strong focus on the local level, culminated in the creation of the LDP, a strategic document outlining a roadmap for achieving sustainability. The LDP was formulated following the SWOT analysis outcomes. Moreover, focusing on the local level offers a distinct advantage: it facilitates a more comprehensive recognition, identification, and mobilisation of potential resources (Bryden & Dawe, 1998). Local development initiatives possess an inherent capacity for self-reinforcement (Bryden & Dawe, 1998).

This self-reinforcing nature is crucial for achieving long-term sustainability, a core objective of the LDP and the sustainable development vision for the Tirreno-Eolie district.

In this regard, the proposed LDP embraces the following sustainable development strategies (numerically ordered) for the Tirreno-Eolie environment: 1. urban redevelopment projects, 2. preservation of historical buildings, 3. environmental awareness initiatives in Sicily, 4. biological diversity programmes, and education, 5. promoting circular economy principles, 6. implementing sustainable corporate governance, 7. developing information system for control and security, 8. establishing partnerships with local associations, 9. leverage European initiatives, 10. deployment of newer and greener technologies, 11. redevelopment of infrastructure (Table 2.3).

Table 2.3. Proposed Sustainable Development Strategies in the LAG Tirreno-Eolie's LDP for Sustainable Development.

Strategy	Goal	Action	Sustainability Impact
1. Urban redevelopment projects	Revitalise urban areas, improve quality of life	Renovation with energy-efficient practices and sustainable materials, creating public spaces, upgrading infrastructure	Reduces energy consumption (environment), creates jobs (social)
2. Preservation of historical buildings	Protect cultural heritage, attract tourism	Restoration of historical buildings	Preserves cultural identity (social), attracts tourism (economic)
3. Environmental awareness initiatives in Sicily	Promote sustainable practices among residents and tourists	Educational campaigns, community events	Encourages responsible behavior (environment), fosters environmental stewardship (social)
4. Biological diversity programmes and education	Protect unique biodiversity of the district	Habitat restoration, endangered species protection, educational programmes	Maintains ecological balance (environment), raises awareness (social)
5. Promoting circular economy principles	Reduce waste and resource consumption	Encouraging recycling, reuse, and repair initiatives	Reduces environmental footprint (environment), promotes resource efficiency (economic)
6. Implementing sustainable corporate governance	Encourage businesses to incorporate environmental, social, and governance (ESG) aspects	Integrating ESG factors into decision-making	Minimises environmental impact (environment), promotes social responsibility (social), fosters long-term economic viability (economic)
7. Developing information system for control and security	Enhance transparency and accountability in resource management	Data collection, monitoring systems, stakeholder engagement	Promotes responsible resource use (environment), builds trust (social)
8. Establishing partnerships with local associations	Leverage expertise and resources for sustainable development	Collaboration with local associations, knowledge sharing	Improves efficiency (environment & economic), strengthens social fabric (social)
9. Leverage European initiatives	Access funding to support sustainability goals	Identifying and applying for relevant grants	Secures financial resources (economic), facilitates implementation (environment & social)

Sustainable Futures

Table 2.3. (*Continued*)

Strategy	Goal	Action	Sustainability Impact
10. Deployment of newer and greener technologies	Address environmental challenges with cleaner technologies	Transitioning to renewable energy, adopting innovative solutions	Reduces pollution and environmental impact (environment), fosters innovation (economic)
11. Redevelopment of infrastructure	Enhance efficiency, promote sustainability, and create a foundation for future growth	Upgrading transportation networks, utilities, and waste management systems	Improves resource use (environment), facilitates economic activity (economic)

Source: Authors.

The provided LDP prioritised the revitalisation of key urban areas within the LAG Tirreno-Eolie framework, to ameliorate the standard of living for inhabitants by enhancing housing options and creating attractive public spaces while fostering economic activity. In particular, the focus was on renovating and restoring existing buildings, and creating new employments, by incorporating energy-efficient practices and sustainable materials. Moreover, new green spaces will be developed to promote social cohesion and environmental well-being. Upgrading infrastructure, including transportation networks and utilities, will further support the revitalised areas. A strong emphasis was posed on community engagement to ensure the projects align with residents' needs and aspirations.

Recognising their inherent cultural and economic value, the LDP emphasised the preservation of historical buildings within the LAG Tirreno-Eolie area. These structures contribute significantly to the local's unique identity, fostering a sense of place for both residents and visitors. Preserving these cultural treasures ensures their protection for future generations while strengthening the area's identity and attracting tourism.

The LDP strategies have recognised that environmental protection is key to the area's long-term success. By promoting environmental awareness and campaigns to encourage responsible behaviour, the LDP's actions aim to establish a durable and sustainable futurity for the region. This is especially important because Tirreno-Eolie's unique environment and culture attract high-value tourists interested in ecotourism and food and wine experiences. A sustainable approach benefits the local economy in several ways: it could stimulate growth in service industries, create jobs, and strengthen the overall economic system against potential downturns (as highlighted by Calvagna et al., 2020).

Improving public transportation is another key aspect of the LDP's environmental strategy. Expanding routes and reducing travel times to coastal areas will encourage tourists and locals to use public transportation instead of private vehicles. This could lead to a healthier environment, especially in protected zones.

In this perspective, LDP focused also on protecting the unique biodiversity of the LAG Tirreno-Eolie district, which encompasses both terrestrial and marine ecosystems, while raising consciousness about environmental issues and promoting sustainable practices among citizens and tourists.

To boot, the topographical ruggedness of the Aeolian archipelagos and the sparse human habitation have historically played a pivotal role in safeguarding the landscape's integrity and biodiversity giving also an important contribution for the development of a high attractive tourist hub with unique and highly prized characteristics for a Mediterranean visitor location, enabling the strategic arrangement of economic endeavours with minimal repercussions on the coastal ecosystem.

Hence, it is imperative to formulate and execute sustainable procedures to manage biodiversity protection and promote the long-term conservation of natural ecosystems. This requires a multi-disciplinary approach that integrates scientific research, traditional knowledge, and environmental-oriented policymaking.

Furthermore, LDP promoted the adoption of circular economy principles. This can be achieved through initiatives that encourage recycling, reuse, and repair within the district. Moreover, this approach emphasises reducing waste and natural resource consumption (Velenturf & Purnell, 2021), by keeping products and materials in use for longer lifecycles.

The territory's natural resources are not only vital for its economic activities but also irreplaceable. Unsustainable practices can damage the environment and endanger local species. Pollution and natural disasters pose additional threats, potentially causing significant biodiversity loss and ecosystem disruption. The LDP agenda aims to prevent these issues by promoting responsible management of natural resources.

Likewise, LDP advocated for the implementation of sustainable corporate governance within the environment. This encourages businesses to incorporate environmental, social, and governance (ESG) aspects into their decision-making processes. Indeed, ESG is increasingly integrated into decision-making processes. This approach prioritises long-term sustainable growth over short-term gains or practices that may have negative environmental or social consequences (Sultana et al., 2018).

What is more, LDP had placed a high priority on developing an information system for control and security. This system could enhance transparency and accountability within the district, promoting responsible resource management and fostering trust among stakeholders.

During the deployment of LDP, the value of collaboration has been acknowledged. Establishing strong partnerships with local associations will leverage the expertise and resources of the LAG. Moreover, building partnerships is a well-established approach to improving the efficiency of governance (Brinkerhoff & Brinkerhoff, 2011).

By establishing a strong framework for partnerships, the unique strengths and resources of both public and private sector partners can be leveraged to foster innovation, improve outcomes, and support sustainable growth. In this sense, PPPs are defined 'as arrangements whereby private parties participate in, or provide support for, the provision of infrastructure, and a PPP project results in a contract for a private entity to deliver public infrastructure-based services' (Grimsey & Lewis, 2007). They play a crucial role in territorial development, enabling collaboration between the public and private sectors to reach shared goals. Additionally, collaboration with universities and research institutions can also be a key factor in territorial development. By working with these institutions, policymakers and development professionals can access the latest research and expertise in areas related to territorial development, such as urban planning, economic development, and environmental sustainability. This can ensure that development projects are informed and based on the most up-to-date evidence.

Besides, LDP embraced the potential of European initiatives. By strategically leveraging these funding opportunities, the district can access resources to support the implementation of its sustainability agenda.

Indeed, European funds are another vital resource for supporting territorial development. These funds furnish economic support for a broad range of development projects across the EU. By pooling resources from multiple sources, these funds can ensure that development projects have the necessary financial support to succeed.

Furthermore, the use of PPPs, European funds, and collaboration with universities and research institutions can be effective tools for supporting territorial development. By working together, public and private sector actors can create thriving, sustainable communities well-positioned for long-term success.

Similarly, LDP had emphasised the deployment of newer and greener technologies. This included transitioning to energy-efficient systems, adopting cleaner production processes, and utilising innovative solutions to address environmental challenges. In fact, emerging technologies like blockchain hold promise for enhancing traceability (Galvez et al., 2018). Specifically, blockchain allows all stakeholders to securely access a transparent and immutable record of a product's journey, from origin to its current location (Galvez et al., 2018).

Ultimately, the LDP recognised the importance of a robust infrastructure network. By redeveloping its infrastructure, the district could improve efficiency, enhance sustainability, and create a foundation for future growth. To evaluate the effectiveness of these LDP strategies in achieving an equilibrium between economic, social, and environmental well-being, the AHP theory was employed. It was used to compare the outlined LDP strategies against each other, considering their contribution to economic development, social cohesion, and environmental sustainability. More in particular, the AHP analysis yielded a prioritised ranking of the LDP strategies based on the stakeholder input. Table 2.4 summarises these weights, with higher values indicating greater importance for achieving sustainable development in the LAG Tirreno-Eolie district.

Interestingly, the top two weighted strategies, 'Promoting Circular Economy Principles' with a weight of 0.1500 and 'Deployment of Newer and Greener Technologies' with a weight of 0.1499, emphasise innovative approaches to resource management and environmental sustainability. This suggests a strong consensus among stakeholders that transitioning towards a circular economy and adopting cleaner technologies are crucial aspects of the district's long-term development.

Table 2.4. Prioritisation of LDP Strategies Using AHP.

LDP Strategies	Weights
5. Promoting circular economy principles	0.1500
10. Deployment of newer and greener technologies	0.1499
11. Redevelopment of infrastructure	0.1217
6. Implementing sustainable corporate governance	0.1150
9. Leverage European initiatives	0.1129
7. Developing information system for control and security	0.1105
8. Establishing partnerships with local associations	0.0669
3. environmental awareness initiatives in Sicily	0.0579
2. Preservation of historical buildings	0.0509
4. Biological diversity programmes and education	0.0266
1. Urban redevelopment projects	0.0214

Source: Authors.

Following closely behind are 'Redevelopment of Infrastructure' with a weight of 0.1217 and 'Implementing Sustainable Corporate Governance' with a value of 0.1150. Indeed, investing in modern infrastructure likely reflects a need for improved transportation, utilities, and waste management systems – essential aspects of building a sustainable future. Furthermore, the emphasis on sustainable corporate governance, ranking a value of 0.1150, suggests stakeholder recognition of the relevance of incorporating environmental, social, and economic considerations into business practices.

Thereafter, 'Leverage European Initiatives', reaching a weight of 0.1129, highlights the strategic importance of accessing financial resources from the European Union to support the LDP's goals. Moreover, this strategy complements the focus on internal collaboration through 'Establishing Partnerships with Local Associations', characterised by a value of 0.0669. Although, both strategies point towards a multi-faceted approach that maximises local expertise and resources while securing external support for sustainable development initiatives.

In addition, the remaining strategies address environmental protection, education, and cultural heritage. 'Environmental Awareness Initiatives in Sicily', ranking 0.0579 as weight, and 'Biological Diversity Programs and Education', with a value of 0.0266, highlight the importance of fostering responsible environmental behaviour and safeguarding the district's unique biodiversity. Furthermore, the 'Preservation of Historical Buildings', reaching 0.0509 as weight, reflects a recognition of the cultural significance of these structures and their potential to contribute to tourism and social identity.

Finally, 'Urban Redevelopment Projects' received the lowest value, registering 0.0214 as weight. This may indicate that stakeholders view other strategies as having a more significant impact on achieving sustainable development in the near term. However, it is important to contemplate the potential long-term benefits of revitalised urban areas, such as improved quality of life and economic growth.

Overall, the AHP results provide valuable insights into stakeholder priorities for the LAG Tirreno-Eolie district's sustainable development. The emphasis on circularity, green technologies, and infrastructure development underscores a commitment to a future-oriented approach. The importance of leveraging external resources alongside local partnerships further strengthens the plan's viability. While environmental protection, education, and cultural preservation receive lower weights, they remain key components of a well-rounded strategy for achieving long-term sustainability.

4. CONCLUSION

This study tackles the multi-faceted ways climate change impacts human health and environmental sustainability, by emphasising the need for proactive sustainability measures at the local level. The examination of the LDP formulated for the LAG Tirreno-Eolie had shed light on the interplay of factors that influence local sustainable development efforts. Employing a case study approach, this research delved into the specific problems and possibilities faced by the LAG highlighting the potential of local initiatives to drive progress towards a more sustainable future. Looking beyond the LAG Tirreno-Eolie, the study's findings offer valuable lessons applicable to local sustainable development efforts worldwide. The importance of a comprehensive and participatory planning process cannot be overstated. A SWOT analysis has been conducted to identify LAG's strengths, weaknesses, opportunities, and threats, providing a solid framework for future action. Furthermore, engaging stakeholders in the planning process ensures that the LDP addresses local needs and priorities, fostering ownership and commitment to its implementation. The LAG Tirreno-Eolie context, with its unique blend of natural beauty, cultural heritage, and economic potential, boasts significant strengths, including its captivating volcanic landscapes, rich biodiversity, and historical sites. These assets hold immense potential for attracting tourists, fostering a strong cultural identity, and stimulating local production. Additionally, the human capital – the skills, knowledge, and traditions of the local population – represents a valuable resource for sustainable development initiatives. However, the path towards sustainability is not without its hurdles. The district grapples with limitations in financial resources and expertise, inadequate infrastructure, and a decline in population, particularly among younger generations. These factors can hinder the adoption of modern technologies, crucial for embracing sustainable practices in agriculture, waste management, and other sectors. Furthermore, potential internal governance issues could pose challenges for effective LDP implementation. Despite these constraints, local stakeholders prioritised innovative approaches such as promoting circular economy principles and deploying newer green technologies. These strategies, as highlighted in the LDP, aim to optimise resource utilisation, minimise environmental impact, and position the district for future growth. The LDP goes beyond environmental considerations, recognising the significance of a balanced approach that integrates economic and social well-being. Initiatives such as urban redevelopment projects and the preservation of historical buildings aim to ameliorate the standard of living for inhabitants, enhance the attractiveness of the territory, and stimulate economic activity. Additionally, the plan emphasises the importance of fostering social cohesion and community engagement, recognising that a united citizenry is a powerful force for positive change. Furthermore, the success of the LDP hinges on effective collaboration and resource mobilisation. The establishment of strong partnerships with local associations, universities, and research institutions can leverage expertise and knowledge, fostering innovation and optimising outcomes. Additionally, strategically leveraging European initiatives provides access to crucial financial resources for implementing the LDP's ambitious goals. The critical role of innovation in achieving sustainable development is another key takeaway. By embracing circular economy principles and deploying newer green technologies, the LAG Tirreno-Eolie could demonstrate a commitment to resource efficiency and environmental responsibility. This forward-thinking approach sets an example for other territories seeking to decouple economic growth from environmental degradation. This study also highlights the importance of fostering a culture of environmental awareness and education. Initiatives promoting responsible behaviour and safeguarding the area's unique biodiversity are fundamental for assuring lasting sustainability of the territory's resources. Additionally, education could be essential in developing a skilled workforce equipped to address the challenges and opportunities of the green economy. Finally, communication and transparency throughout the process are essential for maintaining stakeholder trust and commitment. In essence, the case study of the LAG Tirreno-Eolie offers a microcosm of the opportunities and challenges inherent in local sustainable development efforts. While the specific circumstances of the district may differ from other territories, the core principles identified in this study remain universally applicable. By fostering collaboration, embracing innovation, and prioritising a balanced approach that integrates environmental, social, and economic wellness, local communities can delineate a course towards a more sustainable future. The LDP, with its comprehensive vision and emphasis on stakeholder engagement, provides a valuable roadmap for local actors striving to achieve this ambitious yet vital goal. While the planet combats with the interconnected constraints of climate change and resource depletion, the success of local sustainable development initiatives like the LAG Tirreno-Eolie offers a beacon of hope, demonstrating the power of local communities to take ownership of their future and contribute meaningfully to a global movement towards a more sustainable world. However, acknowledging limitations is essential. The research may be subject to limitations in available information about the LAG. Additionally, the dynamic nature of social and environmental systems poses inherent challenges for long-term planning. This study serves as a springboard for further research. Future investigations could delve deeper into specific aspects of the LDP, such as the feasibility of implementing circular economy projects or the effectiveness of stakeholder engagement strategies. Additionally, comparative studies analysing the LAG Tirreno-Eolie alongside other local sustainable development initiatives across Italy or Europe could provide valuable insights into best practices and transferable models. Moreover, exploring the scalability and adaptability of the LDP framework to diverse contexts could enhance its broader applicability, serving as a model for other communities seeking a more sustainable future. Furthermore, exploring the potential social impacts of the LDP would be a valuable area of future research. The LDP emphasises fostering social cohesion and inclusivity. Examining how the plan's implementation might affect different social groups within the LAG, particularly marginalised communities, would be crucial for ensuring equitable outcomes. Finally, investigating the potential for scaling up successful local initiatives like the LDP holds immense importance. Understanding how local efforts can be replicated or integrated into broader regional or national sustainable development strategies could pave the way for more systemic change. To sum up, the case study of the LAG Tirreno-Eolie provided a rich tapestry of insights into the complexities and possibilities of local sustainable development. The LDP, with its focus on innovation, collaboration, and a balanced approach, offers a valuable framework for local communities striving to create a more sustainable future. By fostering knowledge exchange, promoting best practices, and continuously adapting strategies, local actors can be indispensable in establishing a more resilient and impartial world for all. The success stories, challenges, and lessons learned from the LAG Tirreno-Eolie offer valuable guidance on this collective journey towards a brighter future.

REFERENCES

Abdel-Basset, M., Mohamed, M., & Smarandache, F. (2018). An extension of neutrosophic AHP–SWOT analysis for strategic planning and decision-making. *Symmetry*, *10*(4), 116.

Agovino, M., Casaccia, M., Ciommi, M., Ferrara, M., & Marchesano, K. (2019). Agriculture, climate change and sustainability: The case of EU-28. *Ecological Indicators*, *105*, 525–543.

Atkočiūnienė, V., Dapkuvienė, I., & Ispiryan, A. (2024). Compliance of local development strategies with the leader programme: The case of the Kelme Region Local Action Group. *Management Theory and Studies for Rural Business and Infrastructure Development*, *46*(1), 54–62.

Brinkerhoff, D. W., & Brinkerhoff, J. M. (2011). Public–private partnerships: Perspectives on purposes, publicness, and good governance. *Public Administration and Development*, *31*(1), 2–14.

Bryden, J. M., & Dawe, S. P. (1998, November). Development strategies for remote rural regions: What do we know so far. *OECD international conference on remote rural areas–developing through natural and cultural assets* (pp. 5–6). Albarrain, Spain.

Calvagna, S., Gagliano, A., Greco, S., Rodonò, G., & Sapienza, V. (2020). Innovative multidisciplinary methodology for the analysis of traditional marginal architecture. *Sustainability*, *12*(4), 1285.

CAP 2023–27. (2023). *Agriculture and rural development*. Retrieved April 19, 2024, from https://agriculture.ec.europa.eu/common-agricultural-policy/cap-overview/cap-2023-27_en

Creswell, J. W. (2014). *Research design: Qualitative, quantitative, and mixed method approaches* (4th ed.). SAGE Publications.

Dagilienė, L., Varaniūtė, V., & Bruneckienė, J. (2021). Local governments' perspective on implementing the circular economy: A framework for future solutions. *Journal of Cleaner Production*, *310*, 127340.

Dizdaroglu, D. (2015). Developing micro-level urban ecosystem indicators for sustainability assessment. *Environmental Impact Assessment Review*, *54*, 119–124.

du Plessis, A. (2022). SDG 11: Make cities and human settlements inclusive, safe, resilient and sustainable. *City*, *151*, 152.

Esparcia, J., Escribano, J., & Serrano, J. J. (2015). From development to power relations and territorial governance: Increasing the leadership role of LEADER Local Action Groups in Spain. *Journal of Rural Studies*, *42*, 29–42.

European Commission. (2006). *The leader approach: A basic guide*. Retrieved April 19, 2024, from http://ec.europa.eu/agriculture/rur/leaderplus/pdf/library

GALTIRRENOEOLIE. (2014). Retrieved April 19, 2024, from http://www.galtirrenoeolie.it/

Galvez, J. F., Mejuto, J. C., & Simal-Gandara, J. (2018). Future challenges on the use of blockchain for food traceability analysis. *TrAC Trends in Analytical Chemistry*, *107*, 222–232.

Gasper, R., Blohm, A., & Ruth, M. (2011). Social and economic impacts of climate change on the urban environment. *Current Opinion in Environmental Sustainability*, *3*(3), 150–157.

Grimsey, D., & Lewis, M. (2007). *Public private partnerships: The worldwide revolution in infrastructure provision and project finance*. Edward Elgar Publishing.

Ioppolo, G. (2010). Integrazione di competenze a supporto dei sistemi di gestione costiera: il caso Fish-Gate: progetto integrato di gestione delle risorse. *Integrazione di competenze a supporto dei sistemi di gestione costiera*.

ISTAT. (2011). *15° censimento della popolazione e delle abitazioni 2011*. Retrieved April 19, 2024, from https://www.istat.it/it/censimenti-permanenti/censimenti-precedenti/popolazione-e-abitazioni/popolazione-2011

ISTAT. (2017). *Le Rilevazioni Sperimentali Del 2017*. Retrieved April 23, 2024, from https://www.istat.it/it/censimenti/censimenti-precedenti/popolazione-e-abitazioni/sperimentali-2017

Menconi, M. E., Artemi, S., Borghi, P., & Grohmann, D. (2018). Role of local action groups in improving the sense of belonging of local communities with their territories. *Sustainability*, *10*(12), 4681.

Milán-García, J., Uribe-Toril, J., Ruiz-Real, J. L., & de Pablo Valenciano, J. (2019). Sustainable local development: An overview of the state of knowledge. *Resources*, *8*(1), 31.

Moraga, G., Huysveld, S., Mathieux, F., Blengini, G. A., Alaerts, L., Van Acker, K., de Meester, S., & Dewulf, J. (2019). Circular economy indicators: What do they measure? *Resources, Conservation and Recycling*, *146*, 452–461.

Nations, U. (2015). *Transforming our world: The 2030 agenda for sustainable development* (Vol. 1, p. 41). United Nations, Department of Economic and Social Affairs.

Palm, J., Smedby, N., & McCormick, K. (2019). The role of local governments in governing sustainable consumption and sharing cities. In O. Mont (Ed.), *A research agenda for sustainable consumption governance* (Vol. 1, pp. 172–184). Edward Elgar Publishing.

Palmisano, G. O., Govindan, K., Boggia, A., Loisi, R. V., De Boni, A., & Roma, R. (2016). Local action groups and rural sustainable development. A spatial multiple criteria approach for efficient territorial planning. *Land Use Policy*, *59*, 12–26.

Saaty, T. L. (1980). *The analytic hierarchy process*. McGraw-Hill Book Co.

Saaty, T. L. (1990). How to make a decision: The analytic hierarchy process. *European Journal of Operational Research*, *48*(1), 9–26.

Sacco, P. L., Blessi, G. T., & Nuccio, M. (2009). Cultural policies and local planning strategies: What is the role of culture in local sustainable development? *The Journal of Arts Management, Law, and Society*, *39*(1), 45–64.

Srivastava, P. K., Kulshreshtha, K., Mohanty, C. S., Pushpangadan, P., & Singh, A. (2005). Stakeholder-based SWOT analysis for successful municipal solid waste management in Lucknow, India. *Waste Management*, *25*(5), 531–537.

Sultana, S., Zulkifli, N., & Zainal, D. (2018). Environmental, social and governance (ESG) and investment decision in Bangladesh. *Sustainability*, *10*(6), 1831.

Velenturf, A. P., & Purnell, P. (2021). Principles for a sustainable circular economy. *Sustainable Production and Consumption*, *27*, 1437–1457.

Verma, P., & Raghubanshi, A. S. (2018). Urban sustainability indicators: Challenges and opportunities. *Ecological Indicators*, *93*, 282–291.

WCED, U. (1987). Our common future. World commission on environment and development. *Sustainable Development*, *154*, 1–374.

Zeng, X., Yu, Y., Yang, S., Lv, Y., & Sarker, M. N. I. (2022). Urban resilience for urban sustainability: Concepts, dimensions, and perspectives. *Sustainability*, *14*(5), 2481.

Zhao, Q., Yu, P., Mahendran, R., Huang, W., Gao, Y., Yang, Z., Ye, T., Wen, B., Wu, Y., Li, S., & Guo, Y. (2022). Global climate change and human health: Pathways and possible solutions. *Eco-Environment & Health*, *1*(2), 53–62.

CHAPTER 3

TECHNOLOGICAL INNOVATION AND SUSTAINABLE DEVELOPMENT: ATTRACTING ENVIRONMENTALLY-FRIENDLY AND SOCIALLY RESPONSIBLE INVESTORS

Grațiela-Georgiana Noja[a], Petru Ștefea[b], Andrea Gînguță[b], Alexandra-Mădălina Țăran[c], Irina-Maria Grecu[d] and Andrei Cristian Spulbăr[e]

[a]*Faculty of Economics and Business Administration, Department of Marketing, International Business and Economics, East-European Center for Research in Economics and Business, West University of Timisoara, Timisoara, Romania*
[b]*Faculty of Economics and Business Administration, Department of Management and Entrepreneurship, West University of Timisoara, Timisoara, Romania*
[c]*Faculty of Economics and Business Administration, Department of Finance, Information Systems and Business Modelling, West University of Timisoara, Timisoara, Romania*
[d]*Doctoral School of Economics and Business Administration, West University of Timisoara, Timisoara, Romania*
[e]*"Eugeniu Carada" Doctoral School of Economic Sciences, University of Craiova, Craiova, Romania*

ABSTRACT

Purpose/Objective: *This study aims to investigate the inferences of technological innovations introduced by companies, emphasised by firm investments in innovative products, the use of information technologies (ITs), and the number of innovative products in achieving economic and environmental sustainability.*

Green Wealth: Navigating towards a Sustainable Future
Contemporary Studies in Economic and Financial Analysis, Volume 117, 45–64
Copyright © 2025 by Grațiela-Georgiana Noja, Petru Ștefea, Andrea Gînguță, Alexandra-Mădălina Țăran, Irina-Maria Grecu and Andrei Cristian Spulbăr
Published under exclusive licence by Emerald Publishing Limited
ISSN: 1569-3759/doi:10.1108/S1569-375920250000117004

Design/Methodology/Approach: *Simple regression models with Driscoll–Kraay standard errors processed through the Pooled OLS method, and cluster analysis performed through the Ward method inset on hierarchical clustering. A newly compiled dataset with information extracted from the European Innovation Scoreboard (EIS) 2023 was employed in the analysis, covering the time lapse from 2016 to 2023 and integrating 28 European countries.*

Findings: *A statistically significant relationship between firm investments, technological innovations, and companies' environmental and sustainability credentials. Clusters associated with the impact of innovative technologies on environmental and economic sustainability were identified. The results showed four different clusters, including countries that present similarities among the variables or distinctive tendencies from the countries belonging to other clusters.*

Significance/Implications/Conclusions: *New insights for firms, managers, entrepreneurs, and local or foreign investors and emphasise the need for innovation and technological investments within companies to improve their business activities and support more effective and sustainable development.*

Limitations: *The reduced availability of data and regarding the sample of representative indicators.*

Future Research: *Future research avenues might explore the importance of collaboration among technologists, financiers, policymakers, and environmentalists to harness technology's full potential and navigate the complexities of integrating it with sustainable practices.*

Keywords: Technological innovation; environment; sustainable development; firm investments; information technology

JEL Codes: O33; O31; Q56

1. INTRODUCTION

Innovations in technology have been the cornerstone of industrial and economic development, offering new opportunities for efficiency, growth, and competitiveness. The rise of digital technologies, renewable energy technologies, and advanced manufacturing processes are notable examples of this transformative influence. The relationship between technological innovation and environmental performance is particularly significant. As companies adopt new technologies, they often consider finding ways to reduce waste, lower energy consumption, and minimise their carbon footprint. Notable advancements in this area include energy-efficient technologies, waste recycling systems, and sustainable supply chain practices. Hart and Milstein (2003) have emphasised how sustainable value creation through technological innovation can offer firms for a competitive advantage while addressing critical environmental challenges. The interplay of technological innovation with sustainable development is a critical area of interest. Sustainable development involves balancing economic growth with environmental stewardship and social equity. Technologies like green energy, sustainable agriculture, and smart cities contribute to this balance by providing environmentally friendly and socially responsible solutions that also drive economic growth. The United Nations Sustainable Development Goals explicitly recognise the role of technology in achieving sustainable development, with several goals directly addressing the need for technological innovation in sectors like health, education, and environmental protection. The increased interest of enterprises in addressing environmental issues and their perseverance in reaching environmental sustainability leads to the introduction of new environment-related technologies and innovative products. This research highlights the connections between technological innovations and environmental sustainability and the potential of innovative products and services to contribute fundamentally to reducing the adverse outcomes of industrial activities on the environment.

The present study first explores the theoretical foundation of this research topic using a bibliometric analysis technique. It investigates the most recently published papers in terms of concepts, research objectives, countries, or co-citations, followed by a rigorous literature review of the studies that engaged in the following topics: technological innovations and environmental sustainability. The second part of the paper includes the methodology and indicators' description, followed by a statistical analysis to determine the correlations between the selected variables using Stata software. We processed several unifactorial regression models, using panel data and the Pooled OLS method with Driscoll and Kraay (1998) standard errors, to highlight the connections between each of the dependent variables (economic and environmental sustainability) with the independent variables (the use of IT, product innovations, and firm investments). Furthermore, we included graph illustrations to emphasise the relationship between the variables and to identify the evolution of each indicator during the lapse of time for every selected UE country. To establish a deeper understanding of the variables and to determine the clusters associated with the impact of innovative technologies on environmental and economic sustainability, we performed a cluster modelling analysis using the Ward method. The results showed four different clusters, including countries, present similarities among the variables, or distinctive tendencies from the countries belonging to other clusters.

In this chapter, we have organised the presentation of our research into several sections, each providing a detailed analysis of a specific aspect of our study. In Section 2, we provide an in-depth discussion of the theoretical foundations of both technological innovation and sustainability, exploring the current state of knowledge in these areas and highlighting key debates and controversies. This section aims to provide readers with a clear understanding of the conceptual framework that underpins our research. Moving on to Section 3, we provide a detailed account of the data and methodology used in our study. We describe the data sources, the methods employed to collect and analyse this data, and the key assumptions and limitations of our approach. This section aims to provide readers with a clear understanding of the research design and data analysis procedures used in our study, as well as the quality and reliability of our findings. In Section 4, we present the main findings of our research, which include a detailed analysis of the relationship between technological innovation and sustainability. We discuss key trends and patterns identified in our data and explore the implications of our findings for theory and practice. This section aims to provide readers with a clear understanding of our research results and their significance for the broader field of study. Finally, we offer concluding remarks summarising our key findings and highlighting their implications for practice and future research. We also provide recommendations for future research directions, identifying areas where further research is needed to build on our findings and extend our understanding of the complex relationship between technological innovation and sustainability.

2. BRIEF LITERATURE REVIEW

2.1. Theoretical Groundings of Technological Innovation and Sustainability

The emergence and integration of technological innovations into the environmental sustainability domain have revolutionised how services and products are delivered and consumed and opened new avenues for combating some of the world's most pressing challenges, including climate change. This literature review examines and delves into the transformative potential of technological innovations, exploring their role in promoting sustainable practices and mitigating the impacts of climate change, with a specific focus on achieving environmental sustainability. It aims to synthesise current research, identify areas where technological innovations have significantly contributed to environmental sustainability, and highlight existing gaps and future opportunities in this burgeoning field.

The concept of business sustainability includes the economic sustainability of a business, and it refers to the firm's ability to make profits and contribute to economic growth on a local level, national scale, or international scale (Danciu, 2013). Sustainable development aims to preserve non-renewable resources, and businesses could contribute to reducing these tragic losses of resources by creating innovative products and processes and introducing new technologies that aim to lower these adverse environmental outcomes (Shrivastava & Hart, 1995). Melander (2017) indicates that enterprises often relate to their environmental concerns by measuring the material usage, energy consumption, and pollution generated by their business activities. Their environmental performance could also be analysed by comparing the results of old and new products, the energy saved by using different technologies, the pollution reduction, or the recycled materials used in their development and operational processes (Melander, 2017).

The role and intersection of technological innovations in promoting sustainability and democratising access to finance are areas of increasing interest and importance. Studies by Haddad and Hornuf (2019) and Klapper and Lusardi (2020) highlight how technology facilitates sustainable investment practices, including crowdfunding for green projects and enabling more inclusive financial practices. The rise of green bonds and sustainable investment platforms exemplifies this trend. Green bonds, aimed at funding projects with positive environmental benefits, have experienced exponential growth, financing a range of projects from renewable energy to sustainable agriculture, as the European Parliament (2022) reported. Additionally, the introduction of Robo-advisors, as discussed by Jung et al. (2018), has made sustainable investing more accessible to a broader audience. These automated, algorithm-driven financial planning services focus on sustainability, further illustrating technological innovation's contribution to environmentally conscious investment strategies.

Financial technology's evolution from its early days as a nascent online banking service to a significant force in technological innovation has been rapid and remarkable. This transformation, marked by adopting complex technologies such as blockchain, artificial intelligence (AI), big data, and the Internet of Things, has fundamentally disrupted traditional financial services. Authors like Schueffel (2016), Arner et al. (2015), and Gomber et al. (2018) have extensively traced this evolution. While Schueffel highlights technology's disruptive potential, Arner et al. point to the pivotal role of the 2008 financial crisis in accelerating technological growth, leading to a re-evaluation and subsequent overhaul of traditional financial models. Gomber et al. further discuss reshaping financial services through technology, emphasising the shift towards integrating advanced technologies to create more efficient, accessible, customer-centric, and sustainable financial solutions. Iansiti and Lakhani (2017) also contribute to this narrative by outlining the current trends in technological innovations, underscoring the financial sector's continuous evolution and its impact on financial services' efficiency and accessibility.

Climate change profoundly impacts financial markets, significantly affecting asset values, insurance costs, and investment decisions (Zhang et al., 2020). Studies by Bolton et al. (2020) and research by Worae et al. (2018) emphasise the risks climate change poses to asset prices, investment strategies, insurance liabilities, and investment portfolios. The seminal work of Carney (2015) at the Bank of England has been instrumental in understanding and addressing these risks. He also argues that technologies can aid in identifying and managing these challenges. Additionally, Carney notes that technological innovations play a crucial role in facilitating the transition to a low-carbon economy, highlighting the role of technological innovations in assuring a better risk assessment and management in response to climate-related challenges. According to the authors Antoni et al. (2020), IT capability, which refers to the organisational capacity generated by an IT infrastructure, IT specialists, and IT assets to enhance organisational performance, can be embraced by companies to increase their environmental performance, bring improvements to their profits, and improve their competitive advantage on the market. Studies have shown that IT capability can enhance the efficiency of business operations and can contribute to developing environmental competence within a business (Antoni et al., 2020). Conducting a study on the influence of IT capability on improving a company's environmental performance, the authors' findings reveal that IT infrastructure quality, IT specialists from human resources, and environmental-related IT technologies or equipment can affect the environmental performance of a business (Antoni et al., 2020).

The emergence of innovative technologies such as blockchain and AI has opened up exciting avenues for tackling the pressing challenges related to climate change.

Huang et al. (2020) have expounded on how blockchain technology can serve as a dependable and transparent platform for carbon credit trading, thereby ensuring the market's efficiency and integrity. Moreover, AI and machine learning have become increasingly prevalent in predictive analytics for climate risk assessment and management. Huang et al. (2020) have delved deeply into this application and noted that it facilitates better decision-making and contributes significantly to developing more effective climate change mitigation strategies. These cutting-edge technological solutions are instrumental in addressing the multifaceted challenges posed by climate change.

Climate change is one of the most complex and pressing challenges we face today, and emerging technologies such as blockchain and AI hold great promise in addressing this issue. Huang et al. (2020) have explored the potential of these technologies in detail. Blockchain technology, as they have noted, has the potential to revolutionise the carbon credit trading market by providing a transparent and efficient platform that can enhance its integrity and effectiveness. This technology can help track carbon credits and reduce fraud, making the market more dependable for investors. Similarly, AI and machine learning can be critical in climate risk assessment and management. Huang et al. (2020) have highlighted how these technologies can be used for predictive analytics, enabling us to make more informed decisions about climate change mitigation strategies. Overall, these technological innovations offer a promising path to tackling the multifaceted challenges of climate change. By leveraging the power of blockchain and AI, we can develop more effective strategies for reducing greenhouse gas emissions, promoting sustainability, and safeguarding our planet for future generations.

2.2. Bibliometric Analysis of the Relevant Scientific Literature on Technological Innovation, Environmental Performance, and Sustainable Development

The present study is conducted to provide a comprehensive and in-depth analysis of the theoretical fundamentals of technological innovation and its impact on the environmental sustainability of businesses. The study employs a rigorous bibliometric analysis to identify the fundamental theories, concepts, research directions, authors, organisations/institutes, countries, and co-citation history related to this topic. To achieve this, a large sample of scientific articles, books, and book chapters available in Web of Science and Scopus databases is analysed. We aimed to extract valuable insights into the various dimensions of technological innovation and its impact on the environment and to provide an understanding of the current state of research in this area. The findings of this study will help researchers, policymakers, and business leaders to develop effective strategies for promoting innovation and sustainability in the business sector while minimising the negative environmental impacts.

Hence, we analysed information from 312 documents available on the Web of Science and 293 papers from Scopus for the period 2018–2023. This large amount of data is being processed in VOSviewer. The Web of Science and Scopus search and further extraction were made based on the following keywords: 'innovation', 'sustainable', 'companies', and 'environment'. Using the 'author keyword' searching method on Scopus-indexed articles published between 2018 and 2023, we designed a co-occurrence map presented in Fig. 3.1 that entails innovation, sustainability, sustainable development, and technological innovation at the core of main recent studies on similar topics, combined with mentions of AI, environment, green innovation, and circular economy.

The co-occurrence map resulting after processing the data available in Scopus by analysing several 293 articles indexed on the platform, using the 'all keyword' searching method, is presented in Fig. 3.2. We can observe that sustainable development and innovation were the main topics and basis approached in recent studies published between 2018 and 2023 on this topical subject. The most important keywords used in this research were 'innovation', 'sustainable', 'companies', and 'environment'. Using the 'index keywords' searching method on Scopus-indexed articles, found in Fig. 3.3, there is a clear orientation and concentration of interest for sustainable development and innovation, combined at a particular level with technological innovation, business development, and commerce. Authors such as Porter and van der Linde (1995) also argue that technological innovation can lead to a 'win-win' situation, where environmental improvements result in cost savings and enhanced business competitiveness. On the financial side, technological innovation contributes to enhanced performance through improved operational efficiencies, reduced costs, and new market opportunities.

Schumpeter (1942) highlighted the concept of 'creative destruction', where new technological paradigms disrupt existing markets, leading to the emergence

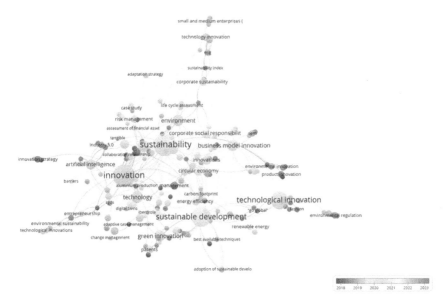

Fig. 3.1. Co-occurrence, Links, and Clustering of Terms/Keywords Approached in Recent Literature About the Technological Innovation Impact on Sustainable Development of Companies, Using 'Author Keyword' Scopus Platform Searching Method. *Source*: Designed by authors in VOSviewer, using Scopus-indexed articles.

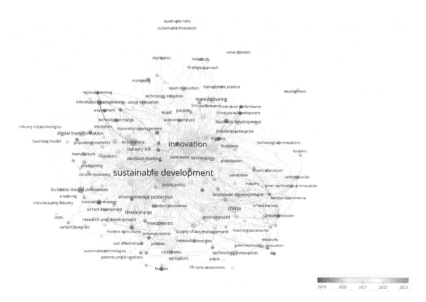

Fig. 3.2. Co-occurrence, Links, and Clustering of Terms/Keywords Approached in Recent Literature on Similar Topics, Using 'All Keyword' Scopus Platform Searching Method. *Source*: Designed by authors in VOSviewer, using Scopus-indexed articles.

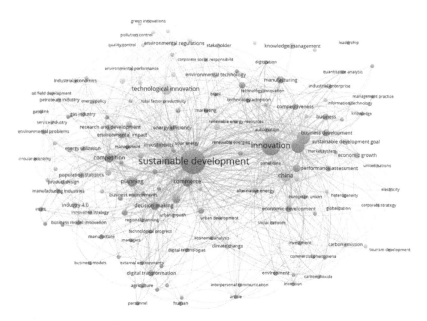

Fig. 3.3. Co-occurrence, Links, and Clustering of Terms/Keywords Approached in Recent Literature About the Technological Innovation Impact on Sustainable Development of Companies, Using 'Index Keywords' Scopus Platform Searching Method. *Source*: Designed by authors in VOSviewer, using Scopus-indexed articles.

of new leaders and the decline of companies that fail to innovate. Other studies, like those by Fama and French (1993), further support this, demonstrating a positive correlation between technological innovation and financial performance.

Fig. 3.4 presents the co-occurrence map of all keywords resulting after processing the data. It entails that innovation, financial and environmental performance, technology, and energy efficiency were the main issues approached in recent studies published on this topical subject.

If we analyse the sample of 312 scientific documents (articles, book chapter) extracted from Web of Science, it is exposed in the co-occurrence map above that the keywords used for this research not only present a high degree of interest for the authors but also for other concepts and fields, such as 'renewable energy', 'digital transformation', and 'financial performance'. Analysing the country of publication of the 312 articles indexed in Web of Science, we can observe in Fig. 3.5 that most are concentrated in and around China. In contrast, others were published in Europe and European Union countries, such as France, Italy, and Romania.

Analysing the country of publication of the 293 articles indexed in Scopus in Fig. 3.6, we can observe that most of them are concentrated in and around China and other Asian countries. In contrast, others were published in Europe and European Union countries, such as France, Italy, or even the Russian Federation, with links to Brazil, Mexico, and Saudi Arabia.

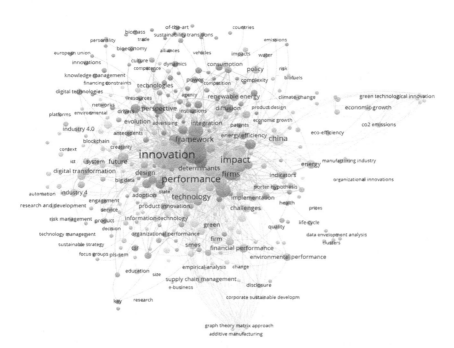

Fig. 3.4. Co-occurrence, Links, and Clustering of Terms/Keywords Approached in Recent Literature on Similar Topics. *Source*: Designed by authors in VOSviewer, using Web of Science-indexed articles.

Fig. 3.5. Co-occurrence, Links, and Clustering of Terms/Keywords Approached in Recent Literature About the Primary Authors' Articles' Country of Publication.
Source: Designed by authors in VOSviewer, using Web of Science-indexed articles.

Fig. 3.6. Co-occurrence, Links, and Clustering of Terms/Keywords Approached in Recent Literature About the Main Authors' Articles' Country of Publication.
Source: Designed by authors in VOSviewer, using Scopus-indexed articles.

3. METHODOLOGY AND RESEARCH OBJECTIVES

Using the EIS 2023, we investigated the influence of technological innovation introduced by companies (emphasised by the firm investments in innovative products, the use of ITs, and the number of innovative products introduced by enterprises) on achieving economic and environmental sustainability. Therefore, we investigated the influence generated by technological innovations on the sales indicator, which measures the financial impact of innovation by taking into consideration the sales resulting from high-tech and innovative products and the sales resulting from knowledge-intensive services. We also analysed the influence of technological innovation (using the same indicators for defining this dimension) on environmental sustainability, which captures the implementation of environment-related technologies, the resource productivity, and the air pollution caused by fine particulate matter (PM2.5) generated by industries, which is considered the pollutant with the most significant effect on human health (EIS, 2023).

Our database contains five indicators with values exported from the EIS 2023 following 28 European countries over eight years (2016–2023). The indicators used in the analysis are described in Table 3.1, and the summary statistics are presented in Table 3.2.

Table 3.1. Indicators Used in the Analysis.

Investments	
Firm investments	This indicator covers research and development investments and other investments that businesses make to introduce innovations, including firms' research and development expenses, other innovation expenses, and innovation expenditures per employee
Use of ITs	This indicator includes the use of IT following the firms' actions that aim to generate and increase employees' information and communication technology (ICT) skills and the number of ICT specialists employed
Business innovations	
Innovators	This indicator captures the share of small- and medium-sized enterprises that have created innovative products and services and introduced them on the market. It also measures the innovations introduced within their organisations, including business process and product innovations
Economic sustainability and environmental impacts	
Sales	This indicator evaluates the economic impact of innovative products and services. It includes several items, such as the exports of medium, high-tech products or knowledge-intensive services and the value generated by selling innovative products
Environmental sustainability	This indicator measures the progress made to reduce the adverse outcomes of industries on the environment. It includes the productivity or the efficient management of resources, the reduction of air pollution, and the increasing interest of businesses in environmental sustainability, reflected by innovative and environment-related technologies introduced on the market

Source: Own processing based on the EIS 2023 indicators (EIS, 2023).

Table 3.2. Descriptive Statistics of the Variables Employed in the Empirical Analysis.

Variable	Obs	Mean	Std. Dev.	Min	Max
FIRM_INV	216	79.55	34.306	14.922	158.448
INF_TECH	216	107.115	44.876	17.591	204.056
INNOV	216	116.403	60.56	0	233.822
SALES_IMP	216	80.085	20.576	33.992	137.73
ENV_SUST	216	87.632	28.561	23.887	149.156

Source: Authors' research in Stata.

Our research endeavour aims to identify if there is a connection between firms' investments in innovations, the use of IT in business processes, and the number of innovative products introduced by enterprises with variables that suggest economic sustainability, such as sales of innovative products, and environmental sustainability, such as pollution reduction or environment-related technologies created by businesses. Therefore, our methodology is based on several statistical methods, such as linear and simple regression models, graph matrix, and cluster modelling, using the environmental sustainability, the sales indicator as dependent variables, and the firm investments, the use of IT, and the innovators as independent variables.

4. RESULTS

Using Stata software, we analysed the influence of the firm investments in innovations, the use of ITs within companies, and the number of innovations introduced by small- and medium-sized organisations on environmental sustainability and economic sustainability (generated by sales of innovative, high-tech, or knowledge-intensive products and services). The pairwise correlations and the Pearson and Spearman correlation matrix can be found in Table 3.3. The Pearson correlation coefficient describes the linear relationship between the selected variables, while the Spearman correlation coefficient determines the monotonic relationship of these variables.

The graph matrix of the correlations is presented in Fig. 3.7. The graph matrix is extensively used to represent the connections in the data and visually illustrate the relationships between the variables.

In Fig. 3.8, we can identify the evolution of the independent variables during the selected period of 2016–2023 for each UE country. We can see that the dynamic of these indicators presents a mostly positive evolution over time, and the innovation indicator presents the most fluctuations over the years, identified in several countries such as Cyprus, Germany, Estonia, Malta, Italy, and Portugal.

Fig. 3.9 presents the evolution of the dependent variable (sales impact) during the eight-year time period considered for the analysis. We can mostly perceive a positive dynamic evolution for this indicator, with slightly fewer exceptions for countries such as France or Hungary.

The evolution of the second dependent variable, environmental sustainability, is identified in Fig. 3.10. This indicator presents more fluctuations over the years, and its evolution follows both positive and negative volatility. Countries such as Germany, Denmark, France, Italy, and the Netherlands maintain a higher score

Table 3.3. Pairwise Correlations and Pearson/Spearman Correlation Matrix.

	Pairwise Correlations				
Variables	(1)	(2)	(3)	(4)	(5)
(1) FIRM_INV	1.000				
(2) INF_TECH	0.601***	1.000			
(3) INNOV	0.569***	0.528***	1.000		
(4) SALES_IMP	0.489***	0.510***	0.406***	1.000	
(5) ENV_SUST	0.434***	0.382***	0.294***	0.477***	1.000

Note: ***$p < 0.01$, **$p < 0.05$, *$p < 0.1$.

	Pearson/Spearman Correlation Matrix				
	FIRM_INV	INF_TECH	INNOV	SALES_IMP	ENV_SUST
FIRM_INV	1.000	0.544	0.562	0.492	0.430
INF_TECH	0.601	1.000	0.513	0.501	0.412
INNOV	0.569	0.528	1.000	0.410	0.297
SALES_IMP	0.489	0.510	0.406	1.000	0.484
ENV_SUST	0.434	0.382	0.294	0.477	1.000

Source: Authors' research in Stata.

Technological Innovation and Sustainable Development 57

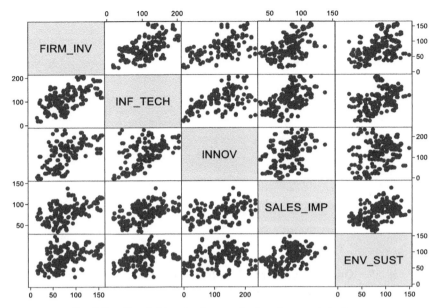

Fig. 3.7. Graph Matrix. *Source*: Authors' research in Stata.

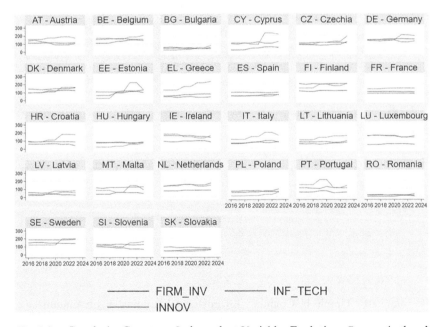

Fig. 3.8. Graphs by Country – Independent Variables Evolution. *Source*: Authors' research in Stata.

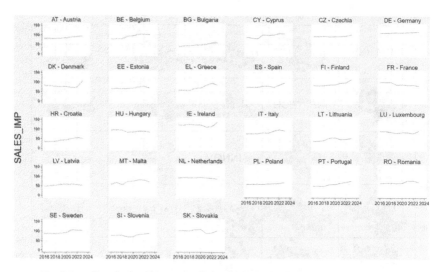

Fig. 3.9. Graphs by Country – Sales Impact Evolution. *Source*: Authors' research in Stata.

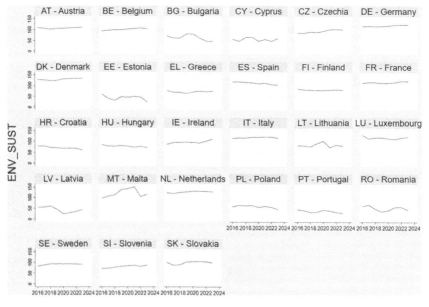

Fig. 3.10. Graphs by Country – Environmental Sustainability Evolution. *Source*: Authors' research in Stata.

over the analysed period and present a mostly positive evolution of this variable, indicating that environmental sustainability benefits from increased attention. This interest is also identified in the bibliometric analysis, where these countries are illustrated in Fig. 3.5, which includes the co-occurrence, links, and clustering of terms/keywords approached in recent literature about the main authors' articles' country of publication.

To further identify the connections and the influence of firm investments, innovations, and ITs on achieving environmental and economic sustainability, we performed a linear and unifactorial regression analysis using a panel data model with the Pooled OLS method, which assumes that all of the countries from the dataset have similar characteristics and do not consider other unobserved variables or country-specific effects. These regression models can be found in Tables 3.4 and 3.5. The results presented statistically significant relationships between the variables (p-values < 0.001) and positive correlations between the independent and dependent variables for both regression models. The R-square value suggests that 32% of the variation in the economic sustainability variable (sales indicator) and 22% of the variation in the environmental sustainability indicator are generated by the variation of the firm investments, the use of IT, and the number of innovations introduced on the market. The innovator indicator does not present an optimum p-value for this simple regression model. Still, we can see that this indicator significantly influences economic and environmental sustainability if it is considered separately from firm investments and the use of IT (in this case, the p-value for both regression models is $p < 0.001$).

Table 3.4. Regression Model – Economic Sustainability (Sales Impacts).

	SALES_IMP	SALES_IMP	SALES_IMP	SALES_IMP
FIRM_INV	0.293*** (0.0120)			0.147*** (0.0187)
INF_TECH		0.234*** (0.00886)		0.141*** (0.0206)
INNOV			0.138*** (0.0162)	0.0354 (0.0183)
_cons	56.77*** (1.112)	55.05*** (2.670)	64.04*** (2.096)	49.18*** (1.660)
N	216	216	216	216
R^2	0.239	0.260	0.165	0.319

Note: Standard errors in parentheses (*$p < 0.05$, **$p < 0.01$, ***$p < 0.001$).
Source: Authors' research in Stata.

Table 3.5. Regression Model – Environmental Sustainability.

	ENV_SUST	ENV_SUST	ENV_SUST	ENV_SUST
FIRM_INV	0.361*** (0.0373)			0.259* (0.0762)
INF_TECH		0.243*** (0.0125)		0.118*** (0.0145)
INNOV			0.139*** (0.0175)	0.00914 (0.0346)
_cons	58.92*** (3.466)	61.57*** (1.457)	71.48*** (1.513)	53.33*** (2.441)
N	216	216	216	216
R^2	0.188	0.146	0.087	0.211

Note: Standard errors in parentheses (*$p < 0.05$, **$p < 0.01$, ***$p < 0.001$).
Source: Authors' research in Stata.

This study uses advanced data collection and analysis techniques to obtain a detailed summary of the data sets. The techniques involve creating clusters of related variables or groups of individuals based on their distinct characteristics, which differ from those of individuals or variables in other clusters. This process is carried out using the Ward method to apply cluster analysis, which yields four specific clusters, as shown in the dendrogram in Fig. 3.11 and Table 3.6.

Cluster analysis results obtained using the Ward method can be found in Tables 3.6 and 3.7. Cluster analysis mainly concentrates on finding a similitude or a discrepancy among the selected variables, and it offers empirically based results that present a specific classification of these variables (Majerova & Nevima, 2017).

Each of these clusters is made up of several EU Member States, grouped according to their performance in terms of technological innovation and sustainability. Using this approach, the study provides a comprehensive understanding of the patterns and trends in the data sets, offering insights into the performance of different countries regarding technological innovation and sustainability. The results of the analysis can be used to identify areas where improvements are needed, as well as to develop strategies to promote sustainable development and

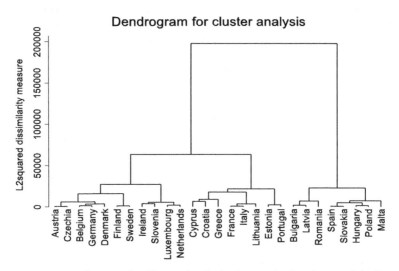

Fig. 3.11. Dendrogram for Cluster Analysis. *Source*: Authors' research in Stata.

Table 3.6. Clusters Associated with the Impact of Innovative Technologies on Environmental and Economic Sustainability.

Clusters (C) 2016–2023	Cluster Modelling – Ward Method
C1	Czechia, Denmark, Sweden, Germany, Finland, Austria, Belgium
C2	Slovenia, Ireland, the Netherlands, Luxembourg
C3	Estonia, France, Italy, Cyprus, Croatia, Lithuania, Greece, Portugal
C4	Latvia, Romania, Malta, Hungary, Bulgaria, Spain, Poland, Slovakia

Table 3.7. Detailed Statistics of the Clusters Associated with the Impact of Innovative Technologies on Environmental and Economic Sustainability.

Indicators	Cluster 1 (C1)			Cluster 2 (C2)			Cluster 3 (C3)			Cluster 4 (C4)			F	R^2
	N	Mean	SD	N	Mean	SD	N	Mean	SD	N	Mean	SD		
	Cluster analysis 2016–2023													
FIRM_INV	7	131.241	13.850	4	70.308	17.164	8	74.239	22.218	8	49.560	22.291	22.5666***	0.7464
INF_TECH	7	151.306	38.787	4	147.860	20.901	8	91.592	29.286	8	81.596	29.304	9.1509***	0.5441
INNOV	7	191.134	16.185	4	152.231	11.831	8	170.740	36.603	8	61.002	25.202	37.0183***	0.8284
SALES_IMP	7	105.548	8.340	4	100.604	24.932	8	77.130	18.733	8	75.231	17.530	5.5981**	0.4220
ENV_SUST	7	106.708	18.215	4	111.866	17.733	8	70.580	35.793	8	70.991	30.488	3.9069*	0.3376

Source: Authors' research in Stata.

innovation in the EU. Overall, the study demonstrates the power and potential of advanced data analysis techniques in generating insights that can inform policy and decision-making processes.

5. CONCLUSION

Business performance is expected to be measured by the firms' economic capacities, and environmental and social capabilities and future-focused companies will tend to commit to improving their sustainability performance and introduce novelties or innovations to achieve sustainable development (Varadarajan, 2017). Sustainability can be a crucial driver of innovation, and in the future, companies will likely face the need to embrace more sustainable methods and practices to thrive and maintain their market position; therefore, their capacity to innovate and introduce new products and services will be essential (Adams et al., 2012). Looking ahead, the challenge for companies will be to align their technological innovation strategies with sustainability goals. This requires not only the adoption of new technologies but also a fundamental shift in corporate culture and business models. Research in this area, evolving rapidly, suggests that a collaborative approach involving governments, businesses, and civil society is essential to leverage technology for sustainable development. Nidumolu et al. (2013) advocate for a new paradigm where businesses view environmental and social challenges as opportunities for innovation, growth, and transformation.

Technological innovations emerge as a key, multifaceted player in the fight against climate change, offering innovative solutions for companies to maintain sustainable developments and risk management. While this field shows great promise, it still evolves, and challenges persist. There is a pressing need for ongoing research to understand the long-term impacts of these technologies and to develop appropriate regulatory frameworks. As technological innovations continue to grow, their potential to contribute to a more sustainable future becomes increasingly evident. This highlights the importance of collaboration among technologists, financiers, policymakers, and environmentalists to harness technology's full potential and navigate the complexities of integrating it with sustainable practices.

Despite its potential, integrating technology with sustainable practices is fraught with challenges. Regulatory issues, as extensively discussed by Zetzsche et al. (2017), pose a significant hurdle. They highlight that current regulations often struggle to keep pace with rapid technological advancements, creating a gap that can impede the alignment of technological developments with sustainable goals. In addition to regulatory hurdles, ethical considerations are equally paramount. Buchanan (2019) emphasises the importance of addressing data privacy and security concerns. Moreover, the digital divide, a critical issue outlined by Chishti and Barberis (2016), may restrict the accessibility of technological solutions, thereby potentially worsening inequalities. These challenges, encompassing regulatory, ethical, and accessibility issues, underscore the complexities involved in harmonising technological innovations with sustainable practices.

ACKNOWLEDGEMENT

This work was supported by a grant from the Romanian Ministry of Research, Innovation, and Digitalisation, the project with the title 'Economics and Policy Options for Climate Change Risk and Global Environmental Governance' (CF 193/28.11.2022, Funding Contract no. 760078/23.05.2023), within Romania's National Recovery and Resilience Plan (PNRR) – Pillar III, Component C9, Investment I8 (PNRR/2022/C9/MCID/I8) – Development of a program to attract highly specialised human resources from abroad in research, development, and innovation activities.

REFERENCES

Adams, R., Jeanrenaud, S., Bessant, J., Overy, P., & Denyer, D. (2012). *Innovating for sustainability – A systematic review of the body of knowledge*. Network for Sustainability. http://nbs.net/knowledge

Antoni, D., Jie, F., & Abareshi, A. (2020). Critical factors in information technology capability for enhancing firm's environmental performance: Case of Indonesian ICT sector. *International Journal of Agile Systems and Management*, 13(2), 159. https://doi.org/10.1504/IJASM.2020.107907

Arner, D. W., Barberis, J. N., & Buckley, R. P. (2015). *The evolution of fintech: A new post-crisis paradigm?* [SSRN Scholarly Paper 2676553]. https://doi.org/10.2139/ssrn.2676553

Bolton, P., Despres, M., Pereira Da Silva, L. A., Samama, F., & Svartzman, R. (2020). *The green swan Central banking and financial stability in the age of climate change*. Bank for International Settlements. https://www.bis.org/publ/othp31.pdf

Buchanan, M. (2019). The limits of machine prediction. *Nature Physics*, 15(4), 304. https://doi.org/10.1038/s41567-019-0489-5

Carney, M. (2015). *Breaking the tragedy of the Horizon – Climate change and financial stability*. https://www.bankofengland.co.uk/speech/2015/breaking-the-tragedy-of-the-horizon-climate-change-and-financial-stability

Chishti, S. & Barberis, J. (Eds.). (2016). *The fintech book: The financial technology handbook for investors, entrepreneurs and visionaries* (1st ed.). Wiley. https://doi.org/10.1002/9781119218906

Danciu, V. (2013). The sustainable company: New challenges and strategies for more sustainability. *Theoretical and Applied Economics*, 9(586), 7–26. https://ideas.repec.org/a/agr/journl/vxxy2013i9(586)p7-26.html

Driscoll, J. C., & Kraay, A. C. (1998). Consistent covariance matrix estimation with spatially dependent panel data. *Review of Economics and Statistics*, 80, 549–560. https://doi.org/10.1162/003465398557825

European Innovation Scoreboard – European Commission. (2023). https://research-and-innovation.ec.europa.eu/statistics/performance-indicators/european-innovation-scoreboard_en

European Parliament. (2022). *European green bonds. A standard for Europe, open to the world*. https://www.europarl.europa.eu/RegData/etudes/BRIE/2022/698870/EPRS_BRI(2022)698870_EN.pdf

Fama, E. F., & French, K. R. (1993). Common risk factors in the returns on stocks and bonds. *Journal of Financial Economics*, 33(1), 3–56. https://doi.org/10.1016/0304-405x(93)90023-5

Gomber, P., Kauffman, R. J., Parker, C., & Weber, B. W. (2018). On the Fintech revolution: Interpreting the forces of innovation, disruption, and transformation in financial services. *Journal of Management Information Systems*, 35(1), 220–265. https://doi.org/10.1080/07421222.2018.1440766

Haddad, C., & Hornuf, L. (2019). The emergence of the global Fintech market: Economic and technological determinants. *Small Business Economics*, 53, 81–105. https://doi.org/10.1007/s11187-018-9991-x

Hart, S. L., & Milstein, M. B. (2003). Creating sustainable value. *Academy of Management Perspectives*, 17(2), 56–67. https://doi.org/10.5465/ame.2003.10025194

Huang, Y., Zhang, L., Li, Z., Qiu, H., Sun, T., & Wang, X. (2020). Fintech credit risk assessment for SMEs: Evidence from China. *IMF Working Paper*, *20*(193), 1–42. https://doi.org/10.2139/ssrn.3721218

Iansiti, M., & Lakhani, K. (2017). The truth about blockchain. *Harvard Business Review*, 1–11. https://enterprisersproject.com/sites/default/files/the_truth_about_blockchain.pdf

Jung, D., Dorner, V., Glaser, F., & Morana, S. (2018). Robo-advisory. *Business & Information Systems Engineering*, *60*(1), 81–86. https://doi.org/10.1007/s12599-018-0521-9

Klapper, L., & Lusardi, A. (2020). Financial literacy and financial resilience: Evidence from around the world. *Financial Management*, *49*, 589–614. https://doi.org/10.1111/fima.12283

Majerova, I., & Nevima, J. (2017). The measurement of human development using the Ward method of cluster analysis. *Journal of International Studies*, *10*(2), 239–257. https://doi.org/10.14254/2071-8330.2017/10-2/17

Melander, L. (2017). Achieving sustainable development by collaborating in green product innovation. *Business Strategy and the Environment*, *26*(8), 1095–1109. https://doi.org/10.1002/bse.1970

Nidumolu, R., Prahalad, C. K., & Rangaswami, M. R. (2013). Why sustainability is now the key driver of innovation. *IEEE Engineering Management Review*, *41*(2), 30–37. https://doi.org/10.1109/emr.2013.6601104

Porter, M. E., & Van Der Linde, C. (1995). Toward a new conception of the environment-competitiveness relationship. *Journal of Economic Perspectives*, *9*(4), 97–118. https://doi.org/10.1257/jep.9.4.97

Schueffel, P. M. (2016). Taming the beast: A scientific definition of fintech. *Journal of Innovation Management*, *4*, 32–54. http://hdl.handle.net/10216/102610

Schumpeter, J. A. (1942). *Capitalism, socialism and democracy* (Vol. 36, pp. 132–145). Harper & Row.

Shrivastava, P., & Hart, S. (1995). Creating sustainable corporations. *Business Strategy and the Environment*, *4*(3), 154–165. https://doi.org/10.1002/bse.3280040307

Varadarajan, R. (2017). Innovating for sustainability: A framework for sustainable innovations and a model of sustainable innovations orientation. *Journal of the Academy of Marketing Science*, *45*(1), 14–36. https://doi.org/10.1007/s11747-015-0461-6

Worae, T. A., Ngwakwe, C. C., & Ambe, C. C. (2018). Threshold effect analysis of the relationship between environmental responsibility and financial performance. *Managing Global Transitions*, *16*(4), 355–377. https://doi.org/10.26493/1854-6935.16.355-377

Zetzsche, D. A., Buckley, R. P., Arner, D. W., & Barberis, J. N. (2017). From FinTech to TechFin: The regulatory challenges of data-driven finance [New York University Journal of Law and Business, Forthcoming, European Banking Institute Working Paper Series 2017 – No. 6, University of Hong Kong Faculty of Law Research Paper No. 2017/007, University of Luxembourg Law Working Paper No. 2017-001]. https://doi.org/10.2139/ssrn.2959925

Zhang, Y., Li, S., Luo, T., & Gao, J. (2020). The effect of emission trading policy on carbon emission reduction: Evidence from an integrated study of pilot regions in China. *Journal of Cleaner Production*, *265*, 121843. https://doi.org/10.1016/j.jclepro.2020.121843doi:10.1016/j.jclepro.2020.121843

CHAPTER 4

ENVIRONMENTAL CHALLENGES AND EFFECTS INDUCED BY THE SHADOW ECONOMY

Sorana Vătavu[a], Cristian Tudorescu[b], Oana-Ramona Lobonţ[a], Nicoleta-Claudia Moldovan[a] and Florin Costea[c]

[a]Faculty of Economics and Business Administration, Department of Finance, Business Information Systems and Modelling, West University of Timisoara, Timisoara, Romania
[b]graduated from West University of Timisoara, Timisoara, Romania
[c]Doctoral School of Economics and Business Administration, West University of Timisoara, Timisoara, Romania

ABSTRACT

Purpose/Objective: *The shadow economy problem comes from the need for governments to increase their revenues, while citizens expect better social protection schemes such as universal basic income, increased spending for social security, and better living standards, including a sustainable and green environment. Our study analyses a complex and multifaced relationship between the shadow economy and the environment.*

Design/Methodology/Approach: *The analysis refers to the shadow economy (% in GDP) and three environmental proxies (Agriculture Methane Emissions, Methane Emissions for the Energy Sector, and Tax on Pollution) for the EU countries over the 2009–2019 period. Firstly, we describe the evolution of the indicators, and then we observe the correlation between the indicators. The last stage considers simple linear regression models, with shadow economy as the independent variable and environmental proxies as dependent variables.*

Significance/Implications/Conclusions: *Our research found that the evolution of the shadow economy is on a downtrend, considering that the fight against corruption developed after the 2009 financial crisis and especially after the Euro crisis 2014. Countries such as Romania, Bulgaria, Italy, Portugal, and Spain have the highest shadow economy due to their political electorate's constant mismanagement and low credibility. On the contrary, countries such as Hungary, Estonia, and Lithuania have a low shadow economy.*

Limitations: *The reliance on limited data and the models applied.*

Future Research: *Future studies could expand the analysis by incorporating additional indicators, considering other econometric models, and incorporating more comprehensive and up-to-date data.*

Keywords: Shadow economy; environment; methane emissions; tax on pollution; correlation; regression analysis; EU

JEL Codes: O17; Q53; C23

1. INTRODUCTION

There is a portion of the huge economic landscape that is mainly shielded from the prying eyes of governments, statisticians, and regulators. This covert industry, often referred to as the shadow economy, is an intricate and elusive network of exchanges that frequently avoids taxation, regulation, and paperwork while taking place outside the scope of official inspection. The shadow economy, which consists of a variety of unofficial, unreported, and clandestine operations, exists in every nation, regardless of its level of economic progress or political structure. The term 'shadow economy', which is often used to describe informal, parallel, or underground economies, covers a broad variety of both illegal and legal operations. Unauthorised employment, unregistered firms, black market transactions, smuggling, tax fraud, money laundering, human trafficking, the sale of illegal drugs, and other types of illicit commerce are a few examples. While some individuals participate in the shadow economy out of need or as a means of survival, others do so on purpose to avoid the law or take advantage of systemic flaws.

The shadow economy's opacity and lack of openness are two of its distinguishing traits. Accurate assessment and quantification of the shadow economy are challenging due to its covert nature. This informal sector's size and influence are sometimes underestimated since traditional economic measures frequently fall short of capturing its full scope. As a result, estimates of the shadow economy's size and contribution to national economies are inconsistent, ranging from a negligible share of GDP to significant amounts in some nations (Davidescu et al., 2022).

The causes for the shadow economy's inception and continued existence are numerous and intricately linked. The expansion of the informal sector may be attributed to a variety of factors, including high taxes, onerous laws, bureaucratic inefficiency, corruption, insufficient social safety nets, and restricted access to official work possibilities. People and enterprises may turn to informal activity as a coping technique for dealing with economic volatility, poverty, unemployment, or exclusion from the formal economy.

The problem of the shadow economy comes, mainly recently, from the need of governments to increase their revenue stream as the citizens are demanding more and more social protection schemes such as universal basic income, increased spending for social security, increase in pensions, salaries, etc. Thus, to increase the revenues, the decrease in the shadow economy (and, of course, the increase in tax revenue that this will bring) is enormously important, especially nowadays when the cost of living has reached unsustainable levels.

The impact of the shadow economy on the environment is complex and multifaced. The environment has not historically benefitted from a lack of oversight, seen in excessive pollution, deforestation, natural disasters, etc. Now, more than ever, given that climate change is a real worldwide destructive phenomenon, governments must be extremely cautious in handling the shadow economy and its repelling effects on the environment. Our paper will continue with an in-depth literature review, reviewing the impact of the shadow economy in Asian and European countries, focusing on the effects on the environment. Then, the case study presents the relationship between the shadow economy and environmental proxies in the EU over the last decade. The final section concludes by offering several benchmarks for how EU member states can apply measures and policies to improve the environment.

2. LITERATURE REVIEW

Air and water pollution have become major issues in developing nations. Human waste and industrial chemicals are contaminating the drinking water supply of many people, and air pollution is also responsible for the premature deaths of around two million individuals each year globally. Pictures of cities in Iran and China shrouded by thick fog have been appearing in newspapers around the globe.

The rapid growth of developing countries has resulted in various environmental problems. Many of these are caused by the use of fossil fuels and coal. In addition, the growth of the shadow economy has affected the economies of other emerging and developing nations such as Peru, Ukraine, and Tanzania. Between 1999 and 2006, over 50% of the gross domestic product of these countries originated from the shadow economy.

According to a study conducted by Schneider et al. (2010), the shadow economy generated around 34.5% of the gross domestic product in over 162 countries from 1999 to 2007. Also, according to Blackman, the informal sector can have significant environmental hazards. Many activities in the shadow economy contribute to pollution, such as brickmaking, leather tanning, and metalworking. In addition, gold uses mercury, which is released into the environment in over a hundred nations (Biswas et al., 2012; Bilan et al., 2021).

In the case of Turkey, from 1970 to 2014, the study conducted by Imamoglu (2018) shows that the existence of informal economic activities can influence the environmental situation. Blackman claims that large underground businesses can result in severe pollution hazards. According to Markandya et al. (2013), underground businesses can lead to various economic consequences. These include higher taxes, reduced revenue for legal taxpayers, competition, and the loss of productivity, but tax revenues from CO_2 are also used to reduce the tax on formal labour. In addition, the lack of transparency in underground business operations can affect companies' efficiency.

In 2010, the International Labor Organization reported that employment from the shadow economy accounts for over 70% of the total in several countries, such as Uganda, Nepal, Thailand, Ghana, and Lithuania. Like other countries with large populations but little advanced economies, employment from illegal businesses may become a problem. Unemployed individuals are forced to take on unauthorised positions with little or no compensation and high pollution consequences. For instance, Biller (1994) states that Brazil's informal gold mining industry has caused severe mercury pollution. Also, globalisation has significant impacts on environmental pollution and degradation through industrialisation and technological progress (Ortiz et al., 2022).

Besides the intensity of the regulation, other factors can contribute to the pollution caused by the shadow economy, such as the tax burden, social security and public sector services, and the official economy. It is, therefore, important to study the multiple effects on the environment. If the other costs exceed the environmental protection tax, then companies will have to turn to shadow production. This issue should be studied to determine if pollution can also have a negative effect on the economy. This can lead to the leakage of pollutants depending on their enforcement.

2.1. Previous Research in Asian Countries

Pang et al. (2020) studied the interplay between shadow economy and pollution with panel data across the provinces of China; the term shadow economy refers to activities that aren't included in the official records of a country. It is a widespread issue that affects countries that are generally law-abiding. One of the main reasons why it is prevalent is that companies can avoid paying taxes by operating in a shadow economy. Due to the cost-saving advantages of shadow operations, many firms are forced to go underground. Even though they are beneficial for profit-making, they can also expose a company to various risks, such as the costly penalties associated with illegal activities. In their research, we find many similarities, such as quotations from Schneider (1994) and Schneider and Enste (2008), where the data are collected from countries like Ukraine, China, Iran, Peru, and Tanzania. In common, they also refer to the use of fossil fuels and coal. In addition, due to the increasing severity of environmental issues, the government is paying more attention to the issue of pollution abatement. This has forced companies to process shadow economy transactions, which can expose them to various risks:

- The lack of regulation and economic activities can lead to the loss of tax revenue, which can be used to fund various public services.
- The growth of the shadow economy can also increase inequality. Individuals involved in it may not have the same protections and benefits they would get in the formal economy.
- The lack of consumer protections and safety standards can also lead to unsafe products and services being offered by the shadow economy.
- The existence of the shadow economy can also encourage corruption, as it provides opportunities for illicit activities and bribes.
- The rise of the shadow economy can also weaken the foundations of democracy. It can provide an alternative to the formal channels of governance and erode public trust in the government.
- The existence of the shadow or informal economy can also contribute to social instability. It can create a feeling of lawlessness and encourage criminal activity.

There have been various studies on the link between shadow economy and environmental regulation, but they have not been able to analyse the relationship between shadow economy and pollution thoroughly. From 2006 to 2016, data collected in China revealed the non-linear relationship between haze pollution and the country's environmental regulations. This suggests that implementing effective regulations cannot immediately reduce pollution levels (Zhang et al., 2019).

It is widely believed that there is a non-linear relationship between pollution and environmental regulation. However, the exact reason behind this relationship may be related to the shadow economy. Baksi and Bose (2010) revealed that the regulation of the informal sector can affect pollution levels. They found that strengthening the regulation can lead to a reduction in overall pollution. The other factor that can affect pollution is the composition effect, as the tighter the regulation, the larger the informal sector will become. This can lead to an increase in the total pollution.

The exact relationship between the regulation and the size of the informal sector can be determined by analysing the effects of different factors on the pollution level. For instance, the tighter the regulation can lead to a reduction in overall pollution. However, the increase in the shadow economy can also lead to a different effect. Besides per capita income, the environment-growth nexus also takes into account other factors such as energy consumption, urbanisation, income inequality, and international trade (Balezentis et al., 2020; Jayanthakumaran et al., 2012).

The rapid growth of trade flows during the 1980s was attributed to the implementation of various trade agreements, which have significantly affected the environment. Despite the growing number of studies examining the link between environmental degradation and trade, the findings are not definitive. Recent studies suggest that trade facilitates the development of more eco-friendly technologies in developing nations. On the other hand, some research states that the trade in manufactured goods mainly causes the adverse effects of trade on the emission of greenhouse gases.

Some countries may experience losses due to trade regulations because of the pollution caused by producing goods for export. Several studies have shown that the relationship between China and the USA affects the emission levels of pollutants in each nation's national inventories. The trade flows between China and the USA are enormous. Both countries have numerous infrastructure projects and trade agreements that can significantly affect the environment. As a result, their decisions can have a significant impact on global pollution. A study conducted by Machado et al. (2001) analysed the effects of trade on CO_2 and energy consumption. According to the authors, trade promotes energy consumption and increases greenhouse gas output. In a study conducted between 1996 and 2007, Ozcan and Ozturk (2019) examined the relationship between various factors such as economic growth, trade, and energy consumption in Turkey. They found that the increase in trade and economic growth can lead to higher pollution per capita. The positive and negative effects of trade can be assessed depending on the regulations in each country and the level of environmental awareness in the population.

As China's rapid economic development continues, it is becoming more and more evident that the country's pollution levels are rising. In 2008, China surpassed the USA as the biggest carbon dioxide emitter. Due to the increasing number of studies on the relationship between environmental pollution and high economic development, the concept of the environmental Kuznets Curve has been widely adopted. The findings of this study suggest that the EKC hypothesis is not entirely accurate when it comes to the link between economic development and income levels. It also shows that the non-income-related factors that can contribute to environmental degradation are still relevant. In 2010, Schneider et al. (2010) estimated that the shadow economy of various developed countries grew at a slower rate than that of developing nations. They noted that the large shadow economy of high-income countries grew at a rate of 16.6% in 2007, while that of developing countries increased by 34.2%. Their paper aimed to analyse the link between economic growth and the size of the shadow economy. It states that the level of the shadow economy will increase at the beginning, but it will decrease once the country's economy has reached the point where it is stable and sound.

Recent studies suggest that trade facilitates the development of more eco-friendly technologies in developing nations. On the other hand, some research states that trade in manufactured goods mainly causes the negative effects of trade on greenhouse gas emissions.

Some countries may experience losses due to trade regulations due to pollution caused by the production of goods for export. Several studies (Fan & Xia, 2012; Minx et al., 2011; Lin et al., 2014; Zhang et al., 2012) have proven that the relationship between China and the USA affects the emission levels of pollutants in each nation's national inventories.

The positive and negative effects of trade can be assessed depending on the regulations in each country and the level of environmental awareness in the population. In Russia, we find that envelope wages and underreporting of business profits stand out as the two largest components of the Russian shadow economy. Underreporting salaries or so-called envelope wages in Russia is approximately 38.7% of the true wage on average in 2018, whereas approximately 33.8% of business income (actual profits) is underreported. Unofficial employees in Russia as a percentage of the actual number of employees are estimated at 28.2% in 2018.

Many companies fail to disclose their employees' salaries or income, which means they contribute to the shadow economy. These entities are estimated to comprise 6.1% of the country's total enterprises. The level of corruption in Russia is very high. According to our findings, the percentage of revenue companies spend on bribes is around 26.4%. On the other hand, the percentage of contract value that they offer as bribes to secure a deal with the government is around 20.6%. Furthermore, over one-third of all companies in the country pay more than 25% of their revenue in bribes. The shadow economy, a type of financial activity the government mainly controls, is estimated to be around 40% of Russia's economy. It is also associated with higher levels of informal activity. This study (Putniņš & Sauka, 2020) employed a regression analysis to determine the characteristics of entrepreneurs who view tax evasion as a form of tolerated behaviour. The findings of this study provide valuable insights into why the size of Russia's shadow economy is so large. It shows entrepreneurs are dissatisfied with the government's tax policy and business legislation. We also find that harsher tax evasion penalties can reduce the evasion level. This suggests that the government should implement better detection methods and increase penalties.

2.2. Previous Research in European Countries

Regarding the situation of the shadow economy in Europe, Schneider (2008; 2012) monitors the evolution of the shadow economy in Germany, stating that the oldest estimate of the shadow economy is based on the survey method used by the IfD in Allensbach, Germany. This indicates that the shadow economy accounted for around 3.6% of gross domestic product in 1974. A study conducted by the two researchers in 2005 and 2008 used the same survey method to estimate the activities of the shadow economy from 2001 to 2006. Using the official wage rate, they estimated that the shadow economy's activities reached a rate of 4.1% in 2001, 3.1% in 2004, 3.6% in 2005, and 2.5% in 2006. Using the lower wage rate, these estimates shrink to 1.3% in 2001 and 1.0% in 2004.

Although the survey method is commonly used to estimate the size of the economy, it underestimates the scope of the shadow economy. A different approach is known as the discrepancy approach, which considers the variations in how various aggregate variables are calculated. This method can help estimate the shadow economy's activity during the 1970s and 1980s. It is widely assumed that the figures presented by the transaction and discrepancy approaches are very large. For instance, the shadow economy, around a third of the GDP during the 1980s, is likely to have been overestimated.

For the national case, Maftei (2014) stated that the transformation of Romania's economy from a planned to a market-based economy had created a favourable environment for expanding the shadow economy. The country's liberalised policies and investments have brought wealth to the government. However, after 1990, the market became more complex, and the activities of illegal enterprises, such as pyramid schemes and exports, became more prevalent. The transition to a market economy was accompanied by the emergence of corruption and the creation of an informal economy.

According to the 2012 Corruption Index, Romania is among the countries with the highest levels of corruption in the Eastern part of the continent. Studies have also proven that illegal economic activities are prevalent in the country.

The size of Romania's underground economy has increased significantly over time due to the effects of the economic crisis. Some of the main factors contributing to its growth are raising taxes, the rising unemployment rate, overregulation, and bureaucracy. These factors are expected to increase the limits of the shadow economy. The evolution of the unofficial economy can be observed in the various changes that have occurred in the market. Some of these include the establishment of a parallel economy that was left behind by the centralised system, the rise of decentralisation and corruption, and the presence of small businesses that can easily evade taxes.

Cosea (in Maftei, 2014), Professor of Economics, also stated in 'An Introduction to the Underground Economy of Romania' that the leading causes of the underground economy can be observed in Romania. The scope of the phenomenon is vast, and its consequences are significant. According to Cosea, the non-observed economy can have various negative consequences. Some of these include the misappropriation of resources for other purposes, the damage to the social assistance system, the growth trend in the budget deficit, the appearance of distrust in government programmes and authority, and the increase in crime and social insecurity. The intensity of Romania's fiscal overregulation is one of the main causes of the non-observed economy. This is because the procedures used for managing the budget are often modified and bureaucratic.

The other factors that can affect the country's economy are the lack of proper fiscal discipline and the high level of corruption (Zaman and Goschin, 2015). This issue is additionally caused by the labour force's use of different activities, which are usually associated with the black market. The complexity of the procedures used to manage the budget and the lack of capital are also some of the factors that can affect the country's economy.

The rise of the underground economy to 30% of the country's GDP is alarming. Although the country's economy has started to improve over the past couple of years, it is still struggling to deal with the various activities related to terrorism and crime. Some of these include drugs, as well as weapons and cigarette trafficking. The government can also not effectively implement the laws against these activities.

The government of Romania recognises the challenge of dealing with the underground economy. It is expected to reduce the country's fiscal pressure and create jobs to improve the economy. Some of the measures that the government can implement to combat illegal activities are the use of electronic payments and online transactions. Despite the various solutions the government can implement to combat the underground economy, it is still important to note that the country needs first-class public services and regulations. This is because the money that the underground economy generates is spent in the real economy. The market functions with dirty money and black money, which is why construction, retail, and tourism are some of the sectors that are affected by tax evasion.

In Italy, Contini and Grand (2010), with 'Disposable Workforce in Italy', considered the labour market approach to analyse the irregular economy in Italy. It defines irregular labour as semi-hidden activities that pay lower wages. These include undocumented construction, overtime work, unauthorised apprentice work, and illegal personal services. According to Contini and Grand, many types of workers fall under the irregular economy. These include those who are not working, are holding temporary positions while looking for a permanent job, and are officially employed. Different methods have been used to measure the number of irregular workers in Italy. In 1974, it was estimated that around 5.5% of the country's labour force had two or more jobs. Other estimates have been made by the Quarterly Survey on the labour force, as well as the QSLF. In 1978, the figure was estimated to be 44.7%. This figure is higher because many unemployed individuals also participate in the informal economy. In 1979 and 1981, Contini studied the determinants and characteristics of the irregular economy. They used various factors to determine the labour force's potential. These include the types of jobs available in the industry, agriculture, services, and official unemployment. By estimating the labour force through surveys, Contini came up with an estimate of the irregular labour forces to the total employment ratio during the 1970s. In his study, he also analyses the various factors that affect the employment ratio, such as the exchange rate, flight from agriculture, and the unit labour cost. He found that the flight to the south accounts for over 55% of the variations in the total employment rate. Italy's shadow economy experienced small fluctuations over the years, but from the 2000s until 2022, it maintained at approximately 22%.

Mauleon and Sarda (2017) prove that in Italy, the evasion of taxes and the shadow economy are major issues threatening the country's public finance and national economy. The losses caused by tax evasion are estimated at around 183 billion annually. In 2011, about 41.3 million individuals in Italy filed their tax returns. Of these, only 0.1% declared an annual income of more than 300,000. Many claimed their yearly income was less than 26,000, while 27% avoided paying taxes by exploiting various tax reliefs and deductions. The most significant sources of tax evasion are free professions and entrepreneurs. It is estimated that over 56.3% of them avoid paying taxes by claiming they don't have enough money to pay. Despite the high number of taxpayers suspected of tax fraud, the Italian tax administration has not effectively addressed the issue. The court system is one of the main allies of tax evaders. It can take taxpayers around 903 days to get their first sentence after they are charged with a crime. This is because appeals can prolong the process. Only 1.7% of taxpayers are apprehended for tax fraud each year.

According to the UK's Her Majesty's Revenue & Customs administration, the tax gap between what was due and what was paid during the 2011–2012 period was about £25 billion. This is approximately 42 billion Euros. The amount is computed by considering various factors, such as the types of tax evasion, the failure of taxpayers to pay taxes, and the difficulties in recovering dues. In cross-sectional terms, the UK's tax gap is mainly due to fraudulent activities linked to VAT, as well as unpaid income tax, corporate taxes, and losses due to uncollected excise. In fiscal 2011, the losses caused by tax evasion reached £5.1 billion. This was mainly due to the avoidance of taxes with tax optimisation techniques.

The state budget also suffered from criminal activities, which amounted to around £4.7 billion. The figure is claimed to be a gross underestimation, implying that the UK lost about 74 billion Euros due to the various factors that affected the country's budget in 2006. He estimated that the country's corporate tax avoidance caused the budget losses in 2006 to be around £12 billion.

On the other hand, he believed that the losses caused by private taxpayers amounted to around £13 billion. The losses caused by tax evasion amounted to around 7.6% of the country's tax revenues in 2006. The government's decision to reduce the number of tax officers by about 12,000 over the next couple of years was a mistake. Reducing the number of tax officers will severely affect the UK's ability to fight tax evasion. It will also deprive the country of tax revenues, already struggling with a public finances crisis.

Moreover, Sweden's fiscal services are focusing on the issue of international corporations using tax avoidance techniques. It has been estimated that the country's corporate tax avoidance has caused losses totalling almost SEK 47 billion. This is mainly due to the actions of multinational companies, which have resorted to various strategies to reduce their tax burden. In 2012, the country was estimated to lose about SEK 43 billion due to micro-business activities. This is equivalent to the budget revenues lost due to tax evasion by these entities.

The unofficial economy of the three countries outside the European Union, namely, Turkey, Switzerland, and Norway, continues to grow at around 15%. However, these countries have varying levels of economic development. In this group, Switzerland is regarded as the leader. Since 2010, it has been actively reducing the participation of its residents in illegal activities. Similar trends can be observed in Turkey and Norway. Although the former's shadow economy differs from the latter, it accounts for 27.2% and 13.1% of the country's GDP, respectively.

Despite the number of studies that examine the causes of shadow economy activities (Frey and Weck-Hanneman, 1984; Dell'Anno et al., 2006, Kelmanson et al., 2019), societies still try to control these through various measures such as education, punishment, and economic growth. However, further instruments such as economic growth and prosecution are also needed. It is essential to conduct our investigations using other factors, such as local autonomy, as this can give us a deeper understanding of the causes of shadow economies. The two main factors that influence tax morale are the level of autonomy and the willingness of the citizens to pay. Having a high level of autonomy allows one to express their preferences and, in turn, enhance their identification with the state's institutions. This can counteract the temptation to be part of the shadow economy. The level of autonomy can also improve the effectiveness of the government by encouraging the interaction between the authorities and the citizens. This can help improve the system's efficiency and prevent the government from being influenced by external factors.

3. CASE STUDY

This section will thoroughly analyse and understand the volatility in the indicators used for our analysis. Firstly, we will start by describing the indicators used for our paper, including the source from which we took the data, while also utilising the Excel graphs to showcase our indicators' evolution better. Lastly, we will apply a Pearson Correlation to observe the correlation between our indicators while continuing to use the Ordinary Least Square (OLS) for our econometric analysis of the simple linear regression model. Starting with a description of the indicators we have utilised in our analysis, Table 4.1 contains the complete information for our indicators.

Furthermore, to better represent the evolution of our indicators and take into consideration the differences between the EU-27 Member States, we have decided to group the EU-27 Member States into two distinct groups: the first one representing the countries that are considered 'Western' and the other representing the countries that are 'Eastern', for example the ones that had a communist regime in place in the 20th century.

The grouping is due to a stark difference in economic development, rule of law, values, environmental consciousness, and regulations between the EU-27 Member States. Therefore, Table 4.2 presents the grouping of countries for our analysis.

Table 4.1. Description of the Indicators Employed.

Indicator	Definition	Unit of Measure	Source
Shadow economy, as % of GDP (SE)	The shadow economy signifies the illegal and non-tax-paying economic activity that is outside the regulatory system of one nation or entity.	%	Schneider (2022). 'New COVID-19-related results for estimating the shadow economy in the global economy in 2021 and 2022'
Agricultural methane emissions (AMEs)	AMEs are from animals, animal waste, rice production, agricultural waste burning (nonenergy, on-site), and savanna burning	(thousand metric tons of CO_2 equivalent)	Eurostat
Methane emissions in the energy sector (MEES)	Methane emissions from energy processes include those from the production, handling, transmission, and combustion of fossil fuels and biofuels	(thousand metric tons of CO_2 equivalent)	Eurostat
Taxes on pollution (TP)	An environmental tax is a tax whose tax base is a physical unit (or a proxy of it) of something that has a proven, specific negative impact on the environment	million EUR	Eurostat

Source: Authors' own process.

Table 4.2. The Groups of Countries Analysed.

Group 1 – Western EU-27 Member States	Group 2 – Eastern EU-27 Member States
Austria, Belgium, Denmark, Finland, France, Germany, Greece, Malta, Ireland, Italy, Luxembourg, The Netherlands, Portugal, Spain, Sweden	Bulgaria, Croatia, Cyprus, Czech Republic, Estonia, Hungary, Latvia, Lithuania, Poland, Romania, Slovakia, Slovenia

Source: Authors' own process.

3.1. Descriptive Analysis

Observing Table 4.2, we can see that two groups were formed based on the geographical positioning within the EU area. To graphically represent the evolution of the indicators employed (Shadow Economy as % of GDP, AMEs, MEES, and TP), we will use the Excel software, more specifically, its graphing capabilities for better visualisation of data. Therefore, we observe the evolution of indicators from Figs. 4.1–4.8.

Analysing Fig. 4.1 and Fig. 4.2, which depict the evolution of the Shadow Economy as % of GDP, gives us a wealth of information on how both Western and Eastern EU-27 Member States deal with the issue of illegal and non-tax-paying economic activity. More precisely, looking at the Western EU-27 Member States, we can observe that the indicator has decreased from the heights of 2009, the earliest date for our data, where countries such as Spain and Portugal had an almost 30% SE (Shadow Economy), this is not particularly groundbreaking findings as Southern Europe has always faced problems in dealing with illegal and non-tax-paying economic activity as those economies were hit especially hard by both the financial crisis of 2007–2009 and the euro crisis.

Moreover, other Southern European countries such as Italy, which had a 29% SE in 2009, and Greece, which stood at 23,5% in 2009, prove that the over-reliance on the tourism industry led to a high informal sector. The tourism sector has

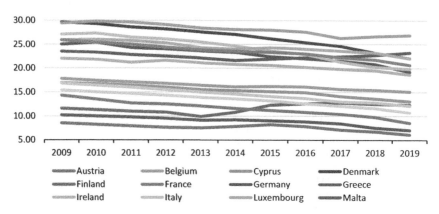

Fig. 4.1. Evolution of the Shadow Economy as % of GDP for Western EU-27 Member States. *Source*: Authors' own computation in Excel.

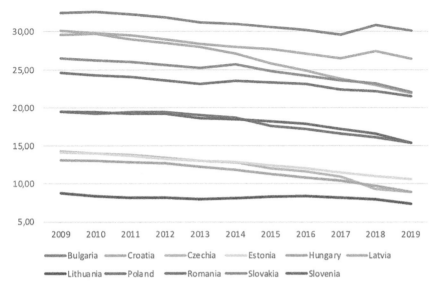

Fig. 4.2. Evolution of the Shadow Economy as % of GDP for Eastern EU-27 Member States. *Source*: Authors' own computation in Excel.

always been susceptible to macroeconomic shocks as it depends on consumers' disposable income. As the disposable income decreases, the first things that are cut back are the leisure activities, especially international ones. Conversely, countries such as Austria, Finland, and Lithuania had the Shadow Economy % of GDP of 8.5%, 11.6%, and 8.8%, respectively, with the lowest values in the entire EU-27. Peculiarly, the major economies of the EU, more precisely, Germany and France, had vastly different SE % at 25% and 14.3%, a difference of 10.7% between two similar and neighbouring countries. Looking specifically at the Eastern EU-27 Member States, we can observe that those countries have a higher SE as % of GDP, compared to the Western countries, at 32.5% in the case of Bulgaria, 30.1% for Croatia, Latvia at 29.6%, and Romania at 24.6%.

It is worth mentioning that in both groups, the SE% has decreased from 2009 to 2019, the latest year of our analysis. This is likely due to governments, through the wishes of their population, becoming increasingly intolerant of corruption and non-tax-paying economic activities, which represent a loss in revenue. As the world increasingly demands socialist reforms, more revenues have to come into the budget, as governmental expenses are ballooning at unsustainable levels.

Thoroughly observing Figs. 4.3–4.8, we can draw many valuable points about how the EU-27 Member States deal with pollution, sustainability, and the circular economy. More precisely, both AME and MEES values are either decreasing or staying at the same level in 2009.

The agriculture methane emissions for countries such as Germany, Belgium, and Romania decreased from their height in 2009. On the contrary, countries such as Cyprus, Slovakia, and Hungary had a higher value in 2019 than in 2009

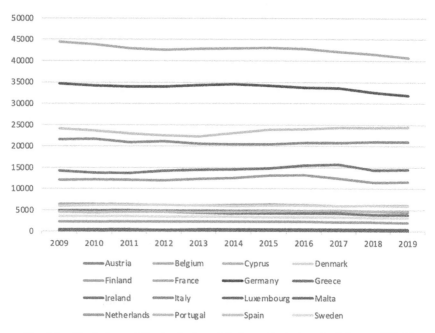

Fig. 4.3. Evolution of the Agriculture Methane Emissions for Western EU-27 Member States. *Source*: Authors' own computation in Excel.

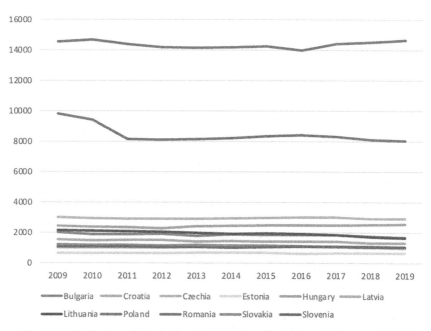

Fig. 4.4. Evolution of the Agriculture Methane Emissions for Eastern EU-27 Member States. *Source*: Authors' own computation in Excel.

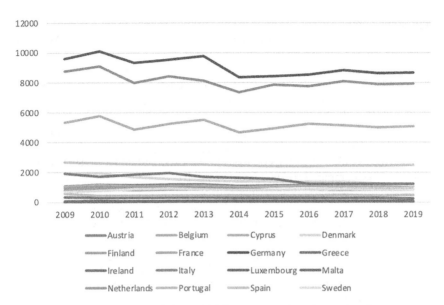

Fig. 4.5. Evolution of the MEES for Western EU-27 Member States.
Source: Authors' own computation in Excel.

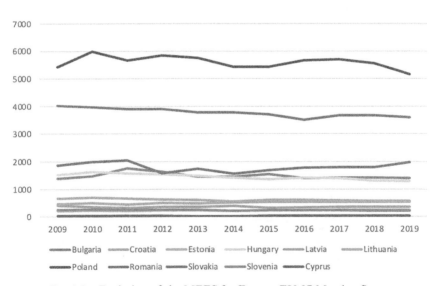

Fig. 4.6. Evolution of the MEES for Eastern EU-27 Member States.
Source: Authors' own computation in Excel.

(a prolonged increase was recorded). This is not surpassing that different EU-27 Member States have recorded a different evolution as countries in the West are more environmentally prone than those in the East.

Considering the MEES, we can observe a decrease from 2009 to 2019 for almost all countries, both from Western and Eastern EU-27 Member States. Countries such as Germany, France, and Italy (the biggest three economies in the EU) are, by far, the biggest emitters. This is not surprising, as there is a correlation between the size and complexity of the economy (whether it is industrially advanced or not) and the emissions of energy.

Nevertheless, almost all the countries in the EU-27 Member States had lower values in 2019 compared to 2009 because the EU is going through a continent-wide transition from polluting energy sources. As we have seen from the current geopolitical events of Russia invading Ukraine, over-reliance on resources that the EU doesn't have is not a responsible energy policy. Lastly, all countries in the EU have started to increase their TP.

This is clearly seen in both Figs. 4.7 and 4.8, where a huge increase can be observed, especially from 2017 onwards. The reason for this is that the EU is going for a net zero future in 2050, where other deterring factors will offset all the EU's CO_2 emissions.

It is worth mentioning that the EU has long desired to reduce CO_2 emissions, but recent macroeconomic shocks have led EU Member States to increase their investment in green energy.

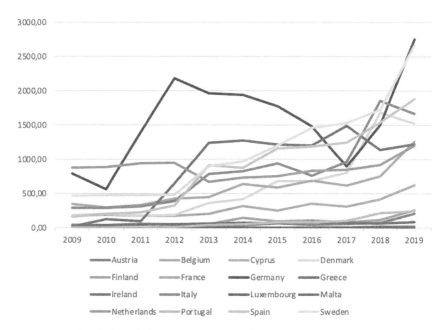

Fig. 4.7. Evolution of the Tax on Pollution for Western EU-27 Member States. *Source*: Authors' own computation in Excel.

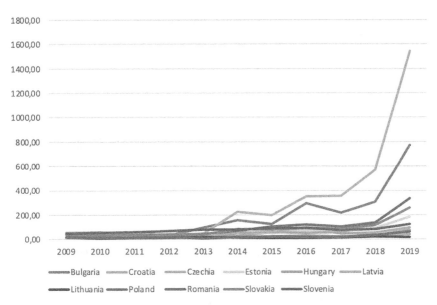

Fig. 4.8. Evolution of the Tax on Pollution for Eastern EU-27 Member States.
Source: Authors' own computation in Excel.

3.2. Correlation and Regression Analysis

Furthermore, to better grasp the evolution and the interconnections of the indicators that we took into consideration for our analysis, we applied the Pearson correlation on our four indicators, namely: Shadow Economy as % of GDP (SE), AME, MEES, and TP.

The results of the Pearson correlation can be observed in Table 4.3. We can expect that the relationship between the Shadow Economy and AMEs and MEES is insignificant, having a correlation coefficient value lower than 0.1. Shadow Economy and TP are weakly and negatively correlated, having a value of -0.12 (if one indicator increases, the other slightly decreases and vice versa).

In the case of the AMEs and the MEES, they are strongly and positively correlated, having a value of 0.71; thus, if one increases, so does the other indicator.

Table 4.3. The Results of the Pearson Correlation.

	SE	AME	MEES	TP
SE	1			
AME	−0.0238	1		
p-Value	0.6833			
MEES	0.0743	0.7109	1	
p-Value	0.2019	0		
TP	−0.1187	0.1639	0.3466	1
p-Value	0.041	0.0046	0	

Source: Authors' own computation in Stata17.

AME and TP are weakly and positively correlated, having a value of 0.16. Lastly, the TP and the MEES are moderately and positively correlated.

To better explain our findings, we employ a simple econometric model and a linear regression model to build a model tailored to our study. Firstly, we will write the general formula of a simple linear regression model that we took into consideration for our analysis:

$$Y = \alpha + \beta_1 X + \varepsilon$$

where Y is the dependent variable, α is the intercept, β is the coefficient of the independent variable, X is the independent variable, and ε is the error term.

We will write a simple linear regression model representative of our intended use to better visualise the model for our indicators.

$$\text{Env. Proxy} = \alpha + \beta \times \text{SE} + \varepsilon$$

where the proxy for the environment (Env. Proxy) represents the dependent variable and will be based on the following indicators:

- AME is the agriculture methane emissions
- MEES is the methane emissions for the energy sector
- TP is the tax on pollution

α is the intercept, SE is the Shadow economy and represents the independent variable, and ε is the error term.

The linear regression results in Table 4.4 were obtained through the OLS model, fixed effect (FE) model, and Random effects (RE) model, which were applied to the entire database. The models consider, as dependent variables, AME, MEES, and TP.

The comparative results from regression models offer us valuable information on the relationship between environmental proxies and the shadow economy. Looking at the R-squared values, our model can barely explain the variance in the Agriculture Methane Emissions, more specifically by the shadow economy. To a limited extent, we can consider the shadow economy to influence methane emissions for the energy sector and tax on pollution. However, despite the shallow R-squared values, the p-values for the independent variable are lower than 0.1. Therefore, we can state that the shadow economy is a statistically significant influencer of the three environmental indicators. Based on the statistically significant regression coefficients, a larger shadow economy would induce higher methane emissions (direct influence on AME and MEES) but lower TP (indirect influence on TP).

Based on the Hausman test, the model with RE would be more suitable for the methane emissions from agriculture and energy. However, for the model explaining TP, we expect countries' characteristics to influence the regression results, and, therefore, the fixed-effects model is more appropriate.

Table 4.4. Regression Results for the Entire Database.

Regression Model	OLS	FE	RE	OLS	FE	RE	OLS	FE	RE
	Dependent Variable: AME			Dependent Variable: MEES			Dependent Variable: TP		
SE	−36.18	34.79***	34.66***	26.23	70.66***	70.01***	−19.43**	−202.7***	−75.63***
	(88.60)	(12.99)	(12.96)	(20.51)	(8.521)	(8.453)	(9.467)	(32.73)	(19.64)
Constant	8.757***	7,425***	7,428***	1,548***	714.6***	726.7	829.9***	4.268***	1,885***
	(1,774)	(244.6)	(2,134)	(410.7)	(160.4)	(514.7)	(189.5)	(615.9)	(403.8)
R-squared	0.001	0.026	0.026	0.006	0.204	0.204	0.014	0.125	0.125
F/Wald test	0.17	7.17***	7.15***	1.64	68.76***	68.6***	4.21**	38.34***	14.82***
Obs.	297	297	297	297	297	297	297	297	297
No. of countries	27	27	27	27	27	27	27	27	27
Hausman chi2 (prob.)		0.02 (0.8874)			0.36 (0.5479)			23.55 (0.0000)	

Standard errors in parentheses; ***$p < 0.01$, **$p < 0.05$, *$p < 0.1$.
Source: Authors' own computation in Stata17.

The final stage in our analysis considers the comparative regression models applied to the two sub-samples, referring to Western and Eastern countries within the EU. Comparative results for the Western sub-sample are presented in Table 4.5, and those returned for the Eastern countries are presented in Table 4.6.

For the Eastern and Western countries, the shadow economy may explain the variance in agriculture methane emissions to a minimal extent (up to 2.3% or 3%, respectively, according to the R-squared from the fixed and RE models). It seems that between the two sub-samples, for the Western countries, more of the variance in methane emissions from the energy sector and tax on pollution can be explained by the shadow economy.

The regression coefficients indicate the same relationships within the sub-samples: the shadow economy directly influences methane emissions proxies but indirectly affects the pollution tax.

The Hausman tests indicate that the RE model is more appropriate for the models describing the variance in AME and MEES. The FE model is more appropriate for describing the variance in TP. These results confirm the ones from the overall EU database.

Based on the regression coefficient values, the impact of the shadow economy on MEES is higher in Western countries. In comparison, the impact of the shadow economy on pollution tax is higher in Eastern countries.

4. CONCLUSIONS

To sum up, the shadow economy poses a challenging issue with many facets that significantly impact the economy and the environment. It includes a wide range of illicit and legal operations that frequently occur outside the scope of government control. The shadow economy is distinguished by its clandestine nature and lack of transparency. Although difficult to define, it is estimated to be quite large and contributes significantly to many national economies.

There are many different and interrelated reasons why the shadow economy exists and is growing. Several circumstances encourage unofficial activities, including high taxes, onerous laws, governmental inefficiency, corruption, and a lack of access to regular employment. While some people use the shadow economy because they have no choice, others intentionally do it to break the law or take advantage of structural flaws.

The influence of the shadow economy on tax collections is one of the main issues surrounding it, especially considering the growing need for social security programmes and the rising cost of living. Governments must confront the issue of the shadow economy to increase their revenue sources and assure the viability of social programmes. Reducing the shadow economy and raising tax compliance are top government concerns everywhere.

Our research found that the evolution of the Shadow Economy is on a downtrend, considering that the fight against corruption picked up after the financial crisis of 2009 and especially after the Euro crisis in 2014. Countries such as Romania, Bulgaria, Italy, Portugal, and Spain have a large shadow economy as

Table 4.5. Regression Results for the Western Countries.

Regression Model	OLS	FE	RE	OLS	FE	RE	OLS	FE	RE
	Dependent Variable: AME			Dependent Variable: MEES			Dependent Variable: TP		
SE	−12.60	46.24**	46.14**	69.85**	77.93***	77.85***	7.498	−175.3***	−103.2***
	(145.83)	(21.20)	(21.12)	(32.13)	(11.48)	(11.39)	(6.97)	(15.11)	(13.95)
Constant	12,267***	11,181***	11,183***	940.81	791.7***	793.2	392.7***	3,767***	2,437***
	(286,377)	(392.5)	(3,469)	(631.01)	(212.5)	(786.3)	(137)	(279.9)	(297.4)
R-squared	0.0000	0.0310	0.0310	0.0282	0.2363	0.2363	0.0070	0.4744	0.4744
F/Wald test	0.01	4.76**	4.78**	4.73**	46.09***	46.73***	1.15	134.5***	54.74***
Obs.	165	165	165	165	165	165	165	165	165
No. of countries	15	15	15	15	15	15	15	15	15
Hausman chi² (prob.)		0.00 (0.9574)			0.00 (0.9546)			153.64 (0.0000)	

Standard errors in parentheses; ***$p < 0.01$, **$p < 0.05$, *$p < 0.1$.
Source: Authors' own computation in Stata17.

Table 4.6. Regression Results for the Eastern Countries.

Regression Model	OLS	FE	RE	OLS	FE	RE	OLS	FE	RE
	Dependent Variable: AME			Dependent Variable: MEES			Dependent Variable: TP		
SE	2.715	19.36*	19.28*	−16.45	60.84***	59.13***	−46.78**	−239.5***	−95.88**
	(47.54)	(11.59)	(11.52)	(23.59)	(12.71)	(12.57)	(18.47)	(72.67)	(39.24)
Constant	3,081***	2,762***	2,764**	2,118***	638.2**	671.0	1,279***	4,970***	2,219***
	(974.2)	(222.6)	(1,265)	(631.01)	(212.5)	(786.3)	(137)	(279.9)	(297.4)
R-squared	0.0000	0.0229	0.0229	0.0037	0.1615	0.1615	0.0471	0.0837	0.0837
F/Wald test	0.00	2.79*	2.8*	0.49	22.92***	22.14***	6.42**	10.87***	5.97***
Obs.	132	132	132	132	132	132	132	132	132
No. of countries	12	12	12	12	12	12	12	12	12
Hausman chi² (prob.)		0.00 (0.9523)			0.81 (0.369)			5.52 (0.0188)	

Standard errors in parentheses; ***$p < 0.01$, **$p < 0.05$, *$p < 0.1$.
Source: Authors' own computation in Stata17.

a percentage of GDP due to the constant mismanagement and low credibility of their political electorate. On the contrary, countries like Hungary, Estonia, and Lithuania have a low shadow economy.

When it comes to the pollution indicators that we have considered for our analysis, all of those decreased except for TP. Currently, Europe and the world face increasing levels of natural disaster weather, such as earthquakes, droughts, excessive rain, etc., because of the repelling effects of climate change. Given that the EU, especially its Southern States, are particularly reliant on good weather to grow their crops, measures have been put in place to mitigate the effects of climate change. Precisely, as observed in our analysis as well, the EU has tried to, and successfully done so, reduce their methane emission for both agricultural-related emissions and for the energy sector. Countries such as Romania have reduced their AMEs from almost 10,000 m^2 tones of CO_2 in 2009 to 8,000 m^2 tones of CO_2 in 2019. The only year it showed a slight increase was in 2016, but in the subsequent year, it decreased and stayed relatively constant until 2019. Other Eastern EU-27 Member States have slightly reduced their AME heights in 2009, such as Lithuania, Latvia, Hungary, Estonia, Slovakia, and the Czech Republic. Poland was the only outlier because the Polish government has been particularly not pleased by the EU's directions in reducing the AMEs because of fear of reducing their competitive advantage compared to neighbouring countries such as Germany and France, which have a much higher agricultural production base. Western EU-27 Member States have been keener to reduce their AME. This is indicated in both our analysis and media perception. Given their position as leading food producers in the EU, France and Germany were the countries that saw the greatest nominal reduction in AMEs, decreasing constantly from 2009 until 2019.

In the case of methane emission for the energy sector, the EU parliament is very keen on having a green transition for their energy sources. Thus, this is seen in the fact that all the countries in our analysis, whether they were from Western Europe or Eastern, have put in place measures to decrease the pollution of their energy sector. The two countries are not very keen to diversify their energy sources. Poland and Hungary, given their very nationalistic and conservative government, do not see climate change as something that exists despite the increasing push from the EU to have a green revolution. Thus, we can observe that TP have increased for all EU-27 Member States, signalling that to combat climate change, taxes must be raised for very polluting processes and to incentivise companies to innovate their production processes to produce less CO_2.

The dependent variables represented several environmental proxies; the independent variable was the shadow economy. We conducted separate regression analyses for the EU-27 Member States and the Western and Eastern sub-samples.

The regression results for the entire database proved that the models had limited explanatory power, especially for methane emissions from agriculture. However, the shadow economy exhibited statistical significance about the dependent variables for regression models with fixed or RE. When analysing the Western EU-27 Member States, similar patterns emerged. The regression models had limited explanatory power, with more influence on TP and methane emissions from the energy sector. The results for the Eastern EU-27 Member States followed a similar trend.

Our findings suggest that the relationship between the analysed environmental indicators and the shadow economy is complex and relatively weak. While some statistically significant associations were observed, the models could explain only a small percentage of the variance in the dependent variables. These results highlight the multifaceted nature of the interactions between the environment and the economy, calling for further research and nuanced policy approaches to address environmental challenges effectively.

It is important to note that this research has certain limitations, such as the reliance on limited data and the simplifications made in the regression models. Future studies could expand the analysis by incorporating additional indicators, considering other econometric models, and incorporating more comprehensive and up-to-date data. By doing so, we can gain a deeper understanding of the intricate dynamics between the environment and the economy and develop more informed policies to promote sustainable development.

ACKNOWLEDGEMENTS

This work was supported by a grant from the Romanian Ministry of Research, Innovation and Digitalization, the project with the title 'Economics and Policy Options for Climate Change Risk and Global Environmental Governance' (CF 193/28.11.2022, Funding Contract no. 760078/23.05.2023), within Romania's National Recovery and Resilience Plan (PNRR) – Pillar III, Component C9, Investment I8 (PNRR/2022/C9/MCID/I8) – Development of a programme to attract highly specialised human resources from abroad in research, development, and innovation activities.

REFERENCES

Baksi, S., & Bose, P. (2010). *Environmental regulation in the presence of an informal sector*. Department of Economics working paper number: 2010-03.

Balezentis, T., Liobikienė, G., Streimikiene, D., & Sun, K. (2020). The impact of income inequality on consumption-based greenhouse gas emissions at the global level: A partially linear approach. *Journal of Environmental Management, 267*, 110635. https://doi.org/10.1016/j.jenvman.2020.110635

Bilan, Y., Paliienko, M., Prasol, L., Vasylieva, T., Kubatko, O., & Kubatko, V. V. (2021). Determinants of shadow economy in transition countries: Economic and environmental aspects. *International Journal of Global Energy Issues, 43*(2/3), 166. https://doi.org/10.1504/ijgei.2021.115142

Biller, D. (1994). *Informal gold mining and mercury pollution in Brazil*. http://documents.worldbank.org/curated/en/481431468743647767/Informal-gold-mining-and-mercury-pollution-in-Brazil

Biswas, A. K., Farzanegan, M. R., & Thum, M. (2012). Pollution, shadow economy and corruption: Theory and evidence. *Ecological Economics, 75*, 114–125. https://doi.org/10.1016/j.ecolecon.2012.01.007

Contini, B., & Grand, E. (2010). *Disposable workforce in Italy*. IZA Discussion Papers, No. 4724, Institute for the Study of Labor (IZA), Bonn. http://dx.doi.org/10.2139/ssrn.1545151

Davidescu, A. A., Putnins, T., & Sauka, A. (2022). *Uncovering the main characteristics of shadow economies in romania and moldova for strengthening the labour market resilience* (pp. 183–200). Springer eBooks. https://doi.org/10.1007/978-3-030-87112-3_11

Dell'Anno, R., Gómez-Antonio, M., & Pardo, Á. A. (2006). The shadow economy in three Mediterranean countries: France, Spain and Greece. A MIMIC approach. *Empirical Economics, 33*(1), 51–84. https://doi.org/10.1007/s00181-006-0084-3

Fan, Y., & Xia, Y. (2012). Exploring energy consumption and demand in China, *Energy, 40*(1), 23–30. ISSN 0360-5442. https://doi.org/10.1016/j.energy.2011.09.049

Imamoglu, H. (2018). Is the informal economic activity a determinant of environmental quality? *Environmental Science and Pollution Research, 25*(29), 29078–29088. https://doi.org/10.1007/s11356-018-2925-y

Jayanthakumaran, K., Verma, R., & Liu, Y. (2012). CO2 emissions, energy consumption, trade and income: A comparative analysis of China and India. *Energy Policy, 42.* https://doi.org/10.1016/j.enpol.2011.12.010

Kelmanson, B., Kirabaeva, K., Medina, L., Mircheva, B., & Weiss, J. (2019). Explaining the shadow economy in Europe: Size, causes and policy options. *IMF Working Papers, 2019*(278). https://doi.org/10.5089/9781513520698.001.a001

Lin, J., Pan, D., Davis, S. J., Zhang, Q., He, K., Wang, C., Streets, D. G., Wuebbles, D. J., & Guan, D. (2014). China's international trade and air pollution in the United States. *111*(5), 1736–1741. https://doi.org/10.1073/pnas.1312860111

Machado, G. V., Schaeffer, R., & Worell, E. (2001). Energy and carbon embodied in the international trade of Brazil: An input-output approach. *Ecological Economics, 39*(3), 409–424. https://doi.org/10.1016/S0921-8009(01)00230-0

Maftei, L. (2014, March). *An introduction to the underground economy of Romania* (Vol. 6(1), pp. 110–116). CES working papers, Centre for European Studies, Alexandru Ioan Cuza University.

Markandya, A., González-Eguino, M., & Escapa, M. (2013). From shadow to green: Linking environmental fiscal reforms and the informal economy. *Energy Economics, 40*(1), S108–S118. https://doi.org/10.1016/j.eneco.2013.09.014

Mauleon, I., & Sarda, J. (2017). Unemployment and the shadow economy. *Applied Economics, 49*(37), 3729–3740.

Minx, J. C., Baiocchi, G., Peters, G. P., Weber, C. L., Guan, D., & Hubacek, K. (2011). A "carbonizing dragon": China's fast growing CO2 emissions revisited. *Environmental Science & Technology, 45*, 9144–9153. https://doi.org/10.1021/es201497m

Ortiz, C., Alvarado, R., Méndez, P., & Flores-Chamba, J. (2022). Environmental impact of the shadow economy, globalisation, and human capital: Capturing spillovers effects using spatial panel data approach. *Journal of Environmental Management, 308*, 114663. https://doi.org/10.1016/j.jenvman.2022.114663

Ozcan, B., & Ozturk, I. (2019). Renewable energy consumption-economic growth nexus in emerging countries: A bootstrap panel causality test. *Renewable and Sustainable Energy Reviews, 104*, 30–37. https://doi.org/10.1016/j.rser.2019.01.020

Pang, J., Li, N., Mu, H., & Zhang, M. (2020). Empirical analysis of the interplay between shadow economy and pollution: With panel data across the provinces of China. *Journal of Cleaner Production, 285*(3), 124864. https://doi.org/10.1016/j.jclepro.2020.124864

Putniņš, T. J., & Sauka, A. (2020). *SHADOW ECONOMY INDEX for Russia 2017-2018: Comparison with the size of the shadow economies in Ukraine, Kyrgyzstan, Kosovo, Moldova, Romania, Latvia, Lithuania, Estonia and Poland.* https://www.sseriga.edu/sites/default/files/2020-01/Shadow%20Economy%20Index%20EN%20for%20Russia%202018%20FINAL.pdf

Schneider, F. (1994). Measuring the size and development of the shadow economy. Can the causes be found and the obstacles be overcome? In H. Brandstätter & W. Güth (Eds.), *Essays on economic psychology* (pp. 193–212), Springer. https://doi.org/10.1007/978-3-642-48621-0_10

Schneider, F. (2008). The shadow economy in Germany: A blessing or a curse for the official economy? *Economic Analysis and Policy, 38*(1), 89–111. https://doi.org/10.1016/s0313-5926(08)50008-7

Schneider, F. (2012). *The shadow economy and work in the shadow: What do we (not) know?* Discussion Papers Series, IZA DP No. 6423.

Schneider, F. (2022). New COVID-related results for estimating the shadow economy in the global economy in 2021 and 2022. *International Economics and Economic Policy, 19*(2), 299–313. https://doi.org/10.1007/s10368-022-00537-6

Schneider, F., Buehn, A., & Montenegro, C. E. (2010). *Shadow economies all over the world: New estimates for 162 countries from 1999 to 2007*. Policy research working papers, 5536.

Schneider, F., & Enste, D. H. (2008). Shadow economies: Size, causes, and consequences. *Journal of Economic Literature, 38*(1), 77–114. https://doi.org/10.1257/jel.38.1.77

Zaman, G., & Goschin, Z. (2015). Shadow economy and economic growth in Romania. Cons and Pros. *Procedia Economics and Finance, 22*, 80–87. https://doi.org/10.1016/s2212-5671(15)00229-4

Zhang, M., Liu, X., Ding, Y., & Wang, W. (2019). How does environmental regulation affect haze pollution governance? – An empirical test based on Chinese provincial panel data. *Science of the Total Environment, 695*, 133905. https://doi.org/10.1016/j.scitotenv.2019.133905

Zhang, Q., He, K., & Huo, H. (2012) Cleaning China's air. *Nature, 484*, 161–162. https://doi.org/10.1038/484161a

CHAPTER 5

SUSTAINABLE ECONOMIC STAKE AND COPRODUCTION IN COMPETITION: A DYNAMIC ANALYSIS

Alexandru Jivan[a], Miruna Lucia Năchescu[b] and Mihaela Neamțu[a]

[a]Faculty of Economics and Business Administration, Department of Economics and Modelling, West University of Timisoara, Timisoara, Romania
[b]Faculty of Economics and Business Administration, Department of Finance, West University of Timisoara, Timisoara, Romania

ABSTRACT

Purpose/Objective: In the context of the service economy, the chapter analyses a dynamic model created for a competition market, aiming to reveal changes that take place when the stake of economic activity goes beyond the strictly competitive meanings, a coproduction with the customer being involved.

Design/Methodology/Approach: A mathematical model is analyzed, describing the interactions between potential consumers, suppliers acting in traditional production conditions, and those applying coproduction with customs. The analysis of the model is done in the frame of nonlinear dynamical systems with time delay.

Findings: The positive equilibrium point is determined, and the conditions for stability and the existence of the oscillatory solutions are given. Numerical *simulations verify the theoretical findings, revealing when the system is stable or when it becomes unstable.*

Significance/Implications/Conclusions: *Consistent with the service approach, our chapter considers not just the common private angle of the economic action but also the environment of the economic actor. The mathematical model brings a special conceptual development by involving coproduction in the competition between the providers. It also reveals the systemic effects of such new interaction involvement.*

Limitations: *The present chapter develops a mathematical model for the single case of coproduction with the customer. Two kinds of suppliers are concerned, the third one representing the demand side. Numerical simulation is developed using theoretical scenarios.*

Future Research: *Subsequent developments will make the role of economic entities more complex, with competition and cooperation being assumed among them all. Diverse other types of joint production will also be approached.*

Keywords: Service economy; economic interactions; co-production; dynamic competition system; equilibrium point; stability

JEL Codes: O14; C62; C63

1. INTRODUCTION

Economic activity mainly consists of fulfilling the private objectives of economic actors. Such purposes are aimed in the context of market interaction in rivalry conditions. Individual actions may be strictly individualistic and competitive but may also be concordant with certain environmental stakes, including collaborative attitudes. Therefore, the considered interactions in this chapter are competition and co-production.

We focus on how economic activities take place in the conditions of the service economy when the environment of the economic entity is also taken into account – and here specifically on the joint action with the customer. The chapter points out a main opening for economics, consisting of such an approach to economic activity from a broader angle than that of usual individual concern: it is about the external approach from the point of view of the environment of the economic entity, as a completion to the market competition. Our research aims to materialise such a broadened approach for the particular case involving coproduction in the competition. The analysis is realised by employing a mathematical model. It represents just a starting point for many possible future developments – that are suggested in this chapter. The suitable background is presented explicitly for each issue or topic approached in the respective section.

The present chapter adds to the literature describing the interaction between economic actors in the competition market, with the particular case when coproduction is also involved. A mathematical model analyses the evolutions of the economic actors (suppliers and their customs) when certain of the offerors employ co-production with their beneficiaries. The effects of such evolutions on the system's stability are revealed. Thus, the detection of stable states is beneficial for the topic of sustainability.

Our research provides valuable findings for the diverse participants in the market process.

The chapter is organised as follows: In Section 2, short references to the core of the actual service economy are included, which ground the widening of the economic stake to an external (environmental) approach; the joint economic action with the customer is here included. When collaborative acting takes place in the production process, it may be called co-production, besides the terminological strict limitation that may be revealed in the marketing literature. However, our approach is not limited to the material productive processes; it is valid for any economic activity. Literature was developed on such issues; specific significant references are made to the issue of such co-production.

Concerning the co-producing industry, economics literature is usually scarce, while marketing literature is abundant. We highlight and emphasise certain valuable contributions of the economics literature (see Section 2) that are consistent with the approach concerning value creation in the service economy but are not well known. In such a view, the environment of the economic entity is reconsidered and relationality becomes defining for the service economy (see, for instance, Bressand and Nicolaidis (1988) and Ramirez (1999), in which the issue of the joint development of the productive activity is a core aspect). Research about economic relationships between actors in the market is also mentioned.

The presentation in Section 2 is not a simple preamble to the mathematical model; rather, the model illustrates a market case (for a certain product or service) for the issues in Section 2.

In Section 3, the mathematical model employed for such exemplification analyses the case when co-production is involved in economic activity under rivalry conditions. The model of co-production involvement with the customer in the competition among suppliers, used by the present research, is presented by referring to certain bibliographic sources where such models are developed.

Our mathematical model considers the correlations with the clients of certain providers of a product or service (actors that adopt cooperation with their beneficiaries and competitor actors that keep the initial production-performing way). The present chapter takes a theoretical and generic stand over the economic entities of the model and over the stake of their economic activity.

We mention that, from the modelling perspective, with respect to the existing literature, the time delay is introduced in the equation of the demand and in the equation of the suppliers that perform in the traditional/initial way of relation with the customers. The offerors that propose the new collaborative way of relation with the beneficiaries are initiating such a new method, and, therefore, no time delay should be considered for their equation. The existence of the Hopf bifurcation is analysed to investigate the stability switches when the delay takes the critical value.

Some numerical simulations are provided in Section 4 to justify the theoretical findings. Also, we illustrate the stability or instability of the considered system of equations.

Finally, in Section 5, conclusions and discussions are given, and future research developments are suggested.

2. SATISFACTION AND CO-PRODUCTION IN THE SERVICE ECONOMY

Economic activities aim to satisfy the interests and goals of economic entities. The usual conceptuality was, and still is, focused on productivity, and economics has long maintained its focus on production, especially material production. In the actual service economy, the science of marketing especially noticed the focus of the attention of the economic action on *serving* the customer. For economics, this new conceptuality is firmly taken into account by introducing the concept of servicity (Jivan, 1993) – as an alternative, or completion, to the common productivity: 'We must consider *the beneficiary's point of view, and that of the society as a whole*'. The basis of it is presented as the generalised service (i.e. the functions fulfilled by each economic agent in the economic and social mechanism) that exists under the form of service performed for the beneficiaries, business partners, and society as a whole according to Jivan (1993).

Bastiat had developed the theory of value-service, thus long surpassing his epoch: any social activity is a service as it represents *an effort of a person to satisfy a need or a wish of another person*; exchanges on the market themselves are done through processes of service (Bastiat, 1851, Chapters 2 and 5). For him, the word *service* includes all the ideas and nuances previously (before him) expressed regarding value (labour, utility, etc.).

Starting with Bastiat, the stake of economic activity goes beyond the strictly individual meanings in its theoretical representation. The issue of service implies widening the horizon of interest to the economic actor's environment (Jivan, 2014).

This means that any economic action has a joint impact, not only individual effects. In this way, the inclusion in the analysis of the environment (financial, social, etc.) is achieved as a necessary horizon broadening if compared with the exclusive angle from the point of view of the analysed economic actor. Both the positive effects (pluses) and the negative ones (minuses) concern, in addition to the investigated economic entity, other economic-social components too. Such an approach is also inherently suitable for considering the issue of sustainability.

In a defining way for the actual service economy, in the servicity approach, the clientele's co-participation, directly or mediated, and other factors, active or passive, is implicit. This approach of broadening the horizon begins with the effects on the client served (*servicity in the narrow sense*). The approach from the 'internal' point of view of the economic actor (i.e. defining the productivity indicator) is widened by also taking into account 'external' effects – positive and negative effects. Such an approach is from an angle that is opposite to usual individualism. Servicity is defined as the service performed by the economic entity for the beneficiary or influencing other entities from the environment of such economic actor. Suppose productivity is understood to benefit the economic actor concerning those broadenings. In that case, it may be said that servicity represents the 'productivity in the benefit of such actor's environment'. The focus on the environment is also considered in works such as, for example, Jivan (2014), Jivan and Năchescu (2018), and Jivan et al. (2018). Ceccagnoli et al. (2012) and Grover and Kohli (2012) may also be quoted with connected analyses. The concept of *servicity, in a broad sense,* totalizes these fundamentally divergent approaches.

The service economy considers serving the beneficiary and the external effects. In a generalised market economy, where human activities are made to be supplied to other economic entities (customers), the necessities are covered through indirect exchange of inter-correlation among members of the society (Jivan, 1993). The separation between producers and consumers is accompanied by an interdependence that becomes more complex (Varey, 2010). In the present chapter, we analyse a single case in which co-production with the client is involved in a competitive market.

Attracting customers in co-production relationships benefits entrepreneurs by enabling them to obtain advantages in production and consumption together. Indeed, the idea of co-production emerged within the market policies of entrepreneurial agents.

Including the customers in co-production means elements of the social environment that may provide sustainability. This approach is intended to ensure market success for the economic actor and, at the same time, systemic equilibrium and sustainability.

The satisfaction in business consists in the revenues and diverse other aspects of the economic process of 'production'. The satisfaction of the custom consists in their expenses (corroborated with other aspects of their action to accomplish their needs).

By acting jointly, market actions become co-actions when they are more or less integrated and bring common results. Such actions are called co-actions using the particle 'co' (in words like cooperation, collaboration, co-creation, and co-production).

Scholars deem co-production a dimension of value co-creation, as shown in Blaschke et al. (2018). Co-creation is presented by Terblanche (2014) as being composed of 'co-creation of value' and 'co-production'. Quoting the approach of Vargo and Lusch (2004), this author says that co-production is the second part of co-creation. Co-production may be seen as one of the three facets of value co-creation, as Prebensen and Xie (2017) say. According to Vargo and Lusch (2008) and Lusch and Vargo (2006), 'value is created collaboratively in interactive configurations of mutual exchange'. The link between co-production and co-creation is an essential concern for Ertimur and Venkatesh (2010), too, in the review of the literature on services marketing that those researchers developed. In their paper Saarijärvi et al. (2017), the authors explain that 'Value co-production [...] was embedded in the concept of value cocreation'.

The interrelation between co-creation and other terms, such as co-design and co-production, is pointed out by Oertzen et al. (2018), from references like Lusch and Vargo (2006), Chathoth et al. (2013), and O'Hern and Rindfleisch (2010). The reference Oertzen et al. (2018) provides a very rigorous, professional, deep analysis with a connection to conceptual pluralism concerning the co-creation of services. According to Oertzen et al. (2018), co-production is one of the forms in which co-creation manifests itself, depending on the phases of the service process. Ramaswamy and Ozcan (2018) mention co-production as one of the numerous diverse topics associated with (or referring to) the idea of co-creation.

Ballantyne and Varey (2006) argue that co-production requires known resources and essential capabilities, which distinguishes it from co-creation. Moreover, the two concepts are not connected. According to Etgar (2008), co-production encompasses all cooperation between the customer and the supplier.

The problem of co-production is also addressed by references such as Ramirez (1999) and Bendapudi and Leone (2003). From the angle of the economic producing and offering entities, Kandampully et al. (2016) talk about 'a process that requires collaborative efforts among internal (i.e. employees) and external (i.e. customers) partners'. Tari Kasnakoglu (2016) explains that there are different terms describing interaction in a service relationship, including co-production.

Our approach includes co-production with a simpler meaning (as we'll show towards the end of this subsection). We supposed that collaboration, as a relation between economic entities, is optional. Our chapter is being based precisely upon the delimitation between the choice of adopting collaborative economic actions and, respectively, the choice of adopting a non-collaborative way.

Diverse dimensions and degrees of the importance of the customer are revealed in the literature, like, for instance, in Terblanche (2014), Prebensen and Xie (2017), Bendapudi and Leone (2003), Toffler (1980), Lovelock and Young (1979), Heinonen and Strandvik (2015), Grönroos and Voima (2013), and Grönroos (2008).

The analysis developed by Oertzen et al. (2018) also emphasises joint creation, contrary to mere customer creation. We mention that in contrast with the value that emerges from or is created by the final consumer, Ramaswamy and Ozcan (2018) suggest a more broadened view of value as 'value-in-interactional creation' and take into account the multi-firm partnerships (exemplifying Ceccagnoli et al., 2012; Grover and Kohli, 2012). We consider that this last approach is more consistent with the idea of joint economic acting. The 'coproducing' character is seen by Jivan (2014) for the entire environment (social, natural) – an environment that, by the generalisation of the idea of co-production, will no longer be seen as just a resource to be exploited.

For the present research's purposes, we focus on market relations, the market being, by definition, a competition. From the supply-side angle, the market approach of the suppliers can maintain the production process apart from the client (i.e. without their participation in the production). On the other hand, according to the present trends specific to the service economy, the approach of the suppliers and the production process may be collaborative with the clients.

In the generalised scheme of economic activity (Jivan, 2014), co-production is merely a process of co-acting to jointly realise (producing) goods and services.

Considering a market (competitional) frame, the present research focuses on co-production (we consider co-production as *the joint production of goods or rendering services and, therefore, a possible superior fulfilment of needs, objectives, and* economic wishes). We kept and consequently used in our model the term of *co-production* – otherwise usual – despite a possible deficiency (insufficiency) of terminological rigour, as we consider that such a term better suggests the joint action of the provider-offer and the beneficiary-buyer in the development of the 'production' process. It describes the cooperation between these actors in 'the production (creation) of value', evinced in the fulfilment, at least up to a point, of the sustainable economic stakes of the parties, therefore, in satisfying the economic purposes and wishes.

Anyway – and regardless of the theoretical speculations – the changes generated by the interactions between the economic actors represent increased clients' satisfaction and enlarged benefits for the entrepreneurs.

The satisfaction provided by the economic actions refers to the beneficiaries and to the suppliers-performers, too. It is an economic characteristic that can be measured by or correlated with specific economic measurements or assessments; in our model (see Section 3), we generally consider values of satisfying through consumption-benefitting and/or fulfilling the business purposes through market sales. By particular approaches, developing more applied models is possible.

Considering the common impact mentioned above and the idea of co-participation, a mathematical model is employed in the present chapter – an exemplification of the vision of cooperation/co-production versus mere competition.

3. MATHEMATICAL MODEL AND STABILITY ANALYSIS

Let $x(t)$ the potential number of consumers of a product within an economic system at the moment $t \geq 0$. We suppose that on the market at moment t, $y(t)$ is the quantity of the product manufactured by the classical individual production (using a certain suitable technology), and $z(t)$ is the quantity of the product manufactured by cooperation with the consumer (implying a suitable new production regime or technology).

The evolution rate of the potential consumers depends on the function $g[0,\infty) \to R, g \in C^1([0,\infty))$, which describes the general evolution of the population; it also responds to the past and present classical producer's policy. Function $g(x)$ represents the specific consumer growth rate with $g(0) > 0$ and it is supposed to be a decreasing function. We presume a natural decreasing propensity of the population, as usual in the most developed countries. Such an assumption is made considering exclusively the native evolutions of such nations; we assume it, despite the rate of the whole population, which is usually growing by new coming people from outside the referred nation, people also proving, in plus, higher nativity indices. Such a *decreasing* function assumption also contradicts the *growing* consumption propensity suitable for a consumption economy.

We consider function $f:[0,\infty) \to R, f \in C^1([0,\infty))$ standing for the functional response of the first provider with $f(0)=0$. It is supposed to be an increasing function: in a growing economy, the propensity of production activities may be assumed to increase. Such increasing tendencies respond to the growing expected consumption in modern society. The function f depends not just on the current moment t but also on the past history $t-\tau$:

$$f(x(t)) = f_0(x(t-\tau)) + f_1(x(t)),$$

where $\tau > 0$ is the time delay.

Then, the evolution rate of the potential consumers is:

$$\dot{x}(t) = x(t)g(x(t)) - y^m(t)[f_0(x(t-\tau)) + f_1(x(t))],$$

with $m \geq 0$ the constant of mutual interference.

Applying co-production with the customer causes a reaction from the producer already present in the market, in addition to the evolution rate of the first production entities previously mentioned. We can detail the reaction functions, regarded as functional responses of the groups of manufacturers, performers (of the two defined categories) and demanding consumers. We suppose that $h:[0,\infty) \to R, h \in C^1([0,\infty))$ is the function regarded as the functional response of the provider that wants to cooperate with the consumer, with $h(0)=0$ and it is supposed to be an increasing function. We assume such an increasing tendency is due to the fact that co-production with the consumers is a growing reality of cooperation in various new ways. The dynamics for the quantities of outputs are affected by the competition in the market, that is, by the entrance of new enterprisers who attempt to obtain a part of the market.

Hence, the dynamics of the first production entities' output (entities that use a classical technology) is described by:

$$\dot{y}(t) = y(t)\{cy^{m-1}(t)[f_0(x(t-\tau)) + f_1(x(t))] - r\} - z(t)h(y(t)),$$

where $\tau \geq 0$ is the time delay, c is the portion of profit re-invested in production, r corresponds to the intra-specific competition among providers that use a classical technology.

The dynamics of the new entities' output (that is realised by cooperation with the consumer) is described by:

$$\dot{z}(t) = z(t)[dh(y(t)) - s],$$

where d is the part of profit re-invested in production and s stands for the intra-specific competition among providers that cooperate with the consumer.

Thus, the mathematical model with time delay is described by:

$$\dot{x}(t) = x(t)g(x(t)) - y^m(t)[f_0(x(t-\tau)) + f_1(x(t))]$$
$$\dot{y}(t) = y(t)\{-r + cy^{m-1}(t)[f_0(x(t-\tau)) + f_1(x(t))]\} - z(t)h(y(t)) \quad (1)$$
$$\dot{z}(t) = z(t)[-s + dh(y(t))]$$

where $g, f_0, f_1, h \in C^1([0,\infty), R)$, $\tau \geq 0$, $m \geq 0$, $c > 0, d > 0, r > 0, s > 0$.

If $\tau = 0$, $m = 0$, $f_0 = 0$, $f_1(x(t)) = p(x(t))$, $r = h$, $c = e$, $h(y(t)) = q(y(t))$, the differential system (1) becomes:

$$\dot{x}(t) = x(t)g(x(t)) - y(t)p(x(t))$$
$$\dot{y}(t) = y(t)[-h + ep(x(t))] - z(t)q(y(t))$$
$$\dot{z}(t) = z(t)[-s + q(y(t))]$$

and it is studied in Guo and Jiang (2012).

The particular case: $g(x(t)) = 1 - x(t)$, $m = 1$, $f_0(x(t)) = ax(t)/(x(t) + b)$, $f_1(x) = 0$, $r = 1$, $h = r$, is analysed in Guo and Jiang (2012).

For $m \in (0,1]$, system (1) is analysed in Ritelli et al. (1997) and for $m \geq 1$ in Dos Santos et al. (2014).

In what follows we determine the equilibrium point of system (1) by solving the algebraic system:

$$xg(x) - y^m[f_0(x) + f_1(x)] = 0$$
$$y\{-r + cy^{m-1}[f_0(x) + f_1(x)]\} - zh(y) = 0 \quad (2)$$
$$z[-s + dh(y)] = 0$$

Observation 1. If we consider the following particular functions:

$$g(x) = a - x^3, f_0(x) = a_0 x^3, f_1(x) = a_1 x^3, h(y) = e_1 y^2, a > 0, a_0 > 0, a_1 > 0, e_1 > 0,$$

then the equilibrium points of system (1) are given by solving the algebraic system:

$$x(a - x^3) - y^m(a_0 + a_1)x^3 = 0$$
$$y[-r + cy^{m-1}(a_0 + a_1)x^3] - ze_1 y^2 = 0 \quad (3)$$
$$z(-s + de_1 y^2) = 0$$

We are interested in the positive solution of (3), denoted by $E(x_0, y_0, z_0)$, where the components are:

$$y_0 = \sqrt{\frac{s}{de_1}}, \quad z_0 = \frac{-r + cy_0^{m-1}(a_0 + a_1)x_0^3}{e_1 y_0}$$

and x_0 is the positive root of the equation:

$$x^3 + (a_0 + a_1) y_0^m x^2 - a = 0. \tag{4}$$

If we consider the translation $u_1 = x - x_0, u_2 = y - y_0, u_3 = z - z_0$, the linearised system of (1) at E is given by:

$$\begin{aligned}
\dot{u}_1(t) &= a_{11} u_1(t) + a_{12} u_2(t) + b_{11} u_1(t-\tau) \\
\dot{u}_2(t) &= a_{21} u_1(t) + a_{22} u_2(t) + a_{23} u_3(t) + b_{21} u_1(t-\tau) \\
\dot{u}_3(t) &= a_{32} u_2(t) + a_{33} u_3(t)
\end{aligned} \tag{5}$$

where

$a_{11} = g(x_0) + x_0 g'(x_0) - y_0^m f_1'(x_0)$, $a_{12} = -m y_0^{m-1}(f_0(x_0) + f_1(x_0))$,
$b_{11} = -y_0^m f_0'(x_0)$, $a_{21} = c y_0^m f_1'(x_0)$, $a_{22} = -r + cm y_0^{m-1}(f_0(x_0) + f_1(x_0)) - z_0 h'(y_0)$,
$a_{23} = -h(y_0)$, $b_{21} = c y_0^m f_0'(x_0)$, $a_{32} = d z_0 h'(y_0)$, $a_{33} = 0$.

The characteristic equation of (5) is given by:

$$\lambda^3 + a_2 \lambda^2 + a_1 \lambda + a_0 - (b_2 \lambda^2 + \beta_1 \lambda + \beta_0) e^{-\lambda \tau} = 0, \tag{6}$$

where

$$a_0 = a_{11} a_{23} a_{32},$$
$$a_1 = a_{22} a_{11} - a_{23} a_{32} - a_{12} a_{21}, a_2 = -(a_{11} + a_{22}),$$
$$b_2 = b_{11}, b_1 = -b_{11} a_{22}, b_0 = -b_{11} a_{23} a_{32}$$
$$c_1 = a_{12} b_{21}, \ \beta_0 = b_0 + c_0, \beta_1 = b_1 + c_1.$$

If there is no delay, equation (6) becomes:

$$\lambda^3 + \alpha_2 \lambda^2 + \alpha_1 \lambda + \alpha_0 = 0 \tag{7}$$

where

$$\alpha_0 = a_0 - b_0 - c_0, \alpha_1 = a_1 - b_1 - c_1, \alpha_2 = a_2 - b_2.$$

Using the Routh–Hurwitz criterion, if the parameters of the model satisfy the conditions:

$$\alpha_0 > 0, \alpha_1 > 0, \alpha_2 > 0, \alpha_2\alpha_1 - \alpha_0 > 0 \tag{8}$$

then, the equilibrium point $E(x_0, y_0, z_0)$ is locally asymptotically stable.

If there is delay, the perturbation of parameter τ causes the stationary state to change from stable to unstable, then a Hopf bifurcation occurs and the orbits of system (1) oscillate. In what follows we investigate the existence of the Hopf bifurcation for the parameter τ. Let $\lambda = i\omega, (\omega > 0)$ be a root of (6). Then, ω must satisfy:

$$\begin{cases} (\beta_0 - b_2\omega^2)\cos(\omega\tau) + \omega b_1 \sin(\omega\tau) = a_0 - a_2\omega^2 \\ (\beta_0 - b_2\omega^2)\sin(\omega\tau) - \omega b_1 \cos(\omega\tau) = \omega^3 - a_1\omega \end{cases}$$

that leads to

$$\omega^6 + \gamma_4\omega^4 + \gamma_2\omega^2 + \gamma_0 = 0, \tag{9}$$

where $\gamma_4 = a_2^2 - 2a_1 - b_2^2, \gamma_2 = a_1^2 - b_1^2 - 2a_2 + 2\beta_0 b_2, \gamma_0 = a_0^2 - \beta_0^2$.

If $z = \omega^2$, then equation (9) becomes:

$$z^3 + \gamma_4 z^2 + \gamma_2 z + \gamma_0 = 0. \tag{10}$$

Thus, we have the following lemma (Zhao et al., 2014):

Lemma 1. For equation (10), one of the following results hols:

(i) If $\gamma_0 < 0$, then (10) has at least one positive root;
(ii) If $\gamma_0 \geq 0$ and $\Delta = \gamma_4^2 - 3\gamma_2 \leq 0$, then (10) has no positive;
(iii) If $\gamma_0 \geq 0$ and $\Delta = \gamma_4^2 - 3\gamma_2 > 0$, then (10) has positive roots if and only if $z_1^* = \dfrac{-\gamma_4 + \sqrt{\Delta}}{3} > 0$ and $\left(z_1^*\right)^3 + \gamma_4\left(z_1^*\right)^2 + \gamma_2 z_1^* + \gamma_0 \leq 0$.

We suppose that equation (10) has positive roots, without loss of generality, we assume that it has three positive roots, defined by z_1, z_2, and z_3, respectively. Then, equation (9) has three positive roots

$$\omega_k = \sqrt{z_k}, \ k = 1, 2, 3. \tag{11}$$

We obtain:

$$\cos(\omega\tau) = \frac{A(\omega)}{B(\omega)} \tag{12}$$

where

$$\begin{cases} A(\omega) = (a_0 - a_2\omega^2)(\beta_0 - b_2\omega^2) + (a_1\omega - \omega^3)\omega b_1 \\ B(\omega) = (\beta_0 - b_2\omega^2)^2 + \omega^2 b_1^2 \end{cases}$$

If we denote:

$$\tau_k^{(j)} = \frac{1}{\omega_k}\left[\arccos\frac{A(\omega_k)}{B(\omega_k)} + 2j\pi\right], \quad k=1,2,3, j=0,1,2,\ldots \quad (13)$$

then $\pm i\omega_k$ is a pair of purely imaginary roots of (12) with $\tau_k^{(j)}$ from (13).
We define:

$$\tau_0 := \tau_{k_0}^{(0)} = \min_{k \in \{1,2,3\}}\left\{\tau_k^{(0)}\right\}. \quad (14)$$

Let $\lambda(\tau) = \alpha(\tau) + i\omega(\tau)$ be the root of (6) near $\tau = \tau_k^{(j)}$ satisfying:

$$\alpha\left(\tau_k^{(j)}\right) = 0, \quad \omega(\tau_k^{(j)}) = \omega_k.$$

We can verify the transversality condition by:

Lemma 2. If $l(z) := z^3 + \gamma_4 z^2 + \gamma_2 z + \gamma_0$, $z_k = \omega_k^2$ and $l'(z_k) \neq 0$, then $\dfrac{d(Re\,\lambda(\tau_k^{(j)}))}{d\tau_k^{(j)}} \neq 0$ and $\dfrac{d(Re\,\lambda(\tau_k^{(j)}))}{d\tau_k^{(j)}}$ and $l'(z_k)$ have the same sign.

For the characteristic equation (6) in accordance to Zhao et al. (2014), we have the following theorem.

Theorem 1. The following statements hold:

(i) If $\gamma_0 < 0$, then (10) has at least one positive root.
(ii) If $\gamma_0 \geq 0$ and $\Delta = \gamma_4^2 - 3\gamma_2 \leq 0$, then (10) has no positive roots.
(iii) If $\gamma_0 \geq 0$ and $\Delta = \gamma_4^2 - 3\gamma_2 \leq 0$, then all roots with positive real part of (6) have the same sum to those of the polynomial equation (10) for all $\tau \geq 0$.
(iv) If either $\gamma_0 < 0$ or $\gamma_0 \geq 0$ and $\Delta = \gamma_4^2 - 3\gamma_2 > 0$, $z_1^* > 0$, and $l(z_1^*) < 0$, then $l(z)$ has at least one positive root z_k, and all roots with positive real part of (6) have the same sum to those of the polynomial equation (10) for $\tau \in [0, \tau_0)$.
(v) If the conditions of (ii) are satisfied and $h(z_k) \neq 0$, then system (1) exhibits Hopf bifurcation at the equilibrium E for $\tau = \tau_0$.

Theorem 2. Suppose that (8) holds. The equilibrium point E is locally asymptotically stable if $\tau < \tau_0$. In addition, if (12) holds, then for $\tau = \tau_0$ system (1) exhibits a Hopf bifurcation at the equilibrium point.

4. NUMERICAL SIMULATION

For the numerical simulations of system (1), we use Mathematica, and we consider the following parameters: $e_1 = 1.5, s = 0.8, d = 2, a = 0.8, m = 1.8, r = 0.2, c = 0.4$, $a_0 = 0.6, a_1 = 1.6$. The demographic function and the reaction functions are given by:

$$g(x) = a - x^3, f_0(x) = a_0 x^3, f_1(x) = a_1 x^3, h(y) = e_1 y^2.$$

The components of the positive equilibrium point of system (1) are: $x_0 = 0.66, y_0 = 0.8164, z_0 = 0.055$. If there is no delay $\tau = 0$, conditions (8) are satisfied, and the positive equilibrium point is locally asymptotically stable. For different initial conditions, the orbits of the number of the potential consumers $(t, x(t))$, the quantity of the product with the classical technology $(t, y(t))$ and the quantity of the product in cooperation with the consumer $(t, z(t))$ in the current market are displayed in Fig. 5.1.

When we consider the time delay, using formula (14) we obtain $\tau_0 = 10.59$. The positive equilibrium point is locally asymptotically stable if $\tau < \tau_0$. In Fig. 5.2, for values of the time delay less than the critical value $\tau_0 (\tau \in \{0, 2, 4, 6, 8\})$, we can visualise the orbits of the number of the potential consumers $(t, x(t))$, the quantity of the output realised with the classical production technology $(t, y(t))$, and the quantity of the product or service realised in cooperation with the consumer $(t, z(t))$ in the current market.

When $\tau = \tau_0$ system (1) exhibits a Hopf bifurcation at the positive equilibrium point. In Fig. 5.3, for the critical value of the time delay $\tau_0 = 10.59$,

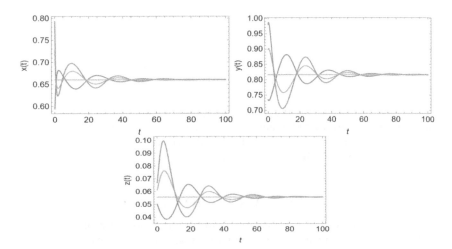

Fig. 5.1. Trajectories of system (1) converge to the asymptotically stable equilibrium point $x_0 = 0.66, y_0 = 0.8164, z_0 = 0.055$, when there is no delay and there are various initial conditions.

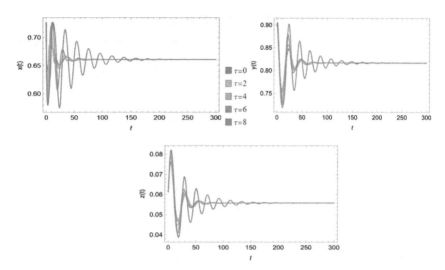

Fig. 5.2. Trajectories of system (1) converge to the asymptotically stable equilibrium point $x_0 = 0.66, y_0 = 0.8164, z_0 = 0.055$ $x_0 = 0.66, y_0 = 0.8164, z_0 = 0.055$, for values of the time delay less than the critical value $\tau \in \{0, 2, 4, 6, 8\}$.

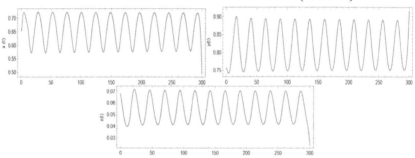

Fig. 5.3. Trajectories of system (1) are periodically, for the critical value of time delay $\tau_0 = 10.59$.

we display the orbits of the number of the potential consumers $(t, x(t))$, the quantity of the output realised with the classical production technology $(t, y(t))$, and the quantity of the product or service realised in cooperation with the consumer $(t, z(t))$ in the current market.

5. CONCLUSIONS

Our research pointed out the issue of broadening the stake of economic action to the actor's environment, materialising it through a mathematical model to the peculiar case of concern for the custom when co-production with the client is involved in the competition of the market. The effects were analysed to reveal the concrete equilibrium and stability of the system.

The emerged changes in the general state of the market, namely of the evolutions of the offers and of the demand, regard the increased satisfaction of the clients and the entrepreneurs' results on the market, which can be concerned in quantitative or qualitative concrete ways.

Our approach in this chapter is theoretical. For the associated mathematical model, we have analysed the existence of equilibrium points and their local stability. Moreover, we have conducted numerical simulations with an exemplification character regarding the evolutions of supply and demand. The numerical simulations are relevant regardless of the considered quantitative or qualitative type of considered economic characteristics.

In the present chapter, we brought to the present some previous economics research, especially on the matter of enlarging the horizon, from the strictly individualistic approach in competition to taking into account the individual actor's environment, the co-production with the customer here included, this being a theoretical important approach for the theory of service economy that allowed the materialisation of the issue, specifically to the involvement of co-production in the market competition.

Thus, our research focused on the coproduction with the customer, introduced by certain suppliers of goods and services, in their market actions, and on its effects on the satisfaction of the economic entities and on the stability of the system.

Such co-production involved in competition was analysed by the mathematical model in a dynamic approach. The evolutions of the demand-side and of the two kinds of suppliers are mathematically described, when consumers choose between the offer of the supply-side that proposes them joining to the process of production-performing, and the offer of the supply-side that remains to the usual/initial organisational way of market relation with the customers.

The demand on the market is influenced by the growth rate concerning the demand-side and by the classical way of relation with clients that initially the supply-side developed.

The reaction to such a usual offer was described by a function depending on past and present choices. Intra-specific competition affects the entities, and a process also takes place by which certain of them choose the new way of production performance, wanting to cooperate with the customers that become co-producers.

Such 'new way' providers or suppliers make co-production to intervene in the market competition.

The equation describing the dynamics of the initial performing entities consists of their own reinvestment in production (from their profits), their relationship with the customers, and the intra-specific competition among those classical providers. The influence of the new intervened (co-productive) way was involved here as well.

The last equation describes the case of entities adopting (proposing to customers) co-production, and analogously, it includes the reinvestment of a part of the profits and the intra-specific competition.

Thus, the mathematical model was described by a nonlinear system with three differential equations and one time delay $\tau \geq 0$. To study the dynamics of the concerned entities, a stability analysis of the positive equilibrium point was carried out. If there is no delay, the system is locally asymptotically stable under some conditions involving the system's parameters. This situation is convenient from an economic point of view and consistent with the favourable functioning of the described economic system.

The critical value of the time delay τ_0 was determined. The equilibrium point is asymptotically stable for $\tau < \tau_0$. Such a case also proves asymptotic stability, which is helpful for the development of economic activities (without significant perturbations). Numerical simulations have verified the theoretical findings.

The present chapter provides theoretical and practical implications. The references to the older or more recent literature also highlight findings with both theoretical and practical relevance. Our study can bring conceptual development to the field of competition and cooperation. The conceptual model that was adopted permits different approaches; thus, the present chapter opens new opportunities for further research by driving the analysis towards more concrete and applied research.

Openings are revealed for other research concerning the relationship between competition and cooperation. Modelling should refer to the competitional aspects of dynamic systems. For instance, co-production not only with the firms' customers but, by adequate development, also with other production-performing collaborations could be analysed.

A limitation of the conceptual model applied in the present research regards the economic collaboration horizon, which cannot be limited to co-production with customers. Correlated with this, another limitation in the present model consists in the fact that the first (group of) economic entities (i.e. the demand-side) is/are outside competition: competition is assumed to occur only between the other two (groups of) economic entities (the enterprisers) and inside the two groups in the supply-side. Next research could capture more complex realities on the market when competition can be assumed among all the participants (more diverse). We consider this to be the logical direction to follow in the future.

Another direction for further development in our research is to consider distributed time delay instead of discrete time delay. Thus, developing our present research could lead to models consistent with capturing more complex dynamic phenomena. Also, the stochastic approach of the deterministic model would capture the perturbations that manifest themselves in the environment.

Apart from the mentioned developments in the use of coproduction and, generally, cooperation in market competition, the horizon broadenings that we theoretically pointed out at the beginning of the chapter (Section 1) can be materialised in multiple other ways, too.

In synthesis, we highlight that starting from a significant economics opening from the last decade of the 20th century, we have analysed the case of the emergence and development of co-production in a competition system, introducing a time-delay in the mathematical model. Such an approach allowed the adequate determination of the effects over the equilibrium of the system functionality.

Also, the present research (as horizon opening) brings forward the possibility of future developments and practical applications, as suggested in the chapter.

REFERENCES

Ballantyne, D., & Varey, R. J. (2006). Creating value-in-use through marketing interaction: The exchange logic of relating, communicating and knowing. *Marketing Theory, 6*(3), 335–348. https://doi.org/10.1177/1470593106066795

Bastiat, F. (1851). *Harmonies Économiques* [Economic Harmonies]. Guillaumin. http://bastiat.org/fr/harmonies.html

Bendapudi, N., & Leone, R. P. (2003). Psychological implications of customer participation in co-production. *Journal of Marketing, 67*(1), 14–28. https://doi.org/10.1509/jmkg.67.1.14.18592

Blaschke, M., Haki, K., Aier, S., & Winter, R. (2018). Value co-creation ontology – A service-dominant logic perspective. *Multikonferenz Wirtschaftsinformatik*, 398–409.

Bressand, A., & Nicolaidis, K. (1988). Les services au cœur de l'économie relationnelle [The services in the core of relational economy]. *Revue d'Economie Industrielle, 43*(1), 141–163. https://doi.org/10.3406/rei.1988.1015

Ceccagnoli, M., Forman, C., Huang, P., & Wu, D. (2012). Cocreation of value in a platform ecosystem: The case of enterprise software. *MIS Quarterly, 36*(1), 263–290. https://doi.org/10.2307/41410417

Chathoth, P., Altinay, L., Harrington, R. J., Okumus, F., & Chan, E. S. (2013). Coproduction versus co-creation: A process based continuum in the hotel service context. *International Journal of Hospitality Management, 32*, 11–20. https://doi.org/10.1016/j.ijhm.2012.03.009

Dos Santos, J. S., Azevedo, K. A., & Torresan, P. (2014). Competition among manufacturers in technological innovation in the market with delayed information. *European Journal of Pure and Applied Mathematics, 7*(2), 156–165. www.ejpam.com

Ertimur, B., & Venkatesh, A. (2010). Opportunism in co-production: Implications for value co-creation. *Australasian Marketing Journal, 18*(4), 256–263. https://doi.org/10.1016/j.ausmj.2010.07.004

Etgar, M. (2008). A descriptive model of the consumer co-production process. *Journal of the Academy of Marketing Science, 36*(1), 97–108. https://doi.org/10.1007/s11747-007-0061-1

Grönroos, C. (2008). Service logic revisited: Who creates value? and who co-creates? *European Business Review*. ISSN: 0955-534X. doi.org/10.1108/09555340810886585

Grönroos, C., & Voima, P. (2013). Critical service logic: Making sense of value creation and co-creation. *Journal of the Academy of Marketing Science, 41*(2), 133–150. https://doi.org/10.1007/s11747-012-0308-3

Grover, V., & Kohli, R. (2012). Cocreating IT value: New capabilities and metrics for multifirm environments. *MIS Quarterly, 36*(1), 225–232. https://doi.org/10.2307/41410415

Guo, S., & Jiang, W. (2012). Global stability and Hopf bifurcation for Gause-type predator-prey system. *Journal of Applied Mathematics, 260798*, 17. https://doi.org/10.1155/2012/260798

Heinonen, K., & Strandvik, T. (2015). Customer-dominant logic: Foundations and implications. *Journal of Services Marketing, 29*(6/7), 472–484. https://doi.org/10.1108/JSM-02-2015-0096

Jivan, A. (1993). Services and servicity. *ServicesWorld Forum Bulletin, 3–4*, 16–24.

Jivan, A. (2014). Productivité et servicité [Productivity and servicity]. Economies et Sociétés, Cahiers de l'ISMEA 4. *Série Economie et Gestion des Services, 15*, 579–599.

Jivan, A., Curea-Pitorac, R., & Tînjală, D. (2018). Serviceable results of five automotive companies. Comparisons concerning certain originally calculated indicators. *Proceedings of the 32nd IBIMA conference*: 15–16 November 2018, Seville, Spain. ISBN: 978-0-9998551-1-9.

Jivan, A., & Năchescu, M. (2018). Environmental approaches in productivity analysis. Improving proposals. CES Working Chapters, Published on-line: January 2019, ISSN: 2067-7693, Volume X, Issue 4, 438–452. https://ceswp.uaic.ro/articles/CESWP2018_X4_JIV.pdf

Kandampully, J., Bilgihan, A., & Zhang, T. C. (2016). Developing a people-technology hybrids model to unleash innovation and creativity: The new hospitality frontier. *Journal of Hospitality and Tourism Management, 29*, 154–164. https://doi.org/10.1016/j.jhtm.2016.07.003

Lovelock, C. H., & Young, R. F. (1979). Look to consumers to increase productivity. *Harvard Business Review, 57*(3), 168–178. https://hbr.org/1979/05/look-to-consumers-to-increase-productivity

Lusch, R. F., & Vargo, S. L. (2006). Service-dominant logic: Reactions, reflections and refinements. *Marketing Theory*, 6(3), 281–288. https://doi.org/10.1177/1470593106066781

Oertzen, A.-S., Odekerken-Schröder, G., Brax, S. A., & Mager, B. (2018). Co-creating services – Conceptual clarification, forms and outcomes. *Journal of Service Management*, 29(1), 641–679. https://doi.org/10.1108/JOSM-03-2017-0067

O'Hern, M. S., & Rindfleisch, A. (2010). Customer co-creation: A typology and research agenda. *Review of Marketing Research*, 6, 84–106. https://doi.org/10.1108/S1548-6435(2009)0000006008

Prebensen, N. K., & Xie, J. (2017). Efficacy of co-creation and mastering on perceived value and satisfaction in tourists' consumption. *Tourism Management*, 60, 166–176. https://doi.org/10.1016/j.tourman.2016.12.001

Ramaswamy, V., & Ozcan, K. (2018). What is co-creation? An interactional creation framework and its implications for value creation. *Journal of Business Research*, 84, 196–205. https://doi.org/10.1016/j.jbusres.2017.11.027

Ramirez, R. (1999). Value co-production: Intellectual origins and implications for practice and research. *Strategic Management Journal*, 20(1), 49–65. https://doi.org/10.1002/(SICI)1097-0266(199901)20:1<49::AID-SMJ20>3.0.CO;2-2

Ritelli, D., Barbiroli, G., & Fabbri, P. (1997). Predation among technologies on the market: A modellistic analysis. *Journal of Mathematical Economics*, 27(3), 347–374. https://doi.org/10.1016/S0304-4068(96)00773-2

Saarijärvi, H., Puustinen, P., Yrjölä, M., & Mäenpää, K. (2017). Service-dominant logic and service logic-contradictory and/or complementary? *International Journal of Services Sciences*, 6(1), 1–25. https://doi.org/10.1504/IJSSCI.2017.088030

Tari Kasnakoglu, B. (2016). Antecedents and consequences of co-creation in credence-based service contexts. *The Service Industries Journal*, 36(1–2), 1–20. https://doi.org/10.1080/02642069.2016.1138472

Terblanche, N. S. (2014). Some theoretical perspectives of co-creation and co-production of value by customers. *Acta Commercii*, 14(2), 1–8. https://doi.org/10.4102/ac.v14i2.237

Toffler, A. (1980). *The third wave*. Morrow, Bantam Books (US).

Varey, R. J. (2010). The economics basis of marketing. *Marketing Theory*, 1(1), 101–120. https://doi.org/10.4135/9781446280096.n5

Vargo, S. L., & Lusch, R. F. (2004). Evolving to a new dominant logic for marketing. *Journal of Marketing*, 68(1), 1–17. https://www.jstor.org/stable/30161971

Vargo, S. L., & Lusch, R. F. (2008). Service-dominant logic: Continuing the evolution. *Journal of the Academy of Marketing Science*, 36(1), 1–10. https://doi.org/10.1007/s11747-007-0069-6

Zhao, W. B., Sun, X. K., & Wang, H. (2014, January). Hopf bifurcation and stability analysis of a congestion control model with delay in wireless access network. In *Abstract and applied analysis* (Vol. 2014). Hindawi. doi.org/10.1155/2014/632564

CHAPTER 6

LESS IS MORE, MORE IS LESS (CLEOPAS MLILO): EXPLORING THE ELUSIVE SUSTAINABILITY IN THE FASHION INDUSTRY

Alexandra-Codruţa Bîzoi and Cristian-Gabriel Bîzoi

West University of Timişoara, Romania

ABSTRACT

Purpose: *This paper investigates how Europe's fast fashion industry's sustainability efforts correlate with socio-economic well-being, focusing on the Human Development Index (HDI), Sustainable Development Goals, and textile waste.*

Design/Methodology/Approach: *Applying Principal Component, Regression, and Spatial Analysis, the study examines cross-European data to identify relationships between development indices and textile waste.*

Findings: *There is a strong link between adherence to Sustainable Development Goals and higher living standards, but the impact of textile waste on well-being is minimal.*

Research Limitations/Implications: *Limitations refer to excluding other socio-economic factors and a narrow metric focus, which may obscure the broader effects of textile waste.*

Practical Implications: *Results advocate for sustainable waste management policies, which were crucial during the European energy crisis, to foster eco-friendly practices in the fashion industry.*

Social Implications: *The study emphasises the need for a circular economy shift in fast fashion, which is vital for environmental sustainability and societal health.*

Originality/Value: *This research enriches the sustainability narrative by correlating it with socio-economic health in European contexts, providing a unique industry perspective.*

Plain Language Summary: *Exploring the connection between sustainability in Europe's fashion industry and quality of life, our study finds that eco-friendly policies match higher living standards. However, fashion waste's direct effect could be much better. Amidst an energy crisis (Kent, 2022), our insights press for greener practices in fashion, underscoring the necessity for a circular economy to support environmental and social well-being.*

Keywords: Sustainability; fashion; waste management; blockchain; Inditex; H&M

JEL Codes: Q01; L67; Q53; L86; L81

1. INTRODUCTION

The European textile waste landscape is on the brink of a significant shift, with fibre-to-fibre recycling emerging as a key strategy in addressing the growing issue of waste, which averages 15 kilograms per citizen each year, with most being consumer discarded (McKinsey, 2022). Despite the concerning levels of waste, predominantly disposed of through incineration and landfills, there is a shift towards sustainable practices, which includes reducing overproduction, promoting conscious consumption, extending textile longevity, and designing for recyclability, with fibre-to-fibre recycling at the forefront, promising to convert waste back into usable fibres.

Current recycling methods, both mechanical for cotton and chemical for materials like polyester, are still nascent, with less than 1% of textile waste undergoing these processes. Challenges such as improving collection and sorting, which stand at 30–35%, must be overcome to meet the exacting purity requirements for recycling (McKinsey, 2022).

In the perspective of 2030, there is potential for recycling rates to climb to 18–26% of total textile waste, which will require an investment of €6–€7 billion but could yield significant economic benefits, including a profit pool of €1.5–€2.2 billion, the creation of roughly 15,000 jobs, and a reduction of around 4 million tons of CO_2 emissions (McKinsey, 2022). The anticipated broader impact is considerable, with a holistic annual benefit of €3.5–€4.5 billion by 2030 and a return on investment of 55–70%, marking the emergence of a sustainable and self-sustaining industry (McKinsey, 2022).

Realising this vision of sustainable textile recycling in Europe calls for achieving economies of scale, collaborative efforts across the value chain, securing transitional funding, and significant investments to develop robust recycling infrastructure. This transition presents an opportunity for innovation, economic growth, and environmental stewardship, turning textile waste from an endpoint into the beginning of a material's lifecycle in a circular economy.

The fast fashion sector, known for rapid production and shifting trends, stands at a crossroads faced with environmental and social challenges, further complicated by the European energy crisis (Euratex, 2022; Global Data, 2022), which affects production costs and consumer spending. This research delves into the relationship between fast fashion sustainability initiatives and the socio-economic well-being of European societies (EC, 2022), focusing on the correlation with the HDI, the impact on Sustainable Development Goals, and the socio-economic role of textile waste management.

This study aims to fill a critical gap in the current literature by exploring the direct effects of European energy policies on the sustainability strategies of fashion brands since the onset of the energy crisis, providing fresh insights into the industry's adaptation to economic pressures.

2. SUSTAINABILITY REVIEW IN FASHION: A CRUCIAL TURNAROUND

The fashion industry's sustainability narrative, woven from diverse academic threads, presents a tapestry of interlinked environmental, economic, and ethical concerns. This literature review critically integrates the findings of pivotal studies, juxtaposing varied insights to illuminate the multifaceted challenges and the industry's response to an evolving sustainability paradigm.

The divergent results across studies, such as the reported improvements in the environmental impact per garment contrasted with the persistent ecological toll of fast fashion, attributable to various factors. Methodological differences are a primary consideration. For instance, Peters et al. (2021) utilize the Eora database, which may capture data differently than Thomas's (2019) and Cline's (2013) approaches, which might rely on case studies or direct industry reports. The geographic focus is another factor; impacts in Southeast Asia may differ from those in Europe due to variances in energy sources, regulatory environments, and production technologies. Temporal scope also plays a role; studies covering different time frames may reflect the changing dynamics of the industry, such as advancements in sustainable materials or shifts in production locales due to trade policies.

Seares (2022) further delivers a timely analysis of the current economic pressures, such as the energy crisis, that are shaping corporate strategies. This analysis shows a landscape where sustainability increasingly intertwines with economic resilience. The assertions of Thomas (2019) and Cline (2013) align with the findings of Niinimäki et al. (2020), who analyze the ecological costs of fast fashion. Methodological differences are a primary consideration. However, such initiatives are sometimes criticised as 'greenwashing' if not accompanied by substantial reductions in overall production volumes (Lopes et al., 2023). For instance, Peters et al. (2021) utilise the Eora database, which may capture data differently than Thomas and Cline's (2023) approaches, which might rely on case studies or direct industry reports. The geographic focus is another factor; impacts in Southeast Asia may differ from those in Europe due to variances in energy sources, regulatory environments, and production technologies. Temporal scope also plays a role; studies covering different time frames may reflect the changing dynamics of the industry, such as advancements in sustainable materials or shifts in production locales due to trade policies. Sustainable and slow fashion movements, as advocated by Jung and Jin (2014), propose a shift away from the prevailing fast fashion model. The literature reveals a tension between the urgency of this shift and the industry's incremental adaptations. For example, while Turker & Altuntas (2014) quantify sustainable supply chain practices, Choi & Cheng (2015) offer a more critical view of the fast fashion model's ongoing environmental toll, suggesting that the industry's current efforts may not mitigate its impact.

The economic viability of sustainability within the fashion industry emerges as a contested space. The efficiency gains highlighted by Peters et al. (2021) suggest an industry moving towards reconciling profitability with environmental responsibility. Conversely, the challenges outlined by Seares (2022) reflect a sector under siege from rising costs and market volatility, where sustainability efforts are as much about economic survival as they are about environmental stewardship. The ethical implications of these economic pressures are not to be understated, as Bick et al. (2020) expose the environmental injustices that fast fashion perpetuates.

Meichtry and Strasburg (2022) offer a contemporary view of how energy costs reshape the European industry, highlighting a crucial area where recent policy changes may significantly influence corporate sustainability strategies, which underscores the need for updated empirical research that can track the impacts of these policies on industry practices. The literature indicates that while the fashion industry has taken strides towards sustainability, the depth and effectiveness of these efforts remain uneven and, at times, superficial. The continued reliance on fast fashion, as evidenced by the rapid production cycles of brands like Zara and H&M (Meichtry & Strasburg, 2022), reveals an industry at odds with its proclaimed sustainability goals.

Consumer behaviour is pivotal in driving the industry's approach to sustainability. The consumer culture prioritising variety and affordability sustained the demand for fast fashion (Barnes & Lea-Greenwood, 2006). However, a growing segment advocates for sustainability, influencing brands like Patagonia and Everlane that emphasise ethical production and durability (Goworek et al., 2020). The contrast between these consumer bases can create a dichotomy in market demand, influencing the pace and nature of the industry's sustainability efforts.

Broader socio-economic factors significantly affect the fashion industry's sustainability trajectory. The COVID-19 pandemic, for instance, has prompted a re-evaluation of global supply chains and consumer priorities, potentially accelerating the shift towards local production and online retail (Pissani & Augier, 2021). Global trade tensions, such as those between the USA and China, can also affect sourcing strategies and adopting sustainable practices due to changing cost structures (Sukar & Ahmed, 2019).

The industry could explore solutions such as adopting circular economy principles, where the design stage marks the end of life of products, to advance genuine sustainability (Ellen MacArthur Foundation, 2021). There is also a need for more robust and transparent sustainability reporting standards within the industry, underpinned by blockchain technology, to ensure traceability (Büşra et al., 2022). We need further research to explore the effectiveness of policy interventions, such as extended producer responsibility schemes, in driving sustainable practices (Bocken, 2023).

The critical integration of these studies suggests that while there is progress, substantial work remains to ensure that the industry's sustainability practices are not just reactive measures but proactive strategies embedded in the core business models. The reviewed literature indicates an increasing focus on the environmental impacts of fast fashion. Nevertheless, few studies have utilised advanced statistical techniques, such as PCA and spatial analysis, to evaluate these impacts across the EU systematically. Our study seeks to fill this methodological void.

3. SUSTAINABILITY ENDEAVOURS OF TWO TOP EUROPEAN TEXTILE BRANDS. FASHION INDEXES AND BLOCKCHAIN TECHNOLOGIES TO IMPROVE SUSTAINABILITY

Many companies practising the fast-fashion business model praised their numerous actions for becoming more sustainable. However, they consume enormous resources in their manufacturing and transport sectors (electric energy, oil, gas, water – see Tables 6.1 and 6.2). Producing large amounts of clothing that remain unsold and fill landfills necessitates all these resources and generates more greenhouse gas (GHG) emissions. Therefore, this business model needs redesigning. If we are to analyse the resource consumption of the significant European fast-fashion companies, we conclude that spending these resources can be more rational, having a lower environmental footprint.

Global energy consumption rose by 5% during the pandemic, as Enerdata reported in 2022 (Enerdata, 2022). We compared the international values of total electricity consumption levels of two major European fast-fashion companies with the lowest country values at the EU level.

Inditex and H&M, two significant players in the global fast fashion industry, have a relatively small footprint on global electricity consumption and negligible water and GHG emissions, accounting for only 0.02% of the world's electricity use. However, their impact is more pronounced when compared to individual European countries (Table 6.3). Together, they are responsible for 0.21% of the EU-28's electricity, 0.01% of its water consumption, and 0.01% of its GHG emissions. Their presence in Portugal is significant, with 14.74% of the country's electricity consumption attributed to them, 0.22% of water usage, and 0.78% of GHG emissions. For Romania, the figures are 8.67% for electricity, 0.32% for water, and 0.45% for GHG emissions. Sweden consumes 7.02% of electricity and 0.75% of water, producing 0.84% of GHG emissions. Pointing out that other multinational

Table 6.1. Fast-fashion Companies' Utility Consumption.

Company	Annual Revenue (billion euros)[a]	Electricity[b] (MWh)/ (TWh)	Natural Gas (MWh)	Other Fuels (MWh)	Water Consumption (m³)	Percentage of Energy Coming from Renewable Sources (%)	GHG Emissions (kilotons)
Inditex	27.7	1.678.957/1.678957*10⁶	72.050	5.203	1.886.900	91	62.35[c]
H&M	23.46	1.268.461/1.268461*10⁶	69.012³	41.319⁴	18.219.486 (recycled)	95	478

[a]Expressed in SEK m. Own calculations into millions of euros.
[b]Electricity consumption in Europe and North America comes from renewable energy sources.
[c]Tons of Scope 1 and 2 emissions turned into kilotons. Own calculations.
Source: 2021 Inditex Annual Sustainability Report, 2021 H&M Annual Report, World of Meters (2023).

Table 6.2. Utility Consumption at Global, European, and Country Level.

Company/Country	Electricity (TWh Converted into MWh)	Water Consumption	Percentage of Energy Coming from Renewable Sources (%)	GHG Emissions (kilotons)
Global	1,455*10¹⁰	3.996.757.700.000	28.1	51.199.870
EU-28	1,372*10⁹	214.478.300.000	37.7	3.924.950
America[a]	3,217*10⁹	715.090.000.000	34.4	9.837.821
Asia[b]	6,310*10⁹	1.760.860.000.000	25.3	21.541.360
Portugal	2.0*10⁷	9.151.000.000	65.5	69.552
Romania	3.4*10⁷	6.374.000.000	44.4	118.954
Sweden	4.2*10⁷	2.689.000.000	67.0	64.589

[a]Canada, the United States, Argentina, Brazil, Chile, Colombia, Mexico.
[b]China, India, Indonesia, Japan, Malaysia, South Korea, Taiwan, Thailand.
Source: Electricity – Enerdata, Water – worldofmeteres, GHG emissions – Crippa et al. (2021).

corporations may have equal or better consumption patterns emphasises the need for broader resource savings. Norway stands out on a global and EU scale, with 99% of its energy derived from renewable sources, setting a high benchmark for sustainable energy use that other nations and regions struggle to meet. In stark contrast, China, which accounts for 42.07% of the world's GHG emissions and has the highest rate of water consumption at 44.06%, only sources 25.3% of its energy from renewables, which is particularly concerning given that many textile corporations, including those in the fast fashion sector, have Asian production bases (see Table 6.4). In this region, environmental regulations are often not up to global standards.

The fashion sector bears considerable environmental and social costs, necessitating greater transparency along its global value chains to lessen its harmful impact. In the European Union, the fashion industry was the third-largest consumer of water and land in 2020 and ranked fifth in GHG emissions and raw material usage. Despite this, the industry is a significant economic player, with

Table 6.3. Utility Consumption of Two Fast-fashion Brands Compared to Global and National Levels.

	Electricity	Water	GHG
(Inditex + H&M)/Global	0.02	0.00	0.00
(Inditex + H&M)/EU-28	0.21	0.01	0.01
(Inditex + H&M)/Portugal	14.74	0.22	0.78
(Inditex + H&M)/Romania	8.67	0.32	0.45
(Inditex + H&M)/Sweden	7.02	0.75	0.84

Source: Own calculations.

Table 6.4. Fast-fashion Companies' Number of Suppliers.

Company	Asian No. of Suppliers	Asian No. Factories	Europe and the Rest of the World's Number of Suppliers	Europe and the Rest of the World's Number of Factories
Inditex (2021)	978	4.567	812	4.189
H&M (2022)	802	1.033	223	357

Source: Inditex annual report 2021, H&M – Statista.

around 160,000 businesses employing 1.5 million individuals and generating €162 billion in 2019 (EEA, 2022). There is a pressing need for the industry to adopt innovative and circular business models that promote sustainable production and consumption to combat these environmental challenges, which range from Arctic melting to wildlife extinction. The industry's environmental burden is significant, consuming 98 million tons of non-renewable resources, emitting 1.2 billion tons of GHGs, and using 93 billion cubic metres of water annually (Ellen MacArthur Foundation, 2017). This pattern of textile consumption is mirrored in the EU and has a notable environmental footprint (see Table 6.5).

However, the EU is not the highest textile producer in the world. Mainly, Asian countries are among the world's top 10 textile producers, exporters, and electricity and water consumers. China, India, and the USA are the world's leading producers and exporters of textiles. China is the leading textile producer in the world, with more than half the global share (52.2), and has the maximum export value (118.5 billion $). Regarding export value, China is followed by the EU, with 74 billion $.

Most leading textile production countries are in Asia (Table 6.6). China's textile sector is a significant economic force, growing due to favourable conditions like low labour costs and reduced trade barriers. India is the second-largest textile producer and exporter, with the USA also playing a significant role. In 2022, the EU and the USA were critical in textile exports, making up 25.1% of the global market, showing a steady increase over the previous two years. Notably, the USA exports grew by 5% in 2022, the most substantial growth among the top global exporters. Despite this, global textile recycling into new products remains below 1%, as per 2017 figures (Ellen MacArthur Foundation, 2017), indicating a need for the textile business model to evolve to address its environmental impact more responsibly.

Table 6.5. EU Textile Consumption Pattern in 2020.

EU-27	2020
Produced textile products	6.9 million tons
Imported finished textile products	8.7 million tons
Primary raw materials used to produce the textile products purchased by the EU households	175 million tons
Primary raw materials used to produce the textile products purchased by the EU households per person	391 kg
Consumption of textile products in the EU	6.6 million tons
Consumption of textile products in the EU per person	15 kg
Required blue water to produce the textile products purchased by the EU households	4,000 million m^3
Required blue water to produce the textile products purchased by the EU households per person	9 m^3
Land use in the supply chain of textiles purchased by European households in 2020	180,000 km^2
Land use in the supply chain of textiles purchased by European households in 2020 per person	400 m^2
GHG emissions[a]	121 million tons of carbon dioxide equivalent (CO_2e)
GHG emissions per person	270 kg CO_2e

[a]Production and consumption of textiles generate greenhouse gas emissions, in particular from resource extraction, production, washing and drying, and waste incineration.
Source: Adapted from EEA (2021).

Table 6.6. Textile Output in Global Share/Textile Export Value.

Rank	Country/Region	2019 Textile Output in the Global Share (%)	2022 Export Value ($ billion)	2018 Export Value ($ billion)
1.	China	52.2	148	118.5
2.	European Union	21.7	71	66
3.	India	6.9	19	18.1
4.	The United States	5.3	14	13.8
5.	Pakistan	3.6	9	8.0
6.	Turkey	1.9	15	11.9
7.	South Korea	1.8	8	9.8

Source: WTO (2023).

In Europe, the current geopolitical climate, including the Ukrainian War, is forcing a re-evaluation of energy sources, affecting sustainability strategies and supply chain dynamics in various industries, including fashion. The textile industry in Europe is the fourth most significant contributor to environmental and climate concerns, after food, mobility, and housing (EEA, 2022). A shift towards a circular economy is crucial, emphasising longer product lifecycles and recycling. However, the industry largely depends on new materials with limited recyclable options.

Fashion companies increasingly focus on ecological and social welfare, promoting supply chain transparency and worker welfare initiatives. For instance, Inditex and H&M strive for zero waste and living wages for supply chain workers. Inditex aims to achieve zero waste by 2023 (Inditex, 2017, 2021a, 2021b), while H&M introduced the Zero Waste Dress in 2020 and aims for a net-zero environmental impact by 2040 (H&M, 2018, 2021a, 2021b, 2022).

The Fashion Transparency Index by Fashion Revolution, launched in 2021, rates brands on sustainability based on public data covering 239 indicators, aiding consumers in assessing a brand's commitment to social and environmental responsibilities (Fashion Revolution, 2021). The fashion industry must address several urgent topics:

1. *Consumer engagement*: Encouraging consumers to opt for long-lasting fashion over disposable trends is vital.
2. *Resource efficiency*: The industry must significantly reduce resource consumption by adopting innovative and efficient manufacturing techniques.
3. *Clean energy transition*: Renewable energy use must go hand in hand with reducing overall energy demand and carbon emissions.
4. *Transparent supply chains*: Ensuring that manufacturing standards are eco-friendly across the globe is necessary for maintaining brand integrity.
5. *Geopolitical resilience*: Diversifying supply chains can mitigate the economic impacts of events like the Ukrainian conflict.
6. *Circular economy adoption*: Investing in recyclable and biodegradable materials, alongside initiatives like clothing rentals, is critical for environmental sustainability.
7. *Genuine CSR*: Brands should demonstrate real change through their CSR initiatives, ensuring fair labour practices and minimising ecological damage.
8. *Embracing slow fashion*: Integrating the ethos of slow fashion could help brands meet consumer demands sustainably.

The fashion industry increasingly adopts blockchain technology to ensure supply chain transparency and authenticate sustainability claims. Notable blockchain platforms include Provenance, A Transparent Company, and Loomia. These technologies can verify the origin of materials, track product lifecycles, and confirm the authenticity of sustainability claims (A Transparent Company, 2023; Loomia, 2023; Martine Jarlgaard London, 2023; Provenance, 2023).

Indexes like the Higg Index (Apparel Coalition, 2023) and the Fashion Transparency Index have been instrumental in measuring sustainability in fashion. Blockchain could further enhance these measures by providing verifiable transparency. As blockchain technology advances, experts expect it to become more integral to sustainable fashion practices (Kshetri, 2018; Masi et al., 2017; O'Leary, 2017; Saberi et al., 2019; Tian, 2017).

Although it has many advantages, blockchain technology still poses some challenges (Croman et al., 2016; Kshetri, 2017; Stoll et al., 2019; Tapscott & Tapscott, 2017; Weber et al., 2016; Zohar, 2015):

- It is complex to implement. Integrating blockchain into existing supply chains and systems might be challenging for many fashion companies, especially those without significant technological infrastructure or expertise.

- It raises data privacy concerns and environmental concerns. Blockchain's transparency means that much of the data is public. While this is good for verifying claims, it might raise concerns about data privacy and misuse. Traditional blockchain networks, like Bitcoin, require significant computational power and, thus, have substantial energy demands. The fashion industry, aiming for sustainability, would need more energy-efficient blockchain solutions.
- The vast and dynamic fashion industry needs scalability, speed, and interoperability. Currently, many blockchain solutions can handle a limited number of transactions per second, which could pose challenges for large-scale applications. Different blockchain systems might need help communicating with each other. For a transparent global supply chain, systems must be interoperable.

While blockchain holds enormous potential for revolutionising the fashion industry, especially ensuring transparency and sustainability, its implementation comes with challenges. However, solutions to these challenges will likely emerge as technology evolves and the industry recognises the value of transparent and ethical operations. Brands willing to invest in and pioneer these solutions will likely be at the forefront of the next wave of sustainable fashion (Croman et al., 2016; Kshetri, 2017; Stoll et al., 2019; Tapscott & Tapscott, 2017; Weber et al., 2016; Zohar, 2015).

The study employs statistical techniques such as PCA, regression analysis, and spatial analysis using R econometrics to assess the environmental impact of fashion within the EU.

4. METHODOLOGY OF ANALYSING SUSTAINABLE PRACTICES IN EU MEMBER STATES

An intensified focus on sustainable growth and development characterises the modern era. In the European context, where countries boast diverse socio-economic landscapes, investigating sustainable practices and their links with human development becomes more crucial. This research analyses the relationship between three pivotal metrics: the HDI, the Sustainable Development Goals scores, and textile waste indicators across European countries.

The European energy crisis and its associated challenges heighten the study's urgency. At this juncture, LABFRESH's waste index becomes instrumental, shedding light on the environmental fallout of the fast fashion sector. In a market where brands continually revamp collections, the average lifespan of apparel dwindles, bolstering textile waste. LABFRESH's commendable initiative in spotlighting the gravity of this waste crisis and proposing solutions through textile advancements aligns with this study's emphasis on sustainability. By methodically ranking European nations based on textile waste, LABFRESH furnishes an empirical base, underscoring the urgent call for shifts in consumer behaviour and industry paradigms (LABFRESH, 2023). The index by LABFRESH offers a comprehensive view of the textile waste problem prevalent in Europe. With the fashion industry's dynamism, clothing items have transitioned into transient commodities. This shift towards overconsumption of perishable, mass-manufactured garments intensifies the textile waste challenge.

LABFRESH's pioneering solutions, especially its long-lasting textile collection, aim to combat this by minimising wash cycles and prolonging garment longevity. Their analysis narrows down to the top 15 European nations that bear the brunt of textile waste. The study reveals a grim reality: an overwhelming proportion of textile waste is incinerated or dumped in landfills. Merely a fractional segment undergoes recycling or resurfacing as second-hand attire. LABFRESH's Fashion Waste Index represents a concerted effort to quantify and compare the scale of textile waste across Europe.

To shed light on the severity of the issue, LABFRESH examined the 15 European countries that generate the most significant amounts of textile waste. Their methodology integrates multiple factors: the total annual fashion waste produced, individual spending on new clothing, the fashion industry's contribution to each country's GDP, and the volume of clothing exports. These elements collectively inform the rankings, with higher scores indicating less sustainability. To articulate the impact on a personal scale, they calculated per capita figures for textile waste generation and disposal methods, uncovering that only a tiny fraction of waste re-enters the market or production cycle. At the same time, the incinerated or landfilled bulk causes considerable environmental harm. LABFRESH's scoring system assigns 0 to 100 points to each factor, where 100 represents the least sustainable and 0 is the most sustainable, culminating in an aggregate score that positions each country on its index. This comprehensive approach underscores the need to reduce textile waste, which is imperative for ecological and human well-being. The meticulous methodology of the index leans on data from Eurostat (2016), examining diverse textile waste facets. An evaluative framework scores nations based on these dimensions, with nations showing minor sustainability receiving superior scores. This cumulative scoring system holistically illustrates each country's textile waste sustainability dynamics. Besides the 15 countries included in the LABFRESH index, we added the remaining members of the EU, including the UK. The revised Waste Framework Directive ((EU) 2018/851) is a pivotal step towards a more sustainable approach to waste management within the European Union. With the overarching aim of recognising waste as a valuable resource, the directive mandates that all Member States implement separate collection systems for textile waste by 2025. This legislative action acknowledges the growing urgency to address the environmental impacts of textile waste and fosters a systemic shift towards circular economy principles. Implementing this directive is expected to enhance the quality and availability of data on textile waste, providing a more accurate and harmonised understanding across Member States. Such data collection and reporting improvements are crucial for future assessments and rankings of textile waste production, potentially offering insights not available for the 2016 LABFRESH index. The forthcoming changes underscore the importance of updated and consistent data in evaluating the progress of European countries in mitigating textile waste and promoting sustainability (EEA, 2021).

We started our analysis with the Principal Component Analysis (PCA), a preliminary statistical lens. This tool illuminates overarching patterns, correlations, and variations within textile waste data, especially spotlighting key dimensions where maximum variances occur.

4.1. PCA on Textile Waste Metrics: An Insightful Exploration

Closely examining the PCA results for 'textile_pca' reveals some captivating insights. One of the most remarkable observations is the standard deviation associated with the first principal component (PC1). A value of 2.236 indicates a significant spread in the data along this axis. This high value suggests that PC1 captures a substantial portion of the variance present in the dataset. However, what truly stands out is the proportion of variance captured by PC1. This single component explains an astonishing 100% of the variance. Such observations are rare in PCAs and underline the fact that the selected variables for this PCA – Textile_waste_tonnes, Yearly_incinerated_textile_waste, Yearly_landfilled_textile_waste, Yearly_recycled_textile_waste_kg, and Yearly_reusable_textile_waste_kg – are tightly correlated. These metrics measure closely related facets of textile waste or share a derivative relationship.

Interpreting the underlying patterns: The dominance of PC1, in this case, tells a significant story. Since it captures all the variability in the textile waste metrics, the scores of PC1 for each country serve as a reflection of each country's stance regarding textile waste. These scores synthesise information from the combination of the five original metrics, giving a singular value that encapsulates the textile waste situation of a country. For instance, a country with a PC1 score of –0.2979 exhibits below-average textile waste based on the consolidated metrics, implying that its textile waste scenario is more favourable than the dataset's mean. In contrast, a country with a score of 1.7501 demonstrates a much higher textile waste profile. Given the sheer dominance of PC1 in capturing variance, analysts and researchers can employ this single score as a composite measure of textile waste for each nation. This measure can guide further analyses, comparisons, or visualisations among countries.

For further explorations, visualising the PCA results (Fig. 6.1) offers an effective way to comprehend and present the differences among countries. The derived composite score, 'Textile_Waste_PC1', can also facilitate comparisons with other economic or environmental metrics. For instance, one could examine the relationship between the composite textile waste measure and the HDI to uncover potential patterns or correlations.

Our results confirm the principal polluters of the EU found by LABFRESH, namely, Italy, Germany, France, and the UK. The lowest polluters of the EU are Estonia, Cyprus, Greece, Malta, and Latvia. In conclusion, the PCA on textile waste metrics offers a fresh lens to understand global trends and patterns. While the results paint a clear picture of the textile waste landscape, they also beckon researchers to delve deeper, ensuring that models remain robust and interpretations remain aligned with the underlying data.

While the PCA of textile waste metrics has unveiled some profound insights into the correlations and overarching patterns within the data, it is only one piece of the analytical puzzle. The dominance of the first principal component offers a synthesised perspective. This statistical tool provides a means to predict one

Less Is More, More Is Less (Cleopas Mlilo) 121

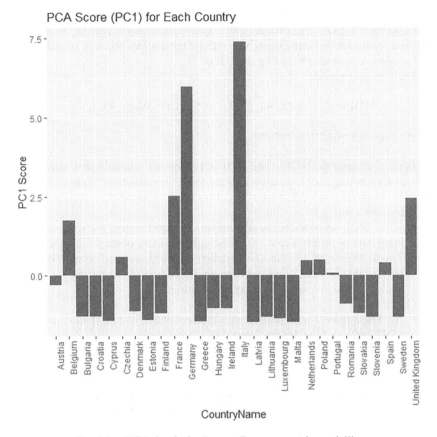

Fig. 6.1. PCA Analysis. *Source*: R econometric modelling.

variable based on another, presenting an opportunity to examine how our synthesised metric from PCA (the PC1 score) might relate to other significant indicators, such as the HDI. By leveraging the consolidated knowledge from PCA in regression models, one can derive a more robust and nuanced understanding of underlying relationships.

Following PCA's foundation, the research journey meanders into two significant analytical techniques: spatial and regression analyses. The former focuses on mapping geographical patterns, offering a spatial perspective to HDI and sustainable practices across European territories. On the other hand, regression analysis provides a more granular look, deciphering potential linear relationships between variables like the HDI and textile waste metrics.

4.2. Regression Analysis Findings

In our analysis, we added data from the EUROSTAT and the UN for the remaining EU member states to understand the relationship between the HDI[1], the Sustainable Development Goals[2], and Textile Waste in European Countries.

We utilised a linear regression model with HDI as the dependent variable, predicted by the SDG_2021 scores and a synthesised metric Textile_Waste_PC1 (derived from various textile waste variables). Our sample consisted of data from 28 European countries (including the UK).

The regression model is:

$$\text{HDI} = \beta_0 + \beta_1 * \text{SDG\_2021} + \beta_2 * \text{Textile\_Waste\_PC1} + \epsilon$$

With the following components:

1. *Dependent variable*: HDI – The HDI is a composite statistic that measures a country's average achievements in three basic dimensions of human development: health, knowledge, and a decent standard of living.
2. *Independent variables*:
   - SDG_2021 – A predictor or feature variable representing the score of alignment with or progress towards the Sustainable Development Goals for 2021.
   - Textile_Waste_PC1 – Another predictor variable derived from a PCA on various textile waste variables is an aggregated metric capturing the significant variance in textile waste across countries.
3. *Coefficients*:
   - β – The intercept represents the predicted value of the HDI when both the SDG_2021 and the Textile_Waste_PC1 are 0.
   - β_1 – The slope or effect size of SDG_2021 on HDI that quantifies the change in HDI for a one-unit change in SDG_2021, keeping the Textile_Waste_PC1 constant.
   - β_2 – The slope or effect size of Textile_Waste_PC1 on the HDI and signifies the change in HDI for a one-unit change in Textile_Waste_PC1, keeping the SDG_2021 constant.
   - ϵ – This is the error term or residual that captures the variation in the dependent variable HDI, not explained by the independent variables and accounts for randomness or unpredictability in the data.

The regression model explores HDI's linear predictability based on SDG_2021 scores and textile waste metrics (Fig. 6.2).

1. *SDG_2021 influence*: A statistically significant relationship emerged between SDG_2021 and HDI. Countries better aligned with the 2021 Sustainable Development Goals exhibited enhanced human development indices.
2. *Textile waste's non-impact*: The aggregated textile waste metric (encapsulated by Textile_Waste_PC1) did not significantly influence HDI.
3. *Model assumptions verification*:
   - *Durbin-Watson test*: A value of 2.1033 endorsed the independence assumption, negating significant autocorrelation in residuals.
   - *Breusch-Pagan test*: The p-value of 0.2763 confirmed homoscedasticity, reinforcing that residuals' variance remains consistent across predicted values.

- *Shapiro-Wilk test*: The model met the normality assumption for residuals with a statistic of 0.93711 and a *p*-value of 0.09334.

Unravelling the spatial landscape of HDI in Europe reveals the intersection of historical, political, and economic influences. The spatial clusters, particularly the high-high clusters, reflect potential historical alliances, shared political experiences, and integrated economic zones. On the regression front, the pronounced influence of a country's alignment with SDG_2021 on its HDI underscores the criticality of sustainable goals. It champions that countries committed to sustainable development boost their societal metrics and foster an environment that catalyses human development. Conversely, the negligible impact of textile waste on HDI may suggest that, within the European context, other factors eclipse its influence on development metrics.

In conclusion, navigating the intricate web of development indicators, this study illuminates the profound influence of sustainable goals on HDI within Europe. Countries championing the Sustainable Development Goals are on an elevated human development trajectory. However, the role of textile waste within this analytical scope still needs to be clarified, beckoning further exploration. The HDI gauges the average achievements in three core dimensions of human development: health, education, and standard of living. Exploring the distribution of the HDI across European countries, this study uncovers the intricate dance between HDI, Sustainable Development Goals (SDG_2021), and textile waste metrics. This investigation uses spatial and regression analysis to illuminate potential determinants of development trajectories across Europe.

The following section will delineate the outcomes derived from the spatial analysis, focusing on geographical patterns and their implications.

5. SPATIAL ANALYSIS FINDINGS

Having analysed the data with PCA and deepened our understanding through regression analysis, another dimension beckons our analytical journey: Spatial Analysis. The world of Spatial Analysis offers a vantage point that traditional statistical methods might miss – geographical patterns and spatial relationships. We aimed to investigate how textile waste metrics manifest spatially across countries or regions, particularly our composite PC1 score. We searched for geographical clusters of high textile waste or specific spatial trends that coincide with other environmental or economic factors. Spatial Analysis allows us to visualise data in the context of geographical space and uncovers patterns and anomalies rooted in location. As we delve into this realm, we embark on a journey that merges the abstract world of numbers with the tangible reality of geography, giving our findings a spatial voice.

Utilising the Moran I test for spatial autocorrelation, the study elucidates:

1. *Significant positive spatial autocorrelation*: A Moran I statistic of approximately 0.743 and a highly significant *p*-value of '2.821e-06' reflect spatially clustered countries with comparable HDI values.

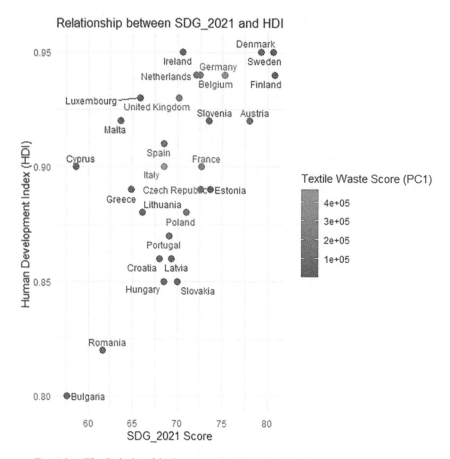

Fig. 6.2. The Relationship Between the HDI, the SDG_2021, and the Textile Waste Metrics. *Source*: R econometric modelling.

2. Spatial clusters (Fig. 6.3):
   - *High-high clusters*: Bulgaria, Greece, Hungary, Romania, and Sweden delineate regions of notable development.
   - *Low-low clusters*: No regions manifested pronounced underdevelopment.
   - *High-low and low-high clusters*: Indicating a discrepancy between a country and its neighbours, countries like Belgium, France, and the UK showcased superior HDI, whereas Italy and Spain manifested the opposite.

The research journey into the dynamics of sustainable practices across European nations offered a multidimensional lens into the intricate dance between environmental concerns and human development. While the results might challenge some preconceived notions, they inevitably highlight the urgent need to prioritise sustainable goals.

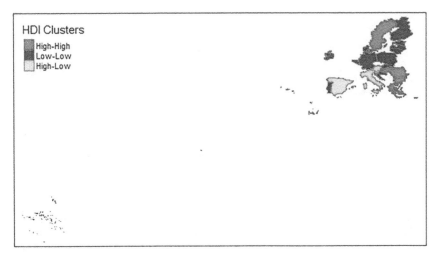

Fig. 6.3. HDI Clusters. *Source*: R econometric, spatial analysis, own findings.

The responsibility now lies with brands and policymakers to take cognizance of these findings and steer the future towards a more sustainable, responsible, and equitable trajectory.

6. CONCLUSIONS

Our study meticulously navigated the multifaceted relationship between HDI, SDG_2021 scores, and textile waste metrics across European nations. While we found a pronounced association between SDG_2021 and HDI, textile waste metrics did not exhibit a marked influence on HDI, contrary to our initial expectations.

This outcome suggests that the fast fashion industry's environmental repercussions still needs to affect broader human development metrics in Europe significantly. Nevertheless, this finding is a cautionary tale for brands, underscoring the increasing importance of sustainable practices and potential long-term consequences if these issues are still needed.

In response to these insights, we propose several recommendations for brands and policymakers:

- Brands should prioritise sustainable sourcing, production, and disposal. Transparently communicating their sustainable efforts can bolster their brand image and consumer loyalty.
- Policymakers need to emphasise waste management regulations, championing circular economy principles. Sustainability is achievable by incentivising responsible practices and enforcing compliance, a notable shift towards industry-wide.

Future research avenues could encompass:

- *Longitudinal studies*: To discern any lagged impacts of textile waste on developmental metrics over time.
- *Socio-economic factors*: Examining the effects of education and public awareness on textile waste generation and management.
- *Granular regional analysis*: Localised studies to unveil any patterns potentially masked at a broader national scope.

Spotlighting trailblazers in the textile industry is a testament to what is achievable. Brands like Patagonia (2023) and Eileen Fisher (2023) exemplify the potential of sustainable initiatives, while countries such as Sweden (Orange, 2016) and France (Jolly, 2023) set national standards that pave the way for responsible waste management.

Drawing upon these illuminating examples, it is evident that foresight and responsibility in the industry can lead to transformative change. Such endeavours, stemming from innovation and ethical commitment, can shape a sustainable future for textiles.

As we reflect on our findings, the study emphasises the importance of sustainability goals. The onus now rests on brands, policymakers, and stakeholders to absorb these insights and architect a trajectory that is both sustainable and equitable.

The research has some limitations, respectively: (i) the PCA indicates highly correlated variables, potentially masking the unique impacts of different textile waste metrics; (ii) the regression analysis might not account for all factors influencing HDI, such as unmeasured variables or lagged effects of textile waste; (iii) the spatial analysis of EU countries may miss global patterns and influences from non-EU regions; (iv) the study's cross-sectional approach may not capture the temporal changes in the relationship between textile waste and human development; (v) the lack of granular data limits understanding of local and regional differences within the identified clusters; (vi) we did not explore the broader environmental impacts of textile waste beyond the scope of HDI.

The study faces challenges due to potential data oversimplification, limited variable inclusion, regional focus, the static nature of the analysis, and a narrower environmental impact scope. Future research could enhance understanding by addressing these limitations through more nuanced data analysis and a broader investigative lens.

NOTES

1. Developed by the UN.
2. Developed by the UN.

REFERENCES

A Transparent Company. (2023, August). http://www.atransparentcompany.com/
Apparel Coalition. (2023, August). *The HIGG index*. https://apparelcoalition.org/the-higg-index/

Barnes, L., & Lea-Greenwood, G. (2006). Fast fashioning the supply chain: Shaping the research agenda. *Journal of Fashion Marketing and Management*, *10*(3), 259–271. https://doi.org/10.1108/13612020610679259

Bick, R., Halsey, E., & Ekenga, C. C. (2020). The global environmental injustice of fast fashion. *Environmental Health*, *17*(1), 1–13. https://ehjournal.biomedcentral.com/articles/10.1186/s12940-018-0433-7

Bocken, N. (2023). *Business models for sustainability*. https://www.researchgate.net/publication/367023438_Business_models_for_Sustainability

Büşra, A., Güner, E., & Son-Turan, S. (2022). Blockchain technology and sustainability in supply chains and a closer look at different industries: A mixed method approach. *Logistics*, *6*(4), 85. https://doi.org/10.3390/logistics6040085

Choi, T. M. & Cheng, T. C. E. (2015). *Sustainable fashion supply chain management*. Springer International Verlag, ISBN 978-3-319-12702-6, DOI https://doi.org/10.1007/978-3-319-12703-3

Cline, E. L. (2013). *Overdressed: The shockingly high cost of cheap fashion*. Penguin.

Crippa, M., Guizzardi, D., Solazzo, E., Muntean, M., Schaaf, E., Monforti-Ferrario, F., Banja, M., Olivier, J. G. J., Grassi, G., Rossi, S., & Vignati, E. (2021). *GHG emissions of all world countries – 2021 Report*, EUR 30831 EN, Publications Office of the European Union, Luxembourg, ISBN 978-92-76-41547-3, doi:10.2760/173513, JRC126363.

Croman, K., Decker, C., Eyal, I., Gencer, A. E., Juels, A., Kosba, A., Miller, A., Saxena, P., Shi, E., Sirer, E. G., Song, D., & Song, D. (2016). On scaling decentralized blockchains. In *Financial cryptography and data security*. Springer. https://fc16.ifca.ai/bitcoin/papers/CDE+16.pdf

EC. (2022). *The European Commission and the IEA outline key energy-saving actions*. Retrieved September 21, 2023, from https://ec.europa.eu/info/news/european-commission-and-iea-outline-key-energy-saving-actions-2022-apr-21_en

EEA. (2021). *Progress towards preventing waste in Europe – The case of textile waste prevention, EEA report no 15/2021*. https://www.eea.europa.eu/publications/progressing-towards-waste-prevention-in

EEA. (2022, August). *Textiles and the environment: The role of design in Europe's circular economy*. https://www.eea.europa.eu/publications/textiles-and-the-environment-the

Eileen Fisher. (2023, August). https://www.eileenfisher.com/?country=RO&currency=RON

Ellen MacArthur Foundation. (2017). *A new textiles economy: Redesigning fashion's future*. Ellen MacArthur Foundation. Retrieved June 22, 2023, from https://emf.thirdlight.com/link/2axvc7eob8zx-za4ule/@/preview/1?o

Ellen MacArthur Foundation. (2021, September). *Circular economy in fashion*. EMF Publications. https://www.ellenmacarthurfoundation.org/fashion-and-the-circular-economy-deep-dive

Enerdata. (2022). *World energy and climate statistics*. https://yearbook.enerdata.net/electricity/electricity-domestic-consumption-data.html

Euratex. (2022). *High energy costs undermine crucial transformation of the textile and clothing industry*. https://euratex.eu/news/high-energy-costs-undermine-crucial-transformation-of-the-textile-and-clothing-industry/

Fashion Revolution. (2021). *Fashion transparency index 2021*. Retrieved June 22, 2023, from https://issuu.com/fashionrevolution/docs/fashiontransparencyindex_2021

Fashion Revolution. (2023). *The fashion transparency index*. https://www.fashionrevolution.org/about/transparency/

Global Data. (2022). *Europe's fashion industry takes a hit amid soaring energy prices*. https://www.globaldata.com/data-insights/consumer/europes-fashion-industry-takes-a-hit-amid-soaring-energy-prices/

Goworek, H., Oxborrow, L., Claxton, S., McLaren, A., Cooper, T., & Hill, H. (2020). Managing sustainability in the fashion business: Challenges in product development for clothing longevity in the UK. *Journal of Business Research*, *117*, 629–641. ISSN 0148-2963. https://doi.org/10.1016/j.jbusres.2018.07.021

H&M. (2018). *The fair living wage strategy: Key impacts and learnings*. https://hmgroup.com/sustainability/fair-and-equal/wages/key-impacts-and-learnings/

H&M. (2021a). *H&M annual and sustainability report*. https://hmgroup.com/wp-content/uploads/2022/03/HM-Group-Annual-and-Sustainability-Report-2021.pdf

H&M. (2021b). *Taking sustainable fashion to a new level with tech.* https://hmgroup.com/our-stories/taking-sustainable-fashion-to-a-new-level-with-tech/

H&M. (2022). *H&M annual and sustainability report.* https://hmgroup.com/investors/annual-and-sustainability-report/

Inditex. (2021a). *Inditex annual report.* Retrieved August 22, 2022, from https://static.inditex.com/annual_report_2021/en/documents/annual_report_2021.pdf

Inditex. (2021b). *Sustainability, the basis for transformation.* https://static.inditex.com/annual_report_2021/en/unique-model/sustainability-basis-transformation.html

Inditex. (2022). *Inditex annual report.* https://static.inditex.com/annual_report_2022/pdf/Inditex-group-annual-report-2022.pdf

Jolly, P. (2023). *French paid to forgo fast fashion in favour of fixing.* https://planetark.org/newsroom/news/french-paid-to-forgo-fast-fashion-in-favour-of-fixing

Jung, S., & Jin, B. (2014). A theoretical investigation of slow fashion: Sustainable future of the apparel industry. *International Journal of Consumer Studies, 38*(5), 510–519. https://onlinelibrary.wiley.com/doi/abs/10.1111/ijcs.12127

Kent, S. (2022). *What Europe's energy crisis means for fashion, business of fashion.* https://www.businessoffashion.com/briefings/retail/europe-energy-crisis-retail-fashion-inflation-russia-gas/

Kshetri, N. (2017). *Can blockchain strengthen the Internet of Things?* IT Professional. Data Privacy Concerns.

Kshetri, N. (2018). 1 Blockchain's roles in meeting key supply chain management objectives. *International Journal of Information Management, 39*, 80–89. https://www.researchgate.net/publication/324139564_1_Blockchain's_roles_in_meeting_key_supply_chain_management_objectives

LABFRESH. (2023). *The fashion waste index.* https://labfresh.eu/pages/fashion-waste-index

Loomia. (2023). https://www.loomia.com/

Lopes, J. M., Gomes, S., & Trancoso, T. (2023). The dark side of green marketing: How greenwashing affects circular consumption? *Sustainability, 15*(15), 11649. https://doi.org/10.3390/su151511649

Martine Jarlgaard London. (2023). https://martinejarlgaard.com/

Masi, D., Day, S., & Godsell, J. (2017). Supply chain configurations in the circular economy: A systematic literature review. *Sustainability, 9*(9), 1602. https://doi.org/10.3390/su9091602

McKinsey. (2022). *Scaling textile recycling in Europe – Turning waste into value.* https://www.mckinsey.com/~/media/mckinsey/industries/retail/our%20insights/scaling%20textile%20recycling%20in%20europe%20turning%20waste%20into%20value/scaling%20textile%20recycling%20in%20europe%20turning%20waste%20into%20value.pdf?shouldIndex=false

Meichtry, S., & Strasburg, J. (2022). Fashion industry gets torn by Europe's soaring energy bills. *The Wall Street Journal.* https://www.wsj.com/articles/energy-crisis-europe-fashion-industry-11666103793

Niinimäki, K., Peters, G., Dahlbo, H., Perry, P., Rissanen, T., & Gwilt, A. (2020). The environmental price of fast fashion. *Nature Reviews Earth and Environment, 1*(4), 189–200. https://www.nature.com/articles/s43017-020-0039-9

O'Leary, D. E. (2017). Configuring blockchain architectures for transaction information in blockchain consortiums: The case of accounting and supply chain systems. *Intelligent Systems in Accounting, Finance, and Management, 24*(4), 138–147. https://ideas.repec.org/a/wly/isacfm/v24y2017i4p138-147.html

Orange, R. (2016). *Waste want not: Sweden to give tax breaks for repairs.* https://www.theguardian.com/world/2016/sep/19/waste-not-want-not-sweden-tax-breaks-repairs

Patagonia. (2023). https://www.patagonia.com/stories/worn-wear/

Peters, G., Li, M., & Lenzen, M. (2021). The need to decelerate fast fashion in a hot climate-A global sustainability perspective on the garment industry. *Journal of Cleaner Production, 295*, 126390.

Pissani, N., & Augier, I. (2021). *The future of the fashion industry in a post-COVID-19 world.* https://hbsp.harvard.edu/download?url=%2Fcatalog%2Fsample%2FIM1154-PDF-ENG%2Fcontent&metadata=e30%3D

Provenance. (2023). https://provenance.io/

Saberi, S., Kouhizadeh, M., Sarkis, J., & Shen, L. (2019). Blockchain technology and its relationships to sustainable supply chain management. *International Journal of Production Research, 57*(7), 2117–2135. https://www.researchgate.net/publication/328345129_Blockchain_technology_and_its_relationships_to_sustainable_supply_chain_management

Seares, E. (2022). *An energy crisis in the fashion supply chain*. Drapers. https://www.drapersonline.com/insight/analysis/an-energy-crisis-in-the-fashion-supply-chain

Statista. (2022). *H&M: Number of manufacturing factories 2022, by country*. Retrieved August 23, 2023, from https://www.statista.com/statistics/1099880/number-of-suppliers-of-h-und-m-group-by-region/

Stoll, C., Klaaßen, L., & Gallersdörfer, U. (2019). The carbon footprint of bitcoin. *Joule, 3*(7), 1647–1661. https://www.sciencedirect.com/science/article/pii/S2542435119302557

Sukar, A., & Ahmed, S. (2019). Rise of trade protectionism: the case of US-Sino trade war. *Transnational Corporations Review, 11*(4), 279–289.

Tapscott, D., & Tapscott, A. (2017). *Blockchain revolution: How the technology behind Bitcoin is changing money, business, and the world*. Penguin.

Thomas, D. (2019). *Fashionopolis: the price of fast fashion–and the future of clothes*. Penguin Press.

Tian, F. (2017). A supply chain traceability system for food safety based on HACCP, blockchain, and the Internet of Things. In: *2017 international conference on service systems and service management*. 2017, (pp. 1–6).

Turker, D., & Altuntaş Vural, C. (2014). Sustainable supply chain management in the fast fashion industry: An analysis of corporate reports. *European Management Journal, 32*. https://doi.org/10.1016/j.emj.2014.02.001. https://www.researchgate.net/publication/261673653_Sustainable_supply_chain_management_in_the_fast_fashion_industry_An_analysis_of_corporate_reports

United Nations. (2023a). *HDI*. https://hdr.undp.org/data-center/human-development-index#/indicies/HDI

United Nations. (2023b). *The sustainable development*. https://sdgs.un.org/goals

Weber, I., Xu, X., Riveret, R., Governatori, G., Ponomarev, A., & Mendling, J. (2016). *Untrusted business process monitoring and execution using blockchain*. International conference on business process management. http://www.imweber.de/downloads/UntrustedBusinessProcessMonitoringAndExecutionUsingBlockchain-BPM2016-authors_copy.pdf

World of Meters. (2023). *Water*. https://www.worldometers.info/water/

WTO. (2023). *World trade statistical review*. https://www.wto.org/english/res_e/booksp_e/wtsr_2023_e.pdf

Zohar, A. (2015). Bitcoin: Under the hood. *Communications of the ACM, 58*(9), 104–113. https://dl.acm.org/doi/fullHtml/10.1145/2701411

CHAPTER 7

BIOECONOMY DEVELOPMENT IN THE EUROPEAN UNION: SOCIAL AND ECONOMIC INFLUENCING FACTORS

Emilia Mary Bălan[a], Cristina Georgiana Zeldea[b] and Laura Mariana Cismaș[c]

[a]*Department of Economics, Law and Human-Environment Interaction, The Institute for Advanced Environmental Research, West University of Timisoara, Romania; The Institute for World Economy, Romanian Academy, Romania*
[b]*The Institute for Economic Forecasting, Romanian Academy, Romania*
[c]*Department of Economics and Economic Modelling, Faculty of Economics and Business Administration, West University of Timisoara, Romania*

ABSTRACT

Introduction: *The bioeconomy is a cross-sectoral domain set out in the dedicated European Commission Strategy 2018, which includes those sectors and systems that are based on biological resources.*

Purpose: *An understanding of the bioeconomy's significance within the EU and the variations in its performance across Member States (MS), thereby informing policymakers and supporting strategic planning efforts to foster sustainable economic growth and resource utilisation within the bioeconomy.*

Methodology: *Quantitative analysis: the value added at factor cost (VAFC), turnover (TRN), and the number of employed persons (NEP). The research used the database of the Joint Research Centre of the European Commission (JRC). The period evaluated was 2008–2021 for the 27 EU MS.*

Findings: *The bioeconomy contributes to the generation of community GDP by approximately 5%, and the sectoral analysis shows that agriculture, hunting, and related services and the food industry are the most relevant from an economic and social point of view. Of the EU MS, those in the Western part of the continent have the most significant contribution to the Community bioeconomy for the bioeconomy component sectors that are focused on value creation, efficient use of resources, and environmentally friendly activities.*

Limitation: *The EU's lack of harmonised statistical data causes difficulties making detailed comparisons between the countries with developed bioeconomies.*

Further Research: *Advanced research could help strengthen the scientific basis for creating national bioeconomy strategies. Other indicators, such as indicators related to agricultural practices in an ecological system, could bring new and valuable insights.*

Keywords: Value added; bioeconomy; European Union; social and economic indicators; number of people employed; turnover; sustainable development

JEL Codes: D24; Q57; F15; J21; D22; Q01

INTRODUCTION

In the European Union (EU) and around the world, talks on sustainable development now often focus on the bioeconomy. This article attempts to give a thorough overview of the state of the bioeconomy in the EU, evaluating the difficulties encountered so far, as well as the opportunities ahead. The bioeconomy's economic, social, and environmental facets will be discussed, emphasising its contribution to environmental goals and sustainable economic growth.

The bioeconomy, which involves the sustainable production and transformation of biomass into value-added products, has recently garnered much attention as a potential solution for pressing social and environmental problems. To promote the bioeconomy, the European Commission (EC) has devised the Bioeconomy Strategy, which outlines EU initiatives and seeks to tap into the economic potential of biological resources, while also addressing job creation and reducing dependence on fossil fuels (European Commission-Directorate General for Research and Innovation [EC-DGRI], 2018). The EU's bioeconomy has grown significantly in recent years, as evidenced by adopting national and European policies and initiatives (Bezama et al., 2019). Adopted in 2018, the European Commission's Bioeconomy Strategy establishes challenging goals for the sustainable utilisation of biological resources and encourages innovation within the bioeconomy industry (EC-DGRI, 2018). To further advance the bioeconomy at the national level, many EU members have created their own programmes and initiatives.

The bioeconomy is increasingly recognised as a driver of innovation and economic growth, providing solutions to current challenges such as food security, climate change, and dependence on finite resources (Organisation for Economic Co-operation and Development, 2009). Considerable advancements have been noted in fields including biotechnology, bioenergy, and biorefineries, which are becoming more economically viable and competitive. Nonetheless, several obstacles are in the way of the EU's bioeconomy's growth. Among these include disparities among MS and market fragmentation resulting from the absence of a consistent approach and cohesive strategy at the European level (Purnhagen et al., 2021). Concerns exist over the effects on ecosystems and biodiversity and the dangers of using natural resources excessively. Developing the bioeconomy sector's infrastructure, capabilities for research and innovation, and financing availability for small- and medium-sized businesses involved in the industry are among the other difficulties. Regulations and policies that are ambiguous or contradictory may also make it more challenging to create and perform bioeconomy initiatives effectively.

Social issues have a significant impact on how the EU's bioeconomy develops. The demand for products from the bioeconomy is influenced by several factors, including cultural norms surrounding resource usage, attitudes towards sustainability, and public awareness and acceptance of bio-based products (Peters et al., 2022). Furthermore, implementing bioeconomy policies and initiatives effectively depends on stakeholder participation and engagement in decision-making processes (Rodriguez & Prestvik, 2020). The EU's bioeconomy development is also heavily influenced by economic reasons. Key factors influencing the expansion of the bioeconomy include funding for research and innovation, availability of supportive regulatory frameworks, and financing for initiatives related to the bioeconomy (Bracco et al., 2018). Furthermore, the bioeconomy sectors' competitiveness and capacity to produce goods with added value that satisfies consumer demand are essential for promoting economic growth (García-Barragán et al., 2019).

Despite its obstacles, the EU still has a lot of room for expansion and innovation in the bioeconomy. Regional bioeconomy promotion strategies can be developed effectively and sustainably with the ongoing co-operation of European institutions and MS. Facilitating the shift to an economy based on the bioeconomy would require investments in infrastructure, innovation, research, and promoting a clear and compelling legislative and policy framework. Furthermore, fostering collaborations among public, private, and academic domains is crucial in promoting innovation and advancing the bioeconomy. In the EU, the sustainable use of biological resources to create food, energy, materials, and services is the focus of the developing and strategically important field of bioeconomy. It entails an integrated strategy that uses existing biological resources, fosters economic expansion and innovation, safeguards the environment, and improves social cohesion.

Analytical documentation of the bioeconomy poses a challenge for scientists and researchers, as official statistics report only data regarding traditional sectors without distinguishing activities related to eco-friendly product manufacturing. For instance, producing synthetic textiles versus eco-friendly textiles presents such a challenge. Consequently, indicators related to the bioeconomy are estimated based on compilations from multiple sources (Ronzon et al., 2015) and found in the JRC statistics.

In analysing the socio-economic indicators of the bioeconomy, we divided some of the EU MS into three groups. The countries included in the first group are Bulgaria, the Czech Republic, Hungary, Poland, and Romania. The second group is formed by Croatia, Estonia, Latvia, Lithuania, Slovenia, and Slovakia. We adopted this method to highlight the position of the two groups of countries in Central and Eastern Europe (CEE) compared to the group of developed Western bioeconomy states. To compare with developed countries among the 27 EU members, 5 of the most relevant states concerning the socio-economic indicators of the bioeconomy were grouped: France, Germany, Italy, Spain, and the Netherlands.

The most recent statistical data (Lasarte López et al., 2022) reveal that in 2021, over 17.2 million people were employed in the bioeconomy sectors of the EU-27, mainly in agriculture and the food industry. The bioeconomy generated over 4% of the EU-27 GDP in the same year and contributed more than 8% to the community workforce. The TRN totalled over 2.5 trillion euros, and the value added was around 728 billion euros. With its potential to stimulate economic growth, create jobs, and safeguard the environment, the bioeconomy is one of the fundamental pillars of sustainable development in the EU.

The chapter is organised as follows: Section 2 provides a literature review of bioeconomy analysis in EU countries, offering a concise summary of relevant indicators for this economic sector and outlining the evolution of key bioeconomy indicators in these countries. Section 3 discusses the data and methodology employed, while Section 4 delves into the results obtained. Finally, the study's key findings and implications are outlined in Section 5.

LITERATURE REVIEW

The pandemic caused by the SARS-CoV-2 virus, the war in Ukraine, the energy crisis in the EU, and a possible food shortage have highlighted that economic development models need to be revised, and there is a need to focus on sustainability and environmental aspects. In rethinking economic development models, much greater emphasis must be placed on the significant role of the bioeconomy. This system utilises terrestrial and aquatic biological resources and waste from the food, non-food, and energy sectors. The strong connections between the bioeconomy and the natural production factor (land), the ability to create multidisciplinary value chains integrated into local areas, and the return of essential soil nutrients because of its circular nature make the bioeconomy one pillar of the new Green Deal launched by the EU (Borgomeo et al., 2020).

In the context of climate change and limited natural resources, the efficient and sustainable use of these resources is a present and future goal for the EU member countries. Transitioning from the current economy, based on depletable resources with highly polluting manufacturing technologies, to a circular economy is particularly necessary. The circular economy and bioeconomy involve keeping all goods, materials, and raw materials in the economy until the end of their life cycle. Recycling waste should become a permanent effort for those involved in economic activity. The EU contributes to developing a shock-resistant, competitive, resource-efficient, and low-carbon emission economy through all its institutions. Such a period of transformation represents an opportunity to change the current economy and achieve new benefits, as well as create competitiveness and sustainability for the EU (EC, 2015). In this context, the bioeconomy represents an alternative to fossil resources, obtaining energy from mineral resources, and can support the transition to the circular economy and the circular bioeconomy.

During economic crisis periods, the bioeconomy can act as a buffer against unemployment, as job loss trends in bioeconomy sectors have been significantly reduced compared to other sectors in EU-27 member countries, such as Bulgaria, Greece, Croatia, Lithuania, and Latvia (EC, 2018). Assessing the bioeconomy is helpful as it provides a way to evaluate progress and improvements that can be made in identified areas and forecasts medium- and long-term objectives. A few case studies demonstrate the various strategies used by EU MS to develop their bioeconomies. Vital bioeconomy sectors have emerged due to large expenditures in bioeconomy research and innovation by nations like Finland, Germany, and the Netherlands. These nations have used their robust research institutes, copious biomass resources, and benevolent legislative frameworks to propel the rise of the bioeconomy (Borychowski et al., 2020).

Regardless of the developments, the EU's bioeconomy still faces various difficulties, such as the requirement for stronger policy coherence amongst MS, the incorporation of sustainability concepts into bioeconomy plans, and the establishment of supply chains for bio-based goods. But these difficulties also offer chances for creativity, teamwork, and the development of fresh markets for goods from the bioeconomy (Kardung et al., 2021).

In specialised articles (Bracco et al., 2018; Zeug et al., 2019), the evolution of the bioeconomy is monitored to facilitate stakeholders in identifying trends, patterns, and associations to make future economic and policy decisions.

The economic approach to the bioeconomy in the EU-27 MS is limited, as the products and activities considered components of the bioeconomy vary significantly from one country to another, regarding national priorities and comparative advantages, due to the lack of a standard methodology for calculating the contribution of the bioeconomy to GDP (Bracco et al., 2018). The contribution of the bioeconomy to the economic development of a region or country is determined by relating VA to GDP (Food and Agriculture Organisation [FAO], 2018). This assessment method is generally accepted by analysts (Bracco et al., 2018; Follador et al., 2019), even though this economic approach has some limitations regarding how the contribution is reflected in the financial sphere, as no standard methodology has been established to allow for international comparison of the bioeconomy's contribution to GDP.

Recent literature studies highlight the significance and complexity of the bioeconomy while considering sustainable development within the EU. Subsequent research endeavours ought to concentrate on precisely identifying and tackling specific challenges and assessing the influence of current practices and rules on the progress of the bioeconomy within the EU.

DATA AND METHODS

From a methodological standpoint, the chapter conducts a quantitative data analysis. We use logical means, such as induction, deduction, and comparative analysis, based on the quantitative analysis, to find new insights. To perform the quantitative research, the relevant indicators of the bioeconomy were studied (Borychowski et al., 2020; Bracco et al., 2018; Kardung et al., 2021; Woźniak et al., 2021), respectively: VAFC, TRN, and the number of persons employed (NPE).

The gross domestic product (GDP) is the most important economic indicator at the macroeconomic level, which shows a country's development level. Our study used GDP at market prices (in million euros), with data sourced from Eurostat. The gross domestic product shows the level of economic growth of a country, and according to researchers (Noja Cristea et al., 2019), government spending as a share of GDP has a positive impact on supporting the environment and the development of a sustainable economy. Bioeconomy research from a GDP perspective at the level of states and sectors is necessary and can contribute to the sustainable development of the economy (Gaigalis & Katinas, 2020).

Value-added (VA) represents the value generated by the economic activities of the bioeconomy after deducting material and capital costs. This is a measure of the sector's contribution to the economy. VAFC is an economic indicator that expresses the difference in value between raw materials and the cost of materials used to produce a high-quality product or service compared to the initial one (U.S. Department of Agriculture [USDA], 2021). According to the National Institute of Statistics (The National Institute of Statistics [NIS], 2021) and Eurostat (2021), VAFC is determined by the difference between gross income from operating activities, operating subsidies, and indirect taxes. According to Olaru (2006), gross value added allows the analysis of contributions to an economic sector by commercial companies and the comparison of these profitable enterprises to measure the economic power of the analysed units. VAFC is a component indicator in the calculation of GDP and presents the financial performance of an activity sector (Capasso & Klitkou, 2020; Ronzon & M'Barek, 2018) due to worker specialisation (Goschin et al., 2015) and the degree of technologisation used in the production process.

TRN is the total sum of revenues generated from selling goods and services within the bioeconomy. It is an essential indicator of this sector's size and economic activity. TRN is defined by Eurostat (Eurostat, 2021) as the difference between the value of production and intermediate consumption. Additionally, Ronzon and M'Barek (2018) argue that high TRN is evident in bioeconomy sectors with high percentages of production factors (or high costs of goods and services purchased to complete the manufacturing process). According to the National Institute of Statistics (NIS, 2021), TRN represents the sum of net income from an economic unit's sale of products and services. TRN is a research method used to qualitatively measure the performance of the bioeconomy at the national, regional, and sectoral levels to provide decision-makers with accurate information (Follador et al., 2019). Furthermore, TRN represents the total value of sales of goods and services within an economic unit, including the costs of production factors (Nowak et al., 2021).

The NPE measures the number of people employed in relevant bioeconomy sectors, such as agriculture, the food industry, biotechnology, etc. It is an important indicator of the workforce in this sector. The average number of persons employed is a socio-economic indicator that allows the quantitative analysis of the bioeconomy in the EU-27 countries. The National Institute of Statistics of Romania (INS) defines this indicator as the total number of people working in a company, regardless of the form of remuneration, as well as seconded employees, but who are paid by the respective profit-making unit (NIS, 2022; Ronzon & M'Barek, 2018). According to the researchers (D'Adamo et al., 2020), NPE is a relevant indicator that determines the evolution of a sector's economic performance by measuring a worker's contribution to the growth of TRN and VA.

In our analysis of the socio-economic indicators of the bioeconomy in the EU, we differentiated the countries of the Central and Eastern European Countries (CEECs) into two groups: East 1 consisting of Bulgaria, the Czech Republic, Hungary, Poland, and Romania, and East 2 comprising Croatia, Estonia, Latvia, Lithuania, Slovenia, and Slovakia. We split the CEECs into two groups that matched geographical, historical, and economic characteristics. We adopted this method to highlight CEEC countries' position within the EU, to compare them to the Western European economies, and to highlight where their bioeconomy attributes converge or diverge. The term 'countries of the CEE' is used by the Organization for Economic Co-operation and Development (Organisation for Economic Co-operation and Development, 2009) to refer to the group of states including Albania, Croatia, Slovenia, the Czech Republic, Poland, Lithuania, Estonia, Latvia, Slovakia, Hungary, Romania, and Bulgaria.

Additionally, to facilitate comparison with the developed countries among the 27 EU MS, we grouped five of the most relevant states regarding the socio-economic indicators of the bioeconomy: France, Germany, Italy, Spain, and the Netherlands. These states are usually referred to as the West countries group.

The most recent statistical data (Lasarte López et al., 2022) reveal that, from 2008 to 2021, over 17 million people were employed in the bioeconomy sectors of the EU-27, primarily in agriculture and the food industry. In the same period, the bioeconomy generated over 4% of the EU-27 GDP and contributed to more than 8% of the community's workforce. The total TRN amounted to over 1.9 trillion euros, with a value added of over 500 million euros. At the same time, the number of people employed in the bioeconomy dropped precipitously. We can attribute the decrease mainly to technological progress if we correlate it with the steady increase in VAFC and TRNO. However, the transition to the service-based economy also affected the bioeconomy sectors (Fig. 7.1).

The Statistical classification of economic activities in the European Community (NACE) system does not particularly indicate activities based on the use of bio and non-bio resources, as noted by Rozon and M'Bareck (2018), who sought indicators that can help create an image of the bioeconomy at the level of a nation or regions. However, some activities are more likely to fall under the scope of bioeconomy than others (Table 7.1). In addition, they note that sectors that use raw materials are commonly referred to as 'hybrid'.

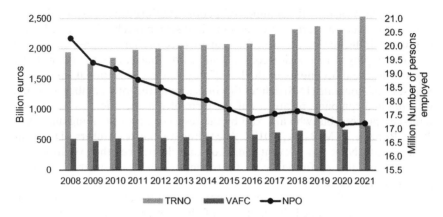

Fig. 7.1. The Evolution of Bioeconomy Indicators in the EU-27 from 2008 to 2021. The Number of Persons Employed, in Millions of People Employed, the TRN and Value Added at Factor Cost, in Billion Euros. *Source*: By the authors, based on Lasarte López et al. (2022).

Table 7.1. NACE Sectors Included in the Bioeconomy.

NACE Code	Bioeconomy Sector
A 01	Agriculture
A 02	Forestry
A03	Fishing and Aquaculture
C10–C12	Food, beverage and tobacco
C13–C15	Bio-based textiles
C16, C31	Wood products and furniture
C17	Paper
C20–C22	Bio-based chemicals, pharmaceuticals, plastics and rubber (excl. biofuels)
C2014, C2059	Liquid biofuels
D3511	Bio-based electricity

Source: Adaptation after Ronzon and M'Barek (2018) and Lasarte López et al. (2022).

RESULTS AND DISCUSSION

Economic Indicators

The Contribution of the Bioeconomy to the Gross Domestic Product

The economic approach to the bioeconomy in the EU-27 MS is limited, as the products and activities considered components of the bioeconomy vary significantly from one country to another in relation to national priorities and comparative advantages (Bracco et al., 2018). The contribution of the bioeconomy to the economic development of a region or country is determined by relating VA to GDP (FAO, 2018). This evaluation method is accepted by analysts (Bracco et al., 2018; Follador et al., 2019), even though this economic approach has some limits in terms of how the contribution is reflected in the economic sphere, as there is no established standard methodology to allow international comparison of the contribution of the bioeconomy to GDP.

In this context, for an overview of the share of the bioeconomy in the generation of the EU-27 GDP in the period 2008–2021, we calculated the importance of the value added and TRN in the bioeconomy. During the period, the share of added value from the bioeconomy in GDP at the EU-27 level had an average of almost 4.7%. Community sectors with significant market shares in GDP are food, beverage, tobacco, and agriculture, which contributed more than 1% to the generation of EU-27 GDP (Table 7.2).

The data analysis revealed that, between 2008 and 2021, the contribution of the bioeconomy to the EU-27 GDP stagnated, as TRN decreased by 0.2 percentage points (pp), while value added increased by only 0.3 pp. This, again, suggests a decrease in agricultural activities due to economic transition. Based on a country-level analysis, Latvia's TRN contributed 8.4 percentage points (pp) to the country's GDP growth throughout the studied period, while the value added was 3.5 pp. According to statistics, Latvia outperformed all other MS by expanding its GDP contribution through the bioeconomy.

According to Eurostat data (2024), in the period 2008–2021, the two groups of East 1 and East 2 states have contributed to the generation of Community GDP with an average of 1.4% East 1 and 0.3% East 2 and West 9%. This reveals how much the Eastern groups lag behind the West. At the same time, it indicates their vast potential to develop and catch on bioeconomy trends. Table AI from the Appendix presents the percentage of TRN and value added from the bioeconomy in national GDP by country across selected country groupings. Looking at the absolute change in 2021, compared to 2008, we see that the VAFC rose significantly. This is suggestive of production processes that become sophisticated and lead to finite products with higher value added.

The differences between the sectoral contribution of TRN in the bioeconomy compared to VA arise because of differences in the cost structure. Purchased goods and services costs are relatively higher in food, beverage, and tobacco

Table 7.2. The Average Contribution of Value Added and TRN per Component Sector of the Bioeconomy to GDP Formation in the EU-27 During the Period 2008–2021.

Indicator/Sector	VAFC	TRN	VAFC	TRN	VAFC	TRN
	Million Euros		% of Bioeconomy		% of GDP	
Bioeconomy	577,583	2,107,433	100	100	4.70	17.14
A01	173,492	405,039	30.04	19.22	1.41	3.29
A02	23,282	46,487	4.03	2.21	0.19	0.38
A03	5,758	12,128	1.00	0.58	0.05	0.10
C10–C12	204,395	1,026,812	35.39	48.72	1.66	8.35
C13–C15	22,704	81,322	3.93	3.86	0.18	0.66
C16 and C31	44,263	162,335	7.66	7.70	0.36	1.32
C17	40,978	170,308	7.09	8.08	0.33	1.38
C20–C22	55,413	171,309	9.59	8.13	0.45	1.39
C2014 and C2059	2,924	13,339	0.51	0.63	0.02	0.11
D3511	4,372	18,354	0.76	0.87	0.04	0.15

Source: Calculated by the authors.

manufacturing (FBT) than in agriculture (Ronzon & M'Barek, 2018). Between 2008 and 2021, the contribution of agriculture to the formation of GDP decreased for the EU-27, from 1.44% to 1.39%, as the tertiary sector (services) expanded, indicating a migration of production factors from agriculture to other sectors of global economies and consumption. Romania and Bulgaria marked the largest decreases in the share of agriculture in GDP by 1.99 pp (from 5.98% in 2008 to 3.99% in 2021) with Romania and, respectively, by 1.47 pp (from 5.42% in 2008 to 3.95% in 2021) with Bulgaria despite their very good agricultural premises and huge untackled potential.

Among the East 1 countries, only Poland contributed to the EU GDP with an average of nearly 1%. In comparison, the other countries in the group recorded shares below 0.5% in their contributions to EU GDP generation. The East 2 group of states has made insignificant bioeconomy contributions to the formation of EU-27 GDP, with shares below 0.5%, which should be interpreted considering the smaller size of their economies. The bioeconomy of the East 1 and East 2 groups of countries has contributed less to the EU GDP because of underdeveloped sectors in regions where value added can be created. These aspects are also reflected in both economic indicators of the bioeconomy, value added, and TRN. As the data reveals, the most significant contribution of bioeconomy sectors to national GDP comes from TRN, as value added has a modest share.

At the level of component sectors of the bioeconomy in the CEECs, quantitative research highlights a significant contribution to the community GDP in terms of TRN and value added compared to other sectors such as A01, A02, A03, C10–C12. The best-performing states in the East 1 group with significant value added from the sectors as a share in the national GDP are as follows: Romania in sectors A01, A02, and A03; Hungary in C20–C22, as well as D3511; Poland in C2014, C2059, C17, and C16, C31; and Bulgaria and the Czech Rep. in C13–C15, respectively, in A02.

On the other hand, the West Group's overall GDP contribution to the EU-27 between 2008 and 2021 was significant, with an average of 11% in TRN and 3% in value added. With an average proportion of almost 3% of the bioeconomy TRN and 0.84% of the value contributed to creating the community GDP, Germany is one of the EU-27's best-performing states.

Value-added Evolution

In terms of VAFC, between 2008 and 2021, the annual average of the indicator for total sectors of the bioeconomy in the EU-27 was almost 600 billion euros, with a clear upward trend from 513.2 billion euros in 2008 (Appendix – Table AII) to 728.3 billion euros in 2021 (+42%). Lithuania and Latvia are the only countries that doubled their value added from the bioeconomy during the analysed period from 2.2 billion euros in 2008 to 4.6 billion euros in 2021, in the case of Lithuania, and from 1.6 billion euros in 2008 to 3.3 billion euros in 2021 in the case of Latvia. Significant contributions came from C10–C12 and A01, with shares in the bioeconomy value added of 35.4% and 30.1%, respectively (Fig. 7.2).

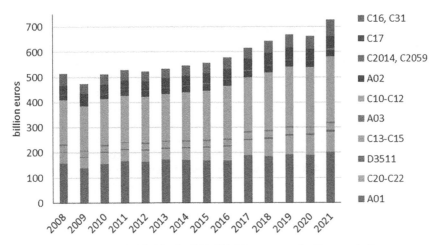

Fig. 7.2. Value Added in the EU-27's Bioeconomy by Economic Sector Components in 2021. *Source*: By the authors, based on Lasarte López et al. (2022).

The quantitative study of statistical data shows that the five countries comprising the West group generated over 64% of the VAFC from the bioeconomy in the EU-27. Significant investments in advanced technologies, as well as the implementation of bioeconomy policies through the application of measures provided in national strategies, have contributed to the evolution of the cross-sectoral domain from values of nearly 333 billion euros in 2008 to over 455 billion euros in the last year of analysis (Table 7.3).

Table 7.3. The Evolution of VAFC Cost from the Bioeconomy in EU-27 Member Countries, Categorised by Group, from 2008 to 2021.

Year/ Country Group	EU-27 (Million Euros)	West (Million Euros)	Share in EU-27 (%)	East 1 (Million Euros)	Share in EU-27 (%)	East 2 (Million Euros)	Share in EU-27 (%)
2008	513,249	333,470	64.97	59,583	11.61	14,219	2.77
2009	474,333	309,544	65.26	51,051	10.76	12,396	2.61
2010	512,978	334,949	65.30	53,443	10.42	13,166	2.57
2011	529,990	344,057	64.92	59,846	11.29	14,185	2.68
2012	523,172	340,151	65.02	56,635	10.83	13,962	2.67
2013	534,200	346,775	64.91	60,264	11.28	14,255	2.67
2014	545,798	352,654	64.61	60,841	11.15	15,253	2.79
2015	556,812	359,163	64.50	60,023	10.78	15,449	2.77
2016	576,765	368,443	63.88	62,522	10.84	15,631	2.71
2017	616,075	397,936	64.59	70,039	11.37	16,437	2.67
2018	644,276	409,497	63.56	73,000	11.33	17,611	2.73
2019	667,684	424,003	63.50	77,273	11.57	18,320	2.74
2020	662,566	415,874	62.77	77,982	11.77	19,134	2.89
2021	728,258	455,331	62.52	85,599	11.75	21,791	2.99

Source: Calculated by the authors.

Moreover, the analysis by groups of states (East 1, East 2, and West) shows that an upward trend in value added in the bioeconomy was observed in both the East 1 and East 2 countries, with each group increasing by 43% in 2021 compared to 2008, reaching 85.6 billion euros and 21.8 billion euros, respectively, while the countries included in the West recorded an overall increase of only 36.5%. This aligns with the convergence laws saying that developing countries have higher growth rates than developed countries. Except for Slovenia, all other states in the East 2 had significant developments in the renewable electricity generation sector (D3511) by attracting European funds made available to MS by the EC. Additionally, another industry that developed in the East 2 countries was that of liquid biofuels (C2014, C2059), which increased eightfold its value added during the period 2008–2021, reaching 105 million euros, with significant growth in Lithuania (111 million euros in 2020, from 10 million euros in 2008). From a sectoral perspective, in the EU-27, A01, A02, A03, and C10–C12 combined account for a 70% share of the value added from the bioeconomy, with the FBT (C10–C12) sector's share being over 35% (Fig. 7.3), representing a value of over 200 million euros.

TRN Dynamics

Between 2008 and 2021, the average TRN generated by the EU-27 bioeconomy was over 2,100 billion euros (Appendix – Table AIII). Germany recorded the highest TRN values, with an average annual TRN of 409 billion euros, followed by France with 348 billion euros and Italy with 300 billion euros. All EU MS registered growth in bioeconomy TRN during the analysed period, but Croatia had the lowest growth rate, only 5.4%. At the other end of the spectrum is Estonia, with an increase in TRN from 4.5 billion euros in 2008 to 9.4 billion euros in 2021 (+108%), Malta (+91%, to 1.5 billion euros), Lithuania (+88%, to 15.4 billion

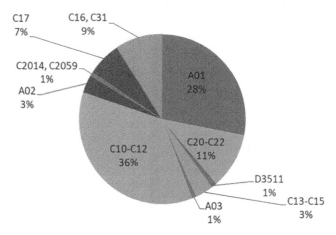

Fig. 7.3. VAFC in the EU-27's Bioeconomy by Economic Sector Components in 2021. *Source*: By the authors, based on Lasarte López et al. (2022).

Bioeconomy Development in the European Union 143

euros), Latvia (+86%, to 10.4 billion euros), Austria (+65%, to 77 billion euros), and Poland, with a 55% increase in TRN to 159 billion euros in 2021.

The West group of states, consisting of Germany, France, Italy, Spain, and the Netherlands, recorded significantly higher TRN values in the bioeconomy among all MS from 2008 to 2021. The cumulative contribution of these five countries to the total TRN of the EU-27 bioeconomy was over 66%. In 2021, the countries in the West group accumulated a TRN value in the bioeconomy of nearly 1,648 billion euros. Germany's average contribution to the EU-27 TRN in the bioeconomy was 19% over the 14 years of analysis, followed in the EU hierarchy by France with a share of 16% and Italy with 14%. Germany's leadership position among EU countries reflects the initiation and implementation of bioeconomy strategies at both national and regional levels. It should also be emphasised that in Germany, the number of patents in the bioeconomy represents 15% of the total number of patents granted annually (Wydra, 2020). France's high TRN value is also determined by a large number of profitable units in the production sector based on ecological products (Ronzon et al., 2017) and the development of industries C10–C12.

Overall, for the countries in the East 1 group, during the analysis period, the average total TRN in the bioeconomy was over 235 million euros, showing a 42% growth from 214 million euros in 2008 to 235 million euros in 2021 (Table 7.4). The share of these states in the total community was approximately 11%, with annual fluctuations ranging between 10% (in 2009) and 12% in 2021. Among the countries included in the East 1 group, between 2008 and 2021, aside from Poland, significant dynamics in bioeconomy TRN were also seen in Bulgaria (+43%, from 12.5 billion euros to 18 billion euros) and Hungary (+33%, from 26.5 billion euros in the first year of analysis to over 35 billion euros in 2021).

Table 7.4. The Dynamics of the Bioeconomy TRN in the EU-27 and by Country Groupings from 2008 to 2021.

Year/ Country Group	EU-27 (Million Euros)	West (Million Euros)	Share in EU-27 (%)	East 1 (Million Euros)	Share in EU-27 (%)	East 2 (Million Euros)	Share in EU-27 (%)
2008	1,937,587	1,292,687	66.72	213,960	11.04	48,287	2.49
2009	1,747,056	1,180,047	67.54	178,838	10.24	41,190	2.36
2010	1,843,610	1,231,482	66.80	193,208	10.48	44,544	2.42
2011	1,973,493	1,314,577	66.61	214,129	10.85	48,699	2.47
2012	1,995,066	1,324,699	66.40	217,367	10.90	49,956	2.50
2013	2,044,424	1,354,369	66.25	224,032	10.96	51,166	2.50
2014	2,051,804	1,356,242	66.10	225,205	10.98	52,835	2.58
2015	2,071,809	1,360,343	65.66	227,549	10.98	53,613	2.59
2016	2,080,027	1,360,863	65.43	229,933	11.05	53,527	2.57
2017	2,235,743	1,470,616	65.78	249,134	11.14	55,875	2.50
2018	2,316,162	1,508,974	65.15	267,260	11.54	59,024	2.55
2019	2,367,922	1,537,956	64.95	277,474	11.72	60,587	2.56
2020	2,309,086	1,501,707	65.03	271,883	11.77	60,950	2.64
2021	2,530,280	1,648,168	65.14	305,821	12.09	71,066	2.81

Source: Calculated by the authors.

Regarding the East 2 group, it generated an average TRN in the bioeconomy of 53.6 million euros, with its share in total EU-27 being only 2.5%. Between 2008 and 2021, Estonia performed well in the renewable electricity production sector (D3511), which in 2021 had a TRN of 330 billion euros (+137 times compared to 2008), in the processing of wood products and furniture manufacturing sector (4 billion euros in 2021, triple the value compared to the first year of the analysed period), and in bio-based chemicals, pharmaceuticals, plastics, and rubber sectors (+89%, reaching 55 million euros in 2021).

Between 2008 and 2021, the sector that recorded a significant TRN in the bioeconomy in the EU-27 is that of C10, C11, and C12, with over 1 billion euros (49% of the total bioeconomy). After the FBT manufacturing (C10–C12) sectors, agriculture holds the largest share of TRN in the bioeconomy, with an average value of 405 billion euros. Over the 14 years analysed, the TRN value in EU-27 FBT manufacturing increased by 27%, from 932 million euros in 2008 to over 1.2 billion euros in 2021, and agriculture by 26%, from 375 million euros in 2008 to over 473 billion euros in 2021 (19% of the total bioeconomy). However, the cumulative share of FBT manufacturing and agriculture in the bioeconomy decreased moderately, with a maximum of 69.5% in 2013 to 65.5% in 2021. Fluctuations in EU-27 FBT manufacturing and agriculture TRN are due to fluctuations in agricultural commodity and food prices. In 2021, the TRN value of EU FBT sectors stood at 1.1 billion euros (47% of the total bioeconomy) and agriculture at 473 billion euros, representing 19% of the bioeconomy (Fig. 7.4).

The EU-27 FBT manufacturing sector's rise in TRN between 2008 and 2021 was contributed to by the following: Austria (+62%, to 29 billion euros), Estonia (+55%, to 2.3 billion euros), Lithuania (+50%, to 5 billion euros), Poland (+48%, to 78 billion euros), Bulgaria (47%, to 7.7 billion euros), and Romania (43%, to 18 billion euros). In the same analysed period, the increase in the TRN of the EU-27 agriculture was supported by the contribution of Latvia (+73%, reaching

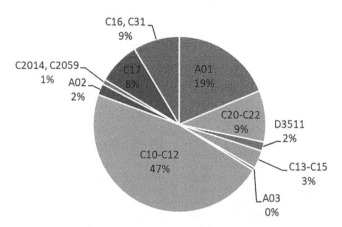

Fig. 7.4. The Sector TRN of the Bioeconomy of the EU-27 in 2021.
Source: By the authors, based on Lasarte López et al. (2022).

2 billion euros), Estonia (+68%, reaching 1.1 billion euros), Ireland (+59%, reaching 10.3 billion euros), the Czech Republic (+56%, reaching 10 billion euros), and Lithuania (+52%, reaching 3.8 billion euros). The most drastic decreases in agricultural TRN between 2008 and 2019 were recorded in Croatia (−10%, reaching 2.9 billion euros), Malta (−9%, reaching 128 million euros), and Romania (−3%, reaching 18.5 billion euros).

Social Indicator

The social dimension of the bioeconomy is determined by the volume of labour employed in its component sectors (Liobikiene et al., 2019), as well as its share within each respective sector. Additionally, the labour force measures the impact of creating new jobs on developing a state's economy (Capasso & Klitkou, 2020). It contributes to calculating its proportion in each sector to compare the financial dynamics of the field (Jander et al., 2020).

In this regard, the subsection examines the evolution of the labour workforce in the bioeconomy by analysing the indicator of the number of persons employed according to Lasarte López et al. (2022).

Between 2008 and 2021, the average NPE in the component sectors of the bioeconomy in the EU-27 was 18.1 million (Appendix – Table AIV), representing 10% of the total employed population in the community economy. In the EU-27 bioeconomy, the trend of NPE marked a decrease during the analysed period by over 15%, to 17.2 million persons in the year 2021 (Table 7.5). Romania, Poland, and Germany had the highest NPE in the bioeconomy from 2008 to 2021, with over two million persons in each mentioned country. Only Romania had an

Table 7.5. The Number of People Employed in the Bioeconomy of the 27 EU MS by Country Groups Between 2008 and 2021.

Year/ Country Group	EU-27 (Thousands of Persons Employed)	West (Thousands of Persons Employed)	Share in EU-27 (%)	East 1 (Thousands of Persons Employed)	Share in EU-27 (%)	East 2 (Thousands of Persons Employed)	Share in EU-27 (%)
2008	20,267	7,792	38.45	8,221	40.56	1,108	5.47
2009	19,388	7,441	38.38	7,873	40.61	1,043	5.38
2010	19,159	7,485	39.07	7,674	40.05	1,036	5.41
2011	18,767	7,403	39.45	7,387	39.36	1,026	5.47
2012	18,494	7,282	39.37	7,372	39.86	975	5.27
2013	18,144	7,202	39.70	7,179	39.57	939	5.18
2014	18,027	7,166	39.75	7,091	39.33	937	5.20
2015	17,687	7,129	40.30	6,860	38.78	942	5.33
2016	17,385	7,297	41.97	6,485	37.30	899	5.17
2017	17,530	7,423	42.34	6,492	37.04	877	5.00
2018	17,626	7,602	43.13	6,422	36.43	861	4.89
2019	17,460	7,641	43.76	6,216	35.60	853	4.88
2020	17,147	7,499	43.73	6,138	35.79	841	4.91
2021	17,188	7,569	44.04	6,073	35.33	851	4.95

Source: Calculated by the authors.

average of nearly three million people employed in the bioeconomy sector. In 2021, compared to 2008, the most drastic decreases in the NEP in the bioeconomy were in Croatia (−38.6%), Romania (−35.5%), Portugal (−27.3%), Bulgaria (−25.2%), and Finland (−23.4%).

In the analysis of state groups, namely, East 1, East 2, and West, it is observed that many employed persons in the bioeconomy, calculated as a proportion of the total employed population, are located in the East 1 states, with an average percentage during the period 2008–2021 of 38%. The other two groups recorded average proportions of 12.3% in the case of East 2 and 6.6% in the West countries. These aspects demonstrate a concentration of the employed population in the bioeconomy in the CEECs due to a massive consolidation of employed persons in the agricultural sectors. All CEECs have recorded decreases in the dynamics of employed persons in the bioeconomy during the analysed period, ranging from 38.6% in Croatia to 2.6% in Hungary. The analysis of the trend in the NEP in the bioeconomy across the three groups of states shows a relatively stagnant trend in the West countries (−4%). In contrast, the East 1 and East 2 states have experienced a downward trend of 26% and 17%, respectively.

In the EU-27, agriculture (A01) contributes a very large NEP among all component sectors of the bioeconomy (Cismaş & Bălan, 2022), accounting for over 50% in 2021, which represented 4.6% of the total employed population at the community level. In the FBT industry (C10–C12), 27% of the total NEP in the bioeconomy were engaged, or 2.5 of the employed population in all economic sectors across the EU-27, while in the other component sectors of the bioeconomy, the proportion was below 10% in 2021 (Fig. 7.5).

The data regarding the evolution of bioeconomy indicators in the EU-27 show that Romania and Poland have the highest number of workers (Cirstea, 2020). The very high proportion of bioeconomy employees in Romania is supported by the concentration of the workforce in agriculture; 83% of bioeconomy

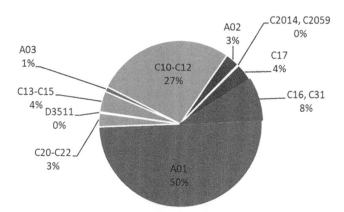

Fig. 7.5. The Share of the Number of Persons Employed in the Bioeconomy of the EU-27, by Component Economic Sectors, in 2021. *Source*: By the authors, based on Lasarte López et al. (2022).

employees came from the agricultural sector (Nowak et al., 2021), but also in Bulgaria, Greece, and Poland, the percentages are significant at 75%, 73%, and 66%, respectively. Throughout the analysed period (2008–2021), the downward trend of the share of employed persons in agriculture in bioeconomy sectors as a whole is evident in most MS, with exceptions only being Italy, Sweden, Denmark, and the Czech Republic.

Sectoral analysis within the EU-27 bioeconomy highlights an increase in the NEP in the renewable energy production sector (D3511). Many MS have seen a rise in the number of employees in this field, notably in Bulgaria, Estonia, Romania, Croatia, Latvia, and Lithuania. These mentioned countries are part of the later stages of EU-27 enlargement and are in the process of developing sustainable economic sectors. Following their accession to the community space, they have benefitted from significant investments through European funds made available to MS by the EC. It is noteworthy that in the East 2 group of states, significant proportions of employed persons in the bioeconomy are reported in forestry sectors (A02), with a combined average percentage of 17%, which is over eight times larger than the EU-27 average. The East 1 group average is supported by a 50% proportion of employed persons in the bioeconomy in the agriculture sector and over 35% in the forestry sector.

In 2021, the NEP in the agricultural sector of the EU-27 decreased by 24% compared to 2008, to 8.6 million people, due to reductions in Croatia (-50%), Romania (-38%), Portugal (-37%), Estonia (-36%), and Lithuania (-33%). Romania, Poland, Italy, France, and Spain had the highest proportion of people employed in agriculture within the bioeconomy, as an average over the 14 years analysed. The country proportions were as follows: Romania 23%, Poland 17%, Italy 8.7%, France, and Spain 7.2% each.

In nominal terms, in 2021, from the group of East 1 states, the greatest number of persons employed in agriculture were in Romania (1.8 million, representing 43.5% of the average of the group states), Poland (1.5 million – 36%), and Bulgaria (536 thousand – 13.2%). In the agriculture of East 2 countries, in the last year of analysis (2021), a significant NEP was recorded in Croatia (91.5 thousand people, representing 28.6% of the average of the group states), Lithuania (64.8 thousand people – 20%), Slovenia (63 thousand people – 19.6%), and Slovakia (44 thousand people – 14%).

CONCLUSIONS

In this study, we sought to assess the development of the bioeconomy and the socio-economic performance of EU MS from this perspective. Our findings revealed varying degrees of development, with certain countries notably surpassing the regional average.

Examining the socio-economic indicators within the bioeconomy, we categorised EU MS into three groups. The first group comprised Bulgaria, the Czech Republic, Hungary, Poland, and Romania. The second group consisted of Croatia, Estonia, Latvia, Lithuania, Slovenia, and Slovakia. For comparison with the developed nations, we grouped five of the most relevant states concerning the socio-economic indicators of the bioeconomy: France, Germany, Italy, Spain, and the Netherlands. We divided the CEECs into two groups based on similar geographical, historical, and economic features. This approach was chosen to underscore the position of CEEC countries within the EU, facilitating comparisons with Western European economies. Additionally, it helps highlight areas of convergence and divergence in their bioeconomy attributes. To conduct quantitative research, we analysed key indicators of the bioeconomy, namely, VAFC, TRN, and the number of persons employed (NPE).

A complicated structure of social and economic forces interacts to shape the growth of the bioeconomy in the EU. The analysis highlights notable disparities in terms of development between the Eastern and Western groups. Yet, it also unveils the significant potential for the Eastern groups to advance and align with emerging bioeconomy trends.

Over time, TRN and value added within the EU's bioeconomy have shown consistent growth while employment figures have declined. Initially, this decline can be largely attributed to technological advancements. As production processes became increasingly sophisticated, they yielded finite products with greater value added. However, the shift towards a service-based economy also affected the bioeconomy sectors. This trend is supported by the decline in the agriculture sector's contribution to the GDP of the EU-27 from 2008 to 2021, coinciding with the expansion of the tertiary sector. This suggests a shift of production factors from agriculture to other sectors within global economies and different consumption patterns. Notably, Romania, and Bulgaria experienced the most significant decreases in the share of agriculture in GDP.

Overall, this study's key finding emphasises the favourable agricultural conditions in CEECs and their substantial, yet untapped, potential to emerge as bioeconomy hubs within the EU.

These findings offer valuable insights for policymakers aiming to establish a robust scientific basis for formulating bioeconomy strategies. They can also aid in assessing and enhancing socio-economic conditions within the bioeconomy sectors at the national level. Policymakers, companies, and stakeholders may collaborate to achieve the bioeconomy's potential to promote sustainable development and economic growth in the EU by understanding and solving these factors.

Subsequent research endeavours could delve into the underlying factors driving the resemblances and disparities among countries. Advanced studies in this area could bolster the scientific underpinnings for crafting national bioeconomy strategies. Exploring additional indicators, such as those pertaining to agricultural practices within ecological systems, has the potential to yield fresh and valuable insights.

REFERENCES

Bezama, A., Ingrao, C., O'Keeffe, S., & Thrän, D. (2019). Resources, collaborators, and neighbours: The three-pronged challenge in implementing bioeconomy regions. *Sustainability*, *11*(24), 7235. https://doi.org/10.3390/su11247235

Borgomeo, L., Campanini, L., Fumagalli, S., Sangalli, I., Trenti, S., & Vitulano, M. R. (2020). *Bioeconomy in Europe. No. 6 Report*. Intesa Sanpaolo. Research Department. https://rebrand.ly/90347

Borychowski, M., Stępień, S., Polcyn, J., Tošović-Stevanović, A., Ćalović, D., Lalić, G., & Žuža, M. (2020). Socio-economic determinants of small family farms' resilience in selected Central and Eastern European countries. *Sustainability*, *12*(24), 10362. https://doi.org/10.3390/su122410362

Bracco, S., Calicioglu, O., Juan, M. G. S., & Flammini, A. (2018). Assessing the contribution of bioeconomy to the total economy: A review of national frameworks. *Sustainability (Switzerland)*, *10*(6), 1698. https://doi.org/10.3390/su10061698

Capasso, M., & Klitkou, A. (2020). Socio-economic indicators to monitor Norway's bioeconomy in transition. *Sustainability*, *12*(8), 3173. https://doi.org/10.3390/su12083173

Cirstea, A. (2020). Measuring Romania's bioeconomy in the context of EU development strategy. *Annals of the 'Constantin Brâncuși' University of Târgu Jiu, Economy Series*, *5*, 247–256. https://rebrand.ly/xl8kbte

Cismaș, L. M., & Bălan, E. M. (2022). Agriculture's contribution to the growth of Romanian bioeconomy: A regional approach. *Eastern European Economics*, *61*(4), 403–419. https://doi.org/10.1080/00128775.2022.2058552

D'Adamo, I., Falcone, P. M., & Morone, P. (2020). A new socio-economic indicator to measure the performance of bioeconomy sectors in Europe. *Ecological Economics*, *176*, 106724. https://doi.org/10.1016/j.ecolecon.2020.106724

European Commission. (2015). *Sustainable agriculture, forestry and fisheries in the bioeconomy – A challenge for Europe*. European Commission. https://doi.org/10.2777/179843

European Commission. Directorate-General for Research and Innovation. (2018). *A sustainable bioeconomy for Europe: strengthening the connection between economy, society and the environment: updated bioeconomy strategy*. Publications Office. https://data.europa.eu/doi/10.2777/792130

Eurostat. (2021). *Annual national accounts (nama10). Eurostat metadata*. Eurostat. https://rebrand.ly/gninqdp

Follador, M., Philippidis, G., Davis, J., & Soares Filho, B. (2019). *Assessing the impacts of the EU bioeconomy on third countries*. Publications Office of the European Union, Luxembourg. ISBN 978-92-76-09820-1, JRC117364 Retrieved from http://doi.org/10.2760/304776.

Food and Agriculture Organisation. (2018). *Assessing the contribution of bioeconomy to countries' economy*. www.fao.org/publicationsC

Gaigalis, V., & Katinas, V. (2020). Analysis of the renewable energy implementation and prediction prospects in compliance with the EU policy: A case of Lithuania. *Renewable Energy*, *151*, 1016–1027. https://doi.org/10.1016/j.renene.2019.11.091

García-Barragán, J. F., Eyckmans, J., & Rousseau, S. (2019). Defining and measuring the circular economy: A mathematical approach. *Ecological Economics*, *157*, 369–372. https://doi.org/10.1016/j.ecolecon.2018.12.003

Goschin, Z., Constantin, D., Roman, M., & Ileanu, B. (2015). Regional specialisation and geographic concentration of industries in Romania. *South-Eastern Europe Journal of Economics*, *7*(1) 99–113. https://rebrand.ly/zxfj0bp

Jander, W., Wydra, S., Wackerbauer, J., Grundmann, P., & Piotrowski, S. (2020). Monitoring bioeconomy transitions with economic–environmental and innovation indicators: addressing data gaps in the short term. *Sustainability*, *12*(11), 4683.

Kardung, M., Cingiz, K., Costenoble, O., Delahaye, R., Heijman, W., Lovrić, M., van Leeuwen, M., M'Barek, R., van Meijl, H., Piotrowski, S., Ronzon, T., Sauer, J., Verhoog, D., Verkerk, P. J., Vrachioli, M., Wesseler, J. H. H., & Zhu, B. X. (2021). Development of the circular bioeconomy: Drivers and indicators. *Sustainability*, *13*(1), 413. https://doi.org/10.3390/su13010413

Lasarte López, J., Piotrowski, S., M'barek, R., Carus, M., & Tamošiūnas, S. (2022). *Jobs and wealth in the EU bioeconomy/JRC-Bioeconomics*. European Commission, Joint Research Centre (JRC). http://data.europa.eu/89h/7d7d5481-2d02-4b36-8e79-697b04fa4278

Liobikiene, G., Balezentis, T., Streimikiene, D., & Chen, X. (2019). Evaluation of bioeconomy in the context of strong sustainability. *Sustainable Development*, *27*(5), 955–964. https://doi.org/10.1002/sd.1984

Noja, G., Cristea, M., Sirghi, N., Hațegan, C. D., & D'Anselmi, P. (2019). Promoting good public governance and environmental support for sustainable economic development. *International Journal of Environmental Research and Public Health*, *16*(24), 4940. https://doi.org/10.3390/ijerph16244940

Nowak, A., Kobiałka, A., & Krukowski, A. (2021). Significance of agriculture for bioeconomy in the member states of the European Union. *Sustainability*, *13*(16), 8709. https://doi.org/10.3390/su13168709

Olaru, G. D. (2006). Enterprise's performance measured by intermediary balance of administration. *Annales Universitatis Apulensis Series Oeconomica*, *8*(2), 43. https://rebrand.ly/vehao3u

Organisation for Economic Co-operation and Development. (2009). *The bioeconomy to 2030: Designing a policy agenda*. Main Findings and Policy Conclusions. OECD Publishing 2009. https://doi.org/10.1787/9789264056886-en

Peters, M. A., Jandrić, P., & Hayes, S. (2022). Biodigital technologies and the bioeconomy: The global new green deal? *Educational Philosophy and Theory*, *55*(3), 251–260. https://doi.org/10.1080/00131857.2020.1861938

Purnhagen, K. P., Clemens, S., Eriksson, D., Fresco, L. O., Tosun, J., Qaim, M., Visser, R. G. F., Weber, A. P. M., Wesseler, J. H. H., & Zilberman, D. (2021). Europe's farm to fork strategy and its commitment to biotechnology and organic farming: Conflicting or complementary goals?. *Trends in Plant Science*, *26*(6), 600–606. https://doi.org/10.1016/j.tplants.2021.03.012

Rodriguez, D. G. P., & Prestvik, A. S. (2020). The need for stakeholder engagement and participative governance to promote bioeconomy. In *The* U. S., Nagothu (Ed.), *The bioeconomy approach: constraints and opportunities for sustainable development*. (pp. 211–236). Routledge. https://doi.org/10.4324/9780429320651

Ronzon, T., Lusser, M., Klinkenberg, M., Landa, L., Sanchez Lopez, J., M'Barek, R., Hadjamu, G., Belward, A., Camia, A., Giuntoli, J., Cristobal, J., Parisi, C., Ferrari, E., Marelli, L., Torres de Matos, C., Gomez Barbero, M., & Rodriguez Cerezo, E. (2017). *Bioeconomy report 2016*. JRC Scientific and Policy Report. EUR 28468 EN. https://doi.org/10.22004/ag.econ.276283

Ronzon, T., & M'Barek, R. (2018). Socioeconomic indicators to monitor the EU's bioeconomy in transition. *Sustainability*, *10*(6), 1745. https://doi.org/10.3390/su10061745

Ronzon, T., Santini, F., & M'Barek, R. (2015). JRC science for policy report – The bioeconomy in numbers, facts and figures on biomass, turnover and employment. 2012, 2011–2014. https://ec.europa.eu/jrc/sites/jrcsh/files/JRC97789 Factsheet_Bioeconomy_final.pdf

The National Institute of Statistics. (2022). *Metadata*. https://rebrand.ly/70v2pbk

U.S. Department of Agriculture. (2021). USDA Value-added Ag Definition. Rural Business Development. https://rebrand.ly/a5693

Woźniak, E., Tyczewska, A., & Twardowski, T. (2021). Bioeconomy development factors in the European Union and Poland. *New Biotechnology*, *60*, 2–8. https://doi.org/10.1016/j.nbt.2020.07.004

Wydra, S. (2020). Measuring innovation in the bioeconomy – Conceptual discussion and empirical experiences. *Technology in Society*, *61*, 101242. https://doi.org/10.1016/j.techsoc.2020.101242

Zeug, W., Bezama, A., Moesenfechtel, U., Jähkel, A., & Thrän, D. (2019). Stakeholders' interests and perceptions of bioeconomy monitoring using a sustainable development goal framework. *Sustainability*, *11*(6), 1511. https://doi.org/10.3390/su11061511

APPENDIX

Table A1. The Share of TRN and Value Added from the Bioeconomy in GDP in East 1, East 2, and West Country Groups (%).

	Country	Indicator/Year	2008	2009	2010	2011	2012	2013	2014	2015	2016	2017	2018	2019	2020	2021
East 1	Bulgaria	TRN	33.74	29.36	29.49	29.84	29.31	30.56	30.11	28.99	28.08	27.57	26.13	24.41	24.08	25.32
		VAFC	9.62	7.68	7.75	8.13	7.99	8.19	8.39	7.99	8.13	7.96	7.33	7.06	7.47	7.72
	Czech Rep.	TRN	20.56	19.20	18.69	20.07	20.63	20.61	20.34	19.31	18.19	17.73	17.32	16.94	17.20	17.83
		VAFC	5.25	5.08	4.69	5.03	5.34	5.36	5.46	5.21	5.15	5.02	4.88	4.79	5.00	4.90
	Hungary	TRN	24.42	23.65	23.17	25.47	26.44	26.27	25.25	24.57	24.65	23.62	22.79	21.79	22.75	23.00
		VAFC	6.70	6.52	6.41	7.35	7.19	7.24	7.30	7.19	7.35	7.24	7.01	6.71	7.03	7.08
	Poland	TRN	27.95	26.87	27.18	28.51	29.33	29.81	29.04	27.47	27.96	28.19	28.52	27.91	28.01	27.54
		VAFC	7.19	7.22	7.23	7.53	7.03	7.43	7.16	6.66	6.93	7.35	6.96	6.93	7.29	6.87
	Romania	TRN	26.82	25.20	24.71	25.32	22.89	24.97	23.46	22.30	21.83	20.89	20.73	19.48	18.69	21.19
		VAFC	9.50	9.18	8.36	8.87	7.38	8.39	7.82	6.74	6.84	6.79	6.94	6.86	6.60	7.43
East 2	Croatia	TRN	24.05	23.61	23.39	24.16	24.43	23.68	23.02	23.49	22.79	22.53	21.97	20.68	21.22	21.08
		VAFC	8.10	8.21	7.72	7.79	7.35	7.49	6.97	6.95	7.10	6.89	7.02	7.14	7.38	7.47
	Estonia	TRN	27.16	24.88	28.83	29.68	28.97	29.65	29.93	30.29	27.92	27.54	27.19	26.66	27.53	30.25
		VAFC	7.69	6.88	7.95	8.31	7.87	7.66	8.16	7.94	7.11	7.11	6.80	6.73	7.04	7.37
	Latvia	TRN	22.69	23.61	29.52	30.14	29.37	30.04	29.54	27.99	27.33	26.16	26.68	26.07	28.01	31.09
		VAFC	6.57	6.72	8.89	7.91	7.59	7.43	7.92	7.91	7.71	7.66	7.81	7.91	8.87	10.02
	Lithuania	TRN	25.04	24.80	26.46	28.76	28.90	29.15	29.14	28.40	27.28	26.93	25.65	25.44	25.95	27.23
		VAFC	6.61	6.55	6.95	7.39	7.69	7.39	7.53	7.96	7.65	7.90	7.33	7.43	8.34	8.22
	Slovakia	TRN	16.82	14.82	15.15	15.28	14.99	15.05	15.89	15.10	14.63	14.25	14.22	13.54	14.00	14.60
		VAFC	4.57	4.15	4.19	4.49	4.07	4.22	4.87	4.29	4.31	4.11	4.18	3.72	3.86	4.06
	Slovenia	TRN	19.05	17.25	17.70	18.40	18.36	18.50	18.38	18.34	17.81	17.48	17.71	17.28	17.46	17.08
		VAFC	5.85	5.46	5.57	5.80	5.58	5.61	5.86	5.92	5.65	5.59	6.02	5.95	6.44	5.88

(Continued)

Table AI. (Continued)

	Country	Indicator/Year	2008	2009	2010	2011	2012	2013	2014	2015	2016	2017	2018	2019	2020	2021
West	France	TRN	16.37	15.56	15.47	15.86	16.09	15.96	15.96	15.49	14.84	16.83	16.02	15.59	16.11	16.22
		VAFC	4.04	3.85	4.15	4.15	4.13	3.92	4.05	4.08	3.93	4.44	4.30	4.20	4.38	4.45
	Germany	TRN	14.24	13.59	13.90	14.36	14.35	14.45	13.89	13.16	12.80	12.86	13.27	13.36	13.54	13.63
		VAFC	3.46	3.34	3.47	3.49	3.35	3.43	3.37	3.15	3.22	3.31	3.44	3.62	3.64	3.74
	Italy	TRN	17.87	16.77	17.08	17.84	17.69	18.29	17.95	17.93	17.48	18.18	18.18	18.23	18.33	18.95
		VAFC	4.76	4.62	4.85	4.93	4.91	5.18	5.08	5.20	5.13	5.26	5.23	5.30	5.40	5.44
	Spain	TRN	17.57	16.86	16.80	17.64	17.86	18.21	17.95	17.57	17.57	17.63	16.97	16.27	16.78	16.52
		VAFC	4.01	4.04	4.23	4.01	4.15	4.20	4.12	4.11	4.24	4.29	4.00	4.05	4.16	3.99
	The Netherlands	TRN	16.37	15.56	15.47	15.86	16.09	15.96	15.96	15.49	14.84	16.83	16.02	15.59	16.11	16.22
		VAFC	4.04	3.85	4.15	4.15	4.13	3.92	4.05	4.08	3.93	4.44	4.30	4.20	4.38	4.45

Source: Calculated by the authors.

Table AII. The Value Added at Factors Cost (VAFC) in the Bioeconomy of the EU-27 States Between 2008 and 2021 (Billion Euros).

VAFC	2008	2009	2010	2011	2012	2013	2014	2015	2016	2017	2018	2019	2020	2021	Average
EU	513.2	474.3	513.0	530.0	523.2	534.2	545.8	556.8	576.8	616.1	644.3	667.7	662.6	728.3	577.6
Austria	13.9	13.0	14.3	15.2	15.3	15.0	15.4	16.0	16.9	17.6	18.8	19.2	19.2	21.6	16.5
Belgium	14.2	15.0	15.2	14.6	15.8	16.6	16.9	17.2	18.7	18.7	21.0	23.5	23.8	25.1	18.3
Bulgaria	3.6	2.9	3.0	3.4	3.4	3.4	3.6	3.7	4.0	4.2	4.1	4.3	4.6	5.5	3.8
Croatia	3.9	3.7	3.5	3.6	3.3	3.3	3.1	3.2	3.4	3.5	3.7	4.0	3.7	4.4	3.6
Cyprus	1.0	1.0	1.0	0.9	0.9	0.8	0.8	0.8	0.9	0.9	0.9	1.0	1.0	1.0	0.9
Czechia	8.5	7.6	7.4	8.3	8.7	8.6	8.6	8.8	9.1	9.8	10.3	10.8	10.8	11.7	9.2
Denmark	10.6	9.9	11.5	11.6	13.1	12.5	13.6	13.3	13.7	15.4	14.7	16.7	17.4	17.1	13.7
Estonia	1.3	1.0	1.2	1.4	1.4	1.4	1.6	1.6	1.5	1.7	1.8	1.9	1.9	2.3	1.6
Finland	11.7	10.2	12.5	12.2	12.2	12.6	13.0	13.0	13.3	14.0	14.8	14.3	13.9	15.7	13.1
France	80.5	74.5	82.7	85.4	86.3	83.0	87.1	89.7	87.8	102.1	101.7	102.4	101.6	111.4	91.2
Germany	88.2	81.6	88.9	94.1	92.1	96.3	98.8	95.3	101.1	108.2	115.8	125.7	123.8	135.4	103.2
Greece	12.6	13.1	12.8	11.6	11.2	10.3	10.6	11.1	10.4	11.5	11.2	11.8	11.5	11.8	11.5
Hungary	7.3	6.2	6.4	7.5	7.2	7.4	7.8	8.1	8.5	9.2	9.5	9.8	9.7	10.9	8.3
Ireland	11.8	10.6	13.4	14.1	13.4	14.7	16.3	16.6	17.0	17.9	17.6	16.8	17.7	20.1	15.6
Italy	78.0	72.8	78.1	81.3	79.7	83.5	82.7	86.0	87.1	91.3	92.6	95.2	89.7	99.1	85.5
Latvia	1.6	1.3	1.6	1.6	1.7	1.7	1.9	1.9	2.0	2.1	2.3	2.4	2.7	3.3	2.0
Lithuania	2.2	1.8	1.9	2.3	2.6	2.6	2.8	3.0	3.0	3.3	3.3	3.6	4.2	4.6	2.9
Luxembourg	0.4	0.4	0.4	0.4	0.5	0.4	0.5	0.5	0.5	0.5	0.5	0.5	0.5	0.5	0.5
Malta	0.2	0.2	0.2	0.2	0.2	0.3	0.3	0.3	0.3	0.3	0.3	0.3	0.3	0.4	0.3
The Netherlands	26.0	25.2	27.0	26.1	27.1	27.7	27.6	28.4	30.0	31.7	31.0	33.0	33.1	34.7	29.2
Poland	26.3	22.9	26.0	28.4	27.1	28.9	29.1	28.6	29.4	34.3	34.7	36.9	38.3	39.6	30.7
Portugal	9.8	9.4	9.9	9.3	9.2	9.7	10.0	10.7	11.0	11.6	12.1	12.1	12.0	13.4	10.7
Romania	13.9	11.5	10.7	12.3	10.3	12.0	11.8	10.8	11.5	12.7	14.3	15.4	14.5	18.0	12.8
Slovakia	3.0	2.7	2.9	3.2	3.0	3.1	3.7	3.4	3.5	3.5	3.8	3.5	3.6	4.1	3.4
Slovenia	2.2	2.0	2.0	2.1	2.0	2.0	2.2	2.3	2.3	2.4	2.8	2.9	3.0	3.1	2.4
Spain	60.8	55.4	58.2	57.2	54.9	56.2	56.4	59.8	62.5	64.7	68.4	67.7	67.7	74.6	61.7
Sweden	18.8	16.7	20.2	21.1	20.5	20.2	20.5	21.0	20.8	20.9	22.9	22.5	22.3	26.0	21.0
Average	**19.0**	**17.5**	**19.0**	**19.6**	**19.4**	**19.8**	**20.2**	**20.6**	**21.1**	**22.7**	**23.5**	**24.4**	**24.2**	**26.5**	

Source: Calculated by the authors.

Table AIII. The TRN Generated by the Bioeconomy in the EU-27 States During the Period 2008–2021 (Billion Euros).

TRN	2008	2009	2010	2011	2012	2013	2014	2015	2016	2017	2018	2019	2020	2021	Average
EU	1,937.6	1,747.1	1,843.6	1,973.5	1,995.1	2,044.4	2,051.8	2,071.8	2,080.0	2,235.7	2,316.2	2,367.9	2,309.1	2,530.3	2,107.4
Austria	46.5	42.6	46.5	50.6	52.2	53.0	53.2	54.1	54.9	57.0	66.0	67.2	66.2	76.8	56.2
Belgium	65.8	64.8	66.2	71.3	74.0	77.4	77.5	78.8	81.0	87.4	83.5	90.6	92.3	100.9	79.4
Bulgaria	12.6	11.0	11.3	12.4	12.4	12.9	13.0	13.3	13.7	14.5	14.7	15.0	14.8	18.0	13.5
Croatia	11.7	10.8	10.7	11.0	10.9	10.5	10.2	10.7	10.8	11.3	11.6	11.5	10.7	12.3	11.1
Cyprus	2.8	2.7	2.7	2.7	2.6	2.4	2.4	2.5	2.6	2.7	2.9	3.0	2.9	3.2	2.7
Czechia	33.3	28.7	29.5	33.2	33.5	32.9	32.1	32.7	32.3	34.4	36.5	38.2	37.1	42.5	34.1
Denmark	43.6	39.5	42.3	44.5	48.0	49.8	52.0	52.1	52.2	55.5	56.1	57.5	59.7	62.0	51.1
Estonia	4.5	3.5	4.2	5.0	5.2	5.6	6.0	6.3	6.1	6.6	7.0	7.5	7.6	9.4	6.0
Finland	43.9	37.2	41.4	43.7	44.5	50.8	50.3	49.8	51.8	48.8	51.4	51.4	47.8	53.9	47.6
France	326.2	301.3	308.7	326.5	336.0	338.0	343.1	340.5	331.6	386.7	378.7	380.1	373.5	405.9	348.3
Germany	362.7	332.3	356.6	386.7	394.1	406.2	406.7	398.2	401.2	420.2	446.6	464.0	461.0	493.1	409.3
Greece	31.4	30.2	30.4	29.8	29.4	29.7	31.7	32.5	31.6	33.1	33.8	34.9	34.1	37.4	32.2
Hungary	26.5	22.4	23.1	26.0	26.5	26.9	26.8	27.7	28.7	30.0	31.0	31.9	31.4	35.4	28.2
Ireland	45.5	39.7	47.1	48.2	48.8	48.1	51.3	52.6	53.2	57.4	56.1	53.6	55.8	64.0	51.5
Italy	292.7	264.5	275.3	294.2	287.4	295.0	292.1	296.7	296.5	315.7	322.1	327.6	304.4	345.4	300.7
Latvia	5.6	4.5	5.3	5.9	6.5	6.8	7.0	6.9	6.9	7.1	7.8	8.0	8.4	10.4	6.9
Lithuania	8.2	6.7	7.4	9.0	9.7	10.2	10.7	10.6	10.6	11.4	11.7	12.5	12.9	15.4	10.5
Luxembourg	1.3	1.3	1.3	1.4	1.6	1.6	1.7	1.7	1.7	1.7	1.7	1.7	1.7	1.8	1.6
Malta	0.8	0.7	0.7	0.7	0.8	0.8	0.8	0.9	0.9	1.0	1.0	1.0	0.9	1.5	0.9
The Netherlands	113.7	105.4	107.4	114.7	116.6	120.3	120.5	121.2	124.5	130.1	131.3	132.3	133.7	143.8	122.5
Poland	102.3	85.2	97.6	107.5	113.0	115.8	118.0	118.1	118.7	131.3	142.3	148.6	147.4	158.7	121.8
Portugal	35.0	32.2	33.6	35.2	35.5	36.1	36.9	38.0	38.6	41.0	42.6	42.8	41.1	46.9	38.3
Romania	39.3	31.6	31.7	35.1	31.9	35.7	35.3	35.7	36.6	38.9	42.7	43.7	41.2	51.2	37.9
Slovakia	11.1	9.5	10.4	11.0	11.0	11.2	12.1	12.1	11.9	12.1	12.8	12.8	13.1	14.6	11.8
Slovenia	7.2	6.3	6.4	6.8	6.7	6.7	6.9	7.1	7.2	7.5	8.1	8.4	8.2	8.9	7.3
Spain	197.3	176.6	183.6	192.4	190.6	194.9	193.8	203.7	207.1	217.8	230.2	234.0	229.1	259.9	207.9
Sweden	67.7	57.7	67.8	73.3	73.2	71.9	69.5	69.7	69.4	71.4	74.1	75.1	76.9	86.9	71.8
Average	71.83	64.77	68.49	73.29	74.17	75.98	76.36	76.82	77.12	82.69	85.35	87.22	85.71	94.83	

Source: Calculated by the authors.

Table AIV. The Workforce (NPE) in the Bioeconomy of the EU-27 Member States During the Period 2008–2021 (Thousands of People).

NPE	2008	2009	2010	2011	2012	2013	2014	2015	2016	2017	2018	2019	2020	2021	Average
EU	1,937.6	1,747.1	1,843.6	1,973.5	1,995.1	2,044.4	2,051.8	2,071.8	2,080.0	2,235.7	2,316.2	2,367.9	2,309.1	2,530.3	18,162.1
Austria	46.5	42.6	46.5	50.6	52.2	53.0	53.2	54.1	54.9	57.0	66.0	67.2	66.2	76.8	343.4
Belgium	65.8	64.8	66.2	71.3	74.0	77.4	77.5	78.8	81.0	87.4	83.5	90.6	92.3	100.9	214.4
Bulgaria	12.6	11.0	11.3	12.4	12.4	12.9	13.0	13.3	13.7	14.5	14.7	15.0	14.8	18.0	844.3
Croatia	11.7	10.8	10.7	11.0	10.9	10.5	10.2	10.7	10.8	11.3	11.6	11.5	10.7	12.3	264.2
Cyprus	2.8	2.7	2.7	2.7	2.6	2.4	2.4	2.5	2.6	2.7	2.9	3.0	2.9	3.2	33.5
Czechia	33.3	28.7	29.5	33.2	33.5	32.9	32.1	32.7	32.3	34.4	36.5	38.2	37.1	42.5	399.2
Denmark	43.6	39.5	42.3	44.5	48.0	49.8	52.0	52.1	52.2	55.5	56.1	57.5	59.7	62.0	173.8
Estonia	4.5	3.5	4.2	5.0	5.2	5.6	6.0	6.3	6.1	6.6	7.0	7.5	7.6	9.4	63.6
Finland	43.9	37.2	41.4	43.7	44.5	50.8	50.3	49.8	51.8	48.8	51.4	51.4	47.8	53.9	196.4
France	326.2	301.3	308.7	326.5	336.0	338.0	343.1	340.5	331.6	386.7	378.7	380.1	373.5	405.9	1,680.5
Germany	362.7	332.3	356.6	386.7	394.1	406.2	406.7	398.2	401.2	420.2	446.6	464.0	461.0	493.1	2,035.7
Greece	31.4	30.2	30.4	29.8	29.4	29.7	31.7	32.5	31.6	33.1	33.8	34.9	34.1	37.4	671.5
Hungary	26.5	22.4	23.1	26.0	26.5	26.9	26.8	27.7	28.7	30.0	31.0	31.9	31.4	35.4	357.9
Ireland	45.5	39.7	47.1	48.2	48.8	48.1	51.3	52.6	53.2	57.4	56.1	53.6	55.8	64.0	178.5
Italy	292.7	264.5	275.3	294.2	287.4	295.0	292.1	296.7	296.5	315.7	322.1	327.6	304.4	345.4	1,918.2
Latvia	5.6	4.5	5.3	5.9	6.5	6.8	7.0	6.9	6.9	7.1	7.8	8.0	8.4	10.4	129.1
Lithuania	8.2	6.7	7.4	9.0	9.7	10.2	10.7	10.6	10.6	11.4	11.7	12.5	12.9	15.4	201.8
Luxembourg	1.3	1.3	1.3	1.4	1.6	1.6	1.7	1.7	1.7	1.7	1.7	1.7	1.7	1.8	10.1
Malta	0.8	0.7	0.7	0.7	0.8	0.8	0.8	0.9	0.9	1.0	1.0	1.0	0.9	1.5	8.5
The Netherlands	113.7	105.4	107.4	114.7	116.6	120.3	120.5	121.2	124.5	130.1	131.3	132.3	133.7	143.8	394.1
Poland	102.3	85.2	97.6	107.5	113.0	115.8	118.0	118.1	118.7	131.3	142.3	148.6	147.4	158.7	2,615.7
Portugal	35.0	32.2	33.6	35.2	35.5	36.1	36.9	38.0	38.6	41.0	42.6	42.8	41.1	46.9	725.1
Romania	39.3	31.6	31.7	35.1	31.9	35.7	35.3	35.7	36.6	38.9	42.7	43.7	41.2	51.2	2,745.6
Slovakia	11.1	9.5	10.4	11.0	11.0	11.2	12.1	12.1	11.9	12.1	12.8	12.8	13.1	14.6	163.2
Slovenia	7.2	6.3	6.4	6.8	6.7	6.7	6.9	7.1	7.2	7.5	8.1	8.4	8.2	8.9	120.2
Spain	197.3	176.6	183.6	192.4	190.6	194.9	193.8	203.7	207.1	217.8	230.2	234.0	229.1	259.9	1,395.2
Sweden	67.7	57.7	67.8	73.3	73.2	71.9	69.5	69.7	69.4	71.4	74.1	75.1	76.9	86.9	261.5
Average	766.5	733.7	724.9	709.1	700.9	687.1	682.8	670.5	659.5	664.1	668.6	660.2	650.0	651.8	

Source: Calculated by the authors.

CHAPTER 8

CHALLENGES IN APPLYING PRINCIPAL ADVERSE IMPACT INDICATORS TO SOVEREIGN DEBT PORTFOLIOS

Bentje Böer[a], Anna Broughel[a] and Mark Kantšukov[b]

[a]*School of Advanced International Studies, Johns Hopkins University, Washington, DC, United States*
[b]*School of Economics and Business Administration, University of Tartu, Tartu, Estonia*

ABSTRACT

Purpose: *This study explores potential effects and challenges of integrating Principal Adverse Impact (PAI) indicators in a sovereign bond portfolio through select exclusion policies.*

Design/Methodology/Approach: *The authors created two model portfolios based on BlackRock's IGOV and EMB ETFs. After recreating the data supplied to asset managers by MSCI, the authors apply two sample policies excluding the worst scoring sovereign bonds. This approach mimics the actual integration of PAI indicators into sustainable investments and, thus, lends itself to discussing the challenges of implementing PAI indicators in practice.*

Findings: *Sovereign PAI indicators disadvantage emerging markets (EMs) and exhibit a regional bias towards European and North American countries. Excluding sovereign bonds belonging to the 10% of the worst-scoring countries does not significantly impact the developed market (DM) portfolio composition, while the same threshold heavily affects the portfolio composition for developing markets. The current indicators have an inherent income bias, with four out of seven numeric indicators substantially correlated with GNI per capita, systematically disadvantaging EMs.*

Implications: *Applying PAI indicators for exclusion raises concerns about sustainable investment in sovereigns where a large transition is still ahead.*

Limitations: *Limitations are associated with the approach adopted by the authors, primarily due to the novelty of the regulation, as well as the absence of relevant data.*

Future Research: *Research is needed to explore the influence of PAI indicators on the composition of financial products, particularly their effects on sovereign bonds, as they remain underexplored in terms of environmental, social, and governance metrics.*

Keywords: SFDR; ESG; sustainable finance; disclosure regulation; sustainable investment; impact materiality

JEL Codes: G18; H63; Q56

LIST OF ABBREVIATIONS

ASCOR	Assessing Sovereign Climate-related Opportunities and Risks
DM	Developed Markets
DNSH	Do No Significant Harm
EC	European Commission
EM	Emerging Markets
EMBI	JPMorgan Emerging Market Bond Index
EMDE	Emerging Markets and Developing Economies
EP	European Parliament
ESEB	J.P. Morgan ESG Emerging Markets Sovereign ETF
ESG	Environmental, Social and Governance
ESMA	European Union Securities and Markets Authority
ETF	Exchange-Traded Fund
EU	European Union
FMP	Financial Market Participant
GHG	Greenhouse gas
GNI	Gross National Income
ICMA	International Capital Market Association
JESG	J.P. Morgan ESG
MSCI	Morgan Stanley Capital International
ND GAIN	Notre Dame Global Adaptation Initiative
SFDR	Sustainable Finance Disclosure Regulation
PAI	Principal Adverse Impact

1. INTRODUCTION

With the Sustainable Finance Action Plan, the EU aims to reform the financial system to support a transitioning world (EC, 2018). The plan underlines the societal and environmental impact of investments, introducing a disclosure regulation (EP and European Council, 2019). This regulation includes PAI indicators to assess potential negative impacts of investments on society and environment. Reporting these indicators is required for the most sustainable financial products and encouraged for all others. Due to the recent introduction of the regulation, academic research on the impact of PAI indicators on financial product structures is limited. Sovereign bonds, in particular, have been underexplored in relation to ESG metrics. This paper aims to fill this gap by analysing the effects of integrating PAI indicators in a sovereign bond portfolio. Building on literature on ESG risk metrics for sovereigns, the paper focuses on identifying dynamics that may disadvantage EMs. The analysis reveals that the current selection of sovereign PAI indicators disadvantages EMs and shows a regional bias towards European and North American countries. Challenges such as data availability and indicator design flaws hinder accurate assessments of the societal and environmental impact of investing in sovereign bonds. To ensure credible assessments, relevant government policies by sovereign issuers must be considered. Otherwise, this approach to integrating impact into investment decisions may disadvantage countries beginning their transition towards more sustainable societies and environments.

The remainder of this chapter is structured as follows. Section 2 offers a literature review that encompasses EU policies on sustainable finance, literature concerning ESG risk metrics, and disclosure theory, providing the foundation for the empirical analysis. Section 3 details the data and method utilised in the analysis. Following this, Section 4 presents the results and accompanying discussion, examining the implications for sovereign bond issuers. Finally, Section 5 offers conclusions that address the current state of sovereign sustainability metrics.

2. LITERATURE REVIEW

2.1. Studies on the EU Policies in Sustainable Finance

The EU's Sustainable Finance Action Plan underscores the financial system's role in advancing Sustainable Development Goals and objectives outlined in the Paris Agreement (EC, 2018). The development of sustainable finance, defined as 'the process of considering ESG factors when making investment decisions, leading to increased longer-term investments into sustainable economic activities and projects' (EC, 2024), is pivotal for enhancing these contributions. With the Action Plan providing a framework for financial sector reforms, the EU aims to assume a global leadership position in combatting climate change (EC, 2018). These reforms aspire to 'redirect capital flows towards sustainable investment to achieve sustainable and inclusive growth', while managing financial risks associated with environmental and social issues, and promoting transparency and 'long-termism' in financial activities (EC, 2018). They address both the impact of investments on society and the environment, as well as the risks posed by social and environmental factors to investment value. Subsequent regulations introduce the term 'double materiality' to capture this dual focus, encompassing 'impact materiality' and 'financial materiality' (EC, 2022a). Impact materiality covers the impacts an organisation has on the environment and society through its operations, products, services, and business relationships across the value chain, while financial materiality refers to ESG matters that can have a material financial impact on the organisation, affecting aspects like cash flows, revenues, expenditures, assets, and liabilities.

One of the mechanisms applying double materiality to advance these goals is the SFDR (EP and European Council, 2019). This regulation mandates disclosures on the integration of sustainability risks and impacts by FMPs, such as asset managers, for their investments. A specific disclosure requirement aims to capture impact materiality by mandating FMPs to disclose whether and how PAI indicators were considered in investments. For each asset class, a list of indicators specifies relevant PAIs, aiming to measure potential negative impacts on the environment and society financed by investments. FMPs may report these indicators on a 'comply or explain' basis for their entire firm and/or on a product level. Additionally, PAI indicators are utilised in the specific disclosures of sustainable investments, comprising two types of financial products contributing to defined sustainability goals as outlined in Article 8 and Article 9 (EP and European Council, 2019), which assert the highest ambitions in financing the transition to a more sustainable economy. Sustainable investments are required to disclose how they 'take PAIs into account' to meet a DNSH requirement for this product class (ESMA, 2023). This heightened transparency aims to facilitate the integration of sustainability impacts into the investment decisions of end investors (see Fig. 8.1).

Academic literature has primarily examined the impact of the SFDR on the labelling of and subsequent demand for financial products. Studies generally conclude that the standardised disclosure of sustainability integration levels in funds has led to increased capital allocation to Article 8 and Article 9 funds (Badenhoop et al., 2023; Becker et al., 2022; Cremasco & Boni, 2022). However, to date, scholarly research has not explored the effects of the SFDR on fund structure and subsequent capital allocation within products. The integration of impact indicators could prompt a 'reorientation of capital flows' (EC, 2018), given their novelty

Fig. 8.1. SFDR increases transparency for end investors. *Source*: Compiled by the authors.

and lower likelihood of already being reflected in investment strategies. Analyses in the grey literature often focus on corporate indicators and highlight challenges related to data availability and timeliness (e.g. Gambetta, 2023). Despite sovereign bonds being almost universally present in investment portfolios, PAI indicators for sovereigns have received comparatively less attention, which is the gap addressed by this chapter. Insights gleaned from academic literature on ESG risk metrics and disclosure theory will guide our exploratory analysis.

2.2. Literature on ESG Risk Metrics

Impact indicators have been poorly examined in academic literature. However, literature on ESG risk metrics bears important insights for the analysis of ESG impact metrics. As ESG factors can impact a company's financial performance and its ability to repay debt, ESG scores have been developed to assess these risks, similar to how credit ratings evaluate creditworthiness. Concerning ESG ratings for companies, various authors have criticised that firms in EMDEs have systematically lower ESG scores after controlling for other factors such as firm size (Ehlers et al., 2022). Similarly, sovereign ESG scores exhibit a substantive income bias, as a series of working papers by the World Bank highlights (Gratcheva et al., 2020, 2021, 2022). This implies that ESG ratings correlate substantially with income measures such as GNI per capita, thus significantly disadvantaging EMDEs. Whether impact indicators lead to a similar systematic disadvantage is explored in Section 4.

2.3. Disclosure Theory

Two important streams of literature on non-financial disclosure are relevant to the analysis. The first, focused on legitimacy theory, revolves around the concept of a social contract or societal license granted to a company, as long as its actions align with societal values and beliefs. Disclosures help companies manage public perception and legitimise the companies' continued operations in a society (see legitimacy theory in Cho & Patten, 2007, and expansion by impression management theory in Barkemeyer et al., 2014). When disclosure is voluntary, companies may be motivated to disclose information rather than explain why they have not in order to maintain legitimacy in the eyes of the public. This logic plausibly influences the extent to which PAI indicators are incorporated in sustainable investments where disclosure of indicator integration is mandatory. Based on legitimacy theory, companies are likely to choose visible and significant integration of PAIs in their products to demonstrate their compliance and maintain their legitimacy.

Another stream of disclosure literature introduces the concept of isomorphism – pressures that lead to the emergence of similar practices, such as disclosure practices, across companies (Bartolacci et al., 2022). DiMaggio and Powell (1983) identify three drivers of isomorphism, one of them being uncertainty, for example in the form of ambiguous goals. Disclosure under the SFDR is marked by substantial uncertainty due to two main factors: the novelty of the regulation itself and the unfamiliarity with the concept of impact indicators, which are often described in vague terms. This encourages imitating the behaviour of large actors in the field, who are seen as more legitimate or successful (DiMaggio & Powell, 1983). In the field of ESG metrics, MSCI ESG is such a large actor (Gratcheva et al., 2020) that it plausibly influences the interpretation of the SFDR beyond the clients of its data products. Potential effects of this dominance are covered in Section 4.

3. DATA AND METHODS

3.1. Data

The guiding principle for all data and methods choices was to enable the discussion of realistic effects of the integration of PAI indicators into sovereign debt portfolios. Wherever possible with publicly available data, the authors mimicked industry practices.

Concerning the data sources for the PAI indicators, the authors used data closely resembling what MSCI offers their clients for PAI reporting. MSCI is a trusted source of ESG data in the industry, a leader in ESG ratings (Gratcheva et al., 2020), and the methodology for its PAI indicators is freely accessible (MSCI, 2023). This makes MSCI a 'large legitimate actor' as described by DiMaggio and Powell (1983), underlining the influence of MSCI's approach on industry-wide practices in the uncertainty surrounding the implementation of a recent regulation. Specific data sources and the explanations of the indicators by the SFDR Regulatory Technical Standards (RTS, EC, 2022b) can be found in Table 8.1.

With respect to the data on sovereign bond portfolios, the authors followed the approach by Teal Emery (2022) and employed publicly available data on the largest BlackRock ETFs for sovereign bonds in hard currency. These ETFs contain sovereign bonds in USD for the developed (IGOV) and emerging (EMB) markets, with 498 million USD and 15,973 million USD net assets as of October 2024, respectively. Both ETFs track indices widely used in the market, the FTSE World Government Bond Index – Developed Markets Capped (USD), and the J.P. Morgan EMBI Global Core Index (BlackRock, 2024a, 2024b). Given their volume and prominence, they lend themselves well for the construction of realistic portfolios. The focus on either DMs or EMs for a product is common practice, as is the focus on hard currency bonds instead of local currency.

The authors used additional data to evaluate the results in the global context of a sustainability transition. On the basis of the World Bank classifications, the authors analyse how effects vary by region or income group (World Bank, 2023a). The Notre Dame Global Adaptation Initiative dataset offers context on the vulnerability to coming climate and societal challenges of states and their readiness to handle them (Notre Dame, 2023). The World Bank's data on GNI per capita commonly supports analyses of income bias in ESG metrics (Gratcheva et al., 2020).

Based on MSCI's PAI methodology (2023), the authors constructed a dataset containing the indicator metrics for 214 countries and the most recent years that would be relevant for the first PAI disclosure and integration effort. Documentation of the data cleaning process of indicator data and additional data (such as income group and ND GAIN vulnerability scores), with links to

Table 8.1. The List of PAI Indicators.

Indicator	Explanation in SFDR Regulatory Technical Standards	Data Sources Used
GHG intensity (mandatory)	Sum of the country's scope 1, 2, and 3 GHG emissions divided by nominal GDP in millions of euros	Only scope 1 due to limited data availability: EDGAR (2022); GDP data by IMF (2024)
Number of investee countries subject to social violations (mandatory)	Absolute number and relative number divided by all investee countries, as referred to in international treaties and conventions, United Nations principles, and where applicable national law	EU trade sanctions (EU External Action Service, 2023)
Political stability	The likelihood that the current regime will be overthrown by the use of force	World Governance Indicators (World Bank, 2023c)
Rule of law	The level of corruption, lack of fundamental rights, deficiencies in civil and criminal justice	World Governance Indicators (World Bank, 2023c)
Corruption	Perceived level of public sector corruption	Corruption Perception Index (Transparency International, 2023)
Freedom of expression	The extent to which political and civil society organisations can operate freely	Freedom House (2023)
Human rights performance	Human rights performance of investee countries	World Justice Project (2023)
Income inequality	Income and economic distribution among participants in a particular economy	World Development Indicators (World Bank, 2023b)
Non-cooperative tax jurisdictions	Investments in jurisdictions on the EU list of non-cooperative jurisdictions for tax purposes	Council of the EU (status: 14 February 2023)
Green securities ratio	The share of bonds not issued under Union legislation on environmentally sustainable bonds	Not included in quantitative analysis due to the lack of data availability

Source: Compiled by the authors.

specific data sources, is available online[1]. Separately, the authors prepared the portfolio data. To construct portfolios solely containing central government debt, all state-owned enterprises included in the original ETFs were excluded, and the weights of the remaining sovereign issuers were normalised. This leads to an EM sovereign bond portfolio with 49 countries and a DM sovereign bond portfolio with 19 countries. Subsequently, the information on portfolio weights was merged with the dataset containing indicator metrics and the additional metrics by country. The resulting dataset comprises 214 countries with country-specific metrics for 33 variables. These include 12 indicators (incorporating 4 distinct sanction metrics), 7 country rank variables per non-binary indicator, 4 alternative metrics for indicators, and 2 country rank variables for corresponding non-binary alternative metrics. Additionally, there are 2 portfolio weight variables and 2 variables indicating EM/DM affiliation, along with 4 supplementary metrics. The data cover the most recent available year for each country and variable, with the oldest data point being income inequality in Trinidad and Tobago from 1992 and the majority of other observations and variables being from 2022.

While the data have some limitations, they still provide valuable insights for the exclusion method and the regulation as a whole. The data cover a wide range of countries and variables, with the majority of observations being from recent years. However, it's important to acknowledge that data coverage and availability are not entirely comprehensive, particularly for metrics such as income inequality, which may have a longer reporting lag or be unavailable for some countries. The potential implications of these data gaps are further explored in Section 4, where they are considered in the context of the regulation's overall effectiveness.

3.2. Methods

As the regulation is new and academic research on impact indicators for sovereigns is still developing, there is no commonly accepted formal method for assessing the effects of regulations, such as the SFDR. Given the lack of established methods, the authors based their approach on current industry practices, which were elicited from publicly available information and personal communication with affected FMPs. By aligning methods with industry practices, the analysis can provide insights into the real-world effects of the regulation. These findings can serve as starting point for discussing the challenges associated with the implementation of the SFDR and potential areas for improvement.

Defining what 'taking PAI indicators into account' (ESMA, 2023) in sovereign debt portfolios could look like required further methodical choices. According to the European Supervisory Authorities, many asset managers opted for 'exclusion policies' and 'screening' when explaining how PAIs are integrated in their products (ESMA, 2023). Recognising the vagueness of this language, they recommend requiring the use and the disclosure of specific PAI thresholds for the DNSH requirement in an updated regulation. However, in the absence of disclosed thresholds and screening criteria, the authors will explore the most likely option: exclusion of a set percentile of worst-scoring issuers, which is commonly practiced, according to personal communication. Regulatory and reputational risks for FMPs reinforce this choice.

Setting individual thresholds per indicator, for example, risks appearing opaque, as it requires end investors to gain extensive background knowledge on each metric to assess the strictness of the threshold. Reweighting a portfolio to keep within certain overall thresholds (since the regulation requires disclosing weighted averages of all holdings within a product) seems even more likely to attract accusation of greenwashing and misleading end investors. More complex approaches would further complicate communicating the commitment to reducing PAI exposure to regulators and end investors. Extensive justifications for individual thresholds would increase the cost of complying with the disclosure regulation.

Therefore, cost, reputational, and regulatory risks make the exclusion of worst-scoring percentiles across all indicators the likeliest option for PAI consideration. This approach is easy to communicate, does not require extensive explanations or background knowledge from end-investors, and keeps disclosure costs low. This approach also mirrors other ESG (risk) integration methods widely used, such as the exclusion of worst-scoring issuers from conventional indexes for ESG indexes by JESG (J.P. Morgan, 2023). This results in the exclusion of ca. 28% of issuers for a standard EM index (based on the comparison of issuers in EMBI and ESEB, which are ETFs following the conventional and respective JESG index). A similar percentage of issuer exclusion is reached when excluding the worst-scoring 5% of issuers from our standard portfolio. Personal communication with asset managers confirms the use of a 5% threshold.

Identifying the 'worst-scoring' issuers highlights a substantial challenge with the PAI indicators: to shape a portfolio according to these indicators, one must know what 'good' values are. It is, however, questionable whether there is consensus on the optimal level of income inequality or the desired level of political stability in an oppressive regime, for example. Thus, the underlying assumptions for any PAI consideration are highly contentious. The authors will discuss the immediate effects of these assumptions in Section 4.

Continuing to mimic industry practice, the authors calculated percentage ranks for covered sovereigns for all non-binary indicators. All percentage ranks are oriented such that percentile 100 is the best and 0 the worst possible percentile[2]. This orientation allows for easier exclusion of different percentiles.

The indicators 'investee countries subject to social violations' and 'non-cooperative tax jurisdictions' are binary and, thus, cannot be assessed using a relative ranking method. The strong reference to norms in the phrasing evokes clear expectations about the behaviour of firms towards the 'violators' or 'non-cooperative' actors. Incentives according to legitimacy theory suggest that 'taking into account' these indicators should entail reducing exposure to these states to zero. Thus, the authors define PAI integration as the exclusion of 'social violators' or 'non-cooperative tax jurisdictions'.

Building on the direct effects of PAI integration, the authors also examine the effects of exclusion thresholds on the average indicator scores disclosed by FMPs. The authors simulate the disclosed values by applying different thresholds of exclusion. These portfolio indicator values are calculated as the investment-weighted average of the sovereign scores[3]. To adjust for incomplete data coverage, the authors excluded uncovered sovereigns and rebased the remaining positions to 100%. Then, the reweighted average for the respective indicator was calculated. This method is widely employed and is consistent with MSCI's approach to handling incomplete data (MSCI, 2023).

To demonstrate the impact of individual indicators on overall portfolio values, the authors adopt a step-by-step exclusion approach. For instance, they initially exclude all issuers within the worst-performing 5% on GHG emissions and calculate the portfolio indicator values based on this selection. Subsequently, they introduce another exclusion criterion by removing all issuers within the worst-performing 5% of another indicator and recalculating the metrics for the revised portfolio, and so on. The authors start with the two mandatory indicators but generally integrate all indicators since legitimacy concerns should encourage the broad application of indicators.

The approach employed by the authors exhibits several limitations, primarily stemming from the novelty of the regulation and the corresponding lack of relevant data. Firstly, disclosing the actual thresholds used for exclusion would enhance the precision of the analysis. Secondly, a broader disclosure of the specific metrics utilised, rather than relying on more general data sources, would enable a more comprehensive and precise comparison of the effects of different data selections. The author's reliance on MSCI's data selection likely reflects a general approach due to its prominence and the resulting isomorphic pressures within the field to conform to its choice (DiMaggio & Powell, 1983). A deeper understanding of MSCI's methodologies, such as when citing multiple data sources, could have refined the emulation of their approach. Access to broader fund holdings lists and index structures would have facilitated the creation of additional sample portfolios, potentially yielding more precise insights into the global impact size. However, even more accurate estimates could be achieved with models that integrate actual thresholds, their utilisation across FMPs, and the sizes of product categories employing different thresholds. This information may become accessible in the coming years if the EC adopts the recommendations by ESMA to mandate PAI use and threshold disclosure. Such developments would pave the way for comprehensive research and well-founded estimates regarding the global effects of capital allocation. Despite these limitations, this exploratory analysis serves as a valuable starting point for discussing the general dynamics, anticipated challenges, and the fundamental value of the PAI regulation, laying the groundwork for more comprehensive research as additional data become available.

4. RESULTS AND DISCUSSION

4.1. Exclusion Effects with 5% and 10% Thresholds

Excluding sovereigns belonging to the worst-scoring 5% of countries on any of the PAI metrics does not affect the DM portfolio. The 10% threshold also has no impact on the DM portfolio[4]. DMs would only be affected once thresholds are set higher than 10%. For example, Canada and Australia belong to the worst-scoring 12% on GHG intensity, while all G7 economies are within the worst-scoring 15% on this metric. Across all other metrics, almost all DM economies score within the best 50%, making their exclusion extremely unlikely with this approach. Israel (within worst-scoring 13% on political stability) and Singapore (within worst-scoring 15% on freedom of expression) are the only exceptions.

For the EM portfolio, both 5% and 10% thresholds, as well as the binary indicators on social violations and non-cooperative tax jurisdictions, heavily affect portfolio composition[5]. Even when considering only the exclusion of countries scoring among the worst 5% on GHG intensity or those subject to EU trade sanctions (thus accounting for only the two mandatory indicators, GHG intensity and social violations), Indonesia, Iraq, Lebanon, and China would be excluded. This represents approximately 8% of issuers and around 6% of the original portfolio weight. Applying the 5% threshold to all indicators and excluding non-cooperative tax jurisdictions results in the exclusion of 14 countries, which account for approximately 28% of issuers and 27% of the original portfolio weight (see Fig. 8.2).

Fig. 8.2. Countries in Portfolios Excluded by 5% PAI Threshold. *Source*: Compiled by the authors.

Based on the 10% threshold and only considering mandatory indicators, six countries are excluded, which account for approximately 12% of issuers and represent 15.5% of original portfolio weight. When considering all indicators based on a 10% threshold, only 25 of the original 49 countries remain, with the excluded 24 issuers representing 39% of original portfolio weight. Given the drastic limitation for diversification imposed by the 10% threshold, the application of even more aggressive thresholds across all indicators seems highly unlikely.

4.2. Portfolio Weight Changes

Excluding issuers from the portfolio results in increased concentration among the remaining positions. Under both thresholds, proportionally redistributing the remaining positions leads to more than 10% of the portfolio being concentrated on Turkey. Specifically, Turkey's weight in the portfolio increases by 3.09 percentage points and 5.3 percentage points with a 5% and 10% threshold, respectively. All other weights remain below 10%. The exclusion impacts regions and income groups differently. Among the top 15 countries experiencing the most significant gains, only one is a lower middle-income country (the Philippines, gaining 1.98 percentage points and 3.45 percentage points with a 5% and 10% threshold, respectively). The other top-gaining countries are upper middle- and high-income countries, including Turkey, Peru, Dominican Republic, Colombia (in the upper middle-income group), and Qatar, Oman, Chile, Uruguay, Poland, and Hungary (in the high-income group). Overall, both exclusionary thresholds result in the greatest portfolio weight gains for Europe and Central Asia (increasing by 5 percentage points and 10 percentage points with a 5% and 10% threshold, respectively). East Asia and Sub-Saharan Africa each experience a decrease of between 1.5 and 2 percentage points in both scenarios. Remarkably, Latin America and the Caribbean witness a slight increase with a 5% threshold and a significant decrease of more than 6 percentage points with a 10% threshold (see Fig. 8.3).

The strong regional impact is not accidental, but inherent to the choice of indicators. In fact, when looking at all countries with available data and applying a theoretical 5% or 10% threshold, as much as 40% or 50% of Sub-Saharan Africa

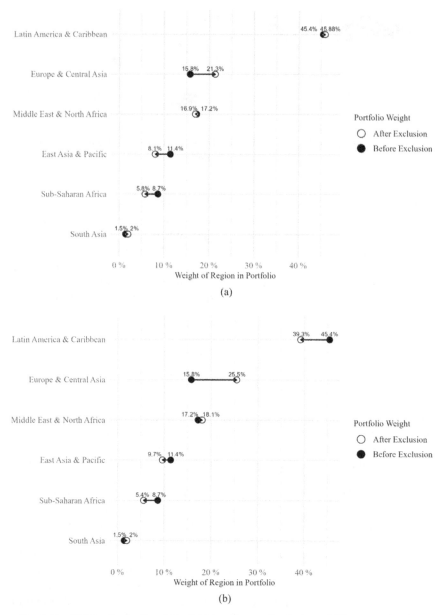

Fig. 8.3. Change in the Portfolio Weights Due to Exclusion of Worst-scoring 5% (a) and Worst-scoring 10% (b) from EMB. *Source*: Compiled by the authors.

Challenges in Applying PAI Indicators 169

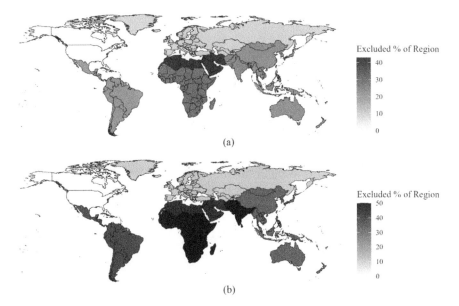

Fig. 8.4. Excluded Percentage of Regions with PAI Threshold of 5% (a) and 10% (b). *Source*: Compiled by the authors.

or the Middle East and North Africa would be excluded (see the 5% threshold in Fig. 8.4a and the 10% threshold in Fig. 8.4b).

This can be partially explained by the inherent income bias of the metrics chosen. Even when only considering the ranks and scores of those countries included in the EM portfolio (and, thus, already excluding the poorest countries without capital market access), four of the seven numeric indicators are substantially correlated with GNI per capita (with correlation coefficients ranging from 55% for corruption to 63% for political stability, see Fig. 8.5).

The choice of indicators is not uncommon for ESG ratings, neither is the inherent income bias. However, in a policy instrument designed to incentivise capital flows for sustainable and inclusive growth, this bias is detrimental to the overarching goal.

4.3. Deterioration of Portfolio PAI Indicators

Applying higher thresholds increases concentration on remaining issuers. If the additionally excluded issuers only barely fall within the exclusionary threshold but belong to top performers on other indicators, this can lead to substantial deterioration on some PAI metrics while others hardly change. The most drastic example is the effect of excluding 10% versus 5% of the worst-scoring sovereigns regarding income inequality on the overall GHG intensity of the portfolio (see the Appendix). When applying one exclusion filter after another, the countries additionally excluded by a 10% threshold on income inequality versus a 5%

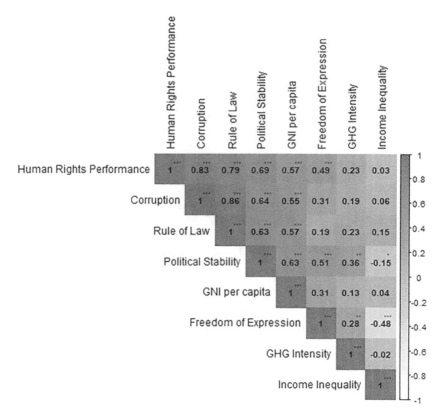

Fig. 8.5. Correlation Matrix of Indicator and GNI per Capita Ranks.
Source: Compiled by the authors.

threshold eliminate valuable opportunities to increase portfolio weights of countries with exceptionally low GHG intensity. In the 5%-PAI portfolio, Colombia's weight increases by 0.74 percentage points due to the income inequality exclusion, contributing to Colombia's rank among the top five gaining countries in the 5%-portfolio overall (total gain is 1.89 percentage points). In contrast, the 10%-portfolio excludes Colombia, Panama, Guatemala, and Angola only due to their income inequality ranks and, thus, loses countries with exceptionally low GHG intensities (and high ranks).

4.4. Limitations of PAI Indicators

Under the premise that the chosen indicators should, indeed, be measured to evaluate PAIs of investments, both poor data availability and poor design choices risk that, in practice, adopted metrics do not measure what was intended. Consequently, exclusions are not based on the intended factors, derailing the desired effect on transparency and capital allocation. Time-lagging and incomplete data do not reflect the impact of funding a current government. The most drastic example is the indicator of income inequality. One of the few global datasets available pertains to the World Development Indicators database by the World Bank (2023b). However, even this dataset does not offer comprehensive and up-to-date values for the Gini index of the income distribution of each country. Creating the most complete dataset by selecting the most recent available value, countries such as Zambia and Guatemala would be among the excluded worst-performing 10% based on data from 2014, South Africa based on values from 2015, and Angola from 2018. These countries would not be excluded by any other indicator. Given the old and likely inaccurate data basis on which they would have to operate, FMPs may opt to report low data availability and exclude data considered outdated. Even if these necessarily arbitrary cut-offs would not lead to allegations of data manipulation, the example still highlights a more substantive issue. Relying on time-lagging, incomprehensive data exacerbates the inability of indicators to reflect (and consequently reward) short-term changes in policies. Addressing income inequality (or any of the other indicators) may take time. Being judged on the basis of decades-old data counteracts the idea of incentivising investments in ambitious governments showing effort to foster sustainable and inclusive growth.

Secondly, vague names and descriptions of indicators lead to a range of possible operationalisations, for example regarding 'Freedom of Expression' and the 'Number of countries subject to social violations'. Operationalising the description rather than the name of the 'Freedom of Expression' indicator would lead to a greater focus on civil society participation than a standard 'Freedom of Expression' metric from Freedom House (the data source for MSCI) offers. Similarly, there are alternatives to interpreting what constitutes a country 'subject to social violations' in addition to the operationalisation as a country subject to (EU trade) sanctions (MSCI's interpretation). However, uncertainty about the regulator's goal with the indicator implies regulatory and reputational risk when opting for an uncommon interpretation. Instead, it encourages orientation towards interpretations by large 'legitimate' actors, such as MSCI. It is at least plausible that the regulator envisioned one (or several) different operationalisations, given that they could have easily clarified the indicator as 'number of countries under EU sanctions' if that was their intention. Describing the indicator as based on international conventions and treaties, points towards a broader intended interpretation. Without further clarification, however, disclosing entities are unlikely to operationalise and integrate the originally intended factor, making these indicators imprecise incentivising instruments.

In addition to design and data issues, the mere inclusion of indicators referring to other EU policy instruments in the list of PAIs harms EU objectives. The indicators in question are the Green Bond Securities ratio based on the EU Green Bond Standard and the indicator on non-cooperative tax jurisdictions. The reliance on EU taxonomy alignment of the Green Bond Standard will lead to a highly selected issuer base, namely consisting of sovereigns which can afford the costly taxonomy alignment assessment and have the necessary expertise to conduct it. It is extremely likely that mostly, if not only, EU issuers will attain the EU Green Bond Standard and thus only investments in them will be able to improve a portfolio's Green Securities Ratio. In the presence of the widely used ICMA Green Bond Standard, insisting on the EU Green Bond Standard thus comes at the cost of greater international fragmentation of standards. This directly counteracts the EU's aspiration to set global standards in sustainable finance disclosures (EC, 2018).

The indicator 'non-cooperative tax jurisdictions' seems even less capable of measuring adverse impacts on sustainability factors since the only criterion for being excluded here is the EU's assessment of insufficient effort to comply with their tax regulation. It reinforces the impression of eurocentrism and further discredits the stated aspiration of the EU to create globally accepted standards on measuring impact materiality. More importantly, the exclusionary impact of this indicator on a sovereign debt portfolio severely contradicts the incentives of other selected indicators. To reduce exposure to non-cooperative tax jurisdictions to zero, Costa Rica, Panama, and Trinidad and Tobago have to be excluded. These would not be excluded by any other indicator. Much to the contrary, given their outstanding performance on the mandatory GHG emissions intensity indicator, one would expect that the regulation aims to incentivise investment in these three countries. Incentivising divestment instead adds to the confusion around the direction in which the regulation aims to reorient capital and seems to undermine the goal of sustainable and inclusive growth.

In general, the utilisation of PAI indicators for exclusion encourages capital allocation towards countries with favourable scores, thereby discouraging investment in sovereigns facing significant transitional challenges. Several unintended consequences compound the severity of this effect. Presently, exclusionary considerations based on PAI indicators have the most pronounced impact on fund structures falling within the Article 8 and Article 9 categories of the SFDR, which demonstrate the highest aspirations toward sustainability objectives and financing the transition to a more sustainable economy. The observed shift in demand for Article 8 and Article 9 funds (Becker et al., 2022) indicates that exclusion driven by PAI indicators will become more widespread. Paradoxically, this means that the expanding category of 'most sustainable' products will substantially hinder inclusive sustainable growth, thus making minimal contributions to the EU's sustainable finance objectives. Moreover, reliance on fund categorisations may lead end investors to overlook the actual impact of their financing. Disclosing the thresholds used poses another challenge, as higher thresholds (resulting in more exclusions) could falsely suggest fewer adverse impacts to end investors while potentially exacerbating them. Additionally, the disclosure framework hampers more nuanced approaches, such as those favoured by impact-oriented investors, as SFDR disclosure practices evolve under significant isomorphic pressures. Making conscious, long-term decisions to support a government's (transition) plans based on comprehensive assessments becomes increasingly challenging when current PAI indicators yield low scores. Taken together, these factors diminish the attractiveness of financing countries' transitions.

If occurring on a large scale, this scenario would elevate the cost of capital for countries in the initial stages or midst of transition, thereby constraining their capacity to finance transitional needs. As depicted in Fig. 8.6, countries excluded

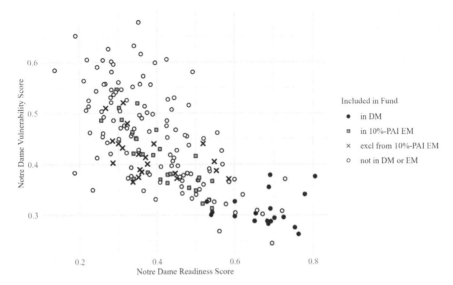

Fig. 8.6. Countries' Portfolio Status and Vulnerability and Readiness Score According to Notre Dame (2023). *Source*: Compiled by the authors.

from the EM portfolio already tend to exhibit greater vulnerability to transition challenges and are less equipped to address them. This readiness is assessed by Notre Dame (2023), specifically evaluating the ability to access and utilise funds in capital markets. Heightened capital costs for excluded countries would not only impede their ability to fund new projects or respond to shocks but also jeopardise existing initiatives. In essence, efforts to mitigate PAI exposure could exacerbate the very conditions that led to exclusion initially – seeking to minimise PAIs may inadvertently result in significant adverse impacts on sustainability factors.

The misalignment stems from the unclear connection between holding sovereign debt from a country, thereby funding the government's spending, and the resulting low PAI score. More refined indicators would encourage investment in issuers dedicated to upholding or attaining a comprehensive sustainability profile.

5. CONCLUSIONS

PAI indicators set a novel regulatory focus on the sustainability impact of sovereign debt. However, scarce data availability and the lack of understanding of secondary consequences stemming from indicator design mean that the current PAI indicators miss their aim. They cannot incentivise ambitious transition policies by governments. Instead, PAI indicators lead to capital allocation away from sovereigns most vulnerable and least ready to confront challenges such as climate change.

This counterintuitive effect is especially worrying given the influence EU regulations have globally. Given the globalisation of financial markets, financial products adapted to the EU market affect what is sold in global markets, in particular, for products benefitting as much from economies of scale as globally sold funds. This de facto regulation of markets outside its borders is sometimes accompanied by a de jure 'Brussels Effect' (Bradford, 2019), increasing the stakes of 'getting it right' at the EU regulatory level. In the case of PAI indicators, this would mean basing indicators on concise indicator descriptions, informed by available data and integrating sovereigns' use of funds.

Responding to the challenges of a transition to a more sustainable world requires large-scale programmes from sovereigns worldwide, particularly in countries less developed and more vulnerable to the impacts of climate change. Orienting capital flows to these sovereigns should be a priority of all actions claiming to 'reorient capital flows towards sustainable and inclusive growth' (EC, 2018). However, vague indicator definitions and scarce availability of high-quality data contribute towards the current PAI indicator list contradicting the overarching aim of the EU Sustainable Finance Action Plan if thoroughly implemented in the market. Given current market practices, financial products categorised as the 'most sustainable' will disadvantage developing countries the most and do the least to enable a sustainable transition. Recent recommendations to the PAI framework (ESMA, 2023) will only scratch the surface of these problems. But if the EU implements its guidance and requires the disclosure of actual exclusion thresholds, this will at least show the scale of the issue of consistent PAI integration for sovereign funds.

Analysing the unintended effects of PAI integration also points towards a larger issue in the sovereign bond world – the question of how to measure impact financed through sovereign bonds. Labelled sovereign bonds, such as green bonds and sustainability-linked bonds, certainly raised awareness around the issue of measuring sovereign sustainability. But it is unlikely that green labelled bonds will completely replace conventional sovereign bonds. If an increasing share of the state budget aligns with transitioning towards a more environmentally and socially sustainable future, this will raise issues around budget tagging and drawing the line between conventional and labelled bonds. General indicators on the sustainability effort and progress of a sovereign could be a way forward, plausibly even requiring a smaller reporting burden than the extended use of labelled bonds, which would, in turn, benefit especially small and developing nation states.

PAI indicators seem to be a first attempt at implementing this approach. Apart from the indicator design and data availability issues, however, they fail on a more fundamental level to measure the impact materiality they aim for. The existing concept lacks a policy dimension that delineates whether holding sovereign debt from a country will fund positive or negative impacts on sustainability factors. More suitable indicators would incentivise investment in issuers committed to maintaining or, more importantly, achieving a holistic sustainability profile, for example by estimating the expected improvement if policies are implemented. Sovereign impact indicators assessing both possible adverse and potential positive impacts would also increase the importance of sovereign bonds in sustainable investment products (Article 8, Article 9), if particularly promising sovereign bonds could count towards the respective share of investments with sustainability goals. Eventually, a set of indicators may even allow for the assessment of subnational issuers such as federal states and municipalities. The ASCOR initiative (ASCOR, 2023) demonstrates that investors are interested in comparable indicators that enable the assessment of financed impact in sovereigns. Sovereign impact indicators would greatly contribute to further establishing the principle of impact materiality and could significantly advance the EU's role as a progressive standard-setter in sustainable finance (if avoiding the pitfalls outlined in this paper).

NOTES

1. https://rpubs.com/beboer/1138241.
2. This means that having a low percentile rank on the corruption score signals high perceived corruption, and a high percentile rank on income inequality means low income inequality.
3. Example GHG intensity: $\sum_{i=1}^{n} \left(\frac{\text{current value of investment}_i}{\text{total current value of all investments} (\text{€M})} \right) \times \left(\frac{\text{country's Scope 1, 2, and 3 GHG emissions}_i}{\text{Gross Domestic Product}_i (\text{€M})} \right)$.
4. See table at https://pai-indicators.com/dm-excl-10.
5. See table on 5% threshold at https://pai-indicators.com/em-excl-05 and table on 10% threshold at https://pai-indicators.com/em-excl-10.

REFERENCES

ASCOR. (2023). *ASCOR country assessment results*. Assessment Date 31 October 2023. https://transitionpathwayinitiative.org/ascor

Badenhoop, N., Hackmann, A., Mucke, C., & Pelizzon, L. (2023). *Quo vadis sustainable funds Sustainable and taxonomy-aligned discolsure in Germany under the SFDR*. Frankfurt a.M.: Leibniz Institute for Financial Research SAFE. SAFE White Paper No. 94. http://hdl.handle.net/10419/273716

Barkemeyer, R., Comyns, B., Figge, F., & Napolitano, G. (2014). CEO statements in sustainability reports: Substantive information or background noise?. *Accounting Forum*, 38(4), 241–257. https://doi.org/10.1016/j.accfor.2014.07.002

Bartolacci, F., Bellucci, M., Corsi, K., & Soverchia, M. (2022). *A systematic literature review of theories underpinning sustainability reporting in non-financial disclosure*. In L. Cinquini & F. De Luca (Eds.), *Non-financial disclosure and integrated reporting - theoretical framework and empirical evidence* (pp. 87–114). Springer Nature. https://doi.org/10.1007/978-3-030-90355-8

Becker, M. G., Martin, F., & Walter, A. (2022). The power of ESG transparency: The effect of the new SFDR sustainability labels on mutual funds and individual investors. *Finance Research Letters*, 47(Part B), 102708. https://doi.org/10.1016/j.frl.2022.102708

BlackRock. (2024a). EMB: iShares J.P: Morgan USD Emerging Markets Bond ETF. https://www.ishares.com/us/products/239572/ishares-jp-morgan-usd-emerging-markets-bond-etf

BlackRock. (2024b). IGOV: iShares International Treasury Bond ETF. https://www.ishares.com/us/products/239830/ishares-international-treasury-bond-etf

Bradford, A. (2019, December). *How the EU became a global regulatory power*. Oxford Academic. pp 7-C1.P56. https://doi.org/10.1093/oso/9780190088583.003.0002

Cho, C. H., & Patten, D. M. (2007). The role of environmental disclosures as tools of legitimacy: A research note. *Accounting, Organizations and Society*, *32*(7), 639–647. https://doi.org/10.1016/j.aos.2006.09.009

Council of the European Union. (2023, February 14). Council conclusions on the revised EU list of non-cooperative jurisdictions for tax purposes. Document Number: 6375/23FISC 29ECOFIN 143. https://data.consilium.europa.eu/doc/document/ST-6375-2023-INIT/en/pdf

Cremasco, C., & Boni, L. (2022). Is the European Union (EU) Sustainable Finance Disclosure Regulation (SFDR) effective in shaping sustainability objectives? An analysis of investment funds' behaviour. *Journal of Sustainable Finance & Investment*, 1–19. https://doi.org/10.1080/20430795.2022.2124838

DiMaggio, P. J., & Powell, W. W. (1983). The iron cage revisited: Institutional isomorphism and collective rationality in organizational fields. *American Sociological Review*, *48*(2), 147–160. https://doi.org/10.2307/2095101

EDGAR (Emissions Database for Global Atmospheric Research). (2022). EDGARv.7. Community GHG database (a collaboration between the European Commission), Joint Research Centre (JRC), the International Energy Agency (IEA), and comprising IEA-EDGAR CO2, EDGAR CH4, EDGAR N2O, EDGAR F-GASES version 7.0, (2022) European Commission, JRC (datasets). https://edgar.jrc.ec.europa.eu/dataset_ghg70

Ehlers, T., Gardes-Landolfini, C., Kemp, E., Lindner, P., & Xiao, Y. (2022). Scaling up private climate finance in emerging market and developing economies. *Global financial stability report: Navigating the high-inflation environment* (pp. 45–64). International Monetary Fund.

Emery, T. (2022). *iShares ETF screener*. https://github.com/t-emery/sais-susfin_data

European Commission (EC). (2018). *Sustainable finance action plan*. COM/2018/097 final (document 52018DC0097). https://eur-lex.europa.eu/legal-content/EN/TXT/?uri=CELEX%3A52018DC0097

European Commission. (2022a). Sustainable finance. 26.07.2022. https://ec.europa.eu/newsroom/fisma/items/754701/en

European Commission. (2022b). *Sustainable finance disclosure regulation commission delegated regulation*. C/2022/1931 (Document 32022R1288). https://eur-lex.europa.eu/eli/reg_del/2022/1288/oj

European Commission. (2024). *Internal market, industry, entrepreneurship and SMEs: Sustainable finance*. https://single-market-economy.ec.europa.eu/industry/sustainability/corporate-sustainability-and-responsibility/sustainable-finance_en

European Parliament and Council. (2019). *Sustainable finance disclosure regulation* (SFDR): Regulation (EU) 2019/2088 of the European Parliament and of the Council of 27 November 2019 on sustainability-related disclosures in the financial services sector. PE/87/2019/REV/1 (Document 32019R2088). https://eur-lex.europa.eu/eli/reg/2019/2088/oj

European Securities and Markets Authority (ESMA). (2023). 'Do No Significant Harm' definitions and criteria across the EU Sustainable Finance framework. ESMA30-379-2281. https://www.esma.europa.eu/sites/default/files/2023-11/ESMA30-379-2281_Note_DNSH_definitions_and_criteria_across_the_EU_Sustainable_Finance_framework.pdf

European Union External Action Service (EEAS). (2023). *EU sanctions map*. Last update 13.05.2024. https://www.sanctionsmap.eu/#/main

Freedom House. (2023). *Freedom in the world*. https://freedomhouse.org/sites/default/files/2023-02/All data FIW 2013-2023.xlsx

Gambetta, G. (2023, August 25). Easy as PAI? Investor frustration over data challenges with new SFDR reports. Responsible Investor. https://www.responsible-investor.com/easy-as-pai-investor-frustration-over-data-challenges-with-new-sfdr-reports/

Giumelli, F., Hoffmann, F., & Ksiazczakova, A. (2021). The when, what, where and why of European Union sanctions. *European Security*, *30*(1), 1–23. https://doi.org/10.1080/09662839.2020.1797685

Gratcheva, E. M., Emery, T., & Wang, D. (2020). *Demystifying sovereign ESG*. IBRD/World Bank. https://openknowledge.worldbank.org/server/api/core/bitstreams/6c664ccf-ba17-59d9-98fa-709118908af7/content

Gratcheva, E. M., Gurhy, B., Emery, T., Wang, D., Oganes, L., Linzie, J. K., … Rink, R. (2021). *A new dawn – Rethinking sovereign ESG*. World Bank and J.P. Morgan. https://hdl.handle.net/10986/35753

Gratcheva, E. M., Gurhy, B., Skarnulis, A., Stewart, F. E., & Wang, D. (2022). *Credit worthy*. The World Bank. https://documents1.worldbank.org/curated/en/812471642603970256/pdf/Credit-Worthy-ESG-Factors-and-Sovereign-Credit-Ratings.pdf

International Monetary Fund. (2024). *World economic outlook databases*. https://www.imf.org/en/Publications/SPROLLs/world-economic-outlook-databases#sort=%40imfdate%20descending

Morgan, J. P. (2023). *J.P. Morgan ESG Index Suite (JESG): Rules and Methodology*. Retrieved April 29, 2024, from https://www.jpmorgan.com/content/dam/jpm/cib/complex/content/markets/composition-docs/JPM_JESG_Index_Methodology.pdf

MSCI. (2023, September). *MSCI SFDR adverse impact metrics methodology*. https://www.msci.com/documents/1296102/23400696/MSCI+SFDR+Adverse+Impact+Metrics+Methodology.pdf/ac60df37-681e6b18-6f9b-fd5196b3fd78?t=1694625178508

Notre Dame. (2023). *Notre dame global adaptation initiative index* (ND GAIN). https://gain.nd.edu/our-work/country-index/download-data/

Transparency International. (2022). *Corruption perception index 2022*. https://www.transparency.org/en/cpi/20232

World Bank. (2023a). *World Bank country and lending groups*. https://datahelpdesk.worldbank.org/knowledgebase/articles/906519

World Bank. (2023b). *World development indicators*. https://datacatalog.worldbank.org/search/dataset/0037712/World-Development-Indicators

World Bank. (2023c). *Worldwide governance indicators*. https://databank.worldbank.org/source/worldwide-governance-indicators

World Justice Project. (2023). *Rule of law index*. https://worldjusticeproject.org/rule-of-law-index/global

APPENDIX

Table AI. PAI Portfolio Metrics Adding Exclusion Screens Step by Step, 10%.

PAI Indicators	Baseline	excl. by GHG intensity	+ by Soc. Viol.	+ by HR Performance	+ by Rule of Law	+ by Freedom of Expression	+ by Corruption	+ by Pol. Stability	+ by Income Inequality	+ by Non-coop. tax jurisd.
10% Exclusion										
GHG Intensity [t/Mln EUR]	146.63	0.89	0.89	0.88	0.88	0.85	0.85	0.85	0.84	0.85
Social Violations [n]	3.00	2.00	0.00	0.00	0.00	0.00	0.00	0.00	0.00	0.00
Human Rights	0.51	0.52	0.52	0.52	0.52	0.52	0.52	0.52	0.52	0.52
Performance Rule of Law	−0.11	−0.06	−0.05	−0.05	−0.05	−0.08	−0.08	−0.08	−0.01	−0.03
Corruption	41.66	42.62	42.72	42.83	42.83	42.26	42.26	42.27	43.26	42.99
Freedom of Expression	10.59	10.66	10.69	10.73	10.73	11.34	11.34	11.35	10.90	10.74
Political Stability	2.13	2.10	2.10	2.09	2.09	2.09	2.09	2.09	2.04	2.04
Income Inequality	42.73	42.16	42.23	42.33	42.33	42.69	42.69	42.71	39.42	39.19
Non-coop. tax jurisdiction [n]	3.00	3.00	3.00	3.00	3.00	3.00	3.00	3.00	2.00	0.00

Source: Compiled by the authors.

Table AIII. PAI Portfolio Metrics Adding Exclusion Screens Step by Step, 5%.

PAT Indicators	Baseline	excl. by GHG intensity	+ by Soc. Viol.	+ by HR Performance	+ by Rule of Law	+ by Freedom of Expression	+ by Corruption	+ by Pol. Stability	+ by Income Inequality	+ by Non-coop. tax jurisd.
5% Exclusion										
GHG Intensity [t/Mln EUR]	146.63	107.22	88.72	89.06	89.06	93.28	93.28	93.28	32.65	35.34
Social Violations [n]	3.00	3.00	0.00	0.00	0.00	0.00	0.00	0.00	0.00	0.00
Human Rights	0.51	0.51	0.51	0.51	0.51	0.51	0.51	0.51	0.51	0.51
Performance Rule of Law	−0.11	−0.10	−0.10	−0.10	−0.10	−0.12	−0.12	−0.12	−0.11	−0.11
Corruption	41.66	41.94	41.96	42.01	42.01	41.82	41.82	41.82	42.08	42.18
Freedom of Expression	10.59	10.65	10.88	10.91	10.91	11.34	11.34	11.34	11.05	10.69
Political Stability	2.13	2.14	2.14	2.14	2.14	2.13	2.13	2.13	2.10	2.12
Income Inequality	42.73	42.93	43.14	43.19	43.19	43.24	43.24	43.24	41.23	40.45
Non-coop. tax jurisdiction [n]	3.00	3.00	3.00	3.00	3.00	3.00	3.00	3.00	3.00	0.00

Source: Compiled by the authors.

CHAPTER 9

THE ROLE OF FINANCIAL INNOVATIONS IN SUSTAINABLE DEVELOPMENT

Agnieszka Majewska and Sebastian Majewski

Institute of Economics and Finance, University of Szczecin, Poland

ABSTRACT

Purpose: Fintech, as part of technological innovation, has evolved from a small industry trend to the main force transforming the financial environment over the past 10 years. In the beginning, it was associated with small start-ups and garage companies focused on bringing new original products and services to the market to improve people's lives. The definition of financial innovation is not as simple as it might seem because it aims at changes in the whole financial sector. Therefore, it includes online and mobile banking, digital payments, cryptocurrency and blockchain, insurtech, neobanks, wealthtech, and artificial intelligence. The aim of this article is to present the role of financial innovation in the processes of change in the global economy for sustainable development.

Methodology: To underline the importance of ongoing changes, trends in fintech subsectors are described using statistical tools. The statistical analysis will be carried out both for time series and for geographical areas, showing the regions with the strongest and weakest positions in the implementation of fintech.

Implications: The classification of financial technologies, with their complicated linkages and relations with other industries, will be a background of the research. In addition, an attempt will be made to diagnose the future of *technological processes in the financial sector, with potential consequences for the sustainable development of countries.*

Keywords: Financial innovations; sustainable development; technology; cryptocurrency; blockchain

JEL Codes: Q55; Q01

INTRODUCTION

One of the most important sectors in the economy today is fintech. It is a platform where financial and technological solutions are combined by means of the internet or other available communication tools. The company could be classified as a financial innovator if it offers financial services and products through online channels. Therefore, some banks, payment and credit institutions, and companies using blockchain technologies are referred to as a fintech.

Despite the fact that the pandemic is a source of great uncertainty, this period of pandemic has created new opportunities for the fintech industry. Global management consultancy McKinsey declared that 'the COVID-19 recovery will be digital' as early as May 2020. A more accurate statement would be that the pandemic itself has been digital, as internet and mobile usage has increased alongside rising infection rates. The COVID-19 pandemic has influenced the acceleration of financial technology development worldwide through a number of important factors, the most important of which can be considered:

1. There has been a huge increase in digital payments due to the need to reduce (limit) physical interactions and the need for cash.
2. There has been an increase in the use of e-commerce and digital financial services during this period, for example there was an increase in fintech financing during the COVID-19 pandemic. High growth in all types of digital financial services [except lending].
3. It is also important to note that digital payments are a gateway to the digital economy. The digital economy can open up additional economic opportunities (earning income, accessing new markets, joining platforms, accessing important information, etc.).
4. An unprecedented acceleration in the process of financial digitisation and a milestone for digital financial inclusion in developing and emerging economies.

Unfortunately, the world is not developing evenly and people in different parts of the world do not have the same access to new technologies. This is why a phenomenon called financial inclusion is emerging. The World Bank defines financial inclusion as the ability of individuals and enterprises to access useful and affordable financial products and services (The World Bank, 2022). Other definitions converge to the following statement that financial inclusion is a process of conducting poorer and marginalised members of society into the framework of a structured financial system to ensure them access to financial products at an affordable price(Table 9.1) (Chithra & Selvam, 2013; Sanderson et al., 2018; Ozili, 2018).

In conclusion, considering the links between sustainable development and financial innovation, it is easy to see that financial exclusion, which destabilises economic development, is caused by basic determinants such as income, education, and gender. Sustainable government policies should aim to eradicate poverty and unemployment, improve education levels, and reduce gender inequalities.

Therefore, the main goal of the article is to present the role of financial innovations in the processes of change in the global economy for sustainable development. In order to achieve this goal, the main elements of the financial sector, which are commonly referred to as fintech, will be presented and briefly described. After that, we will present the development of the financial innovation sector together with forecasts of its further development.

THEORETICAL BACKGROUND

Fintech is defined as an interdisciplinary field which combines financial, technology, and innovation management (Leong & Sung, 2018). The history of fintech can be broken down into three periodic timelines: Fintech 1.0 (analogue industry – 1886–1967), Fintech 2.0 (digitalisation – 1967–2008), and Fintech 3.0 and 3.5 (era of start-ups – 2008–now) (Setiawan & Maulisa, 2020). Fintech is not limited to specific sectors or business models. It encompasses all financial services and products in the traditional sense (Arner et al., 2015).

The financial services industry and its companies are focusing their attention on two general aspects:

- Understanding customer needs
- Using technology in innovative and unique ways.

Fintech has improved sustainable development by making services more accessible and easier to use for people around the world. Financial innovations are perceived as creating new financial products, services, or processes. As a result, many categories of financial innovation can be distinguished. The most important of them are shown in Fig. 9.1.

Online banking (electronic banking, e-banking, virtual banking, or internet banking) is the use of a computer or mobile device to manage bank accounts. This includes the transfer of money, the payment of bills electronically, and the purchase of insurance. In terms of the environment, internet banking makes it possible to improve the efficiency of the use of the technological environment, to reduce the risk of illegal operations through information management, to increase the availability of information on each stage of banking operations, and to detect errors more quickly. In the social area, e-banking primarily enables the inclusion of customers from different geographical regions and hard-to-reach segments and facilitates access to financial education. E-banking influences governance

Table 9.1. Financial Inclusion Connections with Fintech and Sustainable Development.

Term	Description
Unbanked adults	*The objects of financial inclusion* The term closely connected to financial inclusion. They are adults who don't use or can't access traditional financial services such as saving accounts, credit cards, or personal cheques There are some barriers for not having financial institution account (Allen et al., 2016): • the lack of money; • the expensiveness of financial services; • the holding of an account by a family member is sufficient; • the lack of necessary documentation; • the lack of trust to financial institutions; • religious and ethical reasons (Boel & Zimmerman, 2022; Karlan et al., 2021)
Common access to finance	*The economic goal of sustainable development* Access to finance is the ability of individuals or firms to obtain financial services. It includes credit, deposits, payments, insurance, and other risk management services. As one of sustainable goals runs to ensure free access to financial resources for all in need
Financial services	*The fintech sector – the platform for financial cash flows* The element of the fintech branch. Financial services are a broad range of specific activities provided by the financial industry and other specialists (banking, investment and insurance)
Financial institutions	Entities that focus on handling financial and monetary transactions. Their main functions are payments, storage of value, provision of finance, investment opportunities, and risk management such as insurance. By providing financial services, financial institutions empower and secure individuals and businesses. Financial institutions are essential to a functioning capitalist economy because they bring together people seeking funds with those who can lend or invest them
Sustainable development	*The policy of global sustainable economy* Meeting the needs of the present without compromising the ability of future generations to meet their own needs. The four pillars of sustainability are people, society, the economy, and the environment. In many pillars of sustainable development, there are some more important for financial inclusion: *Poverty reduction* can be achieved through the promotion of economic growth in order to increase incomes and employment opportunities for poor people. It requires the government to undertake economic and institutional reforms to increase efficiency and improve the use of resources. This requires access to education and employment opportunities and, of course, the provision of basic services such as health care and housing *Social dimension* refers to the capacity of society to adopt practices that ensure respect for human rights, diversity, cultural traditions, and the rights of communities. It aims to reduce the gap between rich and poor and to ensure social justice by addressing values, norms, rules, and roles *Economic dimension* refers to the ability of public and private sectors to implement profitable practices from an economic perspective. It is important to do this in a way that does not upset the balance with social and environmental practices

Fig. 9.1. Categories of Financial Innovations. *Source*: Own elaboration.

through the possibility of making payments concerning tax and property declarations and other electronic governance services (Sakalauskas et al., 2009).

A digital payment means the transfer of value from one payment account to another using a digital device or channel. It includes all bank transfers, mobile money, QR codes, and all payment instruments such as credit, debit, and prepaid cards. Compared to cash, digital payments have significantly lower environmental costs, in particular through lower CO_2 emissions. Galanti and Özsoy (2022) found that the use of mobile money mitigates the negative impact of CO_2 emissions. Among many services, digital payments are a major driver of financial inclusion across the world. The literature in this area is very extensive. Usually, authors evaluate the impact of financial inclusion on underdeveloped countries and find that access to finance improves a country's general well-being as it allows people to better develop and manage their needs, expand their opportunities, and improve their standard of living (Kim et al., 2018; Park & Mercado, 2015; Van et al., 2021; Yawe et al., 2022). Therefore, digital payments help to foster economic empowerment and reduce environmental impact by keeping carbon footprints low.

Virtual currency is a digital currency with an unregulated status, issued and usually controlled by its creators, and used and accepted among the members of a specific virtual community (European Central Bank, 2012, 2015). It represents value, but is not issued by central banks and, for the most part, is not regulated by financial authorities. Unregulated virtual currencies don't offer legal recourses to investors; therefore, many countries are developing central bank digital currencies (CBDCs), and some have even implemented them. The Bank for International Settlements (BIS) defines CBDS as a central bank liability, expressed in the prevailing unit of account, that serves as a medium of exchange and store of value (Bank for International Settlements, 2018). The main purposes of issuing CBDCs are (Ward & Rochemont, 2019):

- ensuring public access to legal tender if cash were phased out,
- improving the efficiency of payment systems,
- transition towards a less-cash society,
- competition from private e-money,
- improving cross-border payment efficiency.

A balanced approach that encourages the responsible development of innovative technologies with an effective legal and regulatory framework that protects consumers, businesses, and the financial system is needed to stimulate potentially significant benefits (Comizio, 2017).

Money exchanges provide direct money exchange services. They make it possible to convert currencies, send money online, and track exchange rates. They are defined as an online peer-to-peer (P2P) currency exchange marketplace. Carroll and Bellotti consider alternative and complementary currency and exchange innovations in their paper (Carroll & Bellotti, 2015). They consider the implications and directions of the rapidly evolving currency ecosystem, which includes local/community currencies, crypto-currencies, person-to-person collaborative economy micro-businesses, and timebanks. P2P money exchange can be made in two ways. The first allows the exchange of currencies without any associated cryptocurrencies. The second uses a virtual cryptocurrency system for the exchange. One of the paradigms for the P2P resource market was proposed by Turner and Ross early in the 21st century (Turner & Ross, 2004). They pointed out that this paradigm allows applications to tap into a huge pool of surplus peer resources, which could lead to a booming market for P2P resources. In turn, Bhattacharya et al. (2017) outlined the shortcomings of existing foreign currency exchange systems. They also identified the requirements of a potential mobile web application for the exchange of currency through the integration of intelligent systems based on kiosks.

The next category is a neobank. This is a type of direct bank that operates solely on the basis of online banking. There are no traditional physical branch networks, which implies that the range of services provided by neobanks is not as extensive as those provided by traditional banks. Compared to traditional banks, which have high operating costs precisely due to the need for a network of branches and ATMs, neobanks eliminate these costs because they are fully online banks. This means that digital-only banks are seen as serious competitors to traditional, brick-and-mortar-based banks. However, it should be noted that they currently offer basic banking and payment services and cannot be considered a fully-fledged alternative to traditional banking (Clerc et al., 2020). Moreover, the majority of neobank customers today are millennials who are familiar with new technologies and are not afraid to use them (Hopkinson et al., 2019) in contrast to earlier generations who prefer tried and tested practices and often have less confidence in new solutions. Arslanian and Fischer identify three key elements that can have a significant impact on the sustainable development of neobanks. These include the changing economic and regulatory landscape, changing customer expectations, and the evolving technological environment (Arslanian & Fischer, 2019).

The last category listed under financial innovation is a cryptocurrency platform. This category is a general term and can refer to a blockchain protocol, a centralised exchange, as well as a decentralised exchange, a decentralised application, or a crypto wallet. Cryptocurrency platforms operate in a similar way to stock exchanges but allow investors to buy and sell only digital currencies, such as Bitcoin, Ethereum, Tether, BNB, Solana, and others. Therefore, these platforms work only on digital marketplaces such as mobile apps or through desktop functions. Unfortunately, they are often the target of fraud and hacking attacks. Xia and others in their paper identified and conducted a large-scale measurement of cryptocurrency exchange fraud (Xia et al., 2020). The study covered cryptocurrency exchanges, both in the form of domains and mobile applications. They indicated that many attacks are based on social engineering techniques, among which are phishing and trust trading scams. Therefore, the security of the exchange and ensuring the sustainability of the storage are crucial to the long-term feasibility of the platforms. One more element that is also important for sustainable development is reducing the cost of storing cryptocurrencies for miners (Jiang et al., 2022; Liu et al., 2023).

The categories of financial innovation described above include technologies and software that are used to enable, support, and optimise financial services. Therefore, all of them can be described as fintech. Fintech can drive financial inclusion, especially by digitising services, targeting services to underserved populations, building trust, and utilising blockchain. Therefore, actions across different areas of the financial sector are needed. Fig. 9.2 shows the most important areas of financial inclusion by fintech, which include digital innovation in different areas of the financial sector.

As part of the payment services and market infrastructure, in addition to digital payments and electronic money described earlier, an important are overlay services which are built on the existing base infrastructure and deliver increased value to the participants of a payment network. They are helping people to have a smoother payment experience in their everyday lives. Kazan (2015) conducted a comparison of two digital payment platforms Apple Pay and Google Wallet.

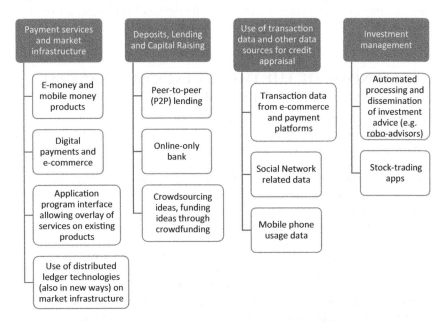

Fig. 9.2. Areas of Financial Inclusion by fintech. *Source*: Own elaboration.

In the area of P2P lending the major problems are information asymmetry, determining the borrower's score, moral hazard, herding behaviour, regulation, and policy (Suryono et al., 2019). Moreover, P2P lending is usually much riskier than a savings account. An important way of raising capital is crowdfunding. It refers to raising funds for a project or venture from a large group of people through a dedicated app or website (Mollick, 2014).

Financial and lending institutions need credit data to make a reliable rating of borrowers. Credit data means any positive or negative data relating to a person. New technologies support their obtaining. One often-used source is obtaining transaction data from e-commerce and payment platforms like PayPal, Amazon Pay, Google Pay, and Apple Pay (Zhang, 2022). Information can also be obtained from social networks (Facebook, Twitter, LinkedIn, or Instagram). These data provide a rich source of information that characterises social media users. Due to the number of smartphone subscriptions significantly exceeding the current number of people in the world, mobile phone is a very important source of data (Shema, 2019).

The last described area accelerating financial inclusion by fintech is investment management. Automated investing offers a convenient and cost-effective way to participate in the financial markets. Two key solutions for investment management are Robo-advisors and stock-trading apps. Robo-advisors use web-based questionnaires that users of their services must complete to obtain the necessary inputs for their investment algorithms (Faloon & Scherer, 2017). Stock trading apps are one of the most popular innovations in investment management. Investors have easy access to the market, where they can buy and sell shares on their mobile devices (Malhotra, 2020; Nair et al., 2023).

DIAGNOSIS OF THE IMPORTANCE OF FINANCIAL INNOVATIONS IN MODERN ECONOMY

The very first variable informing about the importance of financial innovations in the real economy is development of cashless transactions. We used the data from http://www.statista.com. We could observe that the number of cashless transactions indicates on the stable growth. That's why we decided to estimate the trend model to describe this phenomenon. Fig. 9.3 presents empirical data and theoretical values (estimated from econometric logarithmic model) for the number of cashes transactions.

The best approximated model we obtained is the logarithmic model with equation presented in the Table 9.2.

The model shows that the number of cashless transactions will increase by around 14.44% each year. This means that, assuming this rate of change, the number of cashless transactions will reach 1,896 billion in 2027. If we look at the number of transactions in 2014, which was 393.2 billion, we can see that this number will increase by almost five times. This shows the huge importance of this type of transaction in the modern world.

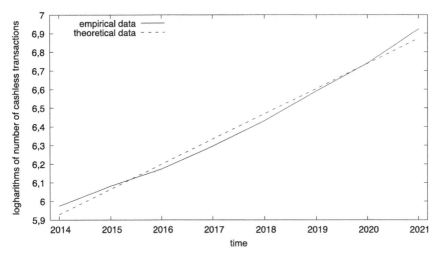

Fig. 9.3. The Theoretical and Empirical Data for Number of Cashless Transactions Worldwide (in Billions). *Source*: Own calculations.

Table 9.2. Estimation OLS for Dependent Variable (Y): log_cashless.

	Coefficient	Standard Error	t-Student Value	p-Value	
const	5.79437	0.0293668	197.3	<0.0001	***
t	0.134863	0.00581550	23.19	<0.0001	***
R-square coefficient	0.988966		Adj. square coefficient	0.987127	
$F(1, 6)$	537.7908		p-value for F-test	4.22e^{-07}	
Likelihood logarithm	16.02637		AIC	−28.05274	
SIC	−27.89386		HQC	−29.12434	
Rho1	0.546183		DW	0.696653	

Source: Own calculations.

According to Statista.com, US$440 billion worth of cashless transactions was conducted in the Asia-Pacific region in 2022. This was followed by Europe and North America, with US$254.6 billion and US$204.4 billion of transactions, respectively. This means that growth at a higher rate is not in the world's strongest economies but in developing countries. In addition, they foresee a significant increase in the number of transactions and their value in Latin America (Brazil, Peru, Colombia) as a result of the implementation of instant payments (https://www.statista.com access on 28.04.2024).

According to estimates by www.statista.com, the fintech industry will be characterised by a steady increase in the value of transactions, which could reach up to US$15.5 trillion in 2028. Table 9.3 shows the breakdown of transaction value by digital payments, neobanking, and digital capital raising (crowdfunding, crowdinvesting, crowdlending, and marketplace lending).

As can be seen, digital payments are the most important component of transaction value (85% on average between 2018 and 2022). However, it is estimated that

Table 9.3. The Structure of Fintech Transactions' Value (in Trillion USD).

Year	Total	Digital Payments	Neobanking	Digital Capital Rising
2018	3.86	3.57	0.23	0.06
2019	4.97	4.46	0.45	0.06
2020	6.24	5.33	0.84	0.07
2021	8.02	6.44	1.52	0.06
2022	10.65	8.04	2.55	0.06
2023	12.27	8.75	3.46	0.06
2024	15.12	10.09	4.96	0.07
2025	17.99	11.55	6.37	0.07
2026	20.87	13.17	7.63	0.07
2027	23.10	14.33	8.70	0.07
2028	25.22	15.53	9.62	0.07

Source: www.statista.com.

this share will fall to up to 60% in favour of transactions generated by neobanks (up to 38%). The average growth rate of transaction value will be between 20% and 30%, falling from the observed 28% to almost 21%.

Another element of the fintech sector to watch is the cryptocurrency market. The most popular cryptocurrency in the world is bitcoin, so we will use bitcoin as an example. Fig 9.4 shows the exchange rate of bitcoin over the period 2020–2024.

The high price volatility of bitcoin can be clearly observed in the figure (the same is true for the other cryptocurrencies). On the one hand, the use of cryptocurrencies enables the development of financial services and the acceleration of transactions in financial markets. However, the high volatility, which implies a high risk of such investments, favours missed investments and influences financial

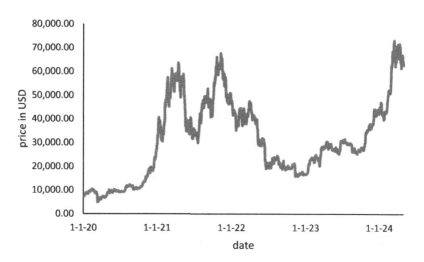

Fig. 9.4. Bitcoin Prices from 1.01.2020 to 29.04.202. *Source*: Own work on the base of data from https://www.investing.com/crypto/bitcoin/historical-data downloaded at 29.04.2024.

Table 9.4. Estimation GARCH(1,1) Model for Dependent Variable (R_t): Rate of Return ($N = 1,580$).

	Coefficient	Standard Error	Statistic z	p-Value	
Const.	0.00662582	0.00135630	4.885	<0.0001	***
DV	−0.115540	0.0283512	−4.075	<0.0001	***
alpha(0)	5.09863e^{-05}	1.19832e^{-05}	4.255	<0.0001	***
alpha(1)	0.094631	0.0188737	5.014	<0.0001	***
beta(1)	0.874564	0.0198593	44.04	<0.0001	***
Likelihood logarithm	3113.439		AIC	−6214.878	
SIC	−6182.687		HQC	−6202.917	

Unconditional variance of model's error = 0.00165513.
Source: Own calculations.

market imbalances. To illustrate the risks of investing in cryptocurrencies, we will present econometric modelling of both bitcoin returns and logarithms of trading volume. The variables used in the models are bitcoin's daily price volatility (DV), return rate (Rt) with lags, and trading volume (Vol.).

In the study, we employed GARCH-type models as the optimal approximation of the volatility of bitcoin prices and trading volumes (see Table 9.4).

This model represents the most accurate approximation of the relationship between bitcoin returns and intraday price volatility. It is based on the logarithmic ratio of the highest and lowest intraday prices and shows a clear inverse relationship. This indicates that as volatility increases, logarithmic daily returns on bitcoin prices decline. The unconditional error variance of this model is remarkably low at 0.00165513, which further validates the model's precision.

The second model (Table 9.5) presented is the ARCH(1) model for trading volume (logarithm), which is explained by intraday price volatility and lagged bitcoin price returns (by 1, 2, and 3 days). The selected variables are characterised by positive parameters. It is of particular significance that the intraday price volatility (10.9173) and the fact that the unconditional variance of the model error is

Table 9.5. Estimation ARCH(1) Model for Dependent Variable (Vol): Trading Volume ($N = 1,577$).

	Coefficient	Standard Error	Statistic z	p-Value	
Const.	−3.03454	0.0361408	−83.96	<0.0001	***
DV	10.9173	0.431212	25.32	<0.0001	***
Rt_1	1.66907	0.347842	4.798	<0.0001	***
Rt_2	2.05693	0.441438	4.660	<0.0001	***
Rt_3	4.18500	0.299784	13.96	<0.0001	***
alpha(0)	0.184567	0.0127204	14.51	<0.0001	***
alpha(1)	1.00000	0.0596688	16.76	<0.0001	***
Likelihood logarithm	−2084,636		AIC	4185,272	
SIC	4228,178		HQC	4201,216	

Unconditional variance of model's error = 4.21658e^{+09}.
Source: Own calculations.

4.21658e^{+09} have the greatest impact on the explanatory variable. While in the first case, this indicates the influence of speculative trading on the increase in trading volume; in the second case, we can speak of a very high instability of the model. This is a consequence of the high volatility in trading volume, which has fluctuated from 20,000 to over 3 billion units.

CONCLUSIONS

This article seeks to illustrate the role of financial innovation in supporting sustainable development. Fintech, as an economic sector, plays a pivotal role, as evidenced by the fact that over 80% of global financial transactions are now cashless. The dynamic development of the entire financial innovation sector will undoubtedly have a positive impact on the economy as a whole. However, the intense growth of the cryptocurrency market may be open to question. The concept of cryptocurrencies has also been acknowledged by global financial institutions, which are seeking to regulate them.

The impact of financial innovation on sustainable development can be pointed out by referring to ESG factors. Concerning to environmental impact, the carbon footprint of fintechs is relatively small compared to manufacturers and bricks-and-mortar retailers. This is because they do not run shops or manufacture products. The greatest impact is in the social area. Fintech lowers the cost of providing financial services, which is especially important for low-income countries. Therefore, it is profitable to provide accounts for low-income individuals and businesses across developing countries. This increases access for poor people, especially women, to basic financial services. Moreover, the possibility of money management can lead to increased income, increased resilience, and improved quality of life. It is also important to note that the use of mobile technology can significantly reduce financial market imperfections and make it easier to extend credit to previously unbanked people. Fintech can also help fill the funding gap for micro-, small-, and medium-sized enterprises through new solutions for raising funds and capital for development.

In the context of sustainable economy, financial innovation fulfils a number of important roles. Firstly, the development of mobile technology has enabled access to banking to be provided to an increasingly broader section of society. Secondly, the use of mobile technology has made it possible for payments to be made and received without the need for special devices. Thirdly, the internet and mobile applications have provided new jobs. Fourthly, they have created new investment opportunities. The emergence of blockchain technology and cryptocurrencies has facilitated access to digital capital raising (crowdfunding, crowdinvesting, crowdlending, and marketplace lending), which represents a source of co-financing or collective financing for investments that do not find funding in classical banking. Furthermore, blockchain technology ensures the rapid transfer of funds between economic sectors, thereby enhancing their competitiveness.

It is important to note that financial innovation also has the potential to have negative impacts on a sustainable economy. One of the most significant of these is the destabilisation of the financial market by speculative activities in the cryptocurrency market. Another related issue is the definite increase in electricity consumption due to the hardware requirements of cryptocurrency mines. Given the still unregulated electricity production and the overly large share of conventional fuels in this production, this has a negative impact on the economics of sustainability.

REFERENCES

Allen, F., Demirguc-Kunt, A., Klapper, L., & Peria, M. S. M. (2016). The foundations of financial inclusion: Understanding ownership and use of formal accounts. *Journal of Financial Intermediation, 27*, 1–30.

Arner, D. W., Barberis, J., & Buckley, R. P. (2015). The evolution of Fintech: A new post-crisis paradigm. *Georgetown Journal of International Law, 47*, 1271.

Arslanian, H., & Fischer, F. (2019). *The future of finance: The impact of FinTech, AI, and crypto on financial services*. Springer.

Bank for International Settlements. (2018, March). *Central bank digital currencies*. Bank for International Settlements, Committee on Payments and Market Infrastructures, Markets Committee.

Bhattacharya, R., White, M., & Beloff, N. (2017, July). A blockchain based peer-to-peer framework for exchanging leftover foreign currency. *2017 Computing conference* (pp. 1431–1435). IEEE.

Boel, P., & Zimmerman, P. (2022). *Unbanked in America: A review of the literature*. Economic Commentary, (2022-07).

Carroll, J. M., & Bellotti, V. (2015, February). Creating value together: The emerging design space of peer-to-peer currency and exchange. *Proceedings of the 18th ACM conference on computer supported cooperative work & social computing* (pp. 1500–1510).

Chithra, N., & Selvam, M. (2013). Determinants of financial inclusion: An empirical study on the interstate variations in India. SSRN 2296096.

Clerc, L., Moraglia, A., & Perron, S. (2020). *Neobanks seeking profitability*. Banque de France.

Comizio, V. G. (2017). Virtual currencies: Growing regulatory framework and challenges in the emerging Fintech ecosystem. *NC Banking Institute, 21*, 131.

Faloon, M., & Scherer, B. (2017). Individualization of robo-advice. *The Journal of Wealth Management, 20*(1), 30.

Galanti, S., & Özsoy, Ç. Y. (2022). Digital finance, development, and climate change. *IFC Bulletin*, 56.

Hopkinson, G. G., Klarova, D., Turcan, R., & Gulieva, V. (2019). *How neobanks' business models challenge traditional banks*.

Jiang, S., Jakobsen, K., Bueie, J., Li, J., & Haro, P. H. (2022). A tertiary review on blockchain and sustainability with focus on Sustainable Development Goals. *IEEE Access, 10*, 114975–115006.

Karlan, D., Osman, A., & Shammout, N. (2021). Increasing financial inclusion in the Muslim world: Evidence from an Islamic finance marketing experiment. *The World Bank Economic Review, 35*(2), 376–397.

Kazan, E. (2015). The innovative capabilities of digital payment platforms: A comparative study of Apple pay & Google wallet. *Proceedings of the 14th international conference on mobile business, ICMB 2015* (p. 4). Association for Information Systems. AIS Electronic Library (AISeL).

Kim, D. W., Yu, J. S., & Hassan, M. K. (2018). Financial inclusion and economic growth in OIC countries. *Research in International Business and Finance, 43*, 1–14.

Leong, K., & Sung, A. (2018). FinTech (financial technology): What is it and how to use technologies to create business value in fintech way?. *International Journal of Innovation, Management and Technology, 9*(2), 74–78.

Liu, Y., Fang, Z., Cheung, M. H., Cai, W., & Huang, J. (2023). Mechanisms design for blockchain storage sustainability. *IEEE Communications Magazine*.

Malhotra, S. (2020). Study of features of mobile trading apps: A silver lining of pandemic. *Journal of Global Information & Business Strategy (JGIBS), 12*(1), 75–80.

Mollick, E. (2014). The dynamics of crowdfunding: An exploratory study. *Journal of Business Venturing*, *29*(1), 1–16.
Nair, P. S., Shiva, A., Yadav, N., & Tandon, P. (2023). Determinants of mobile apps adoption by retail investors for online trading in emerging financial markets. *Benchmarking: An International Journal*, *30*(5), 1623–1648.
Ozili, P. K. (2018). Impact of digital finance on financial inclusion and stability. *Borsa Istanbul Review*, *18*(4), 329–340.
Park, C. Y., & Mercado, R. (2015). Financial inclusion, poverty, and income inequality in developing Asia. *Asian Development Bank Economics Working Paper Series*, 426.
Sakalauskas, V., Kriksciuniene, D., Kiss, F., & Horváth, A. (2009). Factors for sustainable development of E-banking in Lithuania and Hungary. *Proceedings of the EURO-Mini conference* (p. 254). Vilnius Gediminas Technical University, Department of Construction Economics & Property.
Sanderson, A., Mutandwa, L., & Le Roux, P. (2018). A review of determinants of financial inclusion. *International Journal of Economics and Financial Issues*, *8*(3), 1.
Setiawan, K., & Maulisa, N. (2020, March). The evolution of fintech: A regulatory approach perspective. *3rd International conference on law and governance (ICLAVE 2019)* (pp. 218–225). Atlantis Press.
Shema, A. (2019, January). Effective credit scoring using limited mobile phone data. *Proceedings of the tenth international conference on information and communication technologies and development* (pp. 1–11).
Suryono, R. R., Purwandari, B., & Budi, I. (2019). Peer to peer (P2P) lending problems and potential solutions: A systematic literature review. *Procedia Computer Science*, *161*, 204–214.
The World Bank. (2022). *Financial inclusion*. https://www.worldbank.org/en/topic/financialinclusion/overview
Turner, D. A., & Ross, K. W. (2004). A lightweight currency paradigm for the P2P resource market. *Proceedings of electronic commerce research*.
Van, L. T. H., Vo, A. T., Nguyen, N. T., & Vo, D. H. (2021). Financial inclusion and economic growth: An European Central Bank (2015). *Virtual currency schemes – A further analysis*. European Central Bank, Frankfurt.
Ward, O., & Rochemont, S. (2019). Understanding central bank digital currencies (CBDC). *Institute and Faculty of Actuaries*, *13*(2), 263–268.
Xia, P., Wang, H., Zhang, B., Ji, R., Gao, B., Wu, L., Luo, X., & Xu, G. (2020). Characterizing cryptocurrency exchange scams. *Computers & Security*, *98*, 101993.
Yawe, B. L., Ddumba-Ssentamu, J., Nnyanzi, J. B., & Mukisa, I. (2022). Role of mobile money and digital payments in financial inclusion for sustainable development goals in Africa. *Globalization and sustainability-recent advances, new perspectives and emerging issues*. IntechOpen.
Zhang, Y. (2022). An evaluation model of e-commerce credit information based on social big data. *International Journal of Autonomous and Adaptive Communications Systems*, *15*(4), 279–294.

CHAPTER 10

TRANSITION TO A CIRCULAR ECONOMY IN ASEAN-5: INFERENCES ON SUSTAINABLE DEVELOPMENT IN A GLOBALISED WORLD

Grațiela-Georgiana Noja[a], Monica Boldea[b], Maria-Izabela Purdescu[c] and Alina Ionașcu[d]

[a]*Faculty of Economics and Business Administration, Department of Marketing, International Business and Economics, East-European Center for Research in Economics and Business, West University of Timisoara, Timisoara, Romania*
[b]*Faculty of Economics and Business Administration, Department of Marketing, International Business and Economics, West University of Timisoara, Timisoara, Romania*
[c]*Faculty of Economics and Business Administration, West University of Timisoara, Timisoara, Romania*
[d]*Faculty of Economics and Business Administration, Doctoral School of Economics and Business Administration, East-European Center for Research in Economics and Business, West University of Timisoara, Timisoara, Romania*

ABSTRACT

Purpose: *The main purpose of the undertaken research is to analyse the effects induced by the specific coordinates of circular economy (CE), environment, and sustainability on the ASEAN-5 countries by assessing the economic dynamics in the context of this transition.*

Methodology: *The research methodology focuses on robust regression (RREG) models and Gaussian graphical models (GGMs) applied to panel* data, including a complex set of fundamental macroeconomic aggregates as variables. Indicators were compiled for the ASEAN-5 member states: the Philippines, Indonesia, Malaysia, Singapore, and Thailand, over the period 2000–2023, including International Monetary Fund projections for the period 2024–2028.

Findings: *The results highlight the importance of environmental coordinates in modelling the sustainable economic development of the ASEAN countries. Significant positive developments in the transition to a CE have been recorded with the end of the pandemic period, but fluctuations in carbon dioxide emissions (CO_2_EMIS) are still present. Although values have fallen by almost 30% compared to the last decade, countries have failed so far to ensure a downward trend.*

Significance/Implications/Conclusions: *To bring about change, ASEAN-5 countries should focus on implementing a CE framework, enforcing stricter measures, and raising awareness among the population.*

Limitations: *The current research encountered certain limitations primarily due to the lack of data availability and the restricted sample of indicators.*

Future Research: *Innovation, digitalisation, and adopting emerging technologies are indispensable in expediting diverse processes. These facets are fundamental in the assimilation and institutionalisation of CE principles and signify the future trajectory of research.*

Keywords: ASEAN-5; circular economy; sustainability; emissions; pollution

JEL Codes: Q01; F18; F64; O44

1. INTRODUCTION

In the age of globalisation, the whole world faces real threats from climate change and environmental pollution. The world economy faces a lot of challenges in trying to improve as much as possible the footprint of industries that emit environmentally harmful gases or polluting elements in general. The present situation shows how important it is that certain sustainable development measures take hold, especially in developing countries. Economic growth spreads pollutants by some industries, increases population consumerism, and, thus, creates problems for the whole of humanity (Herrador & Van, 2023).

In order to see how these measures influence developing countries, the present study investigates the impact of the transition to a CE in the ASEAN-5 member states of Indonesia, Malaysia, Thailand, Singapore, and the Philippines. Although this is an early-stage initiative, several factors were identified that support the transition to a sustainable development model (Sinay et al., 2023).

The first key issue is the harmonisation of standards and recognition of products and services that comply with the principles of the CE. Next, it is very important to maintain an open market and to encourage trade in goods and services that align with these principles. Innovation, digitisation, and adopting emerging technologies play a key role in accelerating these processes. For example, introducing and producing electric cars, using renewable energy sources, and innovation in state systems such as education and transport. Facilitating these changes requires a strong policy and institutional framework, raising awareness and skills in different sectors, collaboration and strategic partnership, all of which are essential for adopting and mainstreaming CE principles.

In view of these aspects, the undertaken research aims to highlight the fundamental coordinates that define the impact of this transition on the ASEAN-5 countries, analysing the factors shaping economic development in relation to the CE integration process.

The chapter is structured into three comprehensive sections, each of which provides an in-depth analysis of various aspects of the topic. Section 2 presents a theoretical underpinning of the subject matter based on a systematic and bibliometric analysis of the relevant scientific literature. This section aims to provide a comprehensive understanding of the topic by examining the existing body of knowledge in the field. The systematic analysis identifies the key themes, trends, and gaps in the literature, while the bibliometric analysis maps the evolution of the literature and identifies the main concepts and keywords associated with this topic, the most influential authors, journals, and publications. Section 3 presents the data and methodological credentials of the study. This section describes the research design, data collection methods, and analytical techniques used in the study. It also presents the results obtained, which are discussed in light of the theoretical framework presented in Section 2. The section further explores the economic implications of the findings and their potential impact on policy and practice. Finally, Section 4 concludes the chapter by summarising the key findings and their implications for the topic. This section also discusses the limitations of the study and suggests areas for future research.

2. LITERATURE REVIEW

2.1. Systematic Review of the Scientific Literature

The ASEAN grouping of states was established in 1967 to pool the strengths of the five signatories of the Bangkok Declaration: Indonesia, Malaysia, the Philippines, Singapore, and Thailand (Qiu et al., 2022). With much patience and understanding, the foreign ministers managed to set out in just five articles the document that facilitated their new and close collaboration. This created the Association for Regional Cooperation among Southeast Asian Countries, known as the Association of Southeast Asian Nations (ASEAN), which was designed to bring prosperity, active participation in the economic, social, cultural, technical, and educational fields, and in promoting regional peace and stability through respect for justice and the rule of law and adherence to the principles of the United Nations. Over time, the economic development that followed brought about jobs, increased the purchasing power, and, thus, improved the standard of living in that part of Asia. However, with all these benefits, the Southeast also had a large environmental footprint. Sinay et al. (2023) point out that the region's development has led to a rapid increase in carbon emissions, from 1,038 metric tons (Mt) of CO_2 in 2010 to 1,429 Mt CO_2 in 2018. Under these conditions, further long-term economic growth was impossible. To solve the problem, ASEAN needed a new economic model that would change the traditional linear economy (take, make, use, dispose) and emphasise resource efficiency. This is where the CE model based on the 3Rs: reduce, recycle, reuse (Manickam & Duraisamy, 2023) comes in.

Various authors have outlined the definition of the CE as an innovative advanced economic model with a scope to reduce the use of raw materials by reusing products and waste (Crossan et al., 1999); the strategy of changing the linear system of consumption into a circular system for economic sustainability (Smith & Lewis, 2011) and industrial system, which replaces the concept of end-of-life and eliminates the use of environmentally harmful products (Homrich et al., 2018). To join the CE initiative, ASEAN adopted in October 2021 the 'Framework for a Circular Economy'. This is intended to help member states meet their climate targets and achieve a green and resilient recovery especially following the COVID-19 pandemic.

This framework proposes a number of five strategic priorities to accelerate the transition to the CE, such as (i) harmonisation and mutual recognition of circular products and services; (ii) trade opening and facilitation of trade in goods and services; (iii) enhancing the role of innovation, digitisation, and emerging technologies; (iv) sustainable finance and innovative investment; (v) efficient use of energy and other resources. This has had many implications for the economic growth of countries. ASEAN recorded the highest value of foreign direct investment (FDI) in 2022 ($224 billion). According to the ASEAN Investment Report (2023), in 2021–2022, ASEAN member states have adopted 24 investment policy measures (ASEAN Secretariat & UNCTAD, 2023). Of these, 16 were FDI-friendly, 3 were neutral, and the rest were restrictive. Six of the favourable measures focused on investment facilitation. Some Member States liberalised their policies, allowing full foreign ownership in sectors such as insurance, renewable energy, and telecommunications. This has helped strengthen GDP growth and per capita demand, the expansion of the electronics sector, the transition to electric vehicles, and the recovery of the tourism industry. Lee et al. (2023) also explain the concrete ways in which the labour market will be enriched by green jobs. Examples of such jobs are shown in Fig. 10.1.

Transport is the second largest energy-consuming sector in the ASEAN market, and vehicle electrification has become one of the emerging opportunities in many countries. They conclude that increasing CE opportunities are expected to create 6.6 million jobs by 2030. The ASEAN region is, therefore, projected to remain one of the fastest-growing regions of the world economy in the following decade. The declining cost of reusable energy technologies, increasing

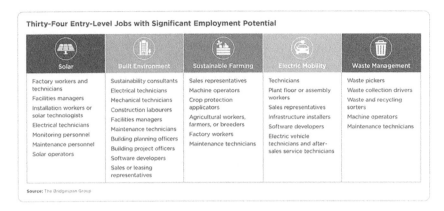

Fig. 10.1. Green Jobs. *Source*: Lee et al. (2023), The Brigespan Group.

opportunities for development through FDI, and jobs generated by the transition to a CE are factors that show the implications of this strategy for the overall economic development of the ASEAN group.

2.2. Bibliometric Analysis of the Scientific Literature

In order to highlight the links between the key concepts related to the analysed topic, we conducted a bibliometric analysis based on information extracted from 1,006 specific articles downloaded from the Web of Science and processed using the VOSviewer software. The graphical representation of the co-occurrence of keywords related to the researched theme is shown in Fig. 10.2, and the main authors of papers published in recent years on this theme and indexed in Web of Science are iterated in Fig. 10.3.

Analysing the connections between the identified keywords ('emissions', 'ASEAN-5', 'community', 'stability', and 'economy'), and the themes addressed in this paper, there is an alignment between current concerns in the literature and research directions. The paper explores how CE principles can contribute to reducing pollution and promoting economic growth in the ASEAN-5 region, showing the importance of adopting innovative economic models. This analysis highlights the relevance of research in the current context of sustainable development and economic growth.

3. CASE STUDY AND RESULTS

In order to undertake the case study, we analysed a complex set of economic indicators, such as the total gross domestic product (GDP_T), the gross domestic product (GDP) per capita (GDP_C), the GDP growth rate (GDP_G), the unemployment rate (UR), the inflation rate (INFL) as proxies of sustainable economic development and of macroeconomic stability, alongside indicators that consider pollution through the volume of CO_2_EMIS, and the frequency of

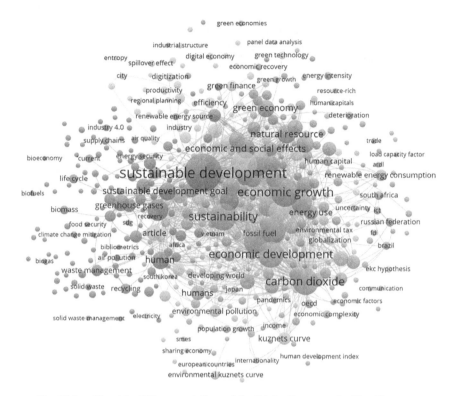

Fig. 10.2. Graphical Representation of the Links Between the Key Concepts Specific to the Theme Addressed. *Source*: Own processing of data extracted from Web of Science using VOSviewer package.

natural disasters caused by climate change (CLIM_D) as proxy of sustainability. The database configured for the empirical research was aimed at the five ASEAN countries – Philippines, Indonesia, Thailand, Malaysia, and Singapore – considered over the period 2000–2028.

Table 10.1 shows the descriptive statistics of the indicators used in the econometric modelling and the related correlation matrix.

GDP is the most widely used indicator of economic growth and long-term development of a country. It describes the sum total of the values of all goods and services intended for final consumption, which are produced in all sectors of a country during a given period. To show a more accurate measure of a state's well-being, GDP per capita is used, which is calculated by dividing the GDP value by the number of inhabitants in that state. In order to have a real picture of these indicators, we considered the data in US dollars as a common currency. The UR shows the percentage of the working population that does not currently have a job. This indicator will suggest how the situation of the unemployed in the ASEAN-5 countries has changed after more 'green jobs' were created. The INFL captures the general rise in prices across the ASEAN states.

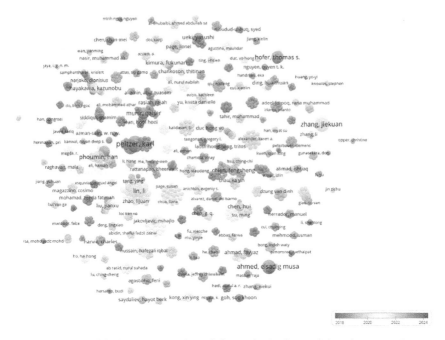

Fig. 10.3. Graphical Representation of the Main Authors of the Literature. *Source*: Own processing of data extracted from Web of Science using VOSviewer package.

Table 10.1. Descriptive Statistics and Correlation Matrix of Variables Used in Modelling.

Variable	Obs	Mean	Std. Dev.	Min	Max
GDP_T (GDP total)	145	4.442e+11	3.705e+11	7.892e+10	2.093e+12
GDP_C (GDP per capita)	145	15,965.614	24,400.923	739	108,204.03
GDP_G (GDP growth)	115	4.549	3.174	−9.52	14.52
UR (unemployment rate)	144	4.319	2.807	0.7	11.825
INFL (inflation rate)	145	3.06	2.461	−1.139	13.101
CLIM_D (disasters induced by climate change)	89	81.91	57.285	10	300
CO_2_EMIS (CO_2 emissions)	115	3.614e+09	2.746e+09	14,477,155	9.843e+09

				Pairwise correlations			
Variables	(1) GDP_T	(2) GDP_C	(3) GDP_G	(4) UR	(5) INFL	(6) CLIM_D	(7) CO_2_EMIS
(1) GDP_T	1.000						
(2) GDP_C	−0.038	1.000					
(3) GDP_G	−0.086	−0.003	1.000				
(4) UR	0.011	−0.408***	0.032	1.000			
(5) INFL	−0.010	−0.196**	0.204**	0.558***	1.000		
(6) CLIM_D	0.278***	−0.467***	0.007	0.526***	0.285***	1.000	
(7) CO_2_EMIS	−0.264***	0.114	0.090	0.451***	0.312***	0.296***	1.000

***$p < 0.01$, **$p < 0.05$, *$p < 0.1$.
Source: Own research of IMF data (2024) using the econometric Stata dataset.

In the current analysis, the volume of emissions shows how many metric tons of CO_2 were released by these countries in the chosen period. The frequency of natural disasters caused by climate change includes the total number of droughts, extreme temperatures, floods, landslides, and storms recorded in a year.

The evolution of the indicators analysed in this study during the period 2000–2028 in the case of the ASEAN countries included in the panel was presented in Fig. 10.4.

Regarding the GDP per capita, it can be noted that most states registered an expansion until the time of the pandemic, and in the years following the pandemic, they managed to reach the initial values or even exceeded them. Thailand is the only exception among the five countries, which in 2022 experienced a decrease

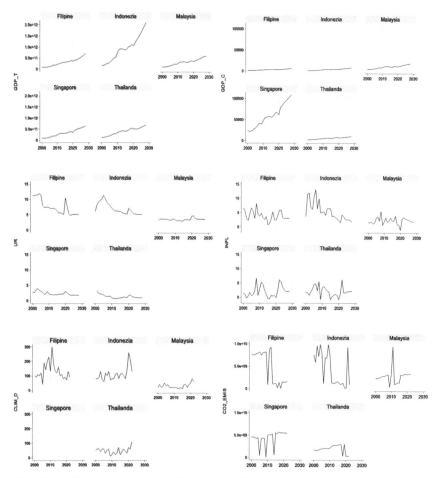

Fig. 10.4. The Evolution of the Economic Indicators Considered in the Analysis at the ASEAN Level, in the Period 2000–2028. *Source*: Own processing of IMF data (2024) with the help of the Stata econometric dataset.

in the GDP per capita caused by the ageing population, the deterioration of the education system, and the low yield of rice cultivation. Likewise, the evolution of the UR also reflects the impact of the pandemic on the labour market, with all states registering increases in this indicator in 2020, some values even doubling (the case of the Philippines). Over the following years, the states managed to fix the problem and considerably reduce the UR by the year 2022.

Analysing the sustainability indicators from the perspective of the environment and climate change recorded by the ASEAN-5 countries, it can be noticed that in the period 2000–2022, there is an upward trend in the case of GDP per capita, indicating an increase in the level of economic prosperity. GDP per capita registered some notable declines in 2009 and 2020, reflecting the impact of the global financial crisis in 2009 and the COVID-19 pandemic in 2020. In terms of CO_2_EMIS, these can be noticed as fluctuating throughout the period. It can be observed that the evolution of the volume of emissions in the period 2010–2015 is 26% higher than in the period 2017–2022. Since 2018, when the ASEAN-5 countries started to adopt CE principles, it has been noted that the CO_2 emissions continue to be unstable, a fact which shows that the measures are still in trial phases to see what will have a real effect on emissions. During this time GDP per capita remained stable and even increased after 2020. This suggests that the ASEAN-5 countries have not yet succeeded in improving resource efficiency and in reducing the negative environmental impact of CO_2 emissions.

The last parameter analysed was the frequency of natural disasters caused by climate problems (natural disasters in this context include floods, droughts, epidemics, storms, landslides, earthquakes, and fires). Indonesia registered the highest number of disasters compared to the other countries and recorded a dramatic peak in the year 2020. The year 2021 showed an overall downward trend in Indonesia and Thailand, but an increase in the Philippines and Malaysia due to the implementation of some more effective prevention measures in some countries than in others. The decline occurred in 2022 continued in all countries except for Thailand, for which the values remained constant. These trends highlight the challenges and successes of different national approaches to managing climate change disasters. From 2017 to 2021, no natural disasters were recorded in Singapore as there were only four recorded events in the past decades.

To further our research approach, emphasis was put on the analysis of the impact induced by the sustainability coordinates focused on the environment and climate change on economic growth and long-term development, respectively, on the performance of the labour market and the macroeconomic stability of the ASEAN states. Thus, we developed a set of RREG models, supplemented by panel correlated standard error correction (PCSE) estimates. At the same time, in order to ensure the robustness of the results so as to interpret them correctly from an economic point of view, we also configured a GGM estimated by the method of partial correlations (PCOR). This model shows the correlational interference between all variables used in the empirical analysis.

The results of the RREG models have been detailed in Table 10.2, and the results of the RREG models compared to the PCSE estimates are to be found in Table 10.3.

Table 10.2. RREG Models Capturing the Effects of Environmental Coordinates on Economic Activity and Sustainable Development of ASEAN Panel States.

GDP_T	Coef.	St. Err.	t-Value	p-Value	[95% Conf	Interval]	Sig
CO_2_EMIS	−0.230	0.065	−3.70	0.000	−0.369	−0.111	***
CLIM_D	0.002	0.001	1.62	0.109	0	0.005	
Constant	31.395	1.398	22.46	0.000	28.616	34.175	***
Mean dependent var			26.414	SD dependent var			0.707
R-squared			0.156	Number of obs			89
F-test			7.931	Prob > F			0.001

GDP_C	Coef.	St.Err.	t-value	p-value	[95% Conf	Interval]	Sig
CO_2_EMIS	−0.204	0.06	−3.40	0.001	−0.323	−0.085	***
CLIM_D	−0.005	0.001	−4.35	0.000	−0.008	−0.003	***
Constant	12.983	1.29	10.06	0.000	10.418	15.548	***
Mean dependent var			8.162	SD dependent var			0.710
R-squared			0.269	Number of obs			89
F-test			15.828	Prob > F			0.000

***$p < 0.01$, **$p < 0.05$, *$p < 0.1$.
Source: Own research in Stata.

Table 10.3. Ascertaining the Robustness of Regression Models by Comparison with the PCSE Correction Method.

	(1)	(2)	(3)	(4)
	GDP_C	GDP_C	GDP_T	GDP_T
	RREG	PCSE	RREG	PCSE
CO_2_EMIS	<0.204** (0.0599)	−0.198** (0.0619)	−0.240*** (0.0649)	−0.235*** (0.0565)
CLIM_D	−0.00525*** (0.00121)	−0.00511*** (0.00111)	0.00211 (0.00131)	0.00249** (0.000903)
_cons	12.98*** (1.290)	12.84*** (1.321)	31.40*** (1.398)	31.27*** (1.207)
N	89	89	89	89
R^2	0.269	0.284	0.156	0.183

	(1)	(2)	(3)	(4)
	UR	UR	INFL	INFL
	RREG	PCSE	RREG	PCSE
CO_2_EMIS	0.699** (0.233)	0.821** (0.277)	0.491* (0.205)	0.570* (0.255)
CLIM_D	0.0309*** (0.00471)	0.0280*** (0.00570)	0.0118** (0.00413)	0.0133** (0.00440)
_cons	−12.62* (5.031)	−14.77* (6.019)	−8.272 (4.416)	−9.738 (5.401)
N	88	88	89	89
R^2	0.386	0.370	0.143	0.138

N.B.: Standard errors in parentheses, *$p < 0.05$, **$p < 0.01$, ***$p < 0.001$.
Source: Own research in Stata.

Analysing the estimates obtained from processing the regression models through the robust method with Huber and biweight iterations, it can be noticed that the negative impact of CO_2 emissions is particularly significant on the economic development of the ASEAN states (negative coefficients, statistically significant), while the negative effects on the economic well-being shown by the level of GDP per capita are highlighted rather by means of the climate change variable (CLIM_D, negative coefficient, and statistically significant at the 0.1% threshold).

To ensure the robustness of the results, we also processed the models by the PCSE correction method. The results obtained have been summarised in Table 10.3 and confirm the significant negative effects induced by environmental pollution (CO_2_EMISSION) reflected by the estimated coefficients showing the reduction of total GDP, GDP per capita, the increase in the UR, and inflationary pressures with the increase in the emissions of carbon dioxide. The same negative economic impact was also highlighted from the perspective of CLIM_D. The estimated coefficients were statistically significant at the 5%, 1%, and 0.1% thresholds.

To validate the results of the regression models with panel data and to better capture the interrelations between all the variables used in the analysis, we also configured a GGM estimated by the method of PCOR. The estimated model is graphically represented in Fig. 10.5. At the same time, the detailed estimates related to the configuration of the GGM model are reported in the Appendices, Fig. A1 and Table AI.

Analysing the configuration of the Gaussian graphic model, we observe the direct and inverse link between the level of total GDP and CO_2 emissions, respectively, between the level of GDP per capita and the number of disasters induced by climate change, respectively, very strong, direct, positive links (according to growth), highlighted through the blue lines between these sustainability indicators and the UR, respectively, the INFL.

These results of network-type analysis using the GGMs reconfirm the estimates obtained in the case of regression models and reinforce the importance of the transition of ASEAN states towards a CE.

4. CONCLUSIONS

The present research presented the directions adopted by the ASEAN-5 states to integrate EC policies into their own economy and the way the transition to a CE brought about a change in the economic growth and welfare of the states. Subsequent to the performed analysis, we note that each ASEAN member country has responded differently to these new influences, but overall, the situation is beginning to improve. The COVID-19 pandemic greatly impacted the economy, and the states we studied managed to overcome that period, registering increases in certain indicators even above the pre-pandemic values.

Fluctuations in CO_2_EMIS have been maintained, but the states are supported by several world institutions such as the IMF and the European Commission and predict a better future through measures designed to introduce circularity in as

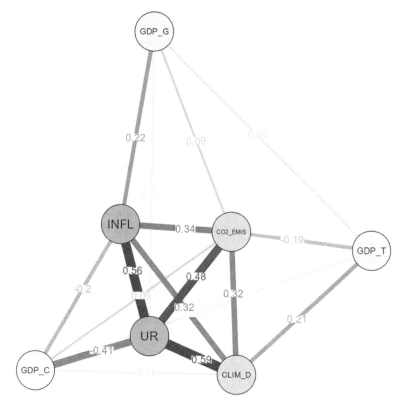

Fig. 10.5. The GGM Estimated by the Method of PCOR. *Source*: Own research in JASP.

many industries as possible. Thus, there would be a continuous flow of goods, without generating polluting waste. Singapore, for example, distinguishes itself by effective environmental policies that have led to stricter control of carbon emissions. It has adopted a number of innovative measures, such as the increased use of renewable energies and the implementation of advanced carbon capture technologies, which have contributed to the stabilisation and even the reduction of emissions per capita. Malaysia and Thailand have also made progress, but fluctuations in carbon emissions point to challenges in the consistency of environmental policies and their long-term enforcement. These countries have benefitted from the implementation of reforestation programmes as well as of programmes regarding the development of renewable energy infrastructure but need to strengthen measures to ensure continued emission reductions. Indonesia faces specific challenges, having one of the highest rates of deforestation, which negatively affects efforts to reduce emissions. However, Indonesia has begun to implement stricter policies to protect forests and promote sustainable agricultural practices, which are critical to achieving emissions reduction targets. The Philippines, although it has pioneered renewable energy activities, is experiencing increases in carbon emissions due to its continued dependence on fossil fuels. Efforts to transition to green energy are still at an early stage, and the country needs to accelerate the adoption of sustainable alternatives.

The frequency of disasters caused by climate change remains difficult to predict and control as can be seen in the analysis. They cause massive destruction and make life difficult for the entire population. In the Philippines, for example, it was found that although climate change adaptation measures have been implemented, the number of natural disasters has remained relatively constant, indicating the need for a more proactive approach to climate risk management.

Another important aspect identified in the data analysis is the link between economic growth and the UR. In Singapore, rapid economic growth and investment in technology have been linked to a significant drop in the UR after the pandemic. This illustrates how economic development and sustainability policies can create jobs and support an active economic recovery.

As development continues, the ASEAN-5 countries should persist in prioritising investments in green technologies and promoting policies that support innovation and digitisation. This will not only help achieve the Sustainable Development Goals but also help their better positioning in the global economy. International cooperation will be essential for the long-term success of the transition to a CE, leading to a prosperous future for all ASEAN-5 countries. This paves the way for a new chapter of economic development, where sustainability and innovation lead to economic growth, ensuring that current environmental protection needs are met.

ACKNOWLEDGEMENTS

This work was supported by a grant from the Romanian Ministry of Research, Innovation, and Digitalisation, the project with the title 'Economics and Policy Options for Climate Change Risk and Global Environmental Governance' (CF 193/28.11.2022, Funding Contract no. 760078/23.05.2023), within Romania's National Recovery and Resilience Plan (PNRR) – Pillar III, Component C9, Investment I8 (PNRR/2022/C9/MCID/I8) – Development of a programme to attract highly specialised human resources from abroad in research, development, and innovation activities.

REFERENCES

Crossan, M., Lane, H. W., & White, R. E. (1999). An organizational learning framework: From intuition to institution. *The Academy of Management Review*, 24, 522–537.

ERIA. (2023). *Circular economy strategies and plans in ASEAN* (No. 18, pp. 102–106). Circular value chains of electrical and electronic equipment in ASEAN, ERIA research project report FY2023.

Herrador, M., & Van, M. L. (2023). Circular economy strategies in the ASEAN region: A comparative study. *Science of the Total Environment*, 908, 168280. https://doi.org/10.1016/j.scitotenv.2023.168280

Homrich, A., Galvão, A., Abadia, L., & Carvalho, M. (2018). The circular economy umbrella: Trends and gaps on integrating pathways, *Journal of Cleaner Production*, 175, 525–543.

Lee, X., Addy, C., Thompson, R., & Farah, R. (2023). *Promoting Equitable and Inclusive Green Job Growth in Southeast Asia*. The Bridgespan Group. https://www.bridgespan.org/insights/equitable-and-inclusive-green-job-growth-in-southeast-asia

Manickam, P., & Duraisamy, G. (2023). *4–3Rs and circular economy* (pp. 77–93). Circular Economy in Textiles and Apparel – Processing, Manufacturing, and Design. https://doi.org/10.1016/B978-0-08-102630-4.00004-2

Qiu, J., Seah, S., & Martinus, M. (2022). Examining climate ambition enhancement in ASEAN countries' nationally determined contributions. *Environmental Development, 49*, 100945. https://doi.org/10.1016/j.envdev.2023.100945

Sinay, J. B., Tumengkol, E. A., & Zendra, O. (2023). *ASEAN transition towards circular economy* (No. 5, pp. 1–10). ASEAN Policy Brief. https://asean.org/wp-content/uploads/2022/12/ASEAN-Policy-Brief-5_Dec2022.pdf

Smith, W. K., & Lewis, M. W. (2011). Toward a theory of paradox: A dynamic equilibrium model of organizing. *Academy of Management Review, 36*(2), 381–403.

The ASEAN Secretariat. (2021). *Framework for circular economy for the ASEAN economic community*. https://asean.org/wp-content/uploads/2021/10/Framework-for-Circular-Economy-for-the-AEC_Final.pdf

The ASEAN Secretariat & UNCTAD. (2023). *ASEAN Investment Report 2023 – International investment trends: Key issues and policy options*. https://asean.org/book/asean-investment-report-2023/.

APPENDIX

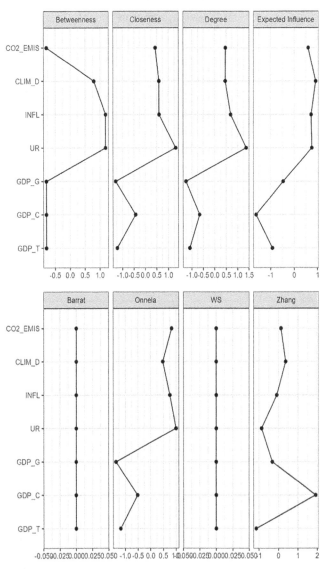

Fig. A1. Centrality and Clustering Indices Specific for the GGM. *Source*: Own contribution in JASP.

Table AI. Features and Measures per Variable of the GGM Estimated Through PCOR.

Summary of Network		
Number of Nodes	Number of Non-zero Edges	Sparsity
7	21/21	0.000

Centrality measures per variable

	Network			
Variable	Betweenness	Closeness	Strength	Expected Influence
GDP_T	−0.795	−1.229	−1.089	−0.928
GDP_C	−0.795	−0.425	−0.661	−1.613
GDP_G	−0.795	−1.294	−1.252	−0.469
UR	1.192	1.315	1.375	0.760
INFL	1.192	0.603	0.696	0.730
CLIM_D	0.795	0.594	0.461	0.921
CO_2_EMIS	−0.795	0.436	0.471	0.599

Clustering measures per variable

	Network			
Variable	Barrat[a]	Onnela	WS[a]	Zhang
GDP_T	0.000	−1.180	0.000	−1.138
GDP_C	0.000	−0.513	0.000	1.923
GDP_G	0.000	−1.367	0.000	−0.318
UR	0.000	0.994	0.000	−0.865
INFL	0.000	0.757	0.000	−0.091
CLIM_D	0.000	0.483	0.000	0.365
CO_2_EMIS	0.000	0.826	0.000	0.125

Weights matrix

	Network						
Variable	GDP_T	GDP_C	GDP_G	UR	INFL	CLIM_D	CO_2_EMIS
GDP_T	0.000	−0.038	−0.061	0.011	−0.010	0.215	−0.187
GDP_C	−0.038	0.000	−0.002	−0.409	−0.196	−0.056	0.091
GDP_G	−0.061	−0.002	0.000	0.034	0.224	0.007	0.090
UR	0.011	−0.409	0.034	0.000	0.560	0.588	0.480
INFL	−0.010	−0.196	0.224	0.560	0.000	0.319	0.343
CLIM_D	0.215	−0.056	0.007	0.588	0.319	0.000	0.319
CO_2_EMIS	−0.187	0.091	0.090	0.480	0.343	0.319	0.000

Note: [a]Coefficient could not be standardized because the variance is too small.
Source: Own contribution in JASP.

CHAPTER 11

ESSENCE AND APPEARANCE: A CRITICAL EXPLORATION OF CORPORATE GREENWASHING THROUGH ETHICAL DILEMMAS IN GLOBAL SUPPLY CHAINS

Alexandra-Codruţa Bîzoi and Cristian-Gabriel Bîzoi

Faculty of Economics and Business Administration, West University of Timişoara, Timişoara, România

ABSTRACT

Purpose: *This study critically explores the phenomenon of corporate greenwashing within global supply chains, aiming to dissect the ethical dilemmas corporations face when their environmental claims do not match their practices. It seeks to understand how corporations navigate the tension between appearing environmentally responsible and implementing sustainable practices.*

Design/Methodology/Approach: *Employing a qualitative analysis framework, the study analyses notable instances of corporate greenwashing case studies. It applies ethical theories such as Utilitarianism, Deontological Ethics, Corporate Responsibility (CR), Global Economic Inequality, stakeholder and shareholder theories, short-term gains versus long-term sustainability, Ethical sourcing, and Economic Realism to evaluate the decisions and behaviours of corporations. This approach allows for a comprehensive examination of greenwashing practices' motives, strategies, and outcomes.*

Findings: *The research uncovers that greenwashing is often a result of the complex interplay between market pressures for environmental responsibility and the challenges of genuinely implementing sustainable practices. Corporations frequently use greenwashing to meet consumer expectations without substantially changing their operations.*

Research Limitations/Implications: *The study acknowledges limitations, primarily due to the selection of case studies and the subjective interpretation of ethical theories. Future research could expand the range of case studies and explore additional ethical frameworks for a more nuanced understanding of greenwashing.*

Practical Implications: *The findings highlight the need for stricter regulatory frameworks and transparent reporting standards to discourage greenwashing. It suggests that corporations adopt a more integrated approach to sustainability, aligning their environmental claims with actual practices.*

Social Implications: *By shedding light on the discrepancy between corporate environmental claims and actions, the study calls for greater corporate accountability. It emphasises the role of informed consumer advocacy in demanding transparency and genuine sustainability efforts from corporations.*

Originality/Value: *This paper contributes to the business ethics literature by providing a detailed analysis of greenwashing within global supply chains through ethical theories. It offers a novel perspective on the ethical considerations involved in corporate environmental claims, enhancing our understanding of corporate sustainability challenges.*

Plain Language Summary: *This research analyses companies that make themselves seem more environmentally friendly than they are – a practice known as greenwashing. By examining real-life examples and using ethical principles, the study reveals why companies do this and how it can mislead consumers. It suggests that to stop greenwashing, there should be stricter rules and more transparent reporting about companies' environmental actions. The research also encourages people to demand truthfulness from companies about their environmental efforts, highlighting the importance of genuine sustainability over mere appearances.*

Keywords: Corporate Social Responsibility; sustainability; greenwashing; global supply chains; business ethics

JEL Codes: M14; Q01; F23

1. INTRODUCTION

Greenwashing represents a significant challenge in corporate sustainability, marked by a dissonance between companies' proclaimed environmental efforts and their actual practices. This discrepancy undermines ethical standards and erodes stakeholder trust, making the investigation of greenwashing's ethical implications timely and crucial. Amid growing environmental consciousness among consumers and its significant impact on corporate reputation, this paper unravels the ethical misalignments promoting greenwashing, guiding corporations towards synchronising their environmental narratives with genuine sustainability actions.

This research scrutinises greenwashing across global supply chains, employing a qualitative analysis of ethical theories such as Utilitarianism, Deontological Ethics, CR, and the dynamics between Shareholder and Stakeholder theories. By selecting case studies from varied industries and regions, we aim to shed light on the motivations behind corporate greenwashing and its resulting ethical dilemmas, thereby understanding its effect on corporate ethics and stakeholder trust. These case studies are pivotal examples to explore how greenwashing distorts corporate ethics, seeking actionable strategies for genuinely reconciling environmental claims with substantive sustainability efforts.

Ultimately, this study aspires to dissect corporate greenwashing by applying ethical theories to examine the behaviours that fuel this practice. Integrating insights from Utilitarianism, Deontological Ethics, CR, and more, our goal is to reveal how these frameworks can illuminate and help mitigate the deceptive practices of greenwashing. The central objective is to bridge the theoretical and practical divide in corporate ethics, offering pathways towards more authentic and sustainable business practices.

2. LITERATURE REVIEW

This section critically explores the interrelation between corporate profitability, ethics, and societal expectations, with an emphasis on the phenomenon of greenwashing. This deceptive practice, where companies overstate their environmental efforts, poses significant ethical challenges. The review highlights how different ethical theories can illuminate the pathways for corporations to align their environmental claims with genuine sustainability efforts.

2.1. Overview of Ethical Theories

2.1.1. Utilitarianism and Deontological Ethics: Combatting Greenwashing with Ethical Insights

Utilitarianism and Deontological Ethics are pivotal frameworks within corporate ethics, particularly in addressing greenwashing. Utilitarianism, as developed by Bentham (1789) and Mill (1863), posits that actions should aim to maximise societal happiness or welfare. This principle urges corporations to critically assess their environmental claims through a cost–benefit lens, ensuring that such claims genuinely contribute to societal well-being rather than merely serving as marketing veneer. The theory's demand for authentic societal benefits directly confronts greenwashing, challenging companies to validate the true impact of their environmental initiatives.

In contrast, Deontological Ethics, drawing from Kant's (1785) foundational philosophy, centres on the inviolability of duty and moral principles independent of the actions' consequences. This ethical stance demands corporate honesty and transparency, establishing a solid moral argument against greenwashing. By upholding ethical integrity, Deontological Ethics compels businesses to report their environmental efforts truthfully, emphasising the inherent value of honesty over manipulating environmental information for competitive advantage.

Applying these theories to the corporate domain underscores a dual mandate: to evaluate the broader societal impacts of business actions and to adhere unwaveringly to ethical principles. This dual perspective enriches the analysis of corporate behaviour in environmental sustainability and offers a direct critique of greenwashing practices.

However, despite the theoretical richness, there is a discernible gap in applying these ethical frameworks to the practical realm of combating greenwashing. Current literature, including works by Bazillier and Vauday (2009), Lyon and Montgomery (2015), and Seele and Gatti (2017), often remains anchored in theoretical exploration, leaving a void in actionable strategies for corporations to align their environmental representations with genuine sustainability efforts, which highlights an essential need for empirical research to translate ethical theories into concrete business practices, offering a roadmap for effectively integrating ethical considerations into corporate environmental strategies.

This synthesis illuminates the theoretical underpinnings necessary for understanding greenwashing and calls for a robust empirical inquiry to bridge the gap between ethical theory and corporate practice. Doing so aims to foster a more authentic approach to corporate sustainability, grounded in the broader impacts of business actions and a steadfast commitment to moral integrity.

2.1.2. CR and Global Economic Inequality: Addressing Greenwashing
In the discourse on corporate ethics, the concepts of CR and Global Economic Inequality are pivotal in formulating responses to greenwashing. This section explores their critical role in ethical corporate conduct and combating the systemic challenges of greenwashing.

As expanded by Freeman's (1984) stakeholder theory, CR shifts the focus from shareholder primacy to a broader stakeholder engagement, including employees, customers, and the wider community. This inclusive approach is instrumental in scrutinising greenwashing, as it mandates corporations to genuinely consider their operations' environmental and social implications, ensuring that sustainability claims are not merely superficial.

Carroll's (1991) Corporate Social Responsibility (CSR) pyramid and Freeman's stakeholder theory provide a framework for businesses to evaluate and refine their practices in light of ethical, legal, and philanthropic responsibilities. These theories challenge corporations to transcend profit-driven motives, advocating for sustainable practices that benefit society and mitigate global economic disparities.

By integrating principles from Piketty (2014), Stiglitz (2002), and Sen (1999), this framework emphasises the need for corporations to address the root causes of economic inequality through ethical sourcing and equitable growth initiatives. Businesses are encouraged to adopt transparent supply chain management, invest in community development, and ensure their environmental initiatives contribute meaningfully to societal well-being to combat greenwashing.

Drawing direct examples from the case studies, such as a company's transition towards genuine sustainability efforts, illustrates how adopting a stakeholder-centric approach can rectify greenwashing. For instance, a firm improving its labour practices in response to stakeholder advocacy highlights the practical application of these ethical theories in real-world scenarios.

Combining CR and examining Global Economic Inequality underpin a comprehensive strategy for confronting greenwashing. These frameworks demand honesty and transparency from corporations and advocate for actions that have a tangible, positive impact on all stakeholders and society. The commitment to addressing greenwashing through this lens underscores the need for businesses to embody their sustainability claims genuinely, paving the way for a more ethical and equitable global economy.

The existing literature underscores a significant gap in directly applying these theories to counteract greenwashing effectively. There is a pronounced need for empirical research to bridge this divide, offering actionable guidance for corporations to authentically integrate these ethical considerations into their environmental strategies (Freeman, 1984; Carroll, 1991; Piketty, 2014; Stiglitz, 2002; Sen, 1999). This approach enhances corporate ethics and contributes to a broader understanding and mitigation of greenwashing practices.

2.1.3. Stakeholder Versus Shareholder Theories: A Lens for Understanding Greenwashing

The ongoing debate between shareholder and stakeholder theories provides a crucial framework for addressing the ethical dimensions of greenwashing within corporate governance. This section aligns these theories with the challenges of greenwashing, offering direct applications, real-world examples, and actionable insights for ethical corporate strategies.

Shareholder theory, primarily associated with Friedman (1970), prioritises maximising shareholder value. In the context of greenwashing, this theory could inadvertently support practices that enhance short-term financial gains at the expense of long-term environmental integrity. Conversely, stakeholder theory, championed by Freeman (1984), expands the corporation's accountability to include a more comprehensive array of stakeholders, offering a broader perspective on combating greenwashing by emphasising transparency and accountability across all business operations.

For instance, the Volkswagen emissions scandal (Ewing, 2017) illustrates a shareholder theory's shortcoming: profit and shareholder value were the priority over environmental truths and stakeholder trust. This case contrasts with stakeholder theory's emphasis on ethical responsibility to all stakeholders, not just shareholders.

Stakeholder theory provides actionable insights for combating greenwashing by advocating for genuine engagement with all stakeholders, including consumers, employees, and the wider community. It suggests that ethical business practices and transparent communication are essential for sustainable success, urging companies to adopt comprehensive sustainability reports and third-party audits to verify their environmental claims.

Both shareholder and stakeholder theories offer unique perspectives on corporate ethics and the fight against greenwashing. Shareholder theory's focus on profit maximisation can lead to ethical compromises, while stakeholder theory promotes a balanced approach that considers the impacts of corporate actions on all stakeholders. The contrast between these theories highlights the need for corporations to adopt financially sound, ethically responsible, and environmentally sustainable strategies.

Piketty (2014) and Stiglitz (2012) further enrich this discussion by linking corporate practices to global economic inequalities, demonstrating the broader implications of ethical corporate conduct. Their work underscores the vital role of businesses in fostering equitable growth and contributing to a more sustainable and just global economy.

Despite the rich discourse, there remains a gap in leveraging these theories to formulate concrete strategies against greenwashing. Future research and corporate practice must bridge this gap, ensuring the fight against greenwashing is grounded in robust ethical frameworks that promote genuine sustainability and transparency (Friedman, 1970; Freeman, 1984; Piketty, 2014; Stiglitz, 2012; Mansell, 2013).

2.1.4. Short-term Gains Versus Long-term Sustainability: Strategies Against Greenwashing

The tension between pursuing short-term gains and committing to long-term sustainability is at the heart of modern corporate strategy, especially when confronting the challenge of greenwashing. This section draws upon the insights of Hart and Milstein (2003), Porter and Kramer (2006), and Laszlo and Zhexembayeva (2011) to explore how strategic sustainability integration can navigate this tension and counteract greenwashing practices.

As Hart and Milstein (2003) argued, sustainability transcends the ethical obligation to become a source of innovation and competitive advantage. This perspective is crucial for understanding greenwashing, as it suggests that genuine sustainability efforts offer not only moral but also strategic benefits, countering the superficial allure of short-term gains presented by greenwashing.

For example, Porter and Kramer's (2006) concept of creating shared value can directly combat greenwashing. Companies like Volkswagen, caught in emissions scandals, illustrate the pitfalls of prioritising short-term financial performance over genuine environmental integrity. This case reinforces the argument for aligning corporate success with genuine societal welfare as a sustainable strategy.

Laszlo and Zhexembayeva (2011) emphasise viewing sustainability pressures as catalysts for innovation, suggesting a proactive approach to transforming greenwashing challenges into opportunities for strategic differentiation and economic benefits. Corporations should leverage transparent, verifiable sustainability initiatives as part of their core strategy, engaging stakeholders in meaningful ways to ensure accountability and genuine environmental stewardship.

This discussion bridges the gap between theoretical sustainability benefits and the tangible challenge of greenwashing. By adopting a long-term sustainability perspective, corporations can navigate the allure of short-term gains while fostering genuine environmental and social responsibility. Future research must explore practical strategies that enable businesses to authentically embed sustainable practices into their operations, moving beyond the superficiality of greenwashing to achieve true resilience and ethical integrity in the global market.

In conclusion, the debate between short-term gains and long-term sustainability underscores the strategic and ethical imperative for corporations to authentically integrate sustainability into their business models. The insights from Hart and Milstein (2003), Porter and Kramer (2006), and Laszlo and Zhexembayeva (2011) offer a comprehensive framework for evaluating and mitigating greenwashing, highlighting the necessity of genuine, strategic sustainability efforts over superficial environmental claims.

2.1.5. Ethical Sourcing Versus Economic Realism: Confronting Greenwashing
Navigating ethical sourcing and economic realism presents a formidable challenge in global supply chain management, where ethical integrity and economic competitiveness often clash. Gereffi et al. (2005) dissect the complexities of global supply chains, highlighting the pivotal role of multinational corporations in balancing economic objectives with ethical sourcing considerations. Their insights underscore the dilemmas faced when striving to uphold ethical standards amidst the relentless pursuit of cost reductions and market competitiveness.

Kaplinsky (2000) delves into this quandary, pointing out the inherent conflict between the drive for profitability and the commitment to ethical sourcing. He articulates how the pressure to minimise costs frequently leads to compromises on ethical principles. Kaplinsky champions innovation and strategic partnerships as avenues to harmonise ethical integrity with economic demands, suggesting a path forward where companies can sustain ethical commitments without sacrificing their competitive edge.

In this context, greenwashing emerges as a critical issue, where companies may superficially adopt sustainable practices without genuine commitment, undermining the essence of ethical sourcing. This practice poses a direct challenge to the principles of ethical integrity, prompting a closer examination of how companies can navigate economic pressures without resorting to misleading environmental claims.

For instance, the Volkswagen emissions scandal (Ewing, 2017) is a poignant example of economic pressures that led to greenwashing, compromising environmental standards and ethical integrity. This case illustrates the consequences of prioritising short-term economic gains over genuine sustainability and ethical conduct.

The analyses by Gereffi et al. (2005) and Kaplinsky (2000) offer actionable insights for businesses striving to combat greenwashing. Companies can effectively balance economic realism with ethical sourcing by fostering transparency in supply chains, investing in innovation, and cultivating strategic partnerships. Such strategies enhance ethical integrity and position businesses as leaders in sustainability, contributing positively to their reputation and long-term success.

Ultimately, the dialogue between ethical sourcing and economic realism enriches our understanding of the corporate battle against greenwashing. By integrating the insights of Gereffi et al. (2005) and Kaplinsky (2000), this discussion illuminates the complex interplay between maintaining economic competitiveness and adhering to ethical principles in supply chain management. It underscores the possibility of achieving a symbiotic relationship between ethical integrity and economic success. It offers a comprehensive framework for companies to navigate the ethical dilemmas of greenwashing in today's global market.

2.2. Greenwashing: Misleading Eco-friendliness in Corporate Practices

Greenwashing, the practice where corporations misleadingly promote their products or policies as environmentally friendly, represents a significant ethical challenge in corporate sustainability efforts. This deceptive marketing strategy, characterised by false claims and superficial environmental initiatives, undermines consumer trust and diminishes the value of genuine sustainability efforts. The phenomenon has garnered considerable scholarly attention, highlighting its impact on consumer perception and CR.

Lyon and Montgomery (2015) provide a critical analysis of greenwashing by introducing a framework to evaluate corporate environmental claims. Their research underscores some corporations' strategic manipulations to appear more environmentally responsible, urging greater transparency and accountability.

Seele and Gatti (2017) delve into the definitional complexities of greenwashing, revealing the challenges in establishing a uniform understanding of the term. Their work emphasises the necessity for clarity and precision in corporate environmental communication, advocating for a nuanced approach to identifying and addressing greenwashing practices.

Bazillier and Vauday (2009) examine the adverse effects of unsubstantiated environmental claims, pointing out how these practices erode consumer trust and contribute to the proliferation of greenwashing. They call for stricter verification processes and enhanced transparency in corporate environmental reporting to combat these misleading practices.

Mitchell and Ramey (2010) explore the concept of selective disclosure, a tactic where companies highlight positive environmental achievements while downplaying negative impacts. This strategy, central to greenwashing, distorts public perception and underscores the ethical obligation of corporations to provide a balanced account of their environmental performance.

The existing literature highlights a significant debate regarding the reconciliation of ethical imperatives with business pragmatics, especially in the context of greenwashing. While various ethical theories offer insights into navigating these challenges, a notable gap exists in integrating these theories with practical strategies to effectively address complex, real-world business dilemmas.

This paper calls for future research to focus on developing dynamic ethical frameworks adaptable to the evolving global business landscape. Empirical studies examining the outcomes of ethical strategies in diverse industry contexts are essential for deepening our understanding of ethical decision-making in business. Such research could provide actionable insights for corporations striving to align their practices with ethical principles and sustainability commitments.

By analysing greenwashing through ethical theories and case studies, our paper contributes to a more nuanced understanding of corporate ethics, highlighting the need for transparency, accountability, and commitment to sustainability. Addressing the challenge of greenwashing is not just a regulatory issue but a fundamental ethical imperative for corporations worldwide.

3. METHODOLOGY

Our methodology adopts a focused approach to explore corporate decision-making's ethical dimensions. Utilising a purposive sampling strategy, we selected five notable case studies of greenwashing across various industries and regions. We chose these case studies based on their prominence in ethical debates, ability to showcase diverse ethical dilemmas, and applicability to our theoretical framework, emphasising the analysis of greenwashing practices.

Data collection was primarily from scholarly papers, reflecting a commitment to academic rigour and ensuring an objective analysis of each case. This approach allowed us to draw on a wealth of academic insights into the ethical issues, avoiding potential biases inherent in corporate-produced reports.

Our analysis method stands out by systematically applying a bespoke ethical, theoretical framework to each case study. This framework, designed specifically for our research, incorporates elements from Utilitarianism, Deontological Ethics, and other relevant ethical theories to dissect the complexities of corporate greenwashing. By doing so, we offer a novel contribution to corporate ethics, illuminating how companies navigate the complex domain of ethical representation and reality.

We recognise the limitations of our qualitative approach, including potential selection bias and the subjective interpretation of complex ethical principles. To mitigate these concerns, we suggest that future studies might expand the scope of research through quantitative methods or by incorporating a more comprehensive array of case studies. Such endeavours could further validate our findings and enrich the academic conversation on corporate ethics and greenwashing.

Our methodology provides a clear and structured pathway to understanding the ethical tensions within corporate strategies against greenwashing. By integrating a unique theoretical framework with in-depth case study analysis, our research contributes valuable insights into reconciling ethical imperatives and practical business considerations in the face of greenwashing.

4. CASE STUDY ANALYSIS

In the labyrinth of global business, where the pursuit of profit frequently intersects with ethical considerations, corporations find themselves at the crossroads of decision-making that can either uphold or undermine moral principles. This section embarks on a detailed analysis of selected case studies representing pivotal moments in contemporary business practices where ethical dilemmas have surfaced and challenged corporate conduct. Through the lens of Utilitarianism, Deontological Ethics, CR, Shareholder versus Stakeholder Theory, Short-term gains versus Long-term sustainability, Ethical Sourcing versus Economic Realism, and Greenwashing, we aim to dissect the actions and decisions of corporations, providing a comprehensive examination of their ethical implications.

The case studies selected for this analysis include the Rana Plaza Factory Collapse, Nike and Sweatshop Allegations, Apple and Foxconn's Labour Practices, the Volkswagen Emissions Scandal, and Cobalt Mining in the Democratic Republic of Congo (DRC). We chose each case meticulously for its significance in highlighting critical ethical challenges within diverse industry contexts, ranging from fashion and technology to automotive and mining. These cases underscore the complexities of navigating ethical conduct in a globalised economy and illustrate corporate decisions' profound impact on human lives, society, and the environment.

As we delve into each case, we will systematically apply the ethical theories outlined in our Ethical Theory Primer to evaluate corporate actions from multiple ethical perspectives. This analysis aims to shed light on the moral dimensions of corporate behaviour, exploring how businesses navigate the complex ethical decision-making process. By critically examining the decisions and actions taken by corporations in these case studies, we will identify where ethical considerations were prioritised or sidelined in the quest for profitability and market dominance.

This journey through the ethical landscape of modern business practices seeks to understand the actions taken and reflect on the lessons learned and the broader implications for corporate ethics. It explores the tension between profit-making and ethical conduct, revealing corporations' strategies to navigate or resolve these tensions. Through this analysis, we contribute to the ongoing dialogue on business ethics, offering insights that may inform academic discourse and practical corporate strategy in pursuing ethical integrity in business operations.

4.1. Case Study Selection

Through the lens of these case studies, this research will dissect the ethical decisions faced by corporations, offering insights into the balancing act between profitability and moral responsibility in the global business environment.

- *Rana Plaza Factory Collapse (Siegle, 2011; Arnold & Bowie, 2003)*: We selected this case for its stark illustration of the conflict between practical views of maximising economic benefits and Deontological Ethics emphasising the rights and safety of workers. It highlights the ethical dilemma of prioritising profit over people, making it a critical study for understanding CR in global supply chains. On 24 April 2013, the Rana Plaza building in Bangladesh collapsed, killing over 1,100 garment factory workers and injuring thousands. This tragedy brought to light the unsafe working conditions and exploitation within the global fashion industry. The factories in the building were manufacturing clothing for many Western brands, raising questions about the ethical obligations of multinational corporations regarding their overseas operations and labour practices.
- *Nike and Sweatshop Allegations (Locke, 2003)*: Nike's experiences with sweatshop allegations probe into the CR towards Global Economic Inequality. This case is pivotal for examining how corporations can influence labour practices globally and the extent of their responsibility in ensuring fair working conditions, especially in lower-income countries. Throughout the 1990s and early 2000s, Nike faced widespread criticism and public backlash over the conditions in its suppliers' factories, with allegations of child labour, poor working conditions, and inadequate wages in countries like Vietnam, China, and Indonesia. This scrutiny forced Nike to reassess and reform its approach to CR, supply chain management, and labour practices.
- *Apple and Foxconn's Labour Practices (Chan et al., 2013)*: The relationship between Apple and its supplier, Foxconn, underscores the tension between shareholder and stakeholder theories. This case is essential for understanding how companies balance the demands for financial returns with their ethical obligations to all stakeholders, including workers in their supply chains. Foxconn Technology Group, a major supplier to Apple, has faced repeated criticism over labour practices at its factories, including reports of excessive overtime, poor working conditions, and a series of worker suicides. These issues raise significant questions about Apple's responsibility towards its workers and corporations' role in ensuring employees' welfare at all levels of the supply chain.
- *Volkswagen Emissions Scandal (Ewing, 2017)*: The Volkswagen emissions scandal exemplifies the dilemma between pursuing short-term gains and committing to long-term sustainability and ethical integrity. This case provides a profound lesson on the consequences of corporate decisions that prioritise immediate financial performance over environmental standards and ethical conduct. In 2015, Volkswagen admitted to installing software in millions of its diesel vehicles to manipulate emissions tests falsely. This deception not only betrayed consumer trust but also highlighted the broader environmental impact of corporate practices, prompting a global discussion on business ethics and sustainability.
- *Cobalt Mining in the DRC (Scheele et al., 2016)*: This case study on cobalt mining in the DRC delves into the dilemma of ethical sourcing versus economic realism. It is critical to explore the complexities of sourcing essential materials

in a manner that respects human rights and the environment amid the pressures of global demand and economic efficiency. The DRC is a primary source of cobalt, a critical component in rechargeable lithium-ion batteries used in electric vehicles and various electronic devices. Reports of hazardous working conditions, child labour, and environmental degradation in cobalt mines pose significant ethical challenges for companies reliant on these materials for their products, underscoring the need for responsible sourcing practices.

4.2. Application of Ethical Theories and Greenwashing

4.2.1. Rana Plaza Factory Collapse

For the Rana Plaza Factory Collapse case study, applying Utilitarianism and Deontological Ethics involves a deep dive into the ethical implications of the actions taken by corporations involved in the tragedy. Utilitarian and Deontological analyses of the Rana Plaza collapse reveal profound ethical failures. Utilitarianism critiques the prioritisation of cost over safety, suggesting that tragedy contradicts achieving the greatest good, as explored by Lucy Siegle (2011). Deontological Ethics, referencing Arnold and Bowie (2003), condemns exploiting workers, stressing adherence to moral duties and respect for human dignity. These perspectives underscore the need for corporations to fundamentally re-evaluate their responsibilities toward workers, highlighting the ethical imperative for safer, more respectful practices in global supply chains.

We applied our theoretical framework to the Rana Plaza Factory Collapse, contrasting Utilitarism and Deontological Ethics. We found Utilitarianism's focus on maximising overall welfare against Deontological Ethics' emphasis on adhering to moral duties and rights, regardless of the consequences. It depicts the ethical conflict between outcome – and principle-based decision-making in addressing and preventing such tragedies. This theoretical analysis suggests that while Utilitarianism would advocate for decisions that prevent the most significant harm, Deontological Ethics insists on the moral imperative to ensure worker safety as a non-negotiable duty, showcasing the ethical complexity in navigating corporate responsibilities (Table 11.1).

The influence of greenwashing on Utilitarianism and Deontological Ethics unveils contrasting perspectives in ethical evaluation and decision-making within the corporate sphere.

In the context of greenwashing, Utilitarianism emphasises the examination of consequences on societal well-being, considering whether the short-term benefits gained by companies outweigh the potential long-term harm to the environment and consumer trust. Decision-making guidelines under Utilitarianism entail assessing immediate gains like enhanced reputation or increased sales against broader societal impacts, such as environmental degradation and erosion of consumer trust. A guided approach within Utilitarianism suggests favouring genuine environmental efforts over greenwashing, as it leads to more significant overall benefits for society. By prioritising authentic initiatives, companies contribute to long-term societal welfare and happiness, aligning with Utilitarian principles that seek the greatest good for the most significant number.

Table 11.1. Comparative Analysis of Utilitarianism and Deontological Ethics in Addressing the Ethical Dilemma of Worker Safety Versus Economic Benefits.

	Utilitarianism focuses on the outcomes of actions, emphasising decisions that maximise overall happiness or minimise harm, and criticises the decision-making that prioritises cost-saving over safety, highlighting a failure in achieving the greatest good for the most significant number	Deontological Ethics emphasises duty and principles over the consequences, focusing on the moral right based on rules and the inherent rights of individuals, and condemns the neglect of workers' safety, emphasising the inherent duty to protect worker rights and dignity, irrespective of economic consequences
Ethical dilemma	The collapse illustrated the ethical conflict between maximising economic benefits and respecting workers' safety and rights	
Decision-making guideline	Choose actions that would have prevented the collapse or minimised the harm to workers, even if it meant incurring higher costs for safety improvements. The correct action is the one that results in the greatest good for the most significant number of people involved	Act following moral duties, such as ensuring safe working conditions, because it is the right thing to do, irrespective of the costs or outcomes
Analysis	The collapse is a failure to prioritise the well-being of employees over profit maximisation. From a Utilitarian perspective, the decision to overlook safety concerns for cost-saving did not result in the most significant overall happiness	The disaster highlights a violation of moral duties towards employees. Under Deontological Ethics, failing to provide safe working conditions is inherently wrong, regardless of the economic rationale
Guided response	To prevent future tragedies, companies should invest in rigorous safety standards and ethical working conditions, evaluating the potential outcomes of their decisions on all stakeholders	Companies must adhere to ethical principles and laws that protect workers' rights and safety, ensuring that all actions respect the dignity and rights of individuals involved

The analysis of greenwashing under Deontological Ethics centres on companies' inherent moral obligations towards honesty and transparency. Greenwashing is condemned as a breach of these duties, regardless of the outcomes or intentions behind such practices. Decision-making guidelines within Deontological Ethics advocate strict adherence to ethical principles that demand truthfulness in environmental claims and policies. Companies are morally obligated to communicate transparently and honestly, ensuring their actions align with ethical standards and principles, even if it entails preceding short-term gains associated with greenwashing.

The influence of greenwashing on Utilitarianism vs. Deontological Ethics underscores the tension between outcome- and principle-based ethical evaluation. While Utilitarianism prioritises the overall consequences and societal welfare, Deontological Ethics emphasises adherence to moral duties and principles. Both frameworks converge in condemning greenwashing and advocating for transparency in corporate practices, albeit through different ethical lenses. Understanding and integrating these perspectives can enrich ethical discourse within corporations, fostering principled decision-making processes that prioritise societal well-being and ethical integrity in the face of greenwashing.

The tragedy underscored corporations' need to reassess their responsibilities towards workers, leading to a broader industry reflection on the importance of ethical practices in supply chains. It highlighted the ethical imperative for companies to invest in safe working conditions and transparent operations, pushing towards more responsible global supply chain management.

This case challenges corporations to balance profitability with ethical imperatives, underscoring the dangers of superficially adopting sustainability measures (greenwashing) without substantive action. It illustrates the need for genuine commitment to ethical principles, transparency, and accountability in corporate practices, emphasising that non-compromising for economic benefits is an ethical conduct. The Rana Plaza collapse is a critical reminder of the real-world implications of ethical failures, driving home the importance of integrating ethical considerations into strategic decision-making to prevent future tragedies.

4.2.2. Nike and Sweatshop Allegations
Analysing Nike's response to sweatshop allegations unveils the intricate interplay between CR and Global Economic Inequality. Locke's (2003) study outlines Nike's transformation from defensiveness to a beacon of ethical globalisation. Nike's adoption of a Code of Conduct, monitoring departments, and external audits epitomise its commitment to labour improvement, reflecting a sense of CR. Conversely, Nike's initial labour practices underscore broader issues of Global Economic Inequality. Exploitation in developing countries mirrors systemic inequalities in supply chains. Nike's reform efforts, driven partly by public pressure, acknowledge the need to confront these disparities. Locke's (2003) case study underscores the potential for corporations to combat global economic inequalities through responsible practices. However, it also underscores ongoing challenges ensuring ethical conduct across global operations. The analysis illustrates the complex journey towards ethical globalisation, necessitating sustained commitment and innovation.

In examining Nike's sweatshop allegations, contrasting CR with Global Economic Inequality offers a multifaceted lens to assess how companies can navigate ethical business practices amid widespread economic disparities. This approach dissects the complex fabric of corporate ethics, revealing how decisions made at the corporate level resonate through the layers of global economic systems. By evaluating this case through the dual perspectives of CR and Global Economic Inequality, we uncover the inherent tensions and potential pathways for more ethical corporate conduct (Table 11.2).

Contrasting CR with Global Economic Inequality in the context of Nike's sweatshop allegations reveals a complex landscape of ethical challenges and opportunities. CR calls for a shift in Nike's internal decision-making processes to prioritise ethical considerations and stakeholder welfare. In contrast, addressing Global Economic Inequality demands an outward-looking approach that

Essence and Appearance

Table 11.2. CR and Global Economic Inequality: A Dual Perspective on Nike's Labour Practices.

	CR underlines the duty of businesses to pursue more than just shareholder profits, highlighting the importance of ethical management, environmental stewardship, and social justice. It urges businesses to weave social and environmental considerations into their operations, explicitly pointing to Nike's responsibility to adopt transparent and fair labour practices as part of its commitment to ethical management and social justice	Global Economic Inequality focuses on the uneven distribution of resources and wealth globally, underscoring the disparities in income, access to education, healthcare, and employment opportunities. It examines the structural factors contributing to these inequalities, like trade policies and globalisation. It reflects on Nike's practices within the broader context of systemic inequalities, highlighting how corporate sourcing strategies can perpetuate or mitigate disparities
Ethical dilemma	Nike faced allegations of sweatshop conditions, underscoring the tension between corporate profitability and the global ethical responsibility to ensure fair working conditions	
Decision-making guidelines	Emphasises the importance of ethical considerations in business operations, urging companies to go beyond profit maximisation to address social justice, environmental stewardship, and ethical management. Decisions should reflect a commitment to the well-being of all stakeholders, including workers, communities, and the broader society	It focuses on understanding and addressing the root causes of economic disparities that businesses operate within. It advocates for corporate actions that contribute to narrowing the wealth gap, such as fair wages, local community investment, and development initiatives
Analysis	Nike's reliance on sweatshops indicates a disconnect between its corporate policies and the practical implementation of its ethical commitments. This situation highlights a failure to fully integrate CR into its operational strategies, leading to practices that undermine workers' rights and welfare	The sweatshop allegations against Nike can be a symptom of broader global economic inequalities. In search of lower production costs, the company's sourcing practices exploit these inequalities, perpetuating cycles of poverty and disadvantage in developing economies
Guided response	Nike should adopt a comprehensive CSR strategy that includes transparent supply chain management, fair labour practices, and active engagement in workers' rights protection. Such a strategy would address current criticisms and set a benchmark for industry-wide practices, demonstrating leadership in ethical corporate behaviour	Nike significantly mitigates economic inequality by leveraging its global presence for positive change, which includes investing in sustainable development projects in sourcing countries, ensuring living wages for all workers, and fostering economic opportunities that elevate local communities

recognises and acts on the company's capacity to influence broader economic systems. Together, these perspectives offer a roadmap for Nike to rectify past oversights and contribute to a more equitable global economy, illustrating the power of corporate actions to effect substantive ethical and economic change.

The influence of greenwashing extends beyond mere ethical considerations, impacting both CR and Global Economic Inequality.

Greenwashing contradicts the core tenets of CR directly by misrepresenting environmental efforts for the sake of corporate gain. Greenwashing deceives consumers and undermines the trust and credibility essential for CR. A guided approach emphasises corporations' need to align their environmental marketing with actual practices, ensuring accountability and transparency.

On the global stage, greenwashing has implications for economic inequality. By misleading consumers and investors with false environmental claims, greenwashing can exacerbate global economic inequalities. Resources allocated to genuinely sustainable initiatives, particularly in developing countries, can be diverted towards deceptive practices instead. This diversion perpetuates economic disparities and hampers progress towards sustainable development goals. Addressing greenwashing necessitates a global perspective acknowledging the interconnectedness of environmental sustainability and economic equality. A guided approach suggests that combating greenwashing requires coordinated efforts to promote transparency, accountability, and genuine environmental stewardship on a global scale.

Nike's journey from denial to becoming a leader in ethical globalisation illustrates a significant shift towards CR. Nike committed to improving labour standards by implementing a Code of Conduct, establishing monitoring departments, and conducting external audits. This transformation addressed the immediate criticisms and set a precedent for industry-wide practices in ethical corporate behaviour.

Nike's case demonstrates the complex interplay between corporate ethics and global economic realities. The shift towards ethical globalisation underscores the importance of corporations acting as agents of positive change. Moreover, Nike's evolution highlights the role of CR in addressing and mitigating economic inequalities, emphasising that genuine sustainability efforts are crucial to overcoming the challenges of greenwashing. This case study showcases the potential for corporations to effect substantial ethical and economic improvements through committed and transparent practices, moving beyond superficial sustainability claims to foster genuine global development.

In conclusion, greenwashing poses significant challenges to CR and Global Economic Inequality. By recognising the detrimental effects of greenwashing on trust, credibility, and resource allocation, corporations and policymakers can work towards fostering genuine environmental stewardship and equitable economic development. Addressing greenwashing through transparent and accountable practices is imperative, ensuring corporate actions align with ethical principles and contribute positively to environmental sustainability and economic equality worldwide.

4.2.3. Apple and Foxconn's Labour Practices
The analysis of Apple's outsourcing practices to Foxconn reflects the contrasting perspectives of Shareholder Theory and Stakeholder Theory. From a Shareholder Theory standpoint, cost reductions, production efficiency, and

Essence and Appearance 227

enhanced shareholder value justifies Apple's strategic decision to outsource production to Foxconn. However, Stakeholder Theory highlights the ethical obligations towards all stakeholders, including workers at Foxconn. Investigations (Chan et al., 2013) reveal that Apple's profit-driven approach has led to labour violations, including illegal overtime and unsafe working conditions, prompting labour activism within Foxconn's factories. This case underscores the tensions between prioritising shareholder interests and broader stakeholder concerns, emphasising the need for a more inclusive approach that considers the well-being of all parties involved. It highlights the complexities of corporate ethics in a globalised economy and the importance of re-evaluating business strategies to ensure ethical and sustainable practices. Exploring the labour practices at Apple and its supplier, Foxconn, through the lenses of Shareholder Theory and Stakeholder Theory provides a rich narrative on corporate ethics and the balance between financial objectives and broader responsibilities. This analysis delves into how these theoretical frameworks influence corporate behaviour and decision-making, particularly in the context of labour practices and worker welfare (Table 11.3).

The contrast between Shareholder Theory and Stakeholder Theory in the context of Apple and Foxconn's labour practices underscores the dynamic tension between prioritising immediate financial returns and acknowledging a broader set of corporate responsibilities. While Shareholder Theory offers a narrowly focused rationale for decision-making based on economic outcomes, Stakeholder Theory provides a more holistic view that considers the long-term implications of corporate actions on all stakeholders. This analysis suggests that navigating the ethical landscape of labour practices requires a nuanced approach that integrates the financial imperatives of Shareholder Theory with the inclusive, ethical considerations of Stakeholder Theory. Adopting such an integrated approach can help Apple and Foxconn address current labour issues more effectively while positioning themselves for sustainable future growth.

The influence of greenwashing extends to both Stakeholder Theory and Shareholder Theory, shaping perspectives on CR and ethical conduct. Greenwashing fails to uphold this principle, as it prioritises short-term gains over the well-being of stakeholders affected by environmental harm and misleading information. A guided approach suggests engaging stakeholders through open dialogue to develop more authentic and effective environmental strategies to address this issue. By involving stakeholders in decision-making processes, companies can foster trust, accountability, and genuine commitment to environmental stewardship, aligning with the principles of Stakeholder Theory.

While greenwashing may initially serve shareholder interests by enhancing a company's image and market value, it poses significant risks to shareholder value in the long run. The potential for reputational damage and legal penalties from greenwashing undermines shareholder trust and erodes market confidence. A guided approach advises that companies prioritise genuine and verifiable environmental initiatives to protect shareholder interests in the long term. By investing in authentic sustainability practices, corporations can enhance their reputation, mitigate risks, and safeguard shareholder value.

Table 11.3. Balancing Shareholder Value and Stakeholder Welfare: Apple and Foxconn's Ethical Dilemma.

	As advocated by R. Edward Freeman (1984), Stakeholder theory suggests corporations owe duties to a wide array of stakeholders – not just shareholders but also employees, customers, suppliers, communities, and the environment. This approach encourages businesses to consider the broader implications of their decisions, moving beyond mere profit maximisation to address societal welfare. It posits that ethical business practices involve contributing positively to society and the environment, with a company's success measured by its societal impact and financial performance. Expressly, in the context of Apple and Foxconn, this theory underlines the importance of ensuring worker welfare and fair treatment alongside shareholder interests, advocating for a balanced consideration of all stakeholders' needs in corporate operations	Shareholder theory posits that a corporation's primary responsibility is to its shareholders, emphasising profit maximization as the ultimate goal. Advocated by Milton Friedman, this theory suggests that ethical obligations are fulfilled by increasing shareholder value under the assumption that a profitable business contributes to societal welfare through economic growth; it supports Apple's outsourcing as a means to enhance profitability and shareholder value, justifying cost-cutting measures that include outsourcing to Foxconn
Ethical dilemma	Apple's outsourcing to Foxconn spotlighted the conflict between cost efficiency for shareholders and ethical responsibilities towards workers, revealing labour rights violations	
Decision-making guidelines	Stakeholder theory expands the scope of CR to include all stakeholders affected by corporate actions, including employees, customers, suppliers, and the community. It emphasises the importance of considering the welfare and interests of these groups in corporate decision-making	Shareholder theory prioritises the interests of shareholders, advocating for decisions that maximise financial returns. Corporate actions are evaluated based on their potential to enhance profitability and shareholder value
Analysis	The labour issues at Apple and Foxconn highlight a misalignment with Stakeholder theory principles, revealing a failure to consider workers' welfare in their operations adequately. This misalignment affects employee well-being and risks damaging customer trust and corporate reputation, which are crucial to long-term success	The labour practices at Apple and Foxconn, under scrutiny for poor working conditions and inadequate wages, can be seen as aligned with Shareholder theory to the extent that they reduce production costs and potentially increase profits. However, this focus on cost minimisation and profit maximisation raises ethical concerns, mainly when it compromises worker welfare and safety
Guided response	Apple and Foxconn should adopt comprehensive stakeholder engagement strategies to improve labour conditions, invest in worker welfare, and ensure fair wages. By integrating stakeholder interests into their business models, they can build a more sustainable and ethical supply chain that supports long-term corporate success and stakeholder satisfaction	To adhere to Shareholder theory while addressing these concerns, Apple and Foxconn might seek efficiency improvements and technological innovations that maintain cost-effectiveness without sacrificing labour standards. This approach requires balancing financial objectives with ethical labour practices to protect long-term shareholder value from reputational risks

Apple's approach initially aligned more closely with Shareholder Theory, prioritising cost efficiencies over workers' welfare. However, public scrutiny and labour activism pushed the company towards adopting a more stakeholder theory perspective, leading to a code of conduct and improved monitoring and auditing of labour practices (Chan et al., 2013). This shift illustrates the tension between enhancing shareholder value and meeting ethical standards for stakeholder welfare.

Apple and Foxconn's case highlights the crucial role of stakeholder engagement and transparency in reconciling financial goals with ethical labour practices. It underscores the need for corporations to integrate Stakeholder Theory into their business strategies, balancing profit with responsibility. This case study shows that ethical considerations and stakeholder welfare are essential for a business's long-term success and reputation. It challenges the idea that prioritising financial returns above everything else is necessary. It also points to the broader implications of greenwashing, showing that genuine commitment to ethical principles is essential for sustainable corporate practices.

In conclusion, greenwashing influences Stakeholder Theory and Shareholder Theory, highlighting the importance of ethical conduct and genuine environmental stewardship in corporate decision-making. By considering the interests of all stakeholders and prioritising long-term shareholder value, companies can navigate the complexities of greenwashing while upholding principles of accountability, transparency, and sustainability.

4.2.4. Volkswagen Emissions Scandal

The Volkswagen emissions scandal, detailed in Jack Ewing's 'Faster, Higher, Farther: The Volkswagen Scandal', from 2017, illustrates a profound ethical dilemma between short-term gains and long-term sustainability and trust. Despite environmental concerns, Volkswagen's 'defeat devices' implementation aimed to dominate the global automotive market by leading in diesel technology. While initially bolstering market position and profitability, this strategy led to substantial costs, legal battles, and damage to reputation exceeding $20 billion. The scandal exposed a toxic corporate culture, prioritising victory at any price, prompting Volkswagen to re-evaluate its values and strategies. Ewing's narrative highlights broader cultural and systemic issues within Volkswagen, emphasising the importance of ethical behaviour and environmental stewardship for long-term success. The case underscores corporations' need to balance ambitions with ethical standards, guiding them towards a sustainable future. In the Volkswagen Emissions Scandal, contrasting short-term gains with long-term sustainability provides a compelling lens to examine the repercussions of prioritising immediate financial advantages over enduring ethical and environmental responsibilities (Table 11.4).

The Volkswagen Emissions Scandal highlights the dangers of prioritising short-term financial gains over ethical and sustainable business practices. While seeking immediate profitability might offer temporary advantages, it poses substantial risks to a company's reputation, legal standing, and customer trust. Conversely, a commitment to long-term sustainability fosters a culture of ethical integrity, regulatory compliance, and innovation supporting environmental

Table 11.4. Balancing Short-term Gains with Long-term Sustainability: Ethical Dilemmas and Decision-Making in Corporate Strategy.

	Short-term gains refer to the immediate financial benefits and competitive edge companies might seek, often at the expense of ethical standards and long-term commitments	Long-term sustainability emphasises the importance of ethical conduct, environmental stewardship, and CR in ensuring a company's longevity and success. It suggests that sustainable practices, though potentially costly or challenging in the short term, lead to lasting benefits
Ethical dilemma	Volkswagen faced a crisis between pursuing short-term financial gains through 'defeat devices' to falsify emissions tests and the long-term implications for sustainability, trust, and ethical integrity	
Decision-making guidelines	This perspective prioritises immediate financial benefits and market advantage, often at the expense of ethical standards and sustainable practices. The potential for quick profitability and competitive positioning guides decisions	Emphasises ethical conduct, environmental stewardship, and sustainable business practices. This approach values decisions that ensure the company's enduring success, reputation, and positive societal impact
Analysis	Volkswagen's choice to install defeat devices to cheat on emissions tests was an apparent pursuit of short-term gains. This strategy aimed to enhance market appeal and sales implied falsely meeting environmental standards, sidestepping the cost and time involved in developing genuinely cleaner technology	The scandal underscored a significant departure from long-term sustainability, damaging Volkswagen's reputation, incurring billions in fines, and eroding customer trust. A commitment to genuine environmental innovation and regulation adherence would have safeguarded its market position and contributed to sustainable industry practices
Guided response	To avoid such pitfalls, companies must incorporate ethical considerations into their strategic planning, ensuring that short-term financial objectives do not overshadow compliance with legal and moral standards	Volkswagen and similar companies should invest in sustainable technologies and transparent business practices. Embracing long-term sustainability involves a genuine commitment to ethical standards and environmental responsibility, aligning corporate strategies with broader societal values

stewardship. This approach secures a company's reputation and market position and aligns it with the evolving expectations of consumers, regulators, and society. The contrast between short-term gains and long-term sustainability in the Volkswagen case serves as a cautionary tale, emphasising the need for ethical decision-making and strategic foresight in navigating the complex landscape of modern business.

The influence of greenwashing lies at the intersection of short-term gains and long-term sustainability, presenting corporations with ethical dilemmas and strategic considerations. In the pursuit of short-term gains, greenwashing might offer an enticing prospect for companies seeking immediate benefits such as enhanced reputation, increased sales, or cost savings. By portraying a facade of environmental responsibility through deceptive marketing tactics, companies may capitalise on consumer demand for sustainable products without making substantial investments in genuine environmental efforts. However, such short-term gains come at a considerable cost to the company's reputation and the environment.

Long-term sustainability emphasises the importance of considering the broader implications of corporate actions on future viability and societal well-being while contrasting with the allure of short-term gains. Greenwashing undermines this principle by neglecting genuine environmental stewardship in favour of superficial appearances. The potential for long-term harm to the company's reputation is significant as consumers become increasingly savvy and intolerant of deceptive practices. Moreover, the environmental consequences of greenwashing, such as resource depletion, pollution, and climate change, pose existential threats to the planet and future generations.

A guided approach to addressing greenwashing advocates for a strategic focus on long-term sustainability, prioritising genuine environmental efforts over deceptive practices. By investing in authentic sustainability initiatives, companies mitigate the risks of reputational damage and align themselves with evolving consumer expectations and regulatory standards. Moreover, genuine environmental stewardship fosters trust, loyalty, and goodwill among stakeholders, contributing to long-term business success and resilience.

Volkswagen's strategic misstep resulted in legal repercussions, financial losses exceeding $20 billion, and a tarnished reputation (Ewing, 2017). This scandal highlighted the peril of sidelining ethical and environmental responsibilities for competitive advantage. Volkswagen's response involved re-evaluating corporate values and a strategic pivot towards sustainable technologies and transparency, indicating a shift from short-term gains to long-term sustainability.

The Volkswagen case illustrates the critical importance of aligning corporate strategies with ethical conduct and environmental stewardship. It demonstrates the high costs of neglecting long-term sustainability for short-term gains, both financially and in terms of corporate reputation. Additionally, this case study serves as a cautionary tale against greenwashing, emphasising the need for genuine environmental initiatives and transparent communication to build and maintain trust among consumers and stakeholders. Volkswagen's journey reflects the broader corporate challenge of balancing immediate financial objectives with the ethical and sustainable practices essential for long-term business viability and societal well-being.

In conclusion, the influence of greenwashing on short-term gains versus long-term sustainability underscores the importance of ethical decision-making and strategic foresight in corporate practices. By prioritising genuine environmental efforts and transparent communication, companies can navigate the complexities of greenwashing while demonstrating a commitment to long-term sustainability and responsible business conduct. Ultimately, businesses and the planet must balance the pursuit of short-term gains with considerations of long-term viability and societal impact to ensure their prosperity.

4.2.5. Cobalt Mining in the DRC

Cobalt mining in the DRC, particularly in Katanga province, is vital for global cobalt supply but faces significant ethical challenges. Despite its importance in consumer electronics and industrial applications, the industry suffers from severe human rights violations and environmental neglect, as highlighted by Scheele and his colleagues (2016) in the 'Cobalt Blues' report (2016). Balancing ethical sourcing with economic pressures is challenging in DRC's cobalt mining sector, where global demand for cobalt, driven by electric vehicles and electronics, often compromises ethical standards. Mining activities in Katanga result in environmental degradation and health risks for communities due to water, air, and noise pollution. Global cobalt demand exacerbates economic pressures, making it difficult for companies to prioritise ethical sourcing without financial consequences. The lack of regulation worsens human rights abuses and environmental degradation. Scheele et al. (2016) emphasise the need for comprehensive action, urging companies to prioritise ethical sourcing and international stakeholders to advocate for responsible mining practices. Reconciling economic interests with human rights and environmental stewardship is crucial, necessitating collaborative efforts from all stakeholders involved.

In Cobalt Mining from the DRC, contrasting Ethical Sourcing with Economic Realism offers a nuanced understanding of the challenges and priorities in securing raw materials for global industries, particularly electronics and electric vehicles (Table 11.5).

The contrast between Ethical Sourcing and Economic Realism in the context of cobalt mining in the DRC illustrates the complex interplay between the moral imperatives of Responsible Sourcing and the economic pressures of maintaining competitiveness in the global market. While Ethical Sourcing demands rigorous adherence to ethical, human rights, and environmental standards, Economic Realism highlights the necessity of pragmatism and adaptability in securing materials essential for technological advancements. Navigating these contrasting perspectives requires a balanced approach that does not sacrifice ethical integrity for economic gains. This analysis underscores the importance of CR in addressing the ethical and economic challenges of cobalt mining in the DRC, advocating for a sustainable model that harmonises the demands of ethical sourcing with the realities of the global economy.

The influence of greenwashing intersects with Ethical Sourcing and Economic Realism, presenting a complex challenge for businesses striving to balance ethical principles with economic pressures.

Ethical sourcing entails the responsible procurement of materials and goods, ensuring the production in a manner that upholds social and environmental standards. However, economic pressures often incentivise companies to cut corners, using greenwashing as a less costly alternative to genuine sustainability efforts. This tension arises from the perceived trade-off between adhering to ethical sourcing standards and meeting financial objectives.

Addressing this tension requires a guided approach that proposes innovative solutions to reconcile ethical sourcing with economic realism. One solution involves leveraging technology and supply chain transparency to ensure

Table 11.5. Ethical Sourcing Versus Economic Realism in Cobalt Mining: Navigating the Challenges of Global Supply Chains.

	Ethical sourcing emphasises the importance of obtaining materials in a manner that is responsible, sustainable, and respects human rights and environmental standards; it stresses obtaining materials responsibly, focusing on human rights, labour standards, and environmental protection	*Economic realism, on the other hand, recognises the practical constraints and competitive pressures of operating within a market economy. It highlights the necessity for cost-effectiveness, efficiency, and market competitiveness, even when sourcing critical materials like cobalt. It acknowledges the market-driven pressures on companies to maintain cost-effectiveness and competitiveness, sometimes at the expense of ethical sourcing principles*
Ethical dilemma	The DRC's cobalt mining faces a clash between ethical sourcing, addressing human rights and environmental concerns, and economic realism, where global demand and competitive market pressures often compromise ethical standards	
Decision-making guidelines	Ethical sourcing emphasises the procurement of materials in a manner that respects human rights, labour standards, and the environment. It involves thorough due diligence to ensure supply chains are free from exploitation and environmental harm	Economic realism focuses on the practical considerations of operating within a competitive market economy, emphasising cost-effectiveness, efficiency, and market competitiveness while navigating ethical sourcing challenges
Analysis	Cobalt mining in the DRC, critical for electronics and electric vehicles, has been marred by reports of child labour, unsafe working conditions, and environmental degradation. Ethical sourcing principles would necessitate re-evaluating sourcing strategies to align with international human rights and environmental standards	Given the high demand for cobalt and the DRC's dominance in cobalt supply, economic realism acknowledges companies' pressures to secure cobalt at competitive prices, which might lead to prioritising cost over strict adherence to ethical sourcing standards
Guided response	Companies must implement transparent supply chain practices, establish traceability, and engage in third-party audits to verify compliance with ethical standards. Collaborating with local communities and NGOs to improve mining practices and investing in sustainable mining technologies are vital	Balancing economic realism with ethical considerations might involve diversifying supply sources, increasing investment in cobalt recycling to reduce dependency, and advocating for industry-wide ethical sourcing standards that do not compromise economic viability

accountability and traceability throughout the sourcing process. Blockchain technology, for example, enables the secure and transparent recording of transactions, providing stakeholders with real-time visibility into the origins and handling of materials.

Additionally, fostering collaboration and partnerships across industries can facilitate the development of sustainable sourcing practices that are economically viable. By pooling resources and expertise, companies can share the costs and risks associated with ethical sourcing initiatives, making them more accessible to a broader range of businesses.

Moreover, consumer demand for ethically sourced products allows businesses to differentiate themselves and command premium prices. By aligning with consumer values and preferences, companies can create value propositions that prioritise ethical sourcing while remaining competitive in the marketplace.

Scheele et al. (2016) call for comprehensive action, urging companies to prioritise ethical sourcing and for international stakeholders to promote responsible mining practices. Strategies include transparent supply chain practices, third-party audits, collaboration with local communities, and sustainable technology investments. Addressing the tension between ethical sourcing and economic pressures necessitates innovative approaches, such as leveraging technology for supply chain transparency, fostering industry partnerships, and meeting consumer demand for ethically sourced products.

The case of cobalt mining in the DRC illustrates the critical need for companies to navigate the ethical complexities of global supply chains. It highlights the importance of a balanced approach that does not sacrifice ethical integrity for economic gains. Furthermore, this case study emphasises the role of CR in combating greenwashing by promoting genuine environmental stewardship and transparent communication. Through collaborative efforts and innovative solutions, businesses can reconcile the demands of ethical sourcing with economic realities, contributing to a sustainable and ethically responsible global market.

In conclusion, the influence of greenwashing on Ethical Sourcing and Economic Realism underscores the need for innovative solutions that do not compromise on ethical standards despite economic pressures. By leveraging technology, fostering collaboration, and responding to consumer demand, businesses can navigate the complexities of ethical sourcing while remaining economically viable. Ultimately, prioritising ethical sourcing is a moral imperative and a strategic advantage that contributes to long-term business success and sustainability.

5. DISCUSSION

In integrating ethical considerations into corporate strategies, it is crucial to champion sustainability and ethical practices and directly confront and weave in the economic challenges these endeavours entail within each case study and ethical theory discussion. The adoption of ethical theories faces scrutiny against the inherent tension between maintaining profitability and investing in sustainability.

Economic challenges, such as the need for significant upfront investments in renewable energy, sustainable raw materials, and fair labour practices, present hurdles especially pronounced in competitive markets with prioritised short-term gains. However, recognising these economic constraints not as insurmountable barriers but as catalysts for innovation and strategic foresight is critical. When viewed through ethical theories applied to real-world case studies, the transition towards sustainable practices underscores the importance of phased strategies and the adoption of innovative business models and technological advancements that can mitigate costs while enhancing long-term benefits.

For instance, when applied to the dilemma of ethical sourcing versus economic pressures in cobalt mining, Utilitarianism emphasises the moral imperatives and the strategic advantage of investing in ethical sourcing practices. This approach aligns with economic realism by highlighting the need for innovative solutions like blockchain for supply chain transparency, which can reconcile ethical sourcing with market competitiveness.

Similarly, applying Deontological Ethics in the context of labour practices showcases the ethical obligation to ensure worker safety and rights, challenging companies to view investments in ethical labour practices not as mere costs but as essential components of long-term brand integrity and market resilience. Innovation in labour management and stakeholder engagement emerges as a strategic response to economic pressures, fostering a culture of ethical integrity that can drive competitive advantage.

Adopting circular economy principles further illustrates how addressing economic challenges within the ethical framework transforms potential cost centres into value-creation opportunities. This approach, coupled with public–private partnerships and incentives, exemplifies how strategic foresight and innovation can ease the transition towards sustainability, making it a compelling investment in future competitiveness rather than a financial burden.

By embedding the acknowledgement of economic challenges within the discussion of each ethical theory and case study, we highlight the nuanced interplay between ethical imperatives and economic realism. This integrated perspective enriches the analysis and positions sustainability and ethical practices as drivers of innovation, efficiency, and long-term financial performance. It shifts the narrative towards viewing sustainable practices as strategic investments that, through innovation and foresight, can overcome economic hurdles and redefine corporate success in the global business landscape.

6. CONCLUSIONS AND FUTURE DIRECTIONS

This research delves into the ethical challenges and dilemmas corporations face amidst pressures to remain profitable while adhering to ethical standards, especially under the scrutiny of greenwashing practices. We have uncovered the critical balance between profit motives and ethical imperatives by applying ethical theories like Utilitarianism, Deontological Ethics, and CR to dissect real-world case studies. Our findings advocate for a holistic ethical framework where decisions serve both financial success and moral obligations, reinforcing the need for corporations to prioritise stakeholder welfare and sustainable, ethical practices to address global economic disparities.

The key insights of our paper underline the necessity for corporations to engage all stakeholders and adopt sustainable practices, which is vital for a more equitable global economy. Moreso, ethical sourcing versus economic pressures underscores the need for innovation, strategic partnerships, and transparency to uphold ethical integrity. Greenwashing impacts consumer trust and sustainability efforts, highlighting the need for more rigorous regulatory frameworks and authentic environmental stewardship.

Future endeavours in corporate ethics and sustainability should concentrate on the following:

1. *Developing adaptable ethical frameworks*: Future research should craft dynamic ethical frameworks that guide corporations through ethical dilemmas, integrating ethical considerations into strategic decisions effectively. These frameworks must adapt to the evolving global business environment, providing a solid basis for ethical decision-making in line with changing societal expectations.
2. *Empirical evaluation of ethical strategies*: There is a critical need for empirical studies assessing ethical strategies' impact across various industries. Such research could illuminate the practical applications of ethical theories, offering corporations actionable insights for embedding ethical practices that bolster decision-making and sustainable success.
3. *Strengthening stakeholder engagement and advocating for regulatory reforms*: Corporations should enhance stakeholder engagement, fostering a participatory ethical decision-making process. Meanwhile, policymakers and regulators should urgently establish and enforce stricter regulations against unethical practices, such as greenwashing. These measures, focused on transparency and accountability, would encourage a business environment where ethical practices are rewarded and expected.

Our study contributes to corporate ethics and sustainability dialogue by highlighting how corporations can navigate ethical complexities. Emphasising stakeholder engagement and the necessity for strict regulations to combat unethical practices, including greenwashing, this research outlines a path toward ensuring that corporate ethics and sustainability are central to business strategies. By focusing on these areas, we can advance the discourse towards actionable insights and practical solutions, ensuring corporations balance profitability with their ethical responsibilities to society and the environment and fostering a more sustainable global economy.

REFERENCES

Arnold, D. G., & Bowie, N. E. (2003). Sweatshops and respect for persons. *Business Ethics Quarterly, 13*(2), 221–242. https://doi.org/10.5840/beq200313215

Bazillier, R., & Vauday, J. (2009). *The greenwashing machine: CSR is more than communication.* Document de Recherche du LEO. 2009-6.

Bentham, J. (1789). *An introduction to the principles of morals and legislation.* Clarendon Press.

Carroll, A. B. (1991). The pyramid of corporate social responsibility: Toward the moral management of organizational stakeholders. *Business Horizons, 34*(4), 39–48.

Chan, J., Pun, N., & Selden, M. (2013). The politics of global production: Apple, Foxconn and China's new working class. *New Technology, Work and Employment, 28*(2), 100–115.

Ewing, J. (2017). *Faster, higher, farther: The inside story of the Volkswagen scandal.* Random House.

Freeman, R. E. (1984). *Strategic management: A stakeholder approach.* Pitman.

Friedman, M. (1970). The social responsibility of business is to increase its profits. *The New York Times Magazine*.
Gereffi, G., Humphrey, J., & Sturgeon, T. (2005). The governance of global value chains. *Review of International Political Economy, 12*(1), 78–104.
Hart, S. L., & Milstein, M. B. (2003). Creating sustainable value. *Academy of Management Perspectives, 17*(2), 56–67.
Kant, I. (1785). *Groundwork of the metaphysics of morals*. Cambridge University Press.
Kaplinsky, R. (2000). Globalisation and unequalisation: What can be learned from value chain analysis? *Journal of Development Studies, 37*(2), 117–146.
Laszlo, C., & Zhexembayeva, N. (2011). Embedded sustainability: A strategy for market leaders. *The European Financial Review, 15*, 37–49.
Locke, R. M. (2003). The promise and perils of globalisation: The case of Nike. *Management: Inventing and Delivering Its Future, 39*, 40.
Lyon, T. P., & Montgomery, A. W. (2015). The means and end of greenwash. *Organization & Environment, 28*(2), 223–249. https://doi.org/10.1177/1086026615575332
Mansell, S. (2013). Shareholder theory and Kantian ethics: On the importance of selecting an appropriate level for ethical analysis. *Business Ethics: A European Review, 22*(4), 377–391.
Mill, J. S. (1863). *Utilitarianism*. Parker, Son, and Bourn.
Mitchell, L., & Ramey, W. (2010). Look how green I am! An individual-level explanation for greenwashing. *Journal of Applied Business and Economics, 12*(6), 40–45. SSRN.. https://ssrn.com/abstract=2409956
Piketty, T. (2014). *Capital in the twenty-first century*. Harvard University Press.
Porter, M. E., & Kramer, M. R. (2006). The link between competitive advantage and corporate social responsibility. *Harvard Business Review, 84*(12), 78–92.
Scheele, F., de Haan, E., & Kiezebrink, V. (2016). *Cobalt blues environmental pollution and human rights violations in Katanga's copper and cobalt mines*. https://www.researchgate.net/publication/346528037_Cobalt_blues_Environmental_pollution_and_human_rights_violations_in_Katanga's_copper_and_cobalt_mines
Seele, P., & Gatti, L. (2017). Greenwashing revisited: In search of a typology and accusation-based definition incorporating legitimacy strategies. *Business Strategy and the Environment, 26*(2), 239–252. https://doi.org/10.1002/bse.1912
Sen, A. (1999). *Development as freedom*. Oxford University Press.
Siegle, L. (2011). *To die for: Is fashion wearing out the world?*
Stiglitz, J. E. (2002). *Globalisation and its discontents*. W. W. Norton & Company.
Stiglitz, J. E. (2012). *The price of inequality: How today's divided society endangers our future*. W. W. Norton & Company.

CHAPTER 12

TECHNOLOGIES PROMOTING THE DIGITAL TOURISM ECONOMY AND STUDENT ATTITUDES TOWARDS ARTIFICIAL INTELLIGENCE IN TOURISM

Simona Biriescu[a] and Laura Olteanu[b]

[a]*Faculty of Economics and Business Administration, Department of Business Information Systems, West University of Timisoara, Timisoara, Romania*
[b]*Faculty of Economics and Business Administration, Department of Business Administration, Babeş-Bolyai University, Cluj Napoca, Romania*

ABSTRACT

Purpose/Objective: *This research aims to ensure that the technologies that promote the digital tourism economy play an important role in its development in the near future, and students will have an open attitude towards digitisation, artificial intelligence (AI), robotisation, and gamification in tourism.*

Design/Methodology/Approach: *A survey questionnaire collected primary data. Simple random sampling was used, and the sample size was 40 students. The questionnaire was distributed via email in March 2024. Data obtained from the questionnaire were analysed based on correlations.*

Findings: *AI usage in the education system for tourism students should be to personalise the learning process as much as possible, provide personalised learning paths according to student's strengths and weaknesses, and adapt learning* materials to the characteristics of students while maintaining the quality of education and the principles of integration into the educational system.

Significance/Implications/Conclusions: *Intelligent IT systems fully support people's needs and intuitively respond to their problems. However, creating such support requires long hours of work and programming. Indeed, the challenge of providing AI that can intelligently interact with humans remains significant. Rephrasing requests to obtain specific and accurate answers is unnecessary.*

Limitations: *Students' attitudes towards AI are not always positive, as attested by their attitudes towards AI in tourism in the research analysis carried out in the chapter. This could lead to limited perspectives on AI in education.*

Future Research: *Specific strategies implemented by companies to offer customers virtual guided tours, allowing them to visualise a place before they get there.*

Keywords: Promotion; technologies; tourism; digitisation; AI; attitude; students; company

JEL Codes: C12; I21; L83; L86; O33; Q55; M21; M15

1. INTRODUCTION

The global COVID-19 epidemic has severely impacted the economy, with tourism being one of the most affected sectors (OECD, 2020). Travel agents, tour operators, hotels, airlines, and other typical businesses were hit hard, with dating experiences plummeting and even being forced to shut down operations. During this period, technology was forced to adapt to this unprecedented situation and reinvent itself to meet the expectations of the tourism market. One of the difficulties for travellers, potential travellers, and professionals in the field at the beginning of the COVID-19 pandemic was finding the right information in the constant stream of data being disseminated by the media.

Smart communities mean new ways to provide tourism, cultural and entertainment services, attract tourists through new promotion and advertising methods, and simplify and streamline access to all the attractions and sights a destination can offer. Even today, obtaining reliable information on the progress of the pandemic, areas at risk, and regulations at the local, national, and international levels is a priority. Accessing and verifying this information, which is essential for both tourism professionals and tourists themselves, is easy thanks to technological initiatives that have emerged rapidly.

Digitisation and the advent of blockchain technology have significantly changed various industries, such as entertainment and gambling. They are now bringing about major changes in many economic sectors, including the world of travel and tourism. The decentralised nature of data in blockchain technology ensures the security of all information and transactions that make travel possible.

Such systems can also provide speed and high efficiency in terms of travel arrangements and bookings, but that is not all. With the help of this technology, travellers can be easily identified with biometric data when they need to travel, thus avoiding wasting time in endless queues at airport security checkpoints, easily tracking their bags, and ensuring the traceability of payments and transactions.

This chapter aims to ensure that the technologies that promote the digital tourism economy play an important role in its development in the near future, and students will have an open attitude towards digitisation, AI, robotisation, and gamification in tourism. Developed during this period, Albatross implemented an API (Application Programming Interface) that provides real-time information on travel restrictions in various countries. By regularly consulting this API, travellers can avoid blockades at airports and other borders and stay informed of the latest official regulations, especially regarding wearing masks and quarantine.

Access to information has been a central concern of travel agents since before the health crisis. Indeed, travel agents must inform travellers, for example, about administrative and health procedures specific to their destination. This information is either manually entered on a registration form given to the customer or set up in a management system. In the latter case, the information is not always up to date since updates remain manual. Yes, that's why we need high-performance digitalisation.

This touches on one of the issues often criticised with new technologies: respect for privacy. Even in the case of COVID-19, it is for a good cause. However, surveillance is much laxer in other countries, such as China and South Korea, where credit card data and facial recognition are used.

This touches on one of the essential points of personal freedom, for which there is no universal solution. However, travellers will face a difficult choice in the months and years ahead: beyond PCR and other tests, countries will take permanent measures to avoid mass transmission of COVID-19 and other viruses. As a traveller, would I cancel a trip or business trip because I believe that the measures taken at my destination would violate my personal liberty? Again, the information provided by the agency would be essential.

It found that new technology was needed to keep businesses running: According to one study, COVID-19 has brought a six-year leap forward for companies in terms of digital transformation. This was the case for tourism operators with little or no online presence and operating in a somewhat 'classic' manner, with POS as their primary distribution and communication channel. Overnight stays, telework, and short working hours were mixed with crisis management, tourist repatriation, and surplus management. Agencies were faced with and had to take advantage of technological solutions to continue working remotely; VPNs, cloud, Zoom, Google Meet, and other private networks were set up, and byte working work was tested as well as possible. Technological solutions for the tourism industry have also met customer expectations, especially in automating receipt management. Most travel agents have benefitted from setting up workstations remotely so that they can access all their tools from home.

Technological and collaborative solutions were largely unknown before the crisis emerged. Zoom, a video-conferencing application, has grown from 14 million users in December 2020 to over 300 million daily meeting participants. Similar applications, such as Google Meet, Microsoft Team, and others, have made it possible to maintain interaction with teams and hold meetings internally, with service providers, or with customers. For example, an application like WhatsApp Messenger will become a natural means of customer contact, just as a phone or a physical interview can be. Tourism stakeholders will struggle to perpetuate and integrate these applications into their information systems. If we stay on the case of WhatsApp, it is an application available exclusively on mobile (use on a computer still requires a mobile). However, few distributors have cell phones for business use. During the health crisis, as everyone became aware of the emergency situation, BYOD (Bring Your Own Device) and PAP (Take your personal devices) made up for the lack of equipment and means of communication. But what will happen in the future? And what will happen to the security of information systems using these devices that the company does not control?

The place of technology in tomorrow's travel plays an important role: AI is a sophisticated digital technology that empowers machines to imitate or surpass certain human practices and abilities that require intelligence. This includes technologies that enable machines to learn and adapt, perceive and interact, reason and plan, and optimise procedures and parameters to extract intelligent insights from large amounts of data and operate autonomously.

AI is a reality that already influences certain human decisions in the fields of tourism, security, marketing, communication strategies, and even medical treatments. Digital technology's development is changing how we live, work, and travel, opening new prospects for the tourism business in the global marketplace. This work analyses the impact of the rise of digital technologies on tourism.

The tourism industry is being transformed by the advancements and applications of digital technology. This transformation is changing the way we live, work, travel, and conduct business. The adoption and diffusion of digital technologies differ from one country, industry, company, and location to another. As a result, there is an uneven playing field, where technology-driven, globally connected tourism businesses have more opportunities than traditional small and micro businesses. These traditional businesses often rely on low-tech practices, which can exacerbate the mismatch between the two types of businesses. So far, the focus has been on digital marketing and e-commerce, which are seen as ways to enter new markets, engage with customers, and develop branding. However, while digital marketing and e-commerce can help improve market access, market understanding, and connectivity and facilitate financial transactions, they are less effective in increasing productivity and innovation in a highly competitive global marketplace.

Productivity-enhancing technologies, such as cloud computing, data analytics, and revenue management software, are not widely used in the tourism industry. However, innovative technologies like augmented reality (AR) are creating new tourism products, services, and offerings, while also increasing originality and personalisation (OECD, 2016). This is leading to new and unpredictable paths for tourism through digital transformation. The impact of digital technologies is significant on businesses of all sizes in the tourism sector, as well as the structure and functioning of tourism value chains as a whole.

2. THEORETICAL AND CONCEPTUAL CONTEXT

The digital revolution has opened up new opportunities for small- and medium-sized enterprises (SMEs) in the tourism sector. They can now access previously untapped markets, develop new products and services, embrace new business models and processes, improve their position in the global tourism value chain, and integrate into the digital ecosystem (Kelly, 2015). For SMEs, there are significant potential benefits, such as becoming more efficient, free in gup time and resources to focus on strategic work, developing new business models, gaining a foothold in new markets, and helping to internationalise their activities (Lockett & Brown, 2006). However, SMEs have been slow to make the digital transition (OECD, 2017b, 2017d), and many traditional small tourism businesses struggle to seise these opportunities and reap the benefits. SMEs that do not invest in digital transformation have no chance of surviving, let alone thriving, in the future. Tourism destinations, businesses, and the overall tourism sector must adopt the latest technologies to stay competitive and leverage their potential for creativity, efficiency, and value generation. Policymakers play a crucial role in aiding tourism businesses of any scale, from the most conventional to the smallest ones, in becoming pioneers in the digital revolution and succeeding amidst the technological paradigm shift.

Digital trends, drivers of change in tourism: Digital development is defined as the process by which technology and data-driven management transform socio-economic systems and our lives. The race to adopt digital technologies is rooted in the convergence of advanced technologies and the increasing socio-economic ties that result from globalisation. The digital revolution has the potential to drive innovation, enhance economic and environmental efficiency, and boost productivity, particularly in the tourism sector, which operates in a highly globalised environment (OECD, 2017a). It is crucial for tourism companies of all sizes to adapt their business models, make the most of digital technologies, and adopt new data-driven approaches to increase their productivity and profitability (Kelly, 2015). As consumers increasingly use digital tools to plan, research, and book their trips, tourism businesses need to integrate these technologies and leverage their advanced capabilities to stay relevant and competitive.

Technologies promoting the digital tourism economy: Technological advancements are significantly impacting the tourism industry. These innovations encompass a broad range of technologies, including business management technologies such as mobile and cloud technologies, advanced automation and robotics, blockchains, and data analytics, as well as technologies that result in inventive tourism products, services, and benefits, such as virtual reality (VR) and AR or the Internet of Things (IoT). Additionally, there are technologies that allow people to benefit from assistance, understand, and communicate with markets, including data analytics, cloud computing, and AI (Ivanov & Webster, 2019).

In the age of technology, both consumers and businesses are generating copious amounts of new data. Companies can use these data to create new business models and increase productivity. By using data analytics, businesses can predict customer preferences and buying behaviour. It is also useful for revenue management and for setting dynamic pricing. As a result, it is important for employees of SMEs to develop the necessary skills to be part of this data-driven ecosystem. However, privacy and data-sharing concerns are a major issue for governments.

In the digital age, consumers and businesses constantly generate new data. Companies can create new business models and productivity gains when they take advantage of these data. Data analysis can predict customer preferences and channel consumer purchasing behaviour. It is also being used to manage venues and establish dynamic pricing. SME employees need to develop the skills to be part of this data-driven ecosystem, and privacy and data-sharing issues are of great concern to governments.

Artificial intelligence: Customers will be able to use AI and voice technologies to access digital concierge services, search the Internet, and retrieve digital records using voice assistants and intelligent cameras.

Internet of Things: IoT will drive a data-rich tourism industry, boost smart tourism, and make cities more efficient. The sensors, data, and automation interoperability will enable real-time access to insights and valuable information for tourism marketing and management, improving tourism offerings and reducing environmental impacts while improving operational and resource efficiency (Biriescu, 2013). AR/VR: AR systems display virtual objects in the real world. In the tourism sector, for example they can replace paper media used for marketing and advertising, be used to improve tourism services in the context of gamification or be used as travel assistants that guide users through complex public transportation networks in real time (Biriescu, 2018a, 2018b).

Blockchain: Blockchain-based smart contracts can be used throughout the supply chain. In the future, user-friendly applications could be widely distributed to travel agencies of all sizes and adapted to increase end-to-end transparency for users. According to a report on online commerce in the EU, more than 70% of internet users have used the blockchain in the past to purchase online goods or services for personal purposes at least once in the past 12 months (Fig. 12.1). More than half (54%) purchase travel and vacation accommodations, with this category trailing clothing and sporting goods by nearly two-thirds (65%). Internet users aged 25–54 are the most likely to purchase travel and vacation (57%).

The report also showed that the percentage of people who shop online varies considerably across the EU, from 29% in Romania to 91% in the UK when people are on vacation (Eurostat, 2020).

They are developing intelligent approaches to tourism: As dematerialisation progresses, new technologies are combined innovatively, pushing digital transformation in new and often unpredictable directions (OECD, 2017c). In the tourism industry, digital convergence takes place in two main areas: the amalgamation of digital technologies and their integration into the physical world (such as wearable technologies, AR, and image recognition). Digital convergence happens when various digital technologies function together in harmony, sharing data and

Technologies Promoting the Digital Tourism Economy

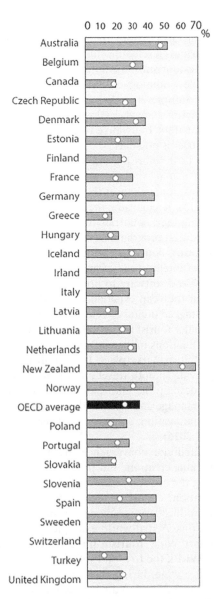

Fig. 12.1. Countries that Use Modern Technology in Tourism (Own Graphics). *Source*: Eurostat data (2020).

information, and giving rise to innovations that facilitate seamless interaction throughout the traveller's journey. For example, once a means of transportation is booked, automatic suggestions for travel, lodging, and activities at a destination are sent based on past behaviour. Users can book a car or restaurant, check into a hotel, or purchase tickets with a few clicks (Melis & Piga, 2016). Automation, AI, and big data analytics facilitate the interoperability of reservation systems. Still, existing partnerships can also ensure that consumer choice is systematically focused on preferred partners, excluding smaller companies offering other products and services. In the tourism industry, digital and physical convergence is expressed in AR, wearable technology, and the IoT to create new hybrid products, services, and offerings. Examples include bicycles, scooters, and electric vehicles. These can be accessed anytime, anywhere through mobile apps, reducing the need for counter presence and staff. Innovative tourism development at the scale of cities, regions, and countries is possible.

Smart tourism aims to develop the information and communication infrastructure and capacity to manage and operate the tourism sector in a coordinated manner that fosters innovation, enhances the lived experience, and increases efficiency (Gretzel et al., 2015). Recognising the transformative economic and social power of intelligent technology, countries such as South Korea, Croatia, Spain, and Portugal have introduced programmes to support the development of innovative tourism destinations. American wine producers' Smart Wine Tourism initiative is an example of intelligent tourism in tourism destinations. This initiative uses Wi-Fi, the IoT, and software to provide geo-location to target tourists near destinations so that they can experience wine during their stay. Providing Internet access and geo-tagged digital directories (such as Tourist Wise) in popular tourist areas and popular tourist routes to facilitate visits to wineries and other attractions will help destinations in increasingly competitive market destinations in an increasingly competitive marketplace. It will only increase in importance as destinations seek to provide smooth travel and improve the traveller experience. Smart tourism aims to develop the information and communication infrastructure and capabilities to manage and operate the tourism sector in a coordinated manner that maintains innovation, enhances the lived experience, and increases efficiency (Gretzel et al., 2015).

Technologies that facilitate convergence are recognised as a significant source of innovation, value creation, and productivity in the tourism industry (Fig. 12.2). Recognising the economic and social power of smart technologies in terms of transformation, countries such as South Korea, Croatia, Spain, and Portugal have introduced programmes to support the development of smart tourism destinations. A real-world example of smart tourism in tourist destinations is the Smart Wine Tourism initiative launched by an American wine producer. It uses Wi-Fi, the IoT, and software to target tourists near their destination to experience wine during their stay and geo-location. Providing Internet access and geo-tagged digital directories (such as Tourist Wise) in popular tourist areas and on popular tourist routes to facilitate visits to wineries and other attractions will help destinations become increasingly competitive.

To develop a tourism model, the knowledge society needs to know:

- The extension and deepening of scientific knowledge and truth.
- *E-tourism*: innovative approaches in the field of tourism.
- The use and management of existing knowledge as technical and organisational knowledge.

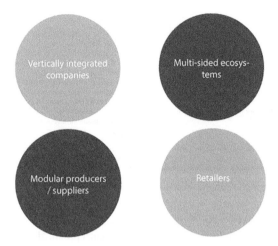

Fig. 12.2. Business Models in the Tourism Sector (Customers-Commercial Relays).

- Production of new technical knowledge through innovation.
- UN precedent dissemination of knowledge to all citizens through new means.
- The use of the Internet, e-books, and e-learning.
- The New Economy is a term that has recently become used daily. It is well known that the information economy is developing in the information society.

In the knowledge society, a new economy, including the Internet economy, is being formed. Thus, the new economy is the information society and the knowledge economy. The knowledge society is a new economy in which the process of innovation (the ability to absorb and transform new knowledge to create new services and products) becomes important (Fig. 12.3).

Mobile/cloud computing technology: Thanks to cloud technology, Wi-Fi, and international mobile projects, mobile devices are now becoming increasingly important and critical travel assistants, including access to real-time destination information and online reservations. Online or mobile payments. Thanks to cloud technology, SMEs can manage their business from anywhere worldwide, as long as they have a high-speed Internet connection.

Data analytics: In the digital age, both consumers and businesses are constantly generating new data. New economic models and productivity gains are being created as companies can leverage these data. Data analysis predicts customer preferences and channels consumer purchasing behaviour. It is also used for revenue management and dynamic pricing. SME employees must develop the skills necessary to become part of this data-driven ecosystem, and privacy and data-sharing issues are of great concern to governments.

Artificial intelligence: AI, conversational agents, and voice technology allow customers to search the Internet, record digital information, and access digital

Strengths	Weaknesses
People at the forefront of artificial intelligence and relevant scientific community (ACIA)	Lack of stable structural funding
Consolidate and strong knowledge system (universities and search centres)	Knowledge fragmentation
Establish agents with transfer capacity	Insufficient non-university training offer
Existing infrastructures (BSC, Labs, 5G, etc.)	Lack of technological vocations and specialised talent
Venue for international events	Regulatory framework
Leading sectors (health, mobility, and tourism)	Immigration to attract talent, creation of start-ups
Agents that can boost innovation and the creation of companies. Start-up creation hub	Public authorities and companies' resistance to change
	Conservative industrial networks with low-risk capacity in technological innovation
	Lack of international influence
Opportunities	**Threats**
European policies to boost artificial intelligence and robotics	Mature policies for driving artificial intelligence in other countries
Increased global investment and decentralisation of major international stakeholders	Limited control over external decision centres
Creation of specialized talent in emerging regions in the AI field	Competitive funding sources in external technology centres
	Very competitive international employment offers

Fig. 12.3. The SWOT Analysis of an AI Ecosystem. *Source*: Government of Catalonia (2019), p. 24, https://participa.gencat.cat/uploads/decidim/attachment/file/932/Document-Bases-Estrategia-IA-Catalunya-_ENversion.pdf.

concierge services, voice assistants, and smart rooms. The technology provides customised, tailored, on-demand services that facilitate a smooth travel experience.

Internet of Things: The IoT can host era data-rich tourism sector and promote smart tourism by increasing urban efficiency. The sensors, data, and automation interoperability can provide real-time indicators and information that can help market and manage tourism, improve tourist offers, increase operational and resource efficiency, and reduce environmental impacts.

Augmented reality/virtual reality: AR systems display virtual objects in the real world. In the tourism sector, for example, they can replace paper media used for marketing and advertising, be used in contexts that enhance entertainment and tourism effectiveness or be used as travel assistants that guide users through complex public transportation networks in real time.

3. RESEARCH METHODOLOGY AND ANALYSIS

3.1. Hypothesis (H)

Starting from a research model in which the attitude of tourism students towards AI is important, we must also take into account the support offered by the University and what controls their behaviour towards AI (Fig. 12.4).

H1. The educational support offered by university studies in the field of tourism specialisation directly and positively influences the students' ability to become managers in tourism and solve situations.

H2. Relational support directly and positively influences the personal attitude of students to become managers in tourism.

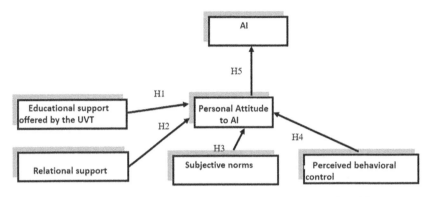

Fig. 12.4. The Model of the Research Hypothesis (Own Graphics).

H3. Subjective norms have a direct and positive impact on students' attitudes towards becoming tourism managers.

H4. Perceived behavioural control has a direct and positive impact on students' attitudes towards becoming tourism managers.

H5. The personal attitude of the students to become managers in tourism has a direct and positive impact on their managerial intention.

Starting from a research model where the attitude of tourism students towards AI is essential, we must also consider the support offered by the faculty and the university and the control of their behaviour towards AI.

3.2. Data Analysis

The type of research used in the case study is a descriptive study, and the method used was a survey through a questionnaire, that is, a collection of primary data. A simple random sampling was used, as the characteristics of the students did not significantly influence the chosen objectives, and the sample size was 40 students. The questionnaire was distributed via email in March of this year.

The questionnaire contained 17 questions, all of which were mandatory. The first question was introductory, and questions 6–17 aimed to obtain the data necessary for the research question. After the response collection period, the responses were exported to the Excel programme, where the encoding and analysis of the data obtained from the questionnaire were carried out based on correlations.

Following the questionnaire responses (database created in Excel), the data analysis was performed by comparing variables.

Some of the relevant charts from the questionnaire (Figs. 12.5–12.7):

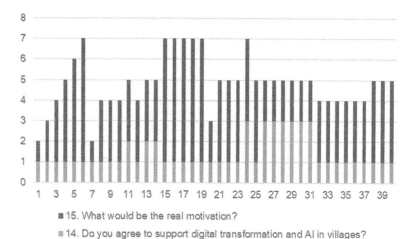

Fig. 12.5. Interpretive Graphics from the Questionnaire (1).

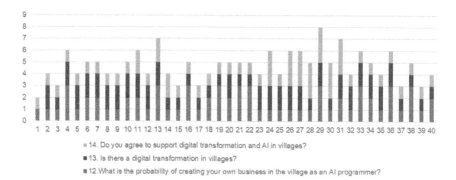

Fig. 12.6. Interpretive Graphics from the Questionnaire (2).

According to the Table 12.1 correlation matrix of the main variables within the model, it can be observed:

- A negative influence can be observed between self-confidence, and the need for achievement (−0.392) between attitudes and entrepreneurial intention is a positive one (0.36) and between subjective norms and entrepreneurial intentions also a positive influence (0.367);
- A low degree of association between control and attitudes (−0.332), respectively between control and entrepreneurial intentions (−0.339);
- An acceptable degree of association between risk predisposition and attitudes (0.331), risk predisposition and perceived behavioural control (0.401), respectively, risk predisposition and subjective norms (0.432);
- A low degree of association between self-confidence and attitudes (−0.125), respectively, between self-confidence and subjective norms (−0.288), and

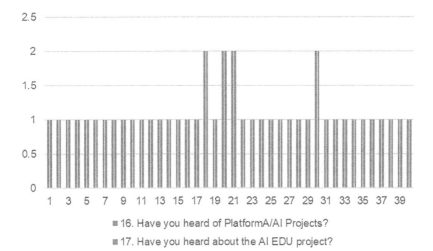

Fig. 12.7. Interpretive Graphics from the Questionnaire (4).

between perceived behavioural control and subjective norms, a positive correlation (0.539);
- An acceptable degree of association between attitudes and perceived behavioural control (0.565) between attitudes and subjective norms (0.384);
- A weak correlation between the variable control and the variable's predisposition to risk (−0.410), self-confidence is acceptable (0.368), the need for achievement is low (−0.438), as well as perceived behavioural control (−0.407) and subjective norms (−0.425), and respect between self-confidence and perceived behavioural control (0.189) an acceptable correlation.

There is a weak correlation between the predisposition to risk and self-confidence (−0.434), but there is an acceptable correlation between the predisposition to risk and the need for achievement (0.189). We note that when asked, 'Have you heard of the AI EDU project?' (Table 12.2). Thirty-six students answered positively out

Table 12.1. Hypothesis Testing – Student's Attitudes Towards AI in Tourism.

	Co	RP	I	S-C	A	Cbp	NA	AI
The correlation matrix of the variables							
Co	1							
RP	−0.41085	1						
I	0.368125	−0.43454	1					
S-C	−0.43868	0.18996	−0.39287	1				
A	−0.33225	0.331613	−0.12556	0.165165	1			
Cbp	−0.4071	0.401719	−0.32623	0.302747	0.565239	1		
NA	−0.42504	0.432961	−0.28842	0.292234	0.384021	0.539237	1	
AI	−0.33978	0.527783	−0.48164	0.563817	0.362994	0.633074	0.367805	1

Source: Authors research in Excel.

Table 12.2. Have You Heard of the AI EDU Project? (Q*, Answers from the Students).

Q*	Column Labels Development	Digitalisation	AI	Innovation	Renew	Transformation	Digital Transformation	Total
Yes	5	1	13	1	6	2	8	36
No	1				2		1	4
Total	6	1	13	1	8	2	9	40

Note: Q* – Have you heard of the AI EDU project?

of 40 respondents. This means that they are knowledgeable about digitisation, innovation, AI, and digital transformation.

The graphical representations were derived from the responses to the survey questions. Notably, for questions Q16/Q17, the results indicate a near parity in responses, with a marginal error of 0.04, as illustrated in Fig. 12.6 and Table 12.3.

According to the research model and considering the determined variables (Table 12.3), we formulated the following equations:

$$A = f(C, RP, S\text{-}C, I, NA),$$

where village students' personal attitude (A) is a behavioural characteristic discerned from their actions, control (C) is a psychological trait of the students, predisposition to risk (RP) is a psychological trait of the students, self-confidence (S-C) is a psychological trait of the students, confidence (Co) is a psychological trait of the students, need for achievement (NA) is a psychological trait of the students.

$$SN = f(C, RP, S\text{-}C, Co, NA)$$

Table 12.3. Data Analysis (Regression) in Parallel with Questions 2 and 17.

Column 1		Column 2	
Statistics	Values	Statistics	Values
Mean	1.1	Mean	1.1
Standard error	0.048038446	Standard error	0.048038446
Median	1	Median	1
Mode	1	Mode	1
Standard deviation	0.30382181	Standard deviation	0.30382181
Sample variance	0.092307692	Sample variance	0.092307692
Kurtosis	5.979137032	Kurtosis	5.979137032
Skewness	2.771707741	Skewness	2.771707741
Range	1	Range	1
Minimum	1	Minimum	1
Maximum	2	Maximum	2
Sum	44	Sum	44
Count	40	Count	40

Source: Authors research in Excel.

where subjective norms (SN) are behavioural characteristics that refer to an individual's perceptions of the general social pressure to act or not to act.

$$Cbp = f(C, RP, S\text{-}C, I, NA)$$

where perceived behavioural control (Cbp) is a characteristic that allows for predicting relatively direct behaviours (i.e. behaviours under will control).

AI (The intention to use AI in tourism) $= f(SN)$
AI $= f(Cbp)$
1). AI $= f(A)$.

Hypothesis verification was achieved using simple linear regression (Table 12.4) between psychological traits and behavioural traits, on the one hand, and between behavioural characteristics and entrepreneurial intentions of village students, on the other hand.

The analysis of the results demonstrates the following:

1. There is a direct, positive, and significant relationship between control (independent variable) and student's attitude towards AI (dependent variable) for students from the city and a negative one if we talk about the students from the village;
2. There is a direct, almost positive and significant relationship between self-confidence (independent variable) and student's attitude towards AI (dependent variable);
3. There is a direct, almost positive and significant relationship between the need for achievement (independent variable) and students' attitude towards AI (dependent variable);

Table 12.4. Hypothesis Testing – Students' AI Usage Intentions.

	Coefficients	Standard Error	t Stat	P-value	Lower 95%	Upper 95%
Intercept	1.020202	0.1395	7.31326	9.3E−09	0.73779877	1.30260526
X Variable 1	0.035354	0.085694	0.41255	0.68225	−0.138125	0.20883247
ANOVA						

	df	SS	MS	F	Significance F
Regression	1	0.012374	0.01237	0.17020	0.68225156
Residual	38	2.762626	0.07270		
Total	39	2.775			
Regression statistics					
Multiple R	0.066776				
R square	0.004459				
Adjusted R square	−0.02174				
Standard error	0.269631				
Observations	40				

Source: Authors research in Excel.

4. There is a direct, almost positive, and significant relationship between control (independent variable) and students' perceived behavioural control towards AI (dependent variable);
5. There is a direct, almost positive, and significant relationship between risk predisposition (independent variable) and perceived behaviour control of students towards AI (dependent variable);
6. There is a direct, almost positive, and significant relationship between self-confidence (independent variable) and perceived behaviour control of students towards AI (dependent variable);
7. There is a direct, almost positive, and significant relationship between the need for achievement (independent variable) and perceived behaviour control of students towards AI (dependent variable);
8. The perceived behavioural control (independent variable) will, in the future, directly, positively, and significantly influence the students' intentions to accept AI (dependent variable); for now, the result is almost positive because we also have negative results (-0.41).

As it appears from the analysis researched in the chapter, students' attitudes towards AI in tourism are not precisely positive. Still, we must note that students come from both urban and rural areas, and their perception of rural areas towards AI is low. However, they are aware that new technologies, digitisation, robotics, gamification, and AI are necessary to promote tourism because tourism is a profitable business, and the turnover can have many zeros.

Digital media must become more and more powerful in shaping digitisation while creating a number of new business opportunities, especially in tourism and its promotion. Thus, as digitisation grows and is implemented, it can promote economic development in digital tourism (McKinsey & Co, 2014). It is important that this development is consistent with the capacity of the tourist area to attract many young people to develop the tourist area through digitisation and innovation with the help of AI.

In the future, computer programmes containing data analysis on various topics will make many more questionnaires with many more variables to support tourism. We will do this together with students when designing a project to develop tourist areas through innovative technologies.

4. CONCLUSION

Web platforms play an essential role in web marketing strategies adapted to the tourism sector (Hagiu & Wright, 2015). The available data make the development of services possible by taking advantage of the latest technologies, particularly AI: optimising access to information, personalising customer journeys, automating certain areas of logistics, saving traveller's time, and creating translation relationships via web interfaces.

AI is already playing an important role in the evolution and renewal of the tourism industry. For several years, tourism/leisure sector web platforms have become essential in the value chain: accommodation rentals, hotel search, catering, transport, and leisure reservations.

Based on our research results, we entail several policy guidelines and recommendations:

- Promotion of tourism with the help of AI in Romania.
- Positioning Romania as one of the engines of AI in Europe.
- Create, retain, and attract AI talents in Romania.
- Promote research and innovation in AI in Romania.
- *Adoption of AI*: Encourage the integration of AI as an innovation engine in the administration and strategic sectors such as agrofood, health and well-being, the environment, mobility, tourism, culture, and industry, among others.
- *Ethics and society*: To promote the development of ethical AI that respects current legality.

REFERENCES

Biriescu, S. (2013). *Ethical marketing for competitive advantage on the internet*. International symposium business information systems – An interdisciplinary challenge of collaboration in Central and Eastern Europe, 20–22 May 2013, Cluj-Napoca, Romania.

Biriescu, S. (2018a). Clusterele în turism reprezintă viitorul. *REVART, 31*(2), 23–31. https://www.ceeol.com/search/article-detail?id=795033

Biriescu, S. (2018b). Estetică și design grafic în turism. *REVART, 31*(2), 32–38. https://www.ceeol.com/search/article-detail?id=795034

Government of Catalonia Ministry for Digital Policy and Public Administration Secretariat for Digital Policy. (2019). *Catalonia's artificial intelligence strategy*. https://participa.gencat.cat/uploads/decidim/attachment/file/932/Document-Bases-Estrategia-IA-Catalunya-_ENversion.pdf

Gretzel, U., Koo, C., Sigala, M., & Xiang, Z. (2015). Special issue on smart tourism: Convergence of information technologies, experiences and theories. *Electronic Markets, 25*(3). https://doi.org/10.1007/s12525-015-0194-x. https://www.researchgate.net/publication/280097713_Special_issue_on_smart_tourism_convergence_of_information_technologies_experiences_and_theories#fullTextFileContent

Hagiu, A., & Wright, J. (2015). Multi-sided platforms. *International Journal of Industrial Organisation, 43*, 162–174. https://doi.org/10.1016/j.ijindorg.2015.03.003

Ivanov, W., & Webster, C. (2019). Robots in tourism: A research agenda for tourism economics. *Tourism Economics, 26*(7), 1–21. https://doi.org/10.1177/1354816619879

Kelly, E. (2015). Business ecosystems come of age. *Business trends series*, Deloitte. https://www2.deloitte.com/content/dam/insights/us/articles/platform-strategy-new-level-business-trends/DUP_1048-Business-ecosystems-come-of-age_MASTER_FINAL.pdf

Lockett, N., & Brown, D. H. (2006). Aggregation and the role of trusted third parties in SME E-business engagement: A regional policy issue. *International Small Business Journal, 24*(4), 379–404. https://doi.org/10.1177/0266242606065509

McKinsey & Co. (2014). *A two-speed IT architecture for the digital enterprise*. https://www.mckinsey.com/business-functions/mckinsey-digital/our-insights/a-two-speed-it-architecture-for-the-digital-enterprise

Melis, G., & Piga, C. (2016). *Are all online hotel prices created dynamic? An empirical assessment*. MPRA paper no. 75896. https://mpra.ub.uni-muenchen.de/75896/

OECD. (2016). *Digital convergence and beyond: Innovation, investment and competition in communication policy and regulation for the 21st century*. Background report for Ministerial Panel 2.1, DSTI/ICCP/CISP(2015)2/FINAL, OECD, Paris.

OECD. (2017a). *La prochaine révolution de la production: Conséquences pour les pouvoirs publics et les entreprises*. Éditions OECD. https://doi.org/10.1787/9789264280793-fr

OECD. (2017b). *Renforcer les contributions des PME dans une économie mondialisée et numérique.* Réunion du Conseil au niveau des Ministres, OECD, Paris.
OECD. (2017c). *Key issues for digital transformation in the G20.* Conférence commune présidence allemande du G20/OECD, Berlin.
OECD. (2017d). *Les politiques d'échanges de services dans une économie mondialisée.* Éditions OECD, Paris. https://doi.org/10.1787/9789264288065-fr
OECD. (2020). *OECD tourism trends and policies 2020.* OECD Publishing, Paris. https://doi.org/10.1787/6b47b985-en

CHAPTER 13

ROLE OF PRO BONO LEGAL SERVICES IN THE SECTOR OF ESG

Aleksandra Klich[a] and Qerkin Berisha[b]

[a]University of Szczecin, Poland
[b]University of Prishtina, Kosovo

ABSTRACT

Purpose: *The Environmental, Social, and Governance (ESG) criteria have become increasingly pivotal for businesses worldwide, shaping their approach to sustainability and societal impact. In response to this trend, the demand for legal guidance within the complex ESG landscape has surged. This paper examines the critical role of pro bono legal services in supporting ESG initiatives within the corporate sector. Beginning with an exploration of the necessity for legal support in the ESG sector, the paper highlights the intricate regulatory environment and the imperative for businesses to align with evolving ESG standards. It then delves into the importance of pro bono legal services in enhancing corporate social responsibility (CSR) and sustainability efforts. Moreover, the paper analyses the benefits and challenges associated with providing pro bono legal services in the ESG sector. It discusses how these services contribute to fostering a culture of responsibility and accountability among businesses while addressing societal and environmental challenges. Furthermore, the paper examines opportunities to develop and improve the effectiveness of pro bono legal services in the context of ESG. It explores avenues for collaboration between legal professionals, businesses, and non-profit organisations to advance ESG goals and address pressing societal and environmental issues.*

Findings: *This paper underscores the vital role of pro bono legal services in supporting ESG initiatives, providing insights into how legal expertise can help businesses meet their ESG commitments while fostering social and environmental progress.*

Keywords: ESG; pro bono; legal services; sustainability; CSR

JEL Codes: K4; O44; A13; G3

INTRODUCTION

The tradition of pro bono practice dates back to ancient and medieval Europe. One of the earliest known examples of pro bono legal services comes from ancient Athens, where the idea of inclusive democracy, civic duty, and justice for the poor was the basis of a kind of legal aid system. Although it was not a comprehensive system, it was relatively common in Athenian cities and clubs to provide legal assistance to people who could not afford to pay for legal representation (Chroust, 1953; Rubinstein, 2000). Usually, this assistance was provided by elected officials, called synegoros, who represented their interests in court (Rubinstein, 2000). In the Middle Ages, the practice of pro bono took the form that is more recognisable today. Initially, Christian men provided free legal services, often referred to as 'pro deo' (for God) (Huls, 1993). Over time, this evolved into the church providing more organised forms of assistance. The first of these was the 'advocatus pauperum deputatus et stipendiatus', an official employed by the church and paid to represent the poor before the church courts (Huls, 1993). A second practice promoted by the church was instructing judges to waive court fees for the poor and sometimes appointing private lawyers to represent them free of charge (Huls, 1993). For centuries, providing legal aid to the needy and impoverished has remained 'an honorable duty of the European legal profession' (Cappelletti & Gordley, 1972).

Pro bono work includes any professional service provided free of charge or for a reduced fee. Although many people equate its provision with those in the legal profession, it can also refer to services provided by translators, doctors, engineers, architects, marketing and PR specialists, and other professionals such as tax consultants, auditors, IT specialists, and education specialists. These professionals can provide pro bono work as part of their skills and experience, helping people in need and non-profit organisations. While pro bono work is not limited to the legal profession and can encompass many different fields and areas of social welfare, there is no doubt that legal professionals are the dominant professional group providing pro bono services. Many countries have developed legal aid programmes to provide people who need legal assistance but cannot afford the costs associated with providing legal services (Gruodytė & Kirchner, 2012). Free legal support can nowadays be provided by those who have the authority to represent clients in courts, the so-called professional attorneys (attorneys, legal advisors), trainees of these professions, academics and law students, law firms, and non-governmental organisations (NGOs).

Pro bono work can be provided in various areas of law, depending on the skills and experience of the lawyer in question. This can include assistance in civil, criminal, family, immigration, labour, tax, etc. It is important that those providing pro bono work act in accordance with applicable ethical standards and adhere to the principles of confidentiality and professionalism. One area where pro bono legal services can be provided is in the ESG sector. This is especially true for those at risk of fiscal and economic exclusion but also for those starting out in a particular area. Access to justice is often limited due to lack of financial resources. Many people who could assert their rights in court are unable to do so due to a lack of funds needed for legal services. What's more, they are often unaware of their rights, or the responsibilities they have (Gruodytė & Kirchner, 2012). There is no doubt that the addressees of pro bono legal assistance in the ESG sector will predominantly be legal entities such as small- and medium-sized enterprises, NGOs and non-profit organisations, start-ups and social enterprises, as well as local communities. However, individuals should not be excluded from this category, as when conducting business, they may also need support in the analysed scope.

Legal services provided in this way play a key role in providing access to justice for individuals and organisations that cannot afford engagement of a private lawyer. They also respond to market demand in the face of the growing popularity and public recognition of responsible business practices. It should be emphasised that both pro bono and ESG activities are rooted in the concept of social responsibility, which has been gaining popularity in recent years. Integrating environmental, social, and corporate governance factors into internal policies is certainly on the rise. Pro bono legal support can play a key role in strengthening and developing a company's ESG credibility. Unpaid legal work can not only broaden a company's offerings to external clients in the ESG field, especially in new and developing areas but also contribute to the internal ingraining of social responsibility values into a company's business practices and culture. This will ensure that internal commitment to ESG issues does not remain a mere formal requirement but becomes an integral part of an entity's operations.

The pro bono work of providing free legal services to a specific group of entities can play a key role in strengthening and developing the firm's credibility in the ESG area. Pro bono work not only, as indicated, expands the firm's offerings to external ESG clients, particularly in new and developing areas of pro bono work (Lochner, 1975), especially in new and developing areas, but also contributes to ingraining social responsibility values into the firm's business practices and culture. In this way, an entity can ensure that internal involvement in ESG issues does not remain a mere formal obligation (in terms of taking responsibility for its environmental and social impact) but becomes an integral part of its business. Such activities can also have tangible benefits for the entity that provides them pro bono. This is because providing such services is a tangible way not only to demonstrate one's own commitment but also to solidify the external image of the entity providing pro bono legal services as socially and environmentally conscious. Treating unpaid legal work as the most privileged form of pro bono can have a reinforcing effect on changing status in the profession (Levin, 2009). In addition, the provision of pro bono legal support can be a key component of ESG strategies by firms and legal industry players.

NECESSARY LEGAL SUPPORT IN THE ESG SECTOR

With increasing regulation of environmental, social, and governance issues, service providers are forced, as indicated, to formulate rules in their area of activity. Those entities that fail to comply with ESG-related regulatory requirements may face financial penalties and reputational damage. For this reason, it seems natural to assume that ESG has become a very popular concept in the business world, influenced by several factors. Firstly, there is a growing public awareness of problems related to climate change, social inequality, or ethical issues. This, in turn, is prompting professional entities to take more responsibility for their actions. Clients, investors, employees, and the public expect activity that is ESG-compliant regardless of the area of services provided. Secondly, effective management of ESG aspects can contribute to the value of the service provider by improving brand image, increasing customer and investor confidence, reducing operational risk, and improving efficiency and long-term profitability. Thirdly, the popularisation of sustainable contributes to investors being more likely to consider ESG criteria when making key decisions. Entities that effectively manage ESG issues can attract more investors and obtain better financing terms.

The concept of ESG is often equated with CSR. Undoubtedly, both issues stem from the development of approaches to corporate responsibility and sustainable development. ESG seems to provide a modern foundation for business strategies, complementing the traditional concept of CSR. Unlike CSR, ESG is not just a voluntary activity, but is becoming a central part of EU regulations, such as the CSRD and ESRS sustainability reporting standards. In practice, CSR focuses on a variety of areas, such as charity, philanthropy, social investment, and maintaining business ethics (Corker, 2015). Entities identifying themselves with this concept strive for social involvement, creating projects that have a positive impact on the community, rather than simply serving to increase profits. In this regard, the need for pro bono legal services, including in the ESG sector, naturally updates.

What needs to be emphasised is that the differences between CSR and ESG are due to the dynamic evolution of the approach to corporate responsibility. Where CSR focused mainly on charitable giving and social action, ESG represents a more comprehensive approach, encompassing social, environmental, and managerial aspects. Social criteria focus on labour standards, diversity, human rights, and data privacy. Environmental criteria include impact on climate change, greenhouse gas emissions, resource management, and pollution. While the governance criteria examine board diversity, executive compensation, anti-corruption measures, and risk management. These criteria are crucial for investors seeking companies with sustainable practices and strong risk management (Henisz et al., 2019). Current regulations such as the CSRD point to the key role of ESG as a risk management tool and promote more sustainable business practices, especially in the context of social activities. Both CSR and ESG are essential elements of modern business operations, having the potential to create value for companies, society, and the environment. As these concepts evolve, companies face the need to adapt their strategies to effectively respond to growing stakeholder expectations and sustainability challenges. Flexibility and commitment to ESG-compliant practices are becoming indispensable elements of effective management, shaping a positive impact on the world around us.

The perceived contemporary trend of creating regulations aimed at increasing transparency and accountability of companies in their social, environmental, and management activities, as well as promoting sustainable development, is fostering initiatives aimed at not only increasing but also building legal awareness among business entities. Although currently the notion of CSR or ESG is catching up with the popularity of EU regulations setting common rules for the processing of personal data, as reflected in the GDPR, in practice, these are still concepts with which there is insufficient legal awareness from a legal perspective. With the regulations being created, companies are required to report on their activities and performance in these areas, which, in turn, influences their approach to CSR and ESG. Although the accessibility to regulations such as the current EU Taxonomy, effective 1 January 2022. EU Taxonomy or the EU's Corporate Sustainability Reporting Directive (CSRD), effective 1 January 2023, is facilitated, if only through access via the websites of the European Parliament or the European Commission, in practice, ESG issues are still defined correctly by those associated with the business world, and the concept is predominantly identified with economic and management activities. A recent survey conducted in 2022 shows a significant increase of regulatory framework related to ESG across the world the past five years prior to 2022. Laws and regulations have surged, with 61.6% of the 337 total surveyed being enacted during this period, including 39% in the last three years alone (Global Regulatory, 2022). Therefore, there is a perceived need to intensify activities in the legal field, related not only to classically perceived legal advice but also to educational and consultative activities, which will be the subject of a later section of the paper.

With the above in mind, when analysing the importance of pro bono legal services in the ESG sector, it is necessary to recognise two fundamental modes of action, that is those related to building and developing legal awareness, as well as those related to classic legal advice and internal policy-making. In attempting to classify pro bono activities in the ESG area, it seems reasonable to start with defining the basic needs and problems resulting in the need for legal support. According to the authors, it is possible to distinguish four basic areas: (1) legal and regulatory compliance, (2) legal and financial risk management, (3) development of sustainability strategies, (4) ESG reporting.

Legal support in the ESG sector is unavoidable as regulations that are not only national and local, but also global in scope, are becoming increasingly stringent and complex. Modern organisations must engage in the analysis, interpretation, and implementation of these regulations in order to gain confidence that their company is operating in compliance with the law. What needs to be emphasised is that a service provider's awareness of the existence of ESG regulations does not automatically justify the assumption that it has adequate resources to cover the costs associated with legal services.

And referring to legal risk management support, it is worth pointing out first that violations of ESG principles can lead to legal and financial risks for the organisation. Therefore, it is important to identify and manage these risks to avoid potential financial losses and legal consequences. In contrast, the area of legal support related to the development of sustainability strategies seems to have the most practical dimension. Legal support in this area involves developing an ESG-compliant action plan that takes into account applicable regulations and organisational goals. The last area where legal support may be necessary is ESG reporting. Legal departments should play a key role in developing ESG reports and corporate communications. This should be preceded by a thorough and comprehensive compliance analysis to minimise the risk of non-compliance and greenwashing.

Analysing the above areas, a certain phasing of the complexity of legal support is discernible, that is from awareness activities, to activities preparing for proper operation, to activity in reporting the degree of implementation of ESG principles every day. There is no doubt that culture and society are constantly evolving and with them the expectations of companies. Aligning a company with the expectations of a new generation of customers is a value that can affect the perception of an organisation.

Pro bono activities also include skill-building initiatives through the implementation of training programmes, legal workshops, educational campaigns, and community legal awareness programmes. These programmes support diverse audiences, including local communities, government officials, employees of other non-profit organisations, lawyers, and legal assistants. Through these initiatives, participants gain the ability to independently navigate legal issues and the ability to act for justice in various contexts.

To summarise the above discussion, it is worth pointing out that pro bono activities can be carried out by individual lawyers and law firms. Both large law firms and smaller local law firms can engage in providing pro bono legal services. Many law firms have special pro bono programmes where their employees can offer their assistance to those in need. Such support can also be provided by individual lawyers who choose to help those in need in their community. Finally, legal support can be underwritten by NGOs that specialise in legal aid or specialise in ESG sector activities. In this area, law clinics and student legal clinics operating at law faculties with a clinical legal education programme should not be overlooked. In this regard, legal support can also be offered by students who, in the future as professional lawyers, would like to focus their practice on sustainability issues.

THE IMPORTANCE OF PRO BONO LEGAL SERVICES IN THE ESG SECTOR

The expression 'pro bono' comes from the Latin pro bono publico, 'for the public good'. For lawyers, it traditionally describes free professional commitment in the service of the public interest (Puel & de Moucheron, 2016). Modern pro bono practice has been reinvented, especially since the 1990s, by NGOs, foundations, and private lawyers. The emergence of modern pro bono practice in Europe was aided by the growth and internationalisation of US and UK law firms committed to institutionalising pro bono in all their offices, which also coincided with the decline of legal aid in Europe (Khadar, 2016). During the 20th century, the principle emerged in Western Europe that the state was obliged to 'affirmatively and effectively guarantee the right to competent legal assistance for all' (Cappelletti & Gordley, 1972). At the beginning of the 21st century, most European countries took steps to implement this principle, introducing a variant of what has been called the 'judicare' model of legal aid. As a result of this process, legal aid became the responsibility of specialised lawyers paid by the state, while private lawyers in Europe no longer considered charitable legal assistance as their professional duty. National legislations provided for ex officio legal support, but the predominant identification of legal services was with their paid nature. Significantly, a lawyer providing pro bono legal assistance has full freedom of choice to engage in such activities (Gruodytė & Kirchner, 2012). It is evident that the pro bono legal services have a more structured approach in the USA with specific guidelines and expectations for pro bono work from lawyers and law firms, which contributes to its more widespread practice compared to Europe. The American Bar Association Model Rule 6.1 establishes professional responsibility for lawyers to provide pro bono legal services, or at reduced fee, primarily aiding individuals of limited means and nonprofit organisations serving them. Being a professional responsibility, it means that is the individual ethical commitment of each lawyer. While the rule is not directly linked to providing services to ESG sector, it aligns with its social component by promoting equitable access to justice (American Bar Association). Pro bono legal services may be provided to social enterprises, to help them address legal challenges, including incorporation, governance, intellectual property, contracts, and compliance, including ESG-related issues.

Modern man functions in many areas and dimensions that did not exist in the past and concern the increasing variability of human activity. Examples include the family, professional and spatial spheres (international migration is an example). Illustrating this with an example that each of us has to deal with, it is worth pointing out that the development of new communication technologies, the popularisation of social networks, the blogosphere, interactive electronic media is also one of the features of the new information society. The use of new technologies requires user knowledge. To cope with the complexities of the ever-changing reality, these new areas entail legal awareness (Danilewicz & Prymakm, 2017). Transferring the above considerations to the ESG sector, it should be emphasised that the growth of the ESG sector in today's society also requires adequate legal awareness. After all, the growth of this sector means, companies increasingly have to deal with complex legal-environmental, social, and management issues. Adequate legal awareness of environmental regulations, labour rights, business ethics, and management standards is, therefore, necessary. The provision of pro bono legal services can be particularly important in this area, as many NGOs, small businesses, and community initiatives that would work for sustainable development may not be able to fund highly qualified legal assistance. With pro bono support, they can get the necessary legal and advisory assistance on ESG issues to better achieve their goals, while remaining compliant with national regulatory framework.

Currently, low legal awareness of society is observed. The problem of so-called social, including legal, exclusion is a challenge not only for the legislation of the European Union member states but also for the activities of public benefit organisations. The need to create a comprehensive system of legal education is inevitable and has been discernible over the past years. The overriding ratio underlying the implementation of this obligation is the need to provide equal opportunities for people who do not have the opportunity to actively participate in social life, who live in areas at risk of social exclusion, who face legal problems of everyday life, which – if they had adequate legal knowledge – could naturally be levelled. This also applies to those starting out in their careers, who do not have sufficient financial resources to cover the costs of professional legal services that guarantee operation in accordance with the applicable norms and rules. For this reason, pro bono services should be seen as a possible form of meeting the needs of the most vulnerable members of society in need of legal assistance (Boon & Abbey, 1997). There is no doubt that increasing legal awareness in the ESG area is crucial to the successful implementation of sustainable business and social practices. A proper understanding of applicable regulations and ESG standards allows companies to better manage their risks, avoid legal conflicts, and build a positive public image.

There is also no doubt that the worst effects of environmental change or unsustainable development are and will increasingly be felt by those with the fewest resources. Consequently, this tends to affect those most in need of legal support (Climate Change and Disaster Displacement, 2022). A lawyer's duty to provide pro bono services to underrepresented people and improve the law is an important aspect of a lawyer's duty to address environmental change and unsustainability (Lindvall, 2021). Therefore, it seems reasonable to assume that the special responsibility of lawyers for the quality of justice also includes the provision of pro bono services to underrepresented parties, as well as the duty to improve the legal system (Dernbach et al., 2023, January 4). It is necessary to create mechanisms that take into account the full participation of these people in society, as well as to build legal awareness among them, not only in terms of obligations but also opportunities involving compliance with the principles of modern business that also takes into account ESG rules. Popularisation of pro bono activities can affect the minimisation, and in the long run – a significant reduction in the barriers preventing the realisation of not only the classically understood right to a court but also to obtain legal support.

The pro bono legal services can, in particular, be targeted towards social enterprises. It argued that social entrepreneurship has gained attention for creating positive social and environmental impact while generating financial returns, while always prioritising impact alongside profitability. While ESG criteria have become crucial for investors assessing sustainability, ESG principles align well with social entrepreneurship's mission of responsible business practices. Social enterprises often struggle to secure funding due to their focus on impact over profits; in this regard, ESG principles can help attract socially conscious consumers, investment, and risk management improvements. It is assumed that most social enterprises may need pro bono legal services to navigate regulatory challenges. A global survey conducted in 2021 by a nonprofit investment fund analysed data from over 150 social enterprises spanning 43 countries and various industries. Social enterprises are designed with social and environmental purposes at their core and have significant and measurable social impact (IKEA, 2021). In fact, 75% of the SEs surveyed tie their impact metrics to the Sustainable Development Goals (IKEA, 2021). Other studies haw identified the similar progress of social enterprises in Europe (The European Social, 2022).

Consequently, it seems reasonable to assume that pro bono legal support in the ESG sector can contribute to: increasing access to legal assistance for organisations and social initiatives working for sustainable development, improving compliance with workers' rights, environmental and ethical standards in companies, and strengthening ESG legal awareness in society. Therefore, the development of pro bono legal services in the ESG field is an important element in building a more sustainable and just society.

BENEFITS AND CHALLENGES OF PROVIDING PRO BONO LEGAL SERVICES IN THE ESG SECTOR

Addressing the benefits of providing pro bono legal services in the ESG sector, it is first necessary to define the catalogue of entities that benefit from the provision of pro bono legal assistance, as well as those that face challenges in providing such legal services. These actors include (a) direct beneficiaries of pro bono legal assistance from the professional sector (i.e. directly related to the business world); (b) legal professionals and organisations providing pro bono legal advice; (c) other individual members of the public.

Undoubtedly, the recipients of the greatest benefits from pro bono legal services are the direct beneficiaries of the legal support provided. On the one hand, they do not incur the costs (or incur them at a much lower amount) of legal services, while on the other hand, in addition to building sustainable policies, they not only build but also increase legal awareness among the team of employees and collaborators. Importantly, individuals and entities with limited financial resources often cannot afford to hire a lawyer for civil, criminal, family, etc., cases. Pro bono legal services provide them with the opportunity to receive legal assistance. As indicated, the beneficiaries of pro bono legal assistance in the

ESG sector include primarily small- and medium-sized enterprises, which often do not have access to specialised legal resources that could help them understand and implement ESG principles. Non-profit legal support can help small- and medium-sized enterprises develop and implement ESG-compliant policies, which will help improve their reputation and competitiveness in the market. On the other hand, in the case of nonprofit organisations (especially those dealing with environmental protection, human rights, social equality, and other ESG issues), beneficiaries of free legal support perceive the need for legal support in drafting contracts, registering organisations, negotiating with business partners, or representing them in court. Free legal support can enable nonprofit organisations to work more effectively in support of their goals. Among the entities that may benefit from free legal assistance, one should not overlook the increasingly popular form associated with start-ups, namely, so-called start-ups and social enterprises seeking to balance profit with a social or environmental mission. These entities, too, may need legal support in developing organisational structures, negotiating investment agreements, or ensuring compliance with ESG rules. And referring to the social benefits, it is worth noting that the beneficiaries of such free legal advice can be both individuals and local communities. In the case of the former, the need to intensify pro bono support is actualised with the definition of the need for legal support on issues such as social inequality, discrimination, environmental protection, or labour rights. Unpaid legal support can enable them to defend their rights in court and access justice. This activity is most often addressed to people at risk of fiscal and economic exclusion. There is no doubt that the common benefit for the above-mentioned entities is that they can work more effectively to promote sustainable development, protect the environment, and promote the principles of social justice.

In addition, the professionalisation of pro bono beneficiaries' activities and activities is also an important factor demonstrating the benefits of pro bono support provided by those with relevant legal training. Thanks to the paid support services offered, entrepreneurs can benefit from high-quality legal and advisory advice that helps them better understand and comply with applicable regulations and sustainability standards. In addition, pro bono legal services allow ESG organisations to better understand their rights and obligations in the areas of environmental protection, labour rights, business ethics, and governance. With the legal support they receive, they can also strengthen their operational and administrative capabilities, allowing them to more effectively achieve their sustainability and CSR goals. Among the benefits of obtaining pro bono legal support, it is also worth noting that their beneficiaries can raise the standards of their operations, including compliance with applicable regulations, sustainability reporting and risk management. Given the above, it seems reasonable to assume that pro bono legal support plays an important role in professionalising the activities of entities in the ESG sector, helping them achieve their goals related to sustainability, CSR, and environmental protection.

Speaking of benefits for companies and law firms, it is worth noting that those that prioritise pro bono work are often seen as more socially responsible and committed to creating a positive impact on society. This reputation can contribute to effective branding among clients and employees who share the same values and are interested in working with entities that prioritise ESG goals. By incorporating pro bono work into their ESG-related strategies, law firms can express their commitment to sustainability, social responsibility, and ethical business practices. It is noteworthy that in the Future Ready Lawyer 2022 Report, as many as 45% of law firms surveyed reported an increase in requirements among corporate clients for ESG guidelines, while as many as 59% anticipate an increase over the next three years (Future Ready Lawyer, 2022). Consequently, it is possible to assume that the growing importance of ESG is not only influencing the type of legal advice and support lawyers provide to clients. There is also an increasingly strong demand for verification from the industry itself regarding what kind of clients it serves, as well as how it cares for its own employees and how it impacts the environment. The approach presented here ties in with the often-expressed belief that it is the insightful understanding of a client's ESG needs and requirements that determines a law firm's value and willingness to provide comprehensive service. Underlying the provision of legal support in this area is an understanding of sustainability, a solid grounding in the principles governing a lawyer's legal and ethical responsibilities, and a willingness to learn and exercise leadership skills in systems (Dernbach et al., 2023).

Lawyers' involvement in pro bono activities demonstrates their active approach to social responsibility, while also being a manifestation of service to the community. Such activity can enhance the firm's reputation among clients and the general public as a socially conscious and ethical organisation. This positive perception can increase brand recognition and a favourable reputation, which can attract new clients and opportunities. Pro bono service can also help individual lawyers build their brand. In addition, pro bono work influences lawyers to develop their skills and gain practical experience and expand their legal knowledge. This allows them to work on a variety of cases and challenges that lawyers may not encounter in their regular practice. This professional development can attract and retain talented lawyers who value the opportunity to make a significant impact through their legal expertise. Pro bono work can also result in the formation of an ability to spot out-of-the-box problems, as well as gaining industry experience and the ability to formulate creative solutions. These skills are undoubtedly among the most valued in the legal profession and are indicative of having and gaining diversity of experience. In addition, among the benefits on the side of law firms and those providing pro bono advice is the ability and ease of networking and relationship building. This is primarily due to the need to collaborate with other lawyers, as well as sometimes with non-profit organisations and other NGOs. Interaction in this regard and a converging goal can lead to the acquisition and development of valuable networking opportunity skills. Many times, through pro bono work, law firms gain the opportunity to connect with influential individuals and organisations in the legal and social sectors. In turn, building these relationships is very likely to lead to recommendations, partnerships on other projects, and even new business opportunities. Participation in pro bono work can affect employees' moral attitudes and job satisfaction at a law firm. Indeed, a source of satisfaction can come from pro bono work, which provides the satisfaction of using one's possession of skills to help people who have no legal recourse.

When analysing the benefits to the beneficiaries of pro bono legal advice, it is also important to refer to the social and environmental benefits. There is also no doubt that thanks to pro bono legal services, people with fewer financial resources have an equal opportunity to assert their rights, which contributes to equalising social inequalities. In this area, the activities of NGOs, especially those working on behalf of local communities, should be clearly highlighted. Many times, they need legal assistance to solve legal problems, and pro bono services allow them to work more effectively for the benefit of society. Their activity generally focuses on awareness-raising and educational activities, with which they can contribute to the social empowerment of entities operating in the ESG sector. This motivation stems from the positive impact on the lives of others, illustrating the broader impact of pro bono services on individual and community well-being.

In this regard, it is possible to distinguish several factors influencing awareness of the obligations of the legal acts regulating standards and rules of operation in the ESG sector. Firstly, there is the complexity of regulations, which can be perceived as complicated and technically complex. This, in turn, can affect their understanding and result in the fact that their implementation can be difficult for entrepreneurs, especially those operating in smaller companies. Secondly, language barriers are perceived. These should be linked to the level of complexity of the legal language, as the texts of legal acts are usually formulated in specialised legal language, which can make them difficult to understand for those outside the legal community. Thirdly, some entrepreneurs may simply not be aware of the existence of the new regulations or may not realise their importance to their business. Fourthly, implementing the new regulations may require time, effort, and resources, especially if the company has no experience in the CSR and ESG area. As has been repeatedly pointed out, increasing awareness among entrepreneurs can be promoted through educational programmes, training, workshops, and other forms of support that help entrepreneurs understand and implement the new regulations. Accordingly, it is important for institutions responsible for implementing these regulations to undertake activities to raise awareness among entrepreneurs and help them understand and implement the required CSR and ESG activities. These activities may include information campaigns, publishing guides, organising training courses and workshops, and providing educational materials on CSR and ESG. In the absence of effective initiatives at the central level, the need for local and regional players to obtain support is being updated.

Despite the many benefits of pro bono legal support in the ESG sector, there are also some challenges, such as a lack of financial and human resources, difficulties in identifying clients' needs, and the need to continuously improve and update legal knowledge. The main challenge that may be associated with hindering the implementation of pro bono support for ESG sector business entities is the lack of highly specialised professionals to undertake educational and training activities, or to provide free legal support. While at the level of educational activities, where the ability to interpret legal texts is sufficient, it is possible to de facto referee the obligations imposed by legislators when it is necessary to develop specific documentation or reporting – theoretical knowledge is insufficient. However, with appropriate measures, such as specialisation in the ESG area, partnerships with NGOs, and training programmes for employees, law firms can effectively counter these challenges and further develop their commitment to pro bono activities for sustainable development and CSR. In addition, a significant challenge may be the lack of belief that pro bono lawyers are characterised by the same level of professionalism and subject matter expertise as those who and the services they provide receive compensation. It should be borne in mind that regardless of whether legal advice is paid or provided free of charge, the duty of a lawyer is to act in the interests of the client, with the due level of professionalism and diligence. Therefore, pro bono activity should not be viewed as inferior or less effective.

OPPORTUNITIES TO DEVELOP AND IMPROVE THE EFFECTIVENESS OF PRO BONO LEGAL SERVICES IN THE CONTEXT OF ESG

Today, more and more educational opportunities, self-assessment tools, and measurement techniques are available to develop and improve the effectiveness of pro bono legal services in the context of ESG. When analysing opportunities for the development in the indicated subject, it is necessary to focus on entities providing pro bono support. Assuming that this type of advice is provided by law firms or legal teams of NGOs and other non-profit organisations, it seems reasonable to emphasise that they can develop specialised departments for pro bono services in the area of ESG, which will enable more effective support for NGOs, small businesses, and community initiatives working for sustainable development. In addition, law firms can establish partnerships with NGOs, foundations, and other ESG stakeholders to better understand their needs and tailor their pro bono services to specific challenges and issues.

The training programmes that are created are of no small importance. Pro bono legal aid providers can organise ESG training programmes for their staff to increase their knowledge and skills in this area and better prepare them to provide pro bono services. In turn, to better respond to the growing needs of local and global communities and support the Sustainable Development Goals, law firms can integrate ESG issues into their pro bono strategy, while putting in place a system to monitor and report on the effectiveness of their pro bono services in the ESG area. To increase the effectiveness of pro bono counsel, it is also possible to engage with other sectors, such as the public sector, the academic sector, and the private sector, to better leverage their resources and competencies in the field of ESG and pro bono service delivery.

Nowadays, all forms of activity and activities undertaken are supported by modern technological solutions, which make it possible to reach a wider audience of the legal support services offered. This can manifest itself, for example, in the organisation of workshops, webinars, and online training on ESG criteria and the practical aspects of their implementation, as well as individual consultations or the development of teaching materials characterised by simple and understandable language (e.g. the development of publications, reports, and analyses on various aspects related to ESG criteria and their importance for business and society). Also, the publication of any graphically designed compilations, information, and their discussion is conducive to building and increasing legal awareness of ESG entities. Those who provide pro bono legal support can more effectively support ESG organisations and initiatives and contribute to building a more sustainable and equitable society.

CONCLUSIONS

The regulatory framework on ESG has increased significantly in recent years. In the context of the growing importance of ESG-related activities, pro bono legal services can play a key role in supporting organisations and initiatives working on sustainability and CSR. Valuable legal support can not only increase access to justice for individuals and groups in need but also contribute to building a positive image for companies and promoting professionalism in the ESG sector. Supporting NGOs, social enterprises, small businesses, and community initiatives working in the ESG field requires not only commitment and determination but also relevant knowledge and experience of laws and sustainability standards. Therefore, pro bono legal support can be an invaluable source of assistance to these entities, enabling them to achieve their goals and missions more effectively while being compliant with national regulatory environment.

Law firms and other entities that engage in providing pro bono services in the ESG area can play a key role in promoting sustainability and CSR. By providing free legal assistance to environmental, human rights and social justice organisations and initiatives, these law firms can contribute to building a more just and sustainable society. There is no doubt that supporting organisations and initiatives working for sustainable development and CSR is not only a moral issue but also a strategic one for law firms and companies operating in the ESG sector.

REFERENCES

American Bar Association, Model Rules of Professional Conduct 6.1 https://www.americanbar.org/groups/probono_public_service/policy/aba_model_rule_6_1/
Amplifying the "S" in ESG (2022). *Global regulatory and legislative frameworks of social indicators* (p. 3). https://esg.trust.org/application/velocity/_newgen/assets/EsgAnnex2.pdf
Boon, A., & Abbey, R. (1997). *Moral agendas? Pro bono publico in large law firms in the United Kingdom.* The Modern Law Review Limited.
Cappelletti, M., & Gordley, J. (1972). *Legal aid: Modern themes and variations part one: The emergence of a modern theme.* Stanford Law Review.
Chroust, A.-H. (1953). *Legal profession in ancient Athens.* Notre Dame Law.
Climate Change and Disaster Displacement. (2022, last visited September). *The un refugee agency.* https://www.unhcr.org/enus/climate-change-and-disasters.html
Corker, J. (2015, September). *Pro bono and corporate social responsibility reputation building, recruitment, retention and client relationships.* NSW Law Society. https://www.probonocentre.org.au/wp-content/uploads/2020/12/Corporate-Social-Responsibility-and-Pro-Bono-Corker-September-2015.pdf

Danilewicz, W., & Prymakm, T. (2017). *From legal awareness of the contemporary youth to legal culture of the information society.* Kultura i edukacja.

Dernbach, J., Russell, I., & Bogoshian, M. (2023, January 4), *Lawyering to make a difference: Ethics and leadership for a sustainable society: Wake forest journal of business & intellectual property law.* https://papers.ssrn.com/sol3/papers.cfm?abstract_id=4318062

Future Ready Lawyer. (2022). *Survey report.* The Wolters Kluwer. https://images.go.wolterskluwerlr.com/Web/WoltersKluwerLRSUS/%7B60c69227-1c9c-45a1-818f-b7cc4863f1f9%7D_LR_white_paper_2022_09-01_FINAL_single.pdf

Gruodytė E., & Kirchner S. (2012, December). Pro bono work vs. legal aid: approaches to ensuring access to justice and the social responsibility of the attorney. *Baltic Journal of Law & Politics.* https://sciendo.com/article/10.2478/v10076-012-0010-2

Henisz, W., Koller, T., & Nuttall, R. (2019). Five ways that ESG creates value: Getting your environmental, social, and governance (ESG) proposition right links to higher value creation. Here's why. *McKinsey Quarterly.* https://www.mckinsey.com/ /media/McKinsey/Business%20Functions/Strategy%20and%20Corporate%20Finance/Our%20Insights/Five%20ways%20that%20ESG%20creates%20value/Five-ways-that-ESG-creates-value.ashx

Huls, N. (1993). From pro deo practice to a subsidized welfare state provision: Twenty-five years of providing legal services to the poor in the Netherlands. *Maryland Journal of Contemporary Legal Issues.*

IKEA Social Entrepreneurship. (2021). *Corporate-ready, how corporations and social enterprises do business together to drive impact.* https://acumen.org/wp-content/uploads/Corporate-Ready-Report.pdf

Khadar, L. (2016). *The growth of pro bono in Europe. Using the power of law for the public interest: DLA paper.* PILnet. https://www.pilnet.org/resource/the-growth-of-pro-bono-in-europe/

Levin, L. (2009). *Pro bono publico in a parellel universe: The meaning of pro bono in solo and small law firm.* Faculty articles and papers. https://digitalcommons.lib.uconn.edu/law_papers/422

Lindvall, D. (2021). *Democracy and the challenge of climate change.* International IDEA Discussion Paper, No. 3. https://doi.org/10.31752/idea.2021.88

Lochner, P. R. Jr. (1975). *The no fee and low fee legal practice of private attorneys.* LAW & SOC'Y REV.

Puel, S., & de Moucheron, B. (2016). *CSR & pro bono report.* Brining meaning to our commitment. 2015–2016. https://www.gide.com/rse/en/1612059-GIDE-GB.pdf

Rubinstein, L. (2000). *Litigation and cooperation: Supporting speakers in the courts of classical Athens.*

The European Social Enterprise Monitor Report 2021–2022. (2022). Euclid Network. https://knowledgecentre.euclidnetwork.eu/european-social-enterprise-monitor-2021-2022/?_gl=1*1ngnic7*_ga*NjMxNTQyNTcuMTcxNTI1NjgzNQ.*_ga_829YQLNDY5*MTcxNTI1Njgz NS4xLjEuMTcxNTI1Njg3MS4yNC4wLjA.*_gcl_au*MTcxMDk1Nzc1OC4xNzE1MjU2 ODM1#

CHAPTER 14

COMPARATIVE ANALYSIS OF CSR AND ESG ACTIONS IN GREECE: A STUDY USING ARTIFICIAL NEURAL NETWORKS AND MACHINE-LEARNING TECHNIQUES

Foteini I. Pagkalou[a], Eleftherios I. Thalassinos[b] and Konstantinos I. Liapis[a]

[a]*Panteion University of Social and Political Sciences, Greece*
[b]*University of Piraeus, Greece*

ABSTRACT

Purpose: *In Greece, large companies have started to focus more and more on corporate social responsibility (CSR) and ESG (environmental, social, and governance) activities, realising the importance of sustainability and social responsibility beyond traditional profits. Using machine-learning (ML) methods and artificial neural networks (ANNs) can enhance the process of measuring performance in these areas in several ways, including data analytics. This paper investigates and explores the correlation between CSR and ESG actions with financial and non-financial factors for the 100 largest companies operating in Greece.*

Methodology: *The study runs from January 2019 until December 2021, and ANNs and ML techniques are employed. The comparison concerns both the control variables and the predictability of the methods.*

Findings: *The main findings that emerged are the confirmation of the correlation between CSR and ESG actions and the financial performance and determinants of corporate responsibility of the companies in the sample. Moreover, good results were obtained for almost all of the techniques examined, but the superiority of deep learning models and gradient-boosted trees (GBTs) was found for the selected variables.*

Significance/Implications/Conclusions: *The findings suggest that using ML techniques and neural networks to measure CSR actions can help companies evaluate their performance and make effective decisions to improve their sustainability. It can also be a valuable tool for institutional investors, banks, and regulators.*

Future Research: *We believe that future research should focus on improving these models, exploring hybrid approaches that combine the strengths of different techniques, and expanding the range of variables considered.*

Keywords: CSR; ESG actions; ANNs; ML methods; financial reporting; non-financial reporting

JEL Codes: G34; M14; M41

1. INTRODUCTION

CSR and environmental, social, and governance (ESG) practices in the contemporary business landscape have become pivotal in shaping corporate strategies. These practices reflect a company's commitment to ethical and sustainable operations and influence investor decisions and stakeholder confidence.

As companies increasingly recognise the importance of integrating sustainable and ethical practices into their operations, there is a growing need to analyse and evaluate the effectiveness and impact of these initiatives and the parameters that would contribute to their interpretation.

Studies focusing on demonstrating the positive correlation between CSR and ESG actions and other economic and non-economic indicators are increasing (see, inter alia, Albuquerque et al., 2019; Dhaliwal et al., 2011; Eccles et al., 2014; Friede et al., 2015; Luo & Bhattacharya, 2006).

However, there is a variation among scholars in both the results and the technical approach to these issues.

Several scholars have chosen to focus on assessing CSR activities by determining their impact and effectiveness, following specific methodologies such as cost–benefit analysis (CBA), balanced scorecard (BSC), triple bottom line (TBL) reporting, social return on investment (SROI), and ESG metrics.

The researches of Boardman et al. (2018), Epstein and Wisner (2001), Slaper and Hall (2011), Millar and Hall (2013), and Friede et al. (2015), and others, are moving in this direction and include the evaluation of both financial and non-financial data.

However, in the last decade, we observe that several studies have used econometric methods such as panel data analysis and structural equation Modelling to analyse their data and assess the corporate responsibility of companies and organisations (Albuquerque et al., 2019; Flammer, 2015; Hsu & Chen, 2015; Jiraporn & Chintrakarn, 2013; Wang et al., 2016). This is because econometric methods are powerful tools for analysing the impact of CSR activities on financial and non-financial outcomes since they offer accuracy and reliability by addressing endogeneity issues and complex causal relationships.

Only recently have studies related to the CSR of companies based on neural networks and ML seen in the light of day. These studies deal with both data analysis and prediction. Among them, we find the study by Chen (2021) that apply the deep learning method interpretation and estimation of CSR, Hernandez et al. (2021) that use the GBTs approach, such as Hernandez et al. (2022a) who make use of algorithms, and so on for all state-of-the-art ML methods.

However, there is a lack of a holistic approach to the issue, controlling both the variables that explain CSR and the modern methods that could yield more complete and reliable results.

This study focuses on Greece, a country with unique economic, social, and environmental challenges, to conduct a comparative analysis of CSR and ESG actions. Adopting ANNs and other ML techniques offers a cutting-edge approach to evaluating and comparing these actions and their influencing factors. Harnessing the power of these advanced analytical tools, this study aims to uncover patterns, correlations, and insights that traditional analyses may overlook. In particular, the use of ANNs allows for processing complex, non-linear relationships in large datasets, providing a fine-grained understanding of CSR and ESG performance across different industries and companies in the country.

The main research question posed in our study is whether and to what extent ML and ANN techniques can contribute to the assessment of CSR of large companies in Greece by controlling for other factors (financial and non-financial) and what these factors should be. More specifically, the objects of this study are (a) to compare the effectiveness of the ANN and ML methods and highlight those that best fit our data. (b) To compare and record those variables that best explain the CSR of the sample companies among several variables (financial and non-financial).

We selected the 100 largest companies operating in Greece in fiscal years 2019, 2020, and 2021 as a sample to investigate the above issues. For our study period, we collected data on 44 variables with which we constructed the index for overall corporate responsibility of the companies and 18 variables with which we tested their correlation with CSR. The reliability of the index was tested using ANNs and other ML techniques. Specifically, the data were tested using GBTs, random forest (RF), deep learning, Naive Bayes, generalised linear model, logistic regression, decision tree, and support vector machine.

The findings demonstrate that these methods can help to interpret CSR and test its correlation with other financial and non-financial factors. However, neural networks and analytical methods offer better results with less measurement error. Also, the variables that most correctly predict our model are the type of corporate responsibility report that each company chooses to record its CSR and ESG data, the responsible body for the implementation and control of corporate responsibility actions by the companies themselves, and the evaluation of the report document with non-financial data.

This research aims to contribute to the existing body of knowledge by presenting a methodological framework that combines the rigour of quantitative analysis with the depth of qualitative evaluation. Through this comparative analysis, the study will provide valuable insights into how Greek companies can monitor, using advanced tools, the effectiveness of their corporate responsibility initiatives through the improvement of other indicators that they can easily monitor, bridging the gap between the theoretical CSR and ESG frameworks, and their practical application in the Greek context. Furthermore, it will highlight best practices and identify areas for improvement, ultimately assisting policy makers, business leaders, and stakeholders in making informed decisions and ultimately promoting sustainable development in Greece.

The rest of the document is organised as follows: Section 2 provides a review of the relevant literature, while Section 3 describes the sample and data collection. Then, in Section 4, the methodology used to construct and test the indicator's reliability is described. Next, in Section 5, the findings are analysed. We conclude with Section 6 and the conclusions of this study.

2. LITERATURE REVIEW

In recent years, CSR and environmental, social, and governance (ESG) practices have gained importance as key elements of corporate strategy and reputation management. The analysis of CSR and ESG activities has become increasingly complex with the proliferation of large data sets and the need for nuanced knowledge in a number of areas. Traditional statistical methods have often been used for these analyses, but recent developments in ANNs and other ML techniques offer promising alternatives. This review summarises the methodology followed to date for assessing corporate responsibility of companies, focusing on recent research on the use of ANNs and ML for CSR and ESG analysis, highlighting the key findings, methodologies, and comparative effectiveness of the different approaches.

Regardless of the method to be followed, however, assessing the CSR activities of companies or organisations requires a multifaceted approach that combines financial analysis with non-financial measurements. To take into account all the information on companies' CSR, it is necessary to first collect data from all documents, financial statements, and corporate responsibility reports.

Several studies have demonstrated a positive correlation between CSR, ESG actions, and other financial and non-financial indicators (Eccles et al., 2014; Flammer, 2015).

In this direction is the study of Friede et al. (2015), which, in their meta-analysis, collected the results of more than 2,000 studies to examine the relationship between ESG criteria and corporate financial performance (CFP) and found a positive correlation between ESG and CFP, indicating that companies with better ESG performance tend to have better financial results. Whereas the study by Albuquerque et al. (2019) investigated the impact of CSR activities on stock market performance, it was found that firms with higher CSR scores exhibit lower stock price volatility and higher stock returns, suggesting that CSR activities can lead to improved financial performance. Previously, Eccles et al. (2014) examined the impact of ESG practices on the operational performance of firms in the European market. The results showed a positive relationship between ESG activities and various operational performances, such as productivity and innovation.

However, in addition to the control variables used in each study, they also differ in their methodological approach.

Methods such as CBA, BSC, TBL reporting, SROI, and ESG metrics provide comprehensive frameworks to assess the impact of CSR initiatives. By employing these methodologies, companies can better understand the value of their CSR activities and make more informed strategic decisions (Boardman et al., 2018; Epstein & Wisner, 2001; Friede et al., 2015; Millar & Hall, 2013).

On the other hand, econometric methods provide reliable frameworks for assessing the impact of CSR activities on financial and non-financial results. Using techniques such as panel data analysis, difference-in-differences, instrumental variables, preference score matching, and structural equation modelling, researchers and practitioners can gain valuable insights into the effectiveness of CSR initiatives. These methods help address issues of endogeneity, selection bias, and complex causal relationships, leading to more accurate and reliable estimates (see, among others, Aguinis & Glavas, 2012; Albuquerque et al., 2019; Chih et al., 2010; Flammer, 2015; Hsu & Chen, 2015; Jiraporn & Chintrakarn, 2013; Jo & Harjoto, 2012; Qiu et al., 2016; Wang et al., 2016).

However, ANNs and ML techniques have revolutionised the analysis of complex datasets, making them invaluable tools in CSR and ESG research. ANNs are computational models inspired by the human brain's neural networks, capable of identifying patterns and relationships within large and complex datasets (LeCun et al., 2015). ML techniques, which include supervised and unsupervised learning, enable predictive modelling and data clustering, providing deeper insights into CSR and ESG performance (Goodfellow et al., 2016).

The application of ANNs and ML in CSR and ESG research is gaining traction. Recent research highlights the application of ANNs and ML in analysing CSR and ESG data for large companies. These techniques are used to evaluate the quality of CSR reports, predict ESG scores, and assess the impact of CSR and ESG practices on financial performance.

Recent studies have demonstrated the efficacy of ANNs and ML in CSR and ESG research due to their ability to model complex, non-linear relationships.

For instance, ML algorithms have been used to analyse CSR reports and assess the impact of CSR activities on financial performance. For example, Li et al. (2020) applied ML to determine the quality of CSR reports from large multinational companies. Their findings indicated that companies with higher quality CSR reports tend to have better financial performance and higher stakeholder trust. Meanwhile, Zhang et al. (2021) analysed the impact of ESG practices on financial performance using ML models. Their research showed that robust ESG practices lead to higher stock returns and lower volatility, highlighting the financial benefits of sustainability. ANNs have also been employed to predict ESG scores and analyse their correlation with company performance metrics. Zhou et al. (2020) used ANNs to predict ESG scores and found that companies with higher predicted ESG scores experienced lower risks and better market performance. Also, Maiti and Singh (2022) demonstrated that ANNs significantly outperform traditional regression models in predicting CSR outcomes, highlighting the importance of their capacity to handle intricate patterns in data. Similarly, Dutta (2023) found that deep learning models, including ANNs, provide higher accuracy in financial forecasting and CSR performance evaluation, emphasising their robustness in processing large datasets with multiple variables.

It stands to reason that these advanced analytical techniques allow researchers to uncover hidden patterns and relationships that traditional statistical methods may overlook. ANNs have been effective in integrating a wide range of variables, including financial metrics, company size, industry sector, and qualitative factors like governance practices and social impact assessments. Research by Kotsantonis and Serafeim (2023) highlighted that combining financial and non-financial data enhances the predictive power of ESG assessments, a capability well-suited to the flexibility of ANNs. This integration allows for a more holistic evaluation of CSR and ESG actions, capturing both quantitative and qualitative dimensions. Another study by Binh (2023) presents a deep-learning framework for assessing CSR activities. The authors used various neural network architectures, including convolutional neural networks (CNN) and recurrent neural networks (RNN), to analyse large datasets and predict CSR performance metrics. Also, the Hernandez et al. (2022b) paper explored the application of deep neural networks for analysing and reporting CSR activities. The authors used a combination of CNNs and RNNs to process textual and numerical data, demonstrating how these models can improve the accuracy and completeness of CSR reports. Moreover, the most recent study by Chen et al. (2021) used deep learning and text-mining techniques to predict CSR ratings based on unstructured data from corporate reports and social media. The authors demonstrate the advantages of using deep neural networks to process and interpret large volumes of text data.

While ANNs offer significant advantages, other ML techniques, such as GBTs, decision trees, and RFs, also play crucial roles. Gupta (2023) reviewed various ML applications in ESG investing and found that ensemble methods like RFs provide robust benchmarks due to their ability to effectively handle variable importance and interaction effects. These methods benefit feature selection and understanding the relative importance of different variables in CSR and ESG performance.

We observe an increase in studies that focus on the application and effectiveness of RF algorithms in estimating CSR metrics or related topics. These research papers mainly explore the use of RFs in the context of CSR, examining their potential in predicting and analysing social responsibility data.

The Minsoo et al. (2020) study presents a methodology for estimating CSR performance using RFs. The authors have used economic, environmental, and social data to predict CSR outcomes, demonstrating the accuracy and robustness of the model compared to traditional linear models. In addition, the empirical study by Brown et al. (2021) investigated the use of RFs to predict CSR ratings. The authors compared the performance of RFs with other ML techniques and highlighted their superior predictive ability and interpretability.

On the other hand, several papers provide a comprehensive overview of how GBTs can be used and optimised for estimating corporate responsibility metrics. The study by Brophy et al. (2023) in which the application of GBT to various forecasting tasks, including corporate liability, was investigated. In their research, they emphasised the importance of tuning and feature selection to enhance the performance of the model. They also provided insights on how GBT can be adapted for CSR metrics by incorporating relevant financial and non-financial indicators. In addition, their study presented methods for understanding and improving GBT predictions. They concluded that customised influence estimation techniques help analyse the impact of different attributes on model predictions, which is crucial for CSR assessment as they allow organisations to understand the driving factors behind their CSR scores. Zhang et al. (2018) introduced a method for handling multiple outputs in GBT models. This is particularly useful for CSR assessment, where multiple CSR-related metrics must be simultaneously predicted. They showed that their proposed method improves the efficiency and accuracy of the models by considering the correlations between the different output variables. Furthermore, the recent study by Lillo et al. (2023), who investigated the use of ML models to analyse the associations between socio-demographic characteristics and CSR perception, concluded that all three models: neural network (NN), RF, and (GBT model provided significant results based on their data.

We note that although several studies have investigated the application of GBTs for assessing CSR among Greek companies, focusing on the relationship between CSR activities and financial performance (Karagiorgos, 2010; Pagkalou et al., 2024) and while there is an increasing body of research using ANNs and ML for CSR and ESG analysis, studies specific to the Greek context are limited. However, even these studies do not focus on estimating CSR through other variables. Most existing studies focus on developed markets, while less attention is paid to emerging economies such as Greece (Skouloudis et al., 2010; Tsalis et al., 2018). It is evident that there is a need for more localised studies that consider the unique economic, social, and regulatory environment in Greece and the difference in the sizes of economic entities.

The literature review revealed the potential of transforming ANN and ML techniques to enhance CSR and ESG practices analysis. Gaps were also identified, particularly in the Greek context.

This study aims to contribute to the literature by proposing a holistic approach to assessing CSR, both theoretically, by considering a multitude of qualitative and quantitative variables, and methodologically, by using modern ML methods.

Following the study of Pagkalou et al. (2024) that documented the set of variables that determine CSR of companies with actions focused on both internal and external environments and considering recent studies, such as Lillo et al. (2023) and Zhang et al. (2021) that demonstrated the usefulness of ML models in the study of CSR, we chose to test the following research hypotheses:

H1. The ANN and ML methods can explain the corporate responsibility of firms.

H2. CSR and ESG actions of large firms are influenced and dependent on other financial and non-financial factors to a lesser or greater extent.

3. DATA DESCRIPTION

We use financial and non-financial information to investigate the corporate responsibility performance of the 100 largest companies operating in Greece between January 2019 and December 2021. The data are recorded annually and collected from the companies' official reports (financial statements and non-financial reports). The information concerns both the format of the documents and their content itself. Our quantitative and qualitative variables can be divided into four broad categories: (a) financial information, (b) general information of the companies in the sample, (c) variables that identify their corporate responsibility with actions related to the internal environment of the companies, and (d) variables that record the CSR actions of the companies towards their external environment according to both ESG criteria. Data for 62 variables (quantitative and qualitative) were collected for the hundred companies in the sample for all three years of the study. The variables and their values are detailed below.

3.1 Variables That Determine Corporate Responsibility

It is known from theory that the CSR actions of companies are divided into those related to their internal environment (employees, etc.) and those related to their external environment (society, economy, governance), also known as ESG factors.

Since the variables that identify CSR are qualitative, it was chosen for comparison purposes to take values from 0 to 5, depending on whether and to what extent information and actions in these areas are implemented and recorded. Specifically, a value of 0 was given when there was no information relevant to the variable, 1 when their action in this area was described in general terms, 2 when it was adequately described but without measurable data, 3 when it was described and included measurable data or costs of actions, 4 in cases where the effectiveness and contribution of actions had been recorded but not measured, and 5 when the companies themselves had also measured these.

Obviously, categorical variables cannot be converted into quantitative ones, but this hierarchical scale allows for comparisons between companies' actions.

In detail, the corporate responsibility actions recorded are as follows by category:

- Internal CSR covers employees, diversity, labour rights, trade union treatment, pay, benefits, training, occupational health and safety, additional employee insurance, profit-sharing and equity schemes, information, consultation and decision-making participation, working environment, natural resource management and environmental impact, free time, and parental protection.
- In terms of external CSR and the environment, these included addressing climate change, creating and implementing renewable energy sources and other alternative environmental technologies, minimising or eliminating carbon emissions, etc., and making efficient use of resources in the production of goods and the delivery of services, including suppliers. It also involves limiting energy, water, steam, materials, packaging, and other resources while promoting eco-friendly alternatives, lowering waste yield, recycling and maintaining local ecological stability.
- Recruitment of individuals from vulnerable social groups, charitable giving, donations, volunteering, protecting public health, supporting and upholding the local economy and ecosystem, human rights, monitoring transparent supply chain operations, empowering youth, promoting culture, games, and sports, lowering environmental costs in the production process, opening up new markets through innovative sustainable technologies and production processes, and providing goods and services to the general public and the environment are the instances recorded concerning external CSR regarding society.
- Concerning external CSR and corporate governance (CG), the following were examined: the Board's structure and composition, decision-making by experienced and independent members, benefits and incentives to meet financial and non-financial targets; leadership ethics (treating stakeholders and shareholders fairly, applying CSR and sustainability principles throughout the hierarchy and all day-to-day operations of the business); and transparency (using international reporting standards and the accuracy, completeness, and dependability of sustainability or CSR reports).

The sum of these variables was the total CSR of the companies (total variable).

3.2. Variables Controlled for Whether and to What Extent They Influence the CSR Actions of Companies

We chose to test the sample companies' CSR on several other financial and non-financial factors.

3.2.1. Data from Their Financial Statements

For the sample companies and our study period, based on their officially published financial statements, the following variables were recorded:

ASS: Assets
ATR: Total asset turnover ratio
DOC: Days of claims
EBI: EBITDA
ICF: Immediate cash flow
LTL: Long-term lending
OM: Operating margin
STL: Short-term lending
TBO: Total debt obligations
TS: Total sales

All of the above variables are purely quantitative. Except for days receivable, all other variables relating to financial information were recorded in millions of euros.

3.2.2. Data from Non-financial Statements

For our sample and the three years studied, we collected the following variables from non-financial statements, which are based on our previous study (Pagkalou et al., 2024):
EMP: number of employees
AD: distinctions, where following the coding of the scoring system in Table 14.1

Table 14.1. The Variable Distinctions (AD) with Corresponding Values.

Values	Explanation
0	No distinctions
1	General distinction/s by Greek organisation/s
2	Distinction/s by Greek organisation/s on a specific methodology
3	Distinction/s by Greek organisation/s by evaluators on a specific methodology
4	General distinction/s by foreign body/bodies
5	General distinction/s by foreign body/bodies on a specific methodology
6	General distinction/s by foreign body/bodies by evaluators on a specific methodology
7	General distinction/s by both a Greek organisation/s and a foreign organisation/s
8	General distinction/s by both a Greek organisation/s and a foreign organisation/s on a specific methodology
9	General distinction/s by both a Greek organisation/s and foreign organisation/s by evaluators on a specific methodology

CG: corporate governance, draw Table 14.2

Table 14.2. The CG with Corresponding Values.

Values	Explanation
0	No or incomplete information
1	General information
2	Indicator description without quantitative information
3	Quantitative and measurable information
4	Recording index efficiency with measurements
5	Whether the efficiency/benefit/effectiveness of the indicator has been measured

EVA: evaluation of reports, as follows (Table 14.3).

Table 14.3. The Variable CSR Reports Assessment (EVA) with Corresponding Values.

Values	Explanation
0	Report that has not been assessed by an external body/auditor
1	Report that has been assessed, but only based on the content they have been given
2	Report that has been assessed both on its basis and with additional audits

LOA: listed on the Athens Stock Exchange, draw Table 14.4

Table 14.4. The Variable 'Listed on the Athens Stock Exchange' with Corresponding Values.

Values	Explanation
0	Not listed on the Athex
1	Listed on the Athex

NEG: risk and negative recording, as follows (Table 14.5)

Table 14.5. The Variable 'Risk and Negative Recording' with Corresponding Values.

Values	Explanation
0	Without significant mention of the negative impact of their actions
1	With significant mention of the negative impact of their actions

RCD: type of report with CSR data, where the relevant values and their explanation are listed in Table 14.6

Table 14.6. The Variable 'Type of Report with CSR Data' with Corresponding Values.

Values	Explanation
0	No or incomplete report
1	Corporate responsibility report
2	CSR report
3	Sustainable development report
4	Sustainable development and CSR report
5	Sustainable development and CSR report with financial information
6	Another type of report

RPM: report preparation manager, where the coding of their scoring system is listed in Table 14.7

Table 14.7. The Variable 'Report Preparation Manager' with Corresponding Values.

Values	Explanation
0	Absence of report or non-reporting of the responsible manager
2	The board of directors of the company
3	The parent company
4	Separate part of the company/organisation
5	Reliable government institutions
6	Private independent bodies

It is evident that all the above variables are qualitative ones that were given numerical values to compare them in the study, with the exception of employees, which is a quantitative variable.

4. METHODOLOGY AND INDEX FRAMEWORK

We investigate the relationship between the corporate responsibility of large companies operating in Greece and other financial and non-financial variables using ML techniques and compare the results. However, it is of primary importance to carefully select the variables that will be used in creating the CSR index.

4.1. Construction of CSR Index

Having chosen the corporate responsibility demonstrated by the companies and organisations in the sample as the dependent variable, we first recorded all the variables mentioned in Section 3.1. The set of variables for CSR actions is qualitative; therefore, for the structure of the indicator, we had to take this parameter into account and not work with sums or averages. For these reasons, clusters were selected as the method. After testing for the number of clusters by elbow method and for interpretability reasons, we chose to have five clusters in which to distinguish the dependent variable CSR. After testing, we concluded that we should follow the unsupervised ML algorithm for the K-Means clustering method to construct the index and division into clusters.

We chose to test the overall CSR of the companies in the sample because in tests that we conducted separately for the CSR actions implemented by the companies towards their internal environment and for the actions towards their external environment (overall as ESG and individually as society, environment, and governance) we did not obtain equally significant results.

4.2. Checking Index Reliability Using ML Techniques

Then, we had to select the independent control variables to interpret the created index. These variables are detailed in Section 3.2. We chose to test the index's

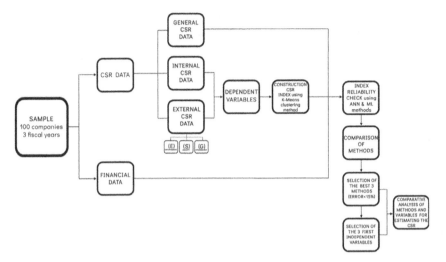

Fig. 14.1. Outline of the Methodological Process of the Study.

effectiveness using neural networks and ML techniques and compare the results. More specifically, we tested with Naive Bayes, generalised linear model, logistic regression, deep learning, decision tree, RF, GBTs, and support vector machine.

As expected, due to the nature of the data, the analytical methods offered better results, especially the GBTs and random forest methods. Deep learning followed this. Consequently, our study was focused on these three methods.

Fig. 14.1 describes the steps required to perform the study, from the data collection and preprocessing to the procedure applied to the ML models and comparing the results.

5. FINDINGS AND EMPIRICAL ANALYSIS

From the methodology developed above, it is clear that we have chosen to assess CSR as a whole rather than in subcategories. Different ML techniques were considered to estimate CSR, and we focused on those that appeared to have the highest accuracy and an estimation error of less than 15%. Afterwards, we present both comparative data of the methods tested and detailed results of the top three in the ranking. By method, those variables that most affect the estimation of CSR in our model are also tested. The comparative approach to the analysis and presentation of the findings applies equally to the techniques and variables, separately and in combination.

5.1. Preliminary Analysis and Descriptive Statistics

The initial observation concerns the accuracy of the analytical techniques examined. For our model, it is noticed that the GBTs method gives the best rate with a measurement error below 10% (accuracy of 90.6%), followed by the random forest method with an accuracy of 88.4% and deep learning with 86.1%, followed in descending order of accuracy by Naïve Bayes (84.9%), generalised linear model (84.7%), logistic regression (78.8%), decision tree (78%), and support vector machine (61.7%). Table 14.8 shows the techniques tested and the accuracy rate of each.

Below is a bar chart illustrating the above results (Fig. 14.2).

Of the above methods that have been recorded for their effectiveness in CSR valuation accuracy, those with an accuracy of more than 85% were selected, and the first three(error<15%) were chosen to deal more extensively.

5.2. Empirical Results

This is followed by controlling the independent variables that seem to influence the sample companies' CSR assessment by the method examined.

Table 14.9 summarises the results by method and variable.

We observe that the variable that most influence the CSR assessment, according to most methods, is the type of corporate responsibility report document, that is the RCD variable with weights ranging between 0.67 (with the decision tree

Table 14.8. Accuracy per Method.

Model	Accuracy (%)
Gradient-boosted trees	90,588
Random forest	88,366
Deep learning	86,0784
Naïve Bayes	84,902
Generalised linear model	84,706
Logistic regression	78,824
Decision tree	77,974

Note: Methods are listed in descending order of value to three decimal places.

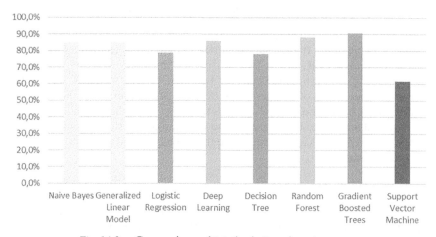

Fig. 14.2. Comparison of Methods Based on Accuracy.

Table 14.9. Attribute of Variables per Method.

Attribute (Variables)	Naïve Bayes	Generalised Linear Model	Logistic Regression	Random Forest	Neural Network	Decision Tree	Gradient-boosted Trees
RCD	0.31	0.56	0.45	0.51	0.47	0.67	0.48
RPM	0.16	0.14	0.04	0.20	0.20	0.01	0.18
EVA	0.16	0.07	0.09	0.20	0.15	0.12	0.19
AD	0.13	0.04	0.02	0.13	0.09	0.08	0.14
CG	0.10	0.14	0.06	0.16	0.05	0.01	0.13
TBO	0.09	0.08	0.21	0.11	0.03	0.03	0.09
LOA	0.09	0.01	0.07	0.08	0.11	0.09	0.06
ATR	0.09	0.10	0.09	0.07	0.01	0.12	0.07
ASS	0.09	0.12	0.13	0.09	0.09	0.11	0.10
LTL	0.08	0.05	0.09	0.02	0.21	0.00	0.01
ICF	0.07	0.05	0.04	0.05	0.10	0.05	0.02
STL	0.06	0.04	0.03	0.11	0.14	0.01	0.13
DOC	0.04	0.05	0.05	0.08	0.05	0.07	0.04
TS	0.03	0.08	0.08	0.04	0.03	0.06	0.02
OM	0.02	0.01	0.03	0.02	0.05	0.01	0.03
EBI	0.02	0.02	0.04	0.12	0.07	0.08	0.10
NEG	0.02	0.02	0.01	0.03	0.02	0.01	0.01
EMP	0.01	0.02	0.04	0.01	0.02	0.02	0.01

method) and 0.31. With a significant difference, this is followed by the variables RPM (e.g. the person responsible for implementing the e.c.e.) and EVA (report evaluation). All three of these variables relate to non-financial parameters and are qualitative, but they seem to lag behind the quantitative data regarding financial variables.

A related chart showing the overall findings is also provided below (Fig. 14.3).

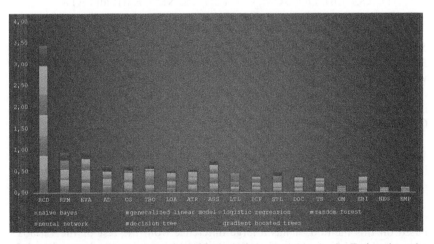

Fig. 14.3. Comparison of the Contribution of the Variables in the Estimation of CSR per Method.

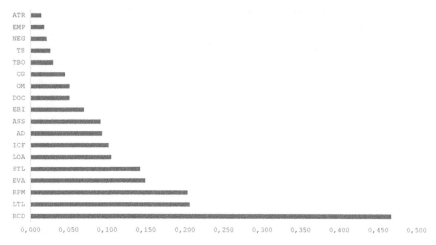

Fig. 14.4. Comparison of Variables Based on Weight Value by Deep Learning Method.

5.2.1. Empirical Results by Method

In this section, we present the results of the most important methods for our model, separately for neural networks and other ML techniques.

The case of ANNs

Fig. 14.4 presents the weights of the most important variables affecting our model according to the deep-learning method in ascending order of importance.

We observe that according to the deep learning method, the variable whose value most influences the overall CSR estimate is RCD, that is the type of report with CSR data. It is followed by LTL and RPM and then by EVA, STL, LOA, ICF, AD, ASS, EBI, DOC, OM, CG, TBO, TS, NEG, EMP, and ATR.

5.2.2. The Case of ML Methods

5.2.2.1. The GBTs Method. Fig. 14.5 presents the weights of the most essential variables affecting our model according to the GBTs method.

We observe that according to the GBTs method, the variable whose value most influences the overall CSR estimate is also RCD, that is the type of report with CSR data. It is followed by EVA and RPM.

5.2.2.2. Random Forest Method. Fig. 14.6 captures the weights of the most important variables affecting our model according to the random forest method.

As Fig. 14.6 demonstrates, RCD is the greatest weight in our model formulation for determining the total CSR of large firms operating in Greece. Also, based on this method, it has a large difference from the rest of the variables. This is followed by the variables EVA and RPM. Contrary to the results of the previous techniques analysed, in this method, quite significant weight is obtained

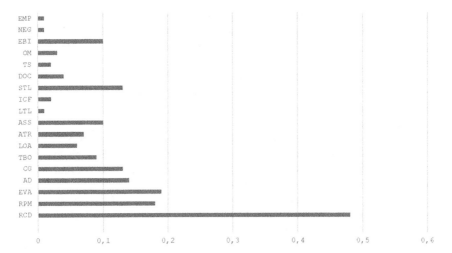

Fig. 14.5. Comparison of Variables Based on Weights Value by GBTs Method.

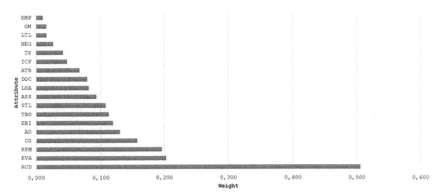

Fig. 14.6. Comparison of Variables Based on Weights Value by Random Forest Method.

in the value of the variables CG, AD, and EVI, confirming our previous study (Pagkalou et al., 2024) followed by a different methodology.

6. DISCUSSION OF THE RESULTS

This study investigates the efficacy of ANNs and other ML techniques in analysing CSR and ESG actions within Greek companies. The comparative analysis of various methods and variables aims to determine the most effective approach for assessing CSR and ESG performance.

The sample's study period runs for three financial years, from January 2019 to December 2021, and the 100 largest companies and organisations operating in Greece during that period are examined. This study focuses on creating an index for corporate responsibility of the sample companies as a whole and testing its reliability. Estimates are made using artificial intelligence and other ML methods. The comparison is between the methods and control variables, jointly or separately.

First of all, it should be noted that our findings are consistent with our first hypothesis that CSR of companies can be estimated by ML methods, providing reliable results and complementing previous empirical evidence (Gupta, 2023; Maiti & Singh, 2022; Zhang et al., 2021; Zhou et al., 2020).

In our analysis, ANNs gave remarkable results in the accuracy of CSR estimation compared to traditional statistical methods such as linear and logistic regression. This aligns with the findings of Dutta et al. (2023), who reported that ANNs and deep learning models provide higher accuracy in economic forecasting and CSR performance evaluation. Our study also confirmed that ML techniques such as GBTs, random forest, and deep learning provide better results, which aligns with other recent studies (Lillo et al., 2023; Thompson & Buertey, 2023).

Examining our second research hypothesis, which is that companies' CSR can be assessed through other financial and non-financial variables, we also agree with our findings. A significant number of variables with which we chose to test the reliability of the CSR index we had created gave high weights. These findings are consistent with those of recent research by Kotsantoni and Serafim (2023), who emphasised the importance of integrating financial and non-financial data to enhance ESG assessments, as well as other researchers (Albuquerque et al., 2019; Eccles et al., 2014; Friede et al., 2015; Pagkalou et al., 2024, and others).

More specifically, the main factors that appeared to influence the assessment of CSR and ESG were the type of report with CSR data (variable RCD), report preparation manager (variable RPM), and evaluation of reports (variable EVA). It was also found that the weights of these and the other variables examined varied from method to method.

However, a general finding is that in this study, variables based on financial data seemed to lag and appear with lower contributions than those based on non-financial data. This superiority of non-financial variables may be related to the nature of qualitative variables, which are better suited to analytical methods.

7. CONCLUSIONS

This study highlights the importance of neural networks and ML techniques in enhancing the analysis of CSR and CSR practices in Greece.

By addressing the gaps identified, especially in the Greek context, this study aims to provide tailored insights and recommendations that can contribute to improving the understanding of large companies' CSR and ESG strategies and the factors that influence them. The study focuses on using ANN and ML techniques to this end with a comparative approach.

A comparative analysis of ML techniques revealed that the effectiveness of these models depends on the quality and completeness of the data used. Inconsistent and incomplete data can significantly undermine the effectiveness of ML models, highlighting the importance of improving data transparency and standardisation in CSR and ESG reporting. In fact, it was found that these methods provide different results for the same control variables. Consequently, depending on our data, careful selection of which techniques should be applied is required.

In our case, we constructed an overall CSR and ESG index by collecting 44 different variables covering the whole spectrum of corporate responsibility. Then, we tested the reliability of this index with 10 quantitative-financial variables and 8 qualitative-non-financial variables. Comparing different ML methods for our sample, we noticed that the following three specific ML regression models (models) outperformed with their respective accuracies: GBTs (90.6%), random forest (88.4%), and deep learning (86.1%). Focusing on these methods, we found that three of the non-financial variables best explain our model: the type of non-financial report document, who has been designated as responsible for policy making and implementation of corporate responsibility actions in each company, and the evaluation or not of the report directly related to the quality of information. We, therefore, consider that efforts to standardise CSR and ESG reporting and improve data transparency are crucial to maximise the potential of ML models in this area.

This study contributes to the literature by concluding that incorporating ML techniques can significantly improve the analysis of CSR and ESG actions. Stakeholders, including policymakers, researchers, and practitioners, should consider adopting these advanced methods to improve the accuracy and depth of their assessments.

Future research should focus on improving these models, exploring hybrid approaches that combine the strengths of different techniques, and expanding the range of variables considered.

REFERENCES

Aguinis, H., & Glavas, A. (2012). What we know and don't know about corporate social responsibility: A review and research agenda. *Journal of Management*, *38*(4), 932–968.

Albuquerque, R., Koskinen, Y., & Zhang, C. (2019). Corporate social responsibility and firm risk: Theory and empirical evidence. *Management Science*, *66*(10), 4451–4469.

Binh, N. (2023). An application of artificial neural networks in corporate social responsibility decision making. *Intelligent Systems in Accounting Finance & Management*, *31*(2), e1542.

Boardman, A. E., Greenberg, D. H., Vining, A. R., & Weimer, D. L. (2018). *Cost-benefit analysis: Concepts and practice*. Cambridge University Press.

Brophy, J., Hammoudeh, Z., & Lowd, D. (2023). Adapting and evaluating influence-estimation methods for gradient-boosted decision trees. *Journal of Machine Learning Research*, *24*(154), 1–48.

Chen, L., Zhang, L., Huang, J., Xiao, H., & Zhou, Z. (2021). Social responsibility portfolio optimization incorporating ESG criteria. *Journal of Management Science and Engineering*, *6*(1), 75–85.

Chih, H.-L., Chih, H.-H., & Chen, T.-Y. (2010). On the determinants of corporate social responsibility: International evidence on the financial industry. *Journal of Business Ethics*, *93*(1), 115–135.

Dhaliwal, D. S., Li, O. Z., Tsang, A., & Yang, Y. G. (2011). Voluntary nonfinancial disclosure and the cost of equity capital: The initiation of corporate social responsibility reporting. *Accounting Review*, *86*(1), 59–100.

Dutta, S. (2023). Predicting CSR performance using artificial neural networks: Evidence from emerging markets. *Financial Innovation*, *9*(4), 57–73.

Eccles, R. G., Ioannou, I., & Serafeim, G. (2014). The impact of corporate sustainability on organizational processes and performance. *Management Science, 60*(11), 2835–2857.
Epstein, M. J., & Wisner, P. S. (2001). Using a balanced scorecard to implement sustainability. *Environmental Quality Management, 11*(2), 1–10.
Flammer, C. (2015). Does corporate social responsibility lead to superior financial performance? A Regression discontinuity approach. *Management Science, 61*(11), 2549–2568.
Friede, G., Busch, T., & Bassen, A. (2015). ESG and financial performance: Aggregated evidence from more than 2000 empirical studies. *Journal of Sustainable Finance & Investment, 5*(4), 210–233.
Goodfellow, I., Bengio, Y., & Courville, A. (2016). *Deep learning*. MIT Press.
Gupta, R. (2023). Machine learning applications in ESG investing: A comprehensive review. *Sustainable Finance and Investment, 13*(1), 112–130.
Hernandez, M., & Gupta, R. (2021). Analyzing the impact of CSR activities on consumer perception using machine learning techniques. *Journal of Business Research, 133*, 1–12.
Hernandez, J., Patel, A., & Li, W. (2022a). Evaluating machine learning techniques for assessing CSR practices: Focusing on interpretability and accuracy. *International Journal of Data Science and Analytics, 14*(2), 123–138.
Hernandez, J., Patel, A., & Li, W. (2022b). A hybrid neural network approach for evaluating corporate social responsibility initiatives. *International Journal of Data Science and Analytics, 13*, 235–250.
Hsu, F. J., & Chen, Y. C. (2015). Is a firm's financial risk associated with corporate social responsibility? *Management Decision, 53*(9), 2175–2199.
Jiraporn, P., & Chintrakarn, P. (2013). How do powerful CEOs view corporate social responsibility (CSR)? An empirical note. *Economics Letters, 119*(3), 344–347.
Jo, H., & Harjoto, M. A. (2012). The causal effect of corporate governance on corporate social responsibility. *Journal of Business Ethics, 106*(1), 3–72.
Karagiorgos, T. (2010). Corporate social responsibility and financial performance: An empirical analysis on Greek companies. *European Research Studies Journal, XIII*(4), 85–108.
Kotsantonis, S., & Serafeim, G. (2023). Integrating financial and non-financial data in ESG assessments. *Harvard Business Review, 101*(1), 45–54.
LeCun, Y., Bengio, Y., & Hinton, G. (2015). Deep learning. *Nature, 521*(7553), 436–444.
Li, Y., Gong, M., & Xu, J. (2020). Big data driven management of corporate social responsibility performance.*Technological Forecasting and Social Change, 153*, 119935.
Lillo, F., Severino-González, P., Rodríguez-Quezada, E., Arenas-Torres, F., & Sarmiento-Peralta, G. (2023). Machine learning approach for predicting corporate social responsibility perception in university students. *Interciencia, 48*(10).
Luo, X., & Bhattacharya, C. B. (2006). Corporate social responsibility, customer satisfaction, and market value. *Academy of Marketing Science Journal, 34*(2), 159–166.
Maiti, M., & Singh, S. (2022). The role of machine learning in analyzing CSR performance. *Journal of Business Ethics, 175*(2), 341–358.
Millar, R., & Hall, K. (2013). Social return on investment (SROI) and performance measurement. *Public Management Review, 15*(6), 923–941.
Minsoo, L., Hyunwoo, P., & Sung, C. (2020). Random forests for predicting corporate social responsibility ratings: An empirical study. *Journal of Business Analytics, 11*(1), 1–19.
Pagkalou, F., Galanos, C., & Thalassinos, E. (2024). Exploring the relationship between corporate governance, corporate social responsibility and financial and non-financial reporting: A study of large companies in Greece. *Journal of Risk Financial Management, 17*(3), 97.
Qiu, Y., Shaukat, A., & Tharyan, R. (2016). Environmental and social disclosures: Link with corporate financial performance. *The British Accounting Review, 48*(1), 102–116.
Skouloudis, A., Evangelinos, K., & Kourmousis, F. (2010). Assessing non-financial reports according to the global reporting initiative guidelines: Evidence from Greece. *Journal of Cleaner Production, 18*(5), 426–438.
Slaper, T. F., & Hall, T. J. (2011). The triple bottom line: What is it and how does it work? *Indiana Business Review, 86*(1), 4–8.
Thompson, E., & Buertey, S. (2023). Which firms opt for corporate social responsibility assurance? A machine learning prediction. *Business Ethics, the Environment & Responsibility, 32*, 599–611.

Tsalis, T. A., Stylianou, M. S., & Nikolaou, I. E. (2018). Evaluating the quality of corporate social responsibility reports: The case of occupational health and safety disclosures. *Safety Science*, *110*(3), 37–49.

Wang, Q., Dou, J., & Jia, S. (2016). A meta-analytic review of corporate social responsibility and corporate financial performance: The moderating effect of contextual factors. *Business & Society*, *55*(8), 1083–1121.

Zhang, D., Hu, M., Ji, Q., & Kou, G. (2021). Systematic literature review on machine learning applications in corporate finance. *Journal of Corporate Finance*, *66*, 110–124.

Zhou, Z., Huang, Z., & Zhou, Y. (2020). ESG performance and stock price crash risk: Evidence from China. *Sustainability*, *12*(4), 1425.

CHAPTER 15

WILLINGNESS TO PAY EXTRA FOR ECO-FRIENDLY PRODUCTS: A SEQUENTIAL MEDIATION ANALYSIS OF BEHAVIOURAL ANTECEDENTS AND ATTITUDE TOWARDS BEHAVIOURAL SUSTAINABILITY

Cuc Lavinia Denisia[a], Rad Dana[b], Hategan Camelia-Daniela[c], Pelau Corina[d] and Szentesi Silviu Gabriel[a]

[a] *Aurel Vlaicu University of Arad, Center for Research and Consultancy in Economics, Arad, Romania*
[b] *Aurel Vlaicu University of Arad, Center of Research Development and Innovation in Psychology, Arad, Romania*
[c] *West University of Timisoara, Department of Accounting and Audit, ECREB – East European Center for Research in Economics and Business, Timisoara, Romania*
[d] *Bucharest University of Economic Studies, Faculty of Business Administration – Foreign Languages, Bucharest, Romania*

ABSTRACT

Purpose: *This study investigates the relationships between environmentally conscious behaviours and intentions among the Romanian population, focusing on the interplay between disposition towards supplementary payment for* eco-friendly products *(DSPEP)*, intention for purchasing green products *(IPGP)*, environmentally aware behaviours *(EAB)*, and anticipated eco-behaviour intention *(AEI)*.

Methodology: *Questionnaire, the participants being selected using a convenience sampling method, taken from the population of Romania in the period 2021–2022, and the final sample being formed from the answers of 759 participants. Data were analysed using SPSS Process Model 6, including confirmatory factor analysis (CFA), correlation analysis, and mediation analysis.*

Findings: *Pearson's correlation coefficients revealed significant positive associations among DSPEP, IPGP, EAB, and AEI, indicating that individuals with a higher disposition towards eco-friendly products are more likely to have stronger intentions and behaviours related to environmental conservation. Mediation analysis further elucidated the mediating roles of EAB and AEI in the relationship between DSPEP and IPGP. Specifically, AEI exerted both direct and indirect effects on DSPEP, with EAB and IPGP acting as significant mediators.*

Implications: *Implications for policymakers and marketers seeking to develop interventions and strategies to foster environmental conservation efforts and promote eco-friendly consumption behaviours.*

Limitations: *The provision of empirical evidence only from the Romanian population. The sampling method and the cross-sectional nature of the data generate methodological limitations, which limit the generalisation and inference of causality of the findings.*

Future Research: *Research can be extended to validate these findings in different cultural contexts and explore additional factors influencing environmentally conscious behaviours and intentions.*

Keywords: Environmentally conscious behaviour; eco-friendly products; sustainable consumption; environmental attitudes; consumer intentions

JEL Codes: Q01; Q56

INTRODUCTION

In the current context, marked by a growing awareness of the impact of human activities on the environment, consumers are becoming more attentive to the products they purchase and their ecological effects. This change in consumer preferences stimulated companies to adopt and promote green products, leading to the emergence of a new field of study in green marketing (Chang & Fong, 2010). Although rich literature explores green consumption behaviours, few studies address the complete chain of sequential mediators that influence the decision to pay a supplement for eco-friendly products.

The central hypothesis of this study proposes that the willingness to pay more for green products is influenced not only by individual awareness and attitudes but also by a series of sequential factors such as anticipated green behaviour intention, green product purchase intention and adoption of a lifestyle oriented towards protecting the environment. Roberts' (1996) study suggests that consumers' green intentions can significantly predict actual purchase behaviours. Gilg et al.'s (2005) research indicates that an environmentally oriented lifestyle is closely related to sustainable consumption decisions.

Therefore, this study aims to explore these relationships in a sequential and systematic manner, providing a deeper insight into how different dimensions of green behaviour interconnect to form a green consumer profile. Understanding these dynamics can help organisations develop more effective marketing strategies and help promote sustainable behaviour globally.

LITERATURE REVIEW

Provision for Additional Payment for Eco-friendly Products

Willingness to pay extra for eco-friendly products is a crucial indicator of consumer attitudes towards environmental responsibility and support for sustainable products. This trend not only is a sign of environmental awareness but also reflects a change in consumer behaviour that several socio-economic and personal factors can influence.

Studies show this disposition varies by demographics, income, and education level. For example, Grankvist et al. (2004) identified that women and people with a higher level of education tend to show a greater willingness to pay for organic products. In addition, Tsakiridou et al. (2008) observed that families with children show an increased concern for organic products, possibly out of a desire to ensure a healthier environment for future generations.

From a marketing impact perspective, brands implementing communication strategies that emphasise their products' environmental benefits can positively influence consumers' willingness to pay more. In their research, Nyilasy et al. (2014) found that advertisements emphasising the positive impact of green purchases on the environment can significantly increase the willingness to pay for a premium product.

In addition, an exciting aspect identified in the specialised literature is the link between the willingness to pay for eco-friendly products and brand loyalty. Hartmann and Apaolaza-Ibáñez (2012) demonstrated that consumers who perceive a brand as sustainable are more willing to pay more for its products and remain loyal to the brand in the long term.

Therefore, the willingness to pay extra for eco-friendly products is not just an isolated phenomenon but an integral part of broader consumption behaviour influenced by personal, cultural, and marketing factors. These findings underscore the importance of integrating sustainability practices into business strategies to meet the demands of a segment that is increasingly aware of the impact of human activities on the environment.

Anticipated Intention of Green Behaviour

Anticipated green behaviour intention is crucial in the process of adopting pro-environmental behaviours and is often considered an indicator of individual commitment to environmental protection. Previous studies have shown that this intention is closely related to personal attitudes and social norms, which directly influence individual decisions and actions regarding environmental protection.

For example, Schwartz (1977) identified that personal attitudes, such as ecological consciousness and concern for environmental issues, are important factors that shape intentions for environmentally friendly behaviour. Likewise, social norms and social pressure exerted by reference groups have a significant impact on the adoption of pro-environmental behaviour (Schultz et al., 2007).

In addition, longitudinal studies have shown that environmental intentions expressed at one point in time can predict the individual's future behaviours. For example, Bamberg and Schmidt (2003) conducted a three-year study. They found that individuals with strong intentions to adopt green behaviours were more likely to engage in concrete actions such as recycling and saving energy in the future.

Although several factors can influence green behaviour intentions, such as age, education, and income level, it is important to emphasise that these intentions can be reshaped and positively influenced by behavioural interventions and ecological awareness campaigns (Steg et al., 2014).

Therefore, understanding and correctly addressing the anticipated intentions of ecological behaviour is essential in promoting more sustainable behaviour and achieving environmental conservation goals.

Intention to Purchase Organic Products

The IPGP is a fundamental aspect of the consumption behaviour of individuals who express concern for the environment through their shopping choices. This intention is closely related to the awareness of environmental issues and the desire to contribute to reducing the negative impact on the global ecosystem.

Recent research has shown a strong association between environmental awareness and the intention to purchase sustainable products. For example, Navalagund et al. (2020) found that individuals with a greater understanding of environmental issues are more likely to seek out and purchase products labelled as green or environmentally friendly.

In addition to awareness, willingness to pay a premium price for green products is another important factor influencing purchase intention. Market studies have shown that a growing segment of consumers are willing to invest more in green products, motivated by the desire to support sustainable business practices and obtain higher-quality products (Wu & Chen, 2014).

Another relevant aspect is the influence of psychological and social factors on the intention to purchase organic products. Research by Zhang et al. (2010) showed that social recognition and group membership with strong environmental values could play a significant role in driving green purchase behaviour.

In conclusion, the IPGP is a complex phenomenon influenced by multiple factors, including awareness, willingness to pay a premium price, and social influences.

Understanding these dynamics is essential for companies that want to develop and promote sustainable products and meet the needs of environmentally conscious consumers.

Environmentally Conscious Behaviours

Environmentally conscious behaviours are tangible manifestations of individual concern for environmental protection and are essential to a sustainable lifestyle. These behaviours involve diverse daily actions and practices that aim to reduce resource consumption and minimise environmental impact.

Previous studies have identified that these behaviours include, among others, saving energy, recycling and responsible waste management, reducing water consumption and carbon emissions, and adopting a more sustainable food diet (Thøgersen, 2005). For example, research by Bamberg and Schmidt (2003) showed that individuals who adopt environmentally conscious behaviours, such as using public transportation or a bicycle instead of their car, are more likely to have future intentions to adopt other green behaviours as well.

In addition, the literature demonstrates the influence of socio-cultural factors on these behaviours. Studies by Wyss et al. (2022) demonstrated that cultural and social norms could play a significant role in determining individual behaviours related to environmental protection. For example, in societies where recycling and environmental conservation are valued and actively promoted, individuals are more likely to adopt green practices in their daily lives.

Moreover, individual environmental attitudes and level of awareness are important factors influencing environmentally conscious behaviours. Research by Hines et al. (1987) showed that people with a higher level of understanding of environmental issues are more likely to adopt pro-environmental behaviours in everyday life.

In conclusion, environmentally conscious behaviours express individual commitment to protecting the environment and are influenced by a wide range of factors, including personal attitudes, cultural norms, and level of awareness. Understanding these dynamics is essential to promoting a sustainable lifestyle and increasing public awareness of the impact of individual actions on the environment.

Relationships Between Concepts

The literature reveals a sequential relationship between these concepts, suggesting that they are interconnected and influence each other in adopting green behaviour. The willingness to pay extra for eco-friendly products is a key factor that can directly affect the anticipated intention of eco-friendly behaviour. Previous studies have shown that individuals who are willing to pay a higher price for green products show a greater intention to adopt environmentally protective behaviours (Roberts, 1996). For example, research by Moser (2015) found that consumers willing to purchase green products are likelier to adopt other pro-environmental behaviours in their daily lives.

In addition, the IPGP can be considered a precursor of environmentally conscious behaviours. Studies by Lee and Shin (2010) showed that individuals who exhibit a strong IPGP are more likely to adopt green practices and engage in environmental conservation behaviours in a variety of contexts.

Empirical research has also revealed a chain of mediation between these concepts, suggesting that their relationships are sequential and cumulative in nature. For example, the studies of Chekima et al. (2016) found that when consumers strongly intend to purchase green products, this is often followed by an increased commitment to adopting a green lifestyle.

Therefore, these findings support the idea that the relationships between willingness to pay extra, green behaviour intention, and environmentally conscious behaviours are complex and interdependent. Understanding these relationships can help develop and implement marketing strategies and behavioural interventions aimed at promoting more consistent and long-term green behaviour.

Methodology

Data analysis was conducted using SPSS Process Model 6. Firstly, CFA was performed to assess the validity of the measurement model by examining the fit of the hypothesised factor structure to the observed data. This analysis allowed for the examination of the relationships between the latent constructs (DSPEP, IPGP, EAB, and AEI) and their respective observed indicators.

Following the CFA, correlation analysis was conducted to explore the relationships between DSPEP, IPGP, EAB, and AEI. Pearson's correlation coefficients were computed to examine the strength and direction of these relationships.

Subsequently, mediation analysis was performed to investigate the potential mediating roles of EAB and AEI in the relationship between DSPEP and IPGP. This analysis allowed for exploring indirect pathways through which DSPEP influences IPGP, mediated by EAB and AEI.

This study employed a combination of CFA, correlation analysis, and mediation analysis to comprehensively examine the relationships between various dimensions of environmentally conscious behaviours and intentions, thereby contributing to a deeper understanding of consumer behaviour towards eco-friendly products.

Participants

Participants were selected using convenience sampling, drawing from the Romanian population from 2021 to 2022. The total sample consisted of 771 individuals. Data from 759 participants were deemed valid for analysis, with 12 responses classified as missing. The demographic characteristics of the participants, including gender, age, and education level, were recorded and analysed (see Table 15.1).

The sample comprised individuals of varying gender, age, and education levels. Gender distribution among participants showed that 20.9% identified as male and 77.6% as female. Regarding age demographics, participants ranged from 18 to over 65 years old, with the largest age group being 25–34 years old (38.8%). Education levels varied among participants, with 52.1% having completed professional education, 24.1% having completed bachelor studies, 16.1% holding a master's degree, and 2.6% having pursued doctoral studies.

Table 15.1. Demographic Characteristics.

Demographic	Category	Frequency	Percent	Valid Percent	Cumulative Percent
Gender					
	Male (1)	161	20.9	21.2	21.2
	Female (2)	598	77.6	78.8	100.0
	Total	759	98.4	100.0	
	Missing	12	1.6		
Age					
	18–24 (1)	185	24.0	24.2	24.2
	25–34 (2)	299	38.8	39.1	63.3
	35–44 (3)	107	13.9	14.0	77.3
	45–54 (4)	93	12.1	12.2	89.4
	55–64 (5)	59	7.7	7.7	97.1
	65+ (6)	22	2.9	2.9	100.0
	Total	765	99.2	100.0	
	Missing	6	0.8		
Education					
	None (0)	19	2.5	2.5	2.5
	Professional (1)	402	52.1	53.5	56.1
	Bachelor (2)	186	24.1	24.8	80.8
	Master (3)	124	16.1	16.5	97.3
	Doctorate (4)	20	2.6	2.7	100.0
	Total	751	97.4	100.0	
	Missing	20	2.6		
Overall total		771	100.0		

Source: Own processing.

Instrument

The survey instrument comprised four factors: DSPEP, IPGP, EAB, and AEI. Reliability of each factor was assessed using Cronbach's alpha, yielding coefficients indicating excellent internal consistency: DSPEP ($\alpha = 0.907$), IPGP ($\alpha = 0.949$), EAB ($\alpha = 0.889$), and AEI ($\alpha = 0.914$), with the overall scale achieving $\alpha = 0.956$.

The scale developed for this study encompasses four distinct factors, each aimed at capturing various dimensions of environmentally conscious behaviours and intentions. The first factor, DSPEP, consists of four items and demonstrates high internal consistency with a Cronbach's α of 0.907. The items in this factor have an average loading of approximately 1.559, with an example item being 'I am willing to pay extra for products that are environmentally friendly'. The second factor, IPGP, includes two items and shows excellent reliability (Cronbach's $\alpha = 0.949$) and an average factor loading of about 1.541. An illustrative item from this scale is: 'I plan to buy more green products in the future'. The third factor, EAB, contains two items and has a good reliability score (Cronbach's $\alpha = 0.889$) with an average loading of roughly 0.972. One example from this scale is: 'I consider that a healthy and clean environment has a major impact on the society I am part of'. Lastly, the AEI factor, which includes two items, reflects strong reliability (Cronbach's $\alpha = 0.914$) with an average loading of about 1.079. An example item here is: 'The purchase of eco-friendly products makes me feel responsible towards the environment'. Together, these scales provide a comprehensive measure of individual dispositions towards eco-friendly practices, assessing everything from behavioural intentions to actual behaviours.

CFA was utilised to validate the measurement model. The factor loadings for each item were significant ($p < 0.001$), supporting the convergent validity of the instrument. The results from Bartlett's test of sphericity ($\chi^2 = 14{,}210.747$, $df = 190$, $p < 0.001$) and the comparative fit indices, such as the comparative fit index (CFI = 0.878) and Tucker–Lewis index (TLI = 0.859). The root mean square error of approximation and the standardised root mean square residual provide additional insights into model fit, with values of 0.117 and 0.083, respectively, suggesting adequate fit between the model and the observed data (see Table 15.2 and Fig. 15.1).

Table 15.2. Reliability Coefficients and Main Factor Loadings.

Factor/Item	Cronbach's α	Estimate	Std. Error	z-Value	p	95% CI Lower	95% CI Upper
DSPEP	0.907						
dspep1		1.556	0.052	29.741	<0.001	1.453	1.658
dspep2		1.570	0.052	30.246	<0.001	1.468	1.671
dspep3		1.591	0.058	27.421	<0.001	1.477	1.704
dspep4		1.521	0.060	25.145	<0.001	1.403	1.640
IPGP	0.949						
ipgp1		1.478	0.052	28.355	<0.001	1.376	1.580
ipgp2		1.604	0.049	32.628	<0.001	1.507	1.700
EAB	0.889						
eab1		0.937	0.050	18.686	<0.001	0.839	1.035
eab2		1.006	0.043	23.604	<0.001	0.922	1.089
AEI	0.914						
aei1		1.058	0.046	23.085	<0.001	0.968	1.148
aei2		1.099	0.047	23.130	<0.001	1.005	1.192

Source: Own processing.

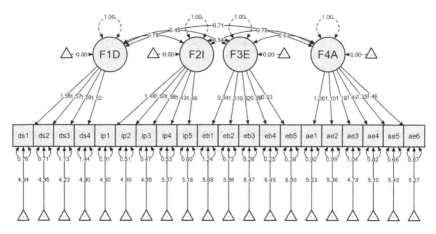

Fig. 15.1. Factorial Structure of the Scale.

The overall findings indicate that the instrument is reliable and valid for measuring environmentally conscious behaviours and intentions, which are crucial for understanding the dynamics in our sequential mediation model. In this model, AEI serves as the independent variable, DSPEP as the dependent variable, with EAB and IPGP functioning as the first and second mediators, respectively.

RESULTS

Correlation analysis was conducted to examine the relationships between the variables of interest: DSPEP, IPGP, EAB, and AEI.

Pearson's correlation coefficients revealed significant positive associations among all variables. Specifically, DSPEP was positively correlated with IPGP ($r = 0.736$, $p < 0.001$), EAB ($r = 0.496$, $p < 0.001$), and AEI ($r = 0.652$, $p < 0.001$). IPGP showed significant positive correlations with EAB ($r = 0.624$, $p < 0.001$) and AEI ($r = 0.743$, $p < 0.001$). Similarly, EAB demonstrated a significant positive correlation with AEI ($r = 0.708$, $p < 0.001$) (see Table 15.3).

These findings suggest that individuals who exhibit a higher DSPEP are also more likely to have stronger intentions to purchase green products, engage in EAB, and anticipate engaging in eco-friendly behaviours in the future.

Further analyses were conducted to explore the potential mediating roles of EAB and AEI in the relationship between DSPEP and IPGP.

The total effect model revealed a significant relationship between AEI and DSPEP ($R = 0.6523$, $R^2 = 0.4254$, $F(1, 769) = 569.4077$, $p < 0.001$). The coefficient for AEI was 0.7605 (SE = 0.0319, $t = 23.8623$, $p < 0.001$), indicating a substantial positive association between AEI and DSPEP.

Regarding the total, direct, and indirect effects, the total effect of AEI on DSPEP was 0.7605 (SE = 0.0319, $p < 0.001$), with a completely standardised indirect effect of 0.3947. The direct effect of AEI on DSPEP was 0.3003 (SE = 0.0468, $p < 0.001$), suggesting a significant relationship between AEI and DSPEP after considering the mediators.

Three indirect effects were observed: AEI → EAB → DSPEP (−0.0348, BootSE = 0.0337), AEI → IPGP → DSPEP (0.4028, BootSE = 0.0405), and AEI → EAB → IPGP → DSPEP (0.0922, BootSE = 0.0180). These results suggest that AEI has both direct and indirect effects on DSPEP, with the mediation paths through EAB and IPGP contributing to the overall relationship (see Table 15.4).

Table 15.3. Correlation Analysis.

Variable		DSPEP	IPGP	EAB	AEI
1. DSPEP – disposition towards supplementary payment for eco-friendly products	Pearson's r	–			
2. IPGP – intention for purchasing green products	Pearson's r	0.736***	–		
3. EAB – environmentally aware behaviours	Pearson's r	0.496***	0.624***	–	
4. AEI – anticipated eco-behaviour intention	Pearson's r	0.652***	0.743***	0.708***	–

*$p < 0.05$, **$p < 0.01$, ***$p < 0.001$.
Source: Own processing.

Table 15.4. Total, Direct, and Indirect Effects.

Effect	Effect	BootSE	BootLLCI	BootULCI
Total	0.7605	0.0319	0.6979	0.8230
Direct	0.3003	0.0468	0.2084	0.3921
Indirect (AEI → EAB → DSPEP)	−0.0348	0.0337	−0.1019	0.0291
Indirect (AEI → IPGP → DSPEP)	0.4028	0.0405	0.3271	0.4852
Indirect (AEI → EAB → IPGP → DSPEP)	0.0922	0.0180	0.0584	0.1294

Source: Own processing.

DISCUSSION

The findings of this study provide valuable insights into the relationships between environmentally conscious behaviours and intentions, particularly in the context of consumer behaviour towards eco-friendly products among the Romanian population. The significant positive correlations observed among DSPEP, IPGP, EAB, and AEI align with previous research highlighting the interconnectedness of these constructs (Osbaldiston & Schott, 2012; Ting et al., 2019).

The correlation analysis revealed robust positive associations among DSPEP, IPGP, EAB, and AEI. These findings suggest that individuals who are more inclined towards paying extra for eco-friendly products also demonstrate stronger intentions to purchase green products, engage in EAB, and anticipate engaging in eco-friendly behaviours in the future. Similar results have been reported in studies conducted in various cultural contexts, indicating the generalisability of these associations across different populations (Chen et al., 2018; Majeed et al., 2022).

Moreover, the mediation analysis uncovered the mediating roles of EAB and IPGP in the relationship between DSPEP and IPGP. Specifically, AEI exerted both direct and indirect effects on DSPEP, with EAB and IPGP acting as significant mediators in this relationship. These findings are consistent with previous research highlighting the importance of considering individuals' environmental attitudes and behaviours in understanding their intentions towards eco-friendly products (Li et al., 2019; Sheng et al., 2019).

While the present study contributes to the existing literature by providing empirical evidence from the Romanian population, it is essential to acknowledge its limitations. The use of a convenience sampling method and the cross-sectional nature of the data limit the generalisability and causality inference of the findings. Future research could employ longitudinal designs and more representative samples to establish causal relationships and enhance the external validity of the results.

In conclusion, this study's findings underline the complex dynamics between individuals' attitudes, behaviours, and intentions towards eco-friendly products. By understanding these relationships, policymakers and marketers can develop targeted interventions and strategies to promote sustainable consumption patterns and foster environmental conservation efforts. Further interdisciplinary research incorporating psychological, sociological, and environmental perspectives is needed to advance our understanding of environmentally conscious behaviours and their implications for society and the environment.

REFERENCES

Bamberg, S., & Schmidt, P. (2003). Incentives, morality, or habit? Predicting students' car use for university routes with the models of Ajzen, Schwartz, and Triandis. *Environment and Behavior*, *35*(2), 264–285.

Chang, N. J., & Fong, C. M. (2010). Green product quality, green corporate image, green customer satisfaction, and green customer loyalty. *African Journal of Business Management*, *4*(13), 2836.

Chekima, B., Wafa, S. A. W. S. K., Igau, O. A., Chekima, S., & Sondoh, S. L. Jr. (2016). Examining green consumerism motivational drivers: Does premium price and demographics matter to green purchasing?. *Journal of Cleaner Production*, *112*, 3436–3450.

Chen, L., Wang, C., & Zhou, K. (2018). Understanding consumers' intention to purchase eco-friendly products: An investigation of perceived consumer effectiveness. *Journal of Environmental Psychology*, *59*, 43–52.

Gilg, A., Barr, S., & Ford, N. (2005). Green consumption or sustainable lifestyles? Identifying the sustainable consumer. *Futures*, *37*(6), 481–504.

Grankvist, G., Dahlstrand, U., & Biel, A. (2004). The impact of environmental labeling on consumer preference: Negative vs. positive labels. *Journal of Consumer Policy*, *27*(2), 213–230.

Hartmann, P., & Apaolaza-Ibáñez, V. (2012). Consumer attitude and purchase intention towards green energy brands: The roles of psychological benefits and environmental concern. *Journal of Business Research*, *65*(9), 1254–1263.

Hines, J. M., Hungerford, H. R., & Tomera, A. N. (1987). Analysis and synthesis of research on responsible environmental behavior: A meta-analysis. *The Journal of Environmental Education*, *18*(2), 1–8.

Lee, K. H., & Shin, D. (2010). Consumers' responses to CSR activities: The link between increased awareness and purchase intention. *Public Relations Review*, *36*(2), 193–195.

Li, G., Li, J., & Sun, X. (2019). Measuring green brand equity in relationship interactions and its impact on brand loyalty. *Revista de Cercetare Si Interventie Sociala*, *66*, 278–297.

Majeed, M. U., Aslam, S., Murtaza, S. A., Attila, S., & Molnár, E. (2022). Green marketing approaches and their impact on green purchase intentions: Mediating role of green brand image and consumer beliefs towards the environment. *Sustainability*, *14*(18), 11703.

Moser, A. K. (2015). Thinking green, buying green? Drivers of pro-environmental purchasing behavior. *Journal of Consumer Marketing*, *32*(3), 167–175.

Navalagund, N., Mahantshetti, S., & Nulkar, G. (2020). Factors influencing purchase intention towards E-vehicles among the potential Indian consumers – A study on Karnataka region. *Journal of the Social Sciences*, *48*(3), 1598–1616.

Nyilasy, G., Gangadharbatla, H., & Paladino, A. (2014). Perceived greenwashing: The interactive effects of green advertising and corporate environmental performance on consumer reactions. *Journal of Business Ethics*, *125*(4), 693–707.

Osbaldiston, R., & Schott, J. P. (2012). Environmental sustainability and behavioural science: Meta-analysis of proenvironmental behavior experiments. *Environment and Behavior*, *44*(2), 257–299.

Roberts, J. A. (1996). Green consumers in the 1990s: Profile and implications for advertising. *Journal of Business Research*, *36*(3), 217–231.

Schultz, P. W., Nolan, J. M., Cialdini, R. B., Goldstein, N. J., & Griskevicius, V. (2007). The constructive, destructive, and reconstructive power of social norms. *Psychological Science*, *18*(5), 429–434.

Schwartz, S. H. (1977). Normative influences on altruism. In L. Berkowitz (Ed.), *Advances in experimental social psychology* (Vol. 10, pp. 221–279). Academic Press.

Sheng, G., Xie, F., Gong, S., & Pan, H. (2019). The role of cultural values in green purchasing intention: Empirical evidence from Chinese consumers. *International Journal of Consumer Studies*, *43*(3), 315–326.

Steg, L., Perlaviciute, G., Van der Werff, E., & Lurvink, J. (2014). The significance of hedonic values for environmentally relevant attitudes, preferences, and actions. *Environment and Behavior*, *46*(2), 163–192.

Thøgersen, J. (2005). How may consumer policy empower consumers for sustainable lifestyles?. *Journal of Consumer Policy*, *28*(2), 143–177.

Ting, C. T., Hsieh, C. M., Chang, H. P., & Chen, H. S. (2019). Environmental consciousness and green customer behavior: The moderating roles of incentive mechanisms. *Sustainability*, *11*(3), 819.

Tsakiridou, E., Boutsouki, C., Zotos, Y., & Mattas, K. (2008). Attitudes and behavior towards organic products: An exploratory study. *International Journal of Retail & Distribution Management*, *36*(2), 158–175.

Wu, S. I., & Chen, Y. J. (2014). The impact of green marketing and perceived innovation on purchase intention for green products. *International Journal of Marketing Studies, 6*(5), 81.

Wyss, A. M., Knoch, D., & Berger, S. (2022). When and how pro-environmental attitudes turn into behavior: The role of costs, benefits, and self-control. *Journal of Environmental Psychology, 79*, 101748.

Zhang, Y., Winterich, K. P., & Mittal, V. (2010). Power distance belief and impulsive buying. *Journal of Marketing Research, 47*(5), 945–954.

CHAPTER 16

GREEN WEALTH IN MOTION: LEVERAGING THE SHARING ECONOMY FOR A CIRCULAR FUTURE

Virginija Grybaitė

Faculty of Business Management, Department of Business Technologies and Entrepreneurship, Vilnius Gediminas Technical University, Vilnius, Lithuania

ABSTRACT

Purpose: *The sharing economy epitomises a paradigm shift by advocating for sustainable consumption practices and resource optimisation. This study investigates the critical factors influencing the burgeoning sharing economy.*

Methodology: *Logical analysis and synthesis methods to glean insights from the existing scholarly literature on the sharing economy and the factors impacting its development. The author establish a comprehensive set of indicators categorised into four key domains: technological infrastructure, political and regulatory landscape, economic context, and socio-cultural environment.*

Findings: *A framework of quantifiable indicators encompassing the critical factors necessary for the sharing economy's development. Indicators encompass a comprehensive spectrum, reflecting the influence of technological advancements, economic conditions, socio-cultural factors, and the prevailing political and regulatory environment.*

Implications: *This evaluation considers the principal factors influencing the development and enables comparative analysis between countries based on the conditions fostering the sharing economy.*

Green Wealth: Navigating towards a Sustainable Future
Contemporary Studies in Economic and Financial Analysis, Volume 117, 307–322
Copyright © 2025 by Virginija Grybaitė
Published under exclusive licence by Emerald Publishing Limited
ISSN: 1569-3759/doi:10.1108/S1569-375920250000117016

Limitations: *This study relies on a literature review, which may not encompass all factors affecting the sharing economy, with a possibility that additional factors not addressed in this study could influence the development of the sharing economy. The indicator framework could be expanded or revised in the future based on new research findings.*

Future Research: *Incorporating dynamic analysis would reveal how fluctuations in identified factors affect the sharing economy over time. Expanding the research to more countries could provide a broader understanding of the global sharing economy landscape, potentially investigating regional or city-level factors for contextual insights. Future research could weight indicators based on their relative importance.*

Keywords: Green wealth; sharing economy; sustainable development; CSR; global finance

JEL Codes: D3; E21

1. INTRODUCTION

The current economic paradigm predicated on linear consumption growth is increasingly recognised as unsustainable. Unsustainable resource extraction and consumption patterns within the contemporary global economic paradigm engender significant environmental degradation (Roberts et al., 2023). It is becoming increasingly clear that reducing environmental degradation is the most effective way to address climate change (Zhu et al., 2023). In recognition of these escalating environmental challenges, a growing consensus is emerging among nations that sustainable development represents the only viable long-term solution to meet the needs of the present generation while simultaneously saving resources, protecting the environment and ensuring the well-being of future generations (Dogan & Pata, 2022).

The evolution of the concept of sustainable development can be traced through a series of key documents and events. The following chronological overview summarises the significant milestones in this evolution. The World Commission on Environment and Development published the report 'Our Common Future' in 1987. This report popularised the term 'sustainable development' and defined it as meeting present needs without compromising future generations' ability to meet their own (United Nations, 1987). In 1992, the United Nations Conference on Environment and Development, also known as the Earth Summit, adopted a comprehensive action plan for sustainable development in every area in which humans impact the environment. This comprehensive action plan is known as Agenda 21 (United Nations, 1992). The United Nations Millennium Declaration was established in 2000, containing a statement of values, principles, and objectives for the international agenda for the 21st century, focused on poverty reduction and other social and environmental issues as a step towards achieving sustainable development (United Nations, 2000). In 2002, the World Summit on Sustainable Development took place in Johannesburg, South Africa, to re-examine the sustainable development agenda after 10 years. It resulted in the Johannesburg Plan of Implementation, reaffirming the commitments made in Agenda 21 and setting new targets (United Nations, 2002). In 2012, guiding principles for the future of sustainable development were agreed upon at the Rio+20 Conference, which took place in Rio de Janeiro, Brazil (United Nations, 2012). Finally, in 2015, a comprehensive framework for achieving sustainable development by 2030, addressing social, economic, and environmental challenges was established. This framework, known as the 2030 Agenda for Sustainable Development, includes 17 Sustainable Development Goals (SDGs) with 169 targets. The SDGs cover a broad range of social, economic, and environmental development issues and are aimed at ending poverty, protecting the planet, and ensuring prosperity for all (United Nations, 2015).

However, despite ongoing efforts, recent data from the SDGs Report indicates insufficient progress (United Nations, 2023). This is evidenced by the continued worsening of the climate crisis and the concerning upward trend in greenhouse gas (GHG) emissions. Therefore, greater attention must be paid to environmental protection and the identification of novel ways to reverse the current deterioration in environmental conditions.

In order to mitigate the threat of rapid resource depletion, novel approaches are required to maximise the utility derived from existing resources, potentially enabling a paradigm shift towards a lower overall resource footprint. In this context, the sharing economy presents a significant opportunity to improve societal well-being without a commensurate increase in resource consumption. Schor (2010) noted that humanity faces an environmental crisis that could potentially reshape people's values, perspectives on consumer goods, and lifestyles. Social innovations and new technologies are believed to enhance people's lives while simultaneously preserving the planet.

Hence, it is imperative to advocate for endeavours that foster the mitigation of environmental pollution and promote practices aligned with sustainable consumption.

The methodology entails selecting indicators that delineate the conditions conducive to the sharing economy's success and guarantee its continued growth. This study examines the pivotal factors that drive the expansion of the sharing economy.

The structure of the article is as follows: Section 2 provides a literature review highlighting the environmental benefits of the sharing economy. Section 3 examines the factors influencing the development of the sharing economy. Section 4 outlines the methodology used to investigate the impact of technological, social, economic, and political factors on access to sharing platforms. Section 5 presents the research findings. Finally, the paper concludes with a discussion and summary of the findings.

2. SHARING FOR A SUSTAINABLE FUTURE: HOW THE SHARING ECONOMY BENEFITS THE ENVIRONMENT

It can be observed that numerous authors have identified the positive impact of the sharing economy on the environment and its potential to contribute to the SDGs. The sharing economy is considered beneficial to the environment

(Piscicelli et al., 2018) as it maximises the utilisation of existing resources, leading to potential energy savings, notably through car-sharing and bike-sharing (Heinrichs, 2013; Martin & Shaheen, 2011; Piscicelli et al., 2018). Kathan et al. (2016) emphasise that sharing economy environmental advantages centred on three key aspects: reduced resource deployment, extended product lifespans, and maximised utilisation. In addition, Toni et al. (2018) highlighted that the sharing economy encourages resource efficiency, waste reduction, and decreased consumption, promoting sustainable consumption practices. Furthermore, the advantage of energy savings in the sharing economy is underscored by Curtis and Lehner (2019), Curtis and Mont (2020), and Skjelvik et al. (2017). For instance, the investigation conducted by Skjelvik et al. (2017) on sharing economy services within the transportation sector unveiled their latent capacity for environmental amelioration. Furthermore, the findings elucidated by Zhu et al. (2023) underscore the role of the sharing economy in diminishing carbon emissions and mitigating pollution, thereby conferring environmental advantages. By employing fixed-effect regressions, Dabbous and Tarhini (2021) study reveals a positive connection between the sharing economy and indicators of sustainable economic development and energy efficiency. These findings suggest that the sharing economy represents a significant socio-economic trend with the potential to stimulate progress towards a more sustainable future.

As noted by Rathnayake et al. (2024), the emergence of the sharing economy signifies a potential paradigm shift in resource consumption patterns. The sharing economy facilitates a transition towards a more circular and potentially sustainable future by promoting access over ownership. Furthermore, Atstaja et al. (2022) highlight the interconnectedness between the sharing economy and the circular economy, which emphasises the reuse of goods and extends their lifespan. Atstaja et al. (2022) further argue that sharing practices are integral components of the circular economy and should be implemented on a societal level to achieve strategic national goals, improve social well-being, and enhance the quality of the ecosystem.

In addition, Zhang et al. (2023) recognise that sharing economy is a pathway to an equality-based and sustainable economy. Furthermore, the findings of Chang and Fang (2023) show a positive correlation between the sharing economy and sustainable development. These results align with the conclusions drawn by Govindan et al. (2020), who state that promoting a sharing economy can generate optimal value by facilitating the sharing of underused or completely unused assets.

On the contrary, cost savings can be achieved while generating revenue by renting resources during idle periods. The authors, for example Botsman and Rogers (2010), noted that a significant benefit of the sharing economy lies in the redistribution of goods and services, leading to a reduction in carbon emissions and waste, as opposed to the continual production of new products or services. The findings of the study (Martin & Shaheen, 2011) indicate that car sharing reduces overall GHG emissions, notwithstanding that most households participating in carsharing experience a slight increase in emissions due to gaining access to automobiles; these increases are small. However, the remaining households reduce emissions by shedding vehicles and driving less. Moreover, Schor and Wengronowitz (2017) asserted that sharing is less resource-intensive.

Further strengthening this argument, Kaushal (2018) and Muñoz and Cohen (2017) point out that the sharing economy promotes both sustainable growth and energy efficiency. In addition, Tu et al. (2023) acknowledge that sharing economy offers a range of economic, social, and environmental benefits that align with the three pillars of the 2030 Agenda for Sustainable Development. Böcker and Meelen (2017) and Strulak-Wójcikiewicz and Wagner (2021) concurred upon and added that the sharing economy exhibits synergies with the core dimensions of sustainable development: economic, social, and environmental.

The sharing economy demonstrates significant potential for environmental sustainability, as highlighted by numerous authors. Maximising resource utilisation, reducing waste, and promoting sustainable consumption practices are key advantages. Studies underscore the role of the sharing economy in energy savings, emissions reduction, and mitigating pollution. Additionally, the sharing economy fosters a transition towards a circular economy, emphasising access over ownership and extending product lifespans. It promotes equality-based and sustainable economic models while generating optimal value through resource sharing. Despite some concerns, such as slight emissions increases due to increased access to shared resources, overall, the sharing economy promotes sustainable growth and energy efficiency, aligning with the goals of the 2030 Agenda for Sustainable Development.

3. UNVEILING THE DETERMINANTS OF THE SHARING ECONOMY DEVELOPMENT

A considerable number of authors have examined the factors that have influenced the growth of the sharing economy, with a particular focus on the impact of technological, economic, social, and political factors on the development of the sharing economy. While prior research has explored the influence of individual environmental dimensions, such as technological infrastructure or economic factors, a dearth of studies exists that comprehensively evaluate the determinants influencing the development of the sharing economy. This research gap extends to the assessment of a nation's potential for fostering a thriving sharing economy based on these multifaceted determinants.

The affordability of internet access and innovative digital technologies is a key factor driving the utilisation of sharing economy services, as highlighted by researchers (Delina & Tkáč, 2015; Hosu & Iancu, 2016; Lingaitienė et al., 2022) Burinskienė et al. (2024) further note that the technological infrastructure, comprising high-speed internet connections, enables the sharing platforms to reach a large number of participants. As Sundararajan (2017) observed, the digital confluence was brought about by the advent of wireless broadband, the proliferation of mass-market smartphones, and the emergence of digitalised social networks. These developments in digital technologies have been identified as a significant factor influencing the emergence of the sharing economy. It is evident that individuals who lack Internet access or a smartphone are unable to participate in the sharing economy through digital platforms (Sundararajan, 2017). The development of sharing economy services is contingent upon integrating smart devices and mobile connectivity. Mobile technologies facilitate the rapid and convenient sharing of information and services through interactions with other users via mobile applications or web platforms (Etter et al., 2019). As Cui et al. (2021) noted, 'technological and regulatory innovation' is crucial for sharing economy development. The rapid evolution of digital technologies is fundamentally reshaping human interaction patterns and consumption behaviours. These advancements introduce novel avenues for individuals to connect with one another while simultaneously influencing the nature and types of goods and services consumed (Hosu & Iancu, 2016). Garud et al. (2022) highlight the transformative impact of the sharing economy on the business landscape. The emergence and widespread adoption of digital technologies primarily drive this transformation. It can be argued that a convergence of research suggests that internet accessibility and user behaviour patterns are paramount factors influencing the sharing economy (Apte & Davis, 2019; Baller et al., 2016; Burinskienė et al., 2024; Huckle et al., 2016; Owyang, 2013). This indicates that both the availability of the internet infrastructure and the habits and frequency of internet use are crucial variables in the development and function of the sharing economy.

While acknowledging the significance of technological factors in the sharing economy's development, the researchers also emphasise the role of social factors (Apte & Davis, 2019; Botsman, 2013; Dervojeda et al., 2013; Owyang, 2013; Toni et al., 2018). These factors encompass cultural characteristics, entrepreneurial spirit, attitudes towards sustainable consumption and sharing, a preference for access over ownership, and trust in others. Cultural context emerges as a significant factor influencing the adoption of sharing economy services. National cultures fostering receptiveness towards online activities and peer-to-peer business models are demonstrably more likely to see higher levels of sharing platform adoption (Owyang, 2013). This suggests the strategic importance of sharing economy companies prioritising operating in regions with cultural norms that embrace such models. Furthermore, population density is regarded as a significant factor in the development of the sharing economy. For instance, re-urbanisation, the concentration of people living in large cities, creates opportunities for the exchange of many assets and activities in the sharing economy (Owyang, 2013; Yeganeh, 2021).

It can be argued that the sharing economy depends on the entrepreneurial intentions of numerous micro-entrepreneurs who utilise sharing economy platforms to operate by providing services. The prevalence of entrepreneurial initiatives further fuels the growth of the sharing economy (Rojanakit et al., 2022). Consumer acceptance is a critical factor influencing the growth of the sharing economy. This acceptance is contingent upon user attitudes and behaviours, specifically their comfort level with the sharing business model and their willingness to engage with services offered through sharing platforms (Mont, 2004). Furthermore, according to Bardhi and Eckhardt (2012) and Möhlmann (2015), consumer awareness, the anti-consumption movement, and the transition towards sustainable consumption have had an impact on the popularity of sharing economy services (Möhlmann, 2015). Furthermore, in the context of green and sustainable consumption and consumer awareness, the sharing economy can bring more opportunities (Cohen & Kietzmann, 2014).

Economic factors have also been identified as contributing to the rise of the sharing economy. Dervojeda et al. (2013) and Goudin (2016) posit that economic downturns, government austerity measures, and environmental anxieties have significantly contributed to this new paradigm of resource utilisation. However, Botsman and Rogers (2010) offer a counterpoint, arguing that the sharing economy represents a broader movement extending beyond mere economic crisis response. They emphasise the growing participation of millions who recognise the consequences of overconsumption and are committed to sustainable consumption practices. Low costs significantly influence consumer adoption of sharing economy services, as evidenced by Yildiz and Altan (2023) and Weng et al. (2020). Furthermore, research by Dervojeda et al. (2013), Apte and Davis (2019), Davis et al. (2015), and Parente et al. (2018) identifies lower transaction costs and the influx of venture capital funding as key drivers propelling the growth of the sharing economy.

Furthermore, emphasis must be placed on the significance of the policy and regulatory landscape in fostering the sharing economy's evolution. Fundamental prerequisites such as a robust legal framework, political stability, safeguarded property rights, and streamlined business establishment and operation procedures are pivotal considerations applicable to any business venture, including those within the sharing economy paradigm. Government policies, regulations, and laws can either facilitate or impede the expansion of the sharing economy. As noted by Belarmino and Koh (2020) and Garud et al. (2022), platform-based business models within the sharing economy encounter distinct regulatory challenges. Whereas most digital platforms grapple with legitimacy concerns upon entry, sharing economy platforms face additional complexities. These complexities stem from their facilitation of transactions involving private assets utilised within public infrastructure.

Consequently, regulatory bodies often mandate compliance with regulations designed for traditional businesses offering similar services through established channels. This results in a convoluted regulatory landscape encompassing multiple levels and jurisdictions, often not tailored to the specificities of the sharing economy. This situation stands in stark contrast to the institutional voids encountered by other business models, further exacerbating the difficulties arising from regulatory mismatches. Notable contributions by Vitkovic (2016) and Singharat et al. (2023) highlight the detrimental impact that inadequate governmental oversight may exert on the sharing economy's development, thereby emphasising the necessity for a robust regulatory framework. Hong and Lee (2020) conducted a study on the development of the sharing economy across 90 countries, revealing a positive correlation between higher levels of governmental quality and the magnitude of sharing economy development. The findings of the study indicate that the role of governments is pivotal in fostering the growth of the sharing economy.

The factors listed in Table 16.1 are considered to be key in promoting the development of the sharing economy, increasing social and economic value. The sharing economy has implications for the environment, the economy, and society, so adapting stakeholder cooperation strategies to integrate circularity principles into sharing economy processes has the potential to simultaneously increase environmental, economic and social value.

Table 16.1. Main Factors.

Group of Factors	Description	Authors
Technological factors	Technological infrastructure enabling sharing platforms to reach a large audience; affordability of internet access and innovative digital technologies; integration of smart devices and mobile connectivity	Delina and Tkáč (2015), Hosu and Iancu (2016), Kathan et al. (2016), Lingaitienė et al. (2022), Burinskienė et al. (2024), Sundararajan (2017), Etter et al. (2019), Cui et al. (2021), Baller et al. (2016), Huckle et al. (2016), Owyang (2013); Cui et al. (2021), Chiang et al. (2021)
Social factors	Cultural characteristics, entrepreneurial intentions and prevalence of micro-entrepreneurs, sustainable consumption attitudes, green and sustainable consumption opportunities, preference for access over ownership, trust in others, population density	Hosu and Iancu (2016), Garud et al. (2022), Rojanakit et al. (2022), Mont (2004), Bardhi and Eckhardt (2012), Kathan et al. (2016), Möhlmann (2015), Cohen and Kietzmann (2014), Owyang (2013), Apte and Davis (2019), Botsman (2013), Dervojeda et al. (2013), Toni et al. (2018), Chiang et al. (2021)
Economic factors	Lower transaction costs, venture capital funding, new opportunities in the market, performance of the country's economy	Dervojeda et al. (2013), Goudin (2016), Botsman and Rogers (2010), Yildiz and Altan (2023), Weng et al. (2020), Apte and Davis (2019), Davis et al. (2015), Parente et al. (2018), Chiang et al. (2021)
Political factors	Importance of policy and regulatory landscape: government policies, regulations, and laws are associated with sharing economy development	Garud et al. (2022), Belarmino and Koh (2020), Vitkovic (2016), Hong and Lee (2020), Singharat et al. (2023)

The sharing economy's growth is influenced by diverse factors, including technological, economic, social, and political elements. While technological advancements, such as internet accessibility and mobile connectivity, drive sharing economy usage, social factors like cultural norms and entrepreneurial initiatives also play pivotal roles. Economic downturns and environmental concerns contribute to the rise of the sharing economy, while low costs and venture capital funding further propel its expansion. Policy and regulatory frameworks significantly impact the sharing economy's evolution, with regulatory challenges posing complexities. Governmental oversight is crucial, with higher governmental quality correlating positively with sharing economy development. This underscores the need for a robust regulatory framework to foster the sharing economy's growth effectively. As the sharing economy holds promise for sustainability, but further research is needed to understand how to best encourage the sharing activities through digital platforms.

4. METHODS AND DATA

The author aimed to identify the technological, social, economic, and political factors and develop a regression model. Regression analysis is a statistical

Green Wealth in Motion

technique primarily employed to model the relationship between an independent variable (predictor) and a dependent variable (outcome). This relationship is often characterised by changes in the dependent variable in response to variations in the independent variable. The regression model itself serves as a mathematical function that captures this mapping between the independent and dependent variables. Table 16.2 summarises the various correlation and regression analysis methods used in research on the sharing economy. The research topics encompass the impact of the sharing economy on various aspects: the hospitality industry (the impact on Lithuanian hotels) and sustainability (the relationship between sharing economy use and sustainable development and the environmental impact of sharing economy involvement. Consumer behaviour (factors affecting rental accommodation choices and influence of host attributes on renter purchases), sharing economy usage (factors driving the intention to use sharing economy services), and other impacts. This variety of methods highlights the multifaceted nature of sharing economy research and the different approaches used to analyse its various impacts.

Table 16.2. Sharing Economy Research: Analysis Methods by Research Focus.

Method	Research Aim	Author
Correlation and regression analysis methods	The evaluation of the impact of the sharing economy on Lithuanian hotel business	Srovnalikova et al. (2020)
Pooled ordinary least square (OLS) technique	The assessing of the relationships between the sharing economy uses and sustainable economic development and energy efficiency	Dabbous and Tarhini (2021)
Poisson regression model	To explore the effects of host attributes on renter purchases made on sharing economy platform	Wu et al. (2017)
Least square models (OLS) and quantile regression estimation techniques	To identify factors affecting consumer choices when selecting rental accommodations	Moreno-Izquierdo et al. (2020)
Least squares regression	To assess the factors driving the sharing economy and their relationship with the intention to use sharing economy services	Chiang et al. (2021)
Generalised least squares estimation	To investigate the relationship between gasoline prices and bikeshare usage	Javed et al. (2020)
OLS regression, Bayesian regression model	To explore how the level of involvement in the sharing economy affects CO_2 emissions and the overall environmental performance	Yin et al. (2021)
OLS regression	To conduct a comparative analysis of Airbnb's offerings relative to traditional hospitality services	Gyódi (2017)
Qualitative comparative analysis (fsQCA), regression; Cramer's V	To investigate the factors influencing the overall perception of tourists who utilise peer-to-peer accommodation	Pappas (2018)
OLS and geography weighed regression analysis	To examine the critical factors of spatial distribution of Airbnb in London	Xu et al. (2020)
Multiple linear regression models	To access if sharing economy has an impact on administrative law governance	Xu (2024)
OLS regression	To examine how sharing economy company Airbnb affects local economy	Mao et al. (2018)

One of the prevailing and frequently employed methodologies is the Least Squares method (Bergh et al., 2018; Hong & Lee, 2020; Wang & Nicolau, 2017; Xu et al., 2020); however, it is acknowledged that it has some important limitations, in particular, it is sensitive to the presence of outliers and may not be robust in such cases (Brossart et al., 2011; Issa Ismail & Abdullah Rasheed, 2021) For the purpose of this study, the author have employed the robust least squares (RLS) method to mitigate the influence of outliers. This technique enables the author to construct a model incorporating technological, social, economic, and political factors, thereby investigating their relative significance in fostering the development of sharing activity. For research purposes, variables from Eurostat, the World Bank, Heritage Foundation, and Global Entrepreneurship Monitor databases were collected for 2012–2023. The selection of indicators was based on a literature review with the objective of maintaining a comparable number of indicators within each group and considering data availability. The author compiled a dataset of 15 indicators (Table 16.3) for nine European Union (EU) member states (Croatia, Czech Republic, Estonia, Hungary, Latvia, Lithuania, Poland, Slovakia, and Slovenia) classified as Central and Eastern European (CEE) countries according to the EuroVoc geographical classification system to examine whether they have an impact on the use on sharing economy platform (Airbnb). The author of the dependent variables selected the number of visits to digital sharing platforms for which data were collected from Google Trends. The author selected the data based on correlation coefficients and associated probabilities derived from a constructed matrix of variables, as presented in Table 16.3.

All variables meeting a significance level of $p < 0.05$ (Table 16.3) were included in the constructed regression model. Furthermore, the author employed a RLS approach to establish the relationship between the dependent variable and the regressors. This methodology facilitated the transformation of regression coefficients into a model representing robust estimation, with a particular focus on a class of techniques known as M-estimators.

The author constructed a regression model to ascertain how technological, social, economic, and political variables affect the number of visits to sharing platform.

$$se_t = \beta_0 + \beta_1\ ane_{(t)} + \beta_2\ gd_{(t)} + \beta_3\ iuip_{(t)} + \beta_4\ iuis_{(t)} + \beta_5\ iuif_{(t)} + \beta_6\ unem_{(t)} + u_t$$

where se_t is the dependent variable of the number of visits to digital sharing platforms in the selected countries in year t; β_0 is the intercept; $ane_{(t)}$ is the annual net earnings in selected countries in year t; $gd_{(t)}$ is the GDP per capita in selected countries in year t; $iuip_{(t)}$ is the individuals using the internet for participating in social networks in year t; $iuis_{(t)}$ is the individuals using the internet for selling goods or services in selected EU countries in year t; $iuif_{(t)}$ is the individuals using the internet for finding information about goods and services in the selected EU countries in year t; $unem_{(t)}$ is the total unemployment rate in the selected EU countries in year t; u_t is the random model error; $\beta_1, \beta_2, \beta_3, \beta_4, \beta_5, \beta_6$ are coefficients of elasticity reflect the influence of independent variables on sharing.

Table 16.3. Correlation Matrix.

Groups	The Number of Visits to Sharing Platform	Abbreviation	Statistics	
Technological	Level of internet access	IA	Corr. coefficient	0.6976
			Probability	0
	Mobile-cellular subscriptions	MS	Corr. coefficient	−0.0865
			Probability	0.3736
	Internet use by individuals	IUI	Corr. coefficient	0.5657
			Probability	0
Social	Cultural and social norms	CSN	Corr. coefficient	0.05261
			Probability	0.5887
	Individuals using the internet for participating in social networks	IUIP	Corr. coefficient	0.5429
			Probability	0
	Population density	PD	Corr. coefficient	0.04255
			Probability	0.6619
	Individuals using the internet for finding information about goods and services	IUIF	Corr. coefficient	0.5198
			Probability	0
	Individuals using the internet for selling goods or services	IUIS	Corr. coefficient	0.3038
			Probability	0.0014
Economic	Annual net earnings	ANE	Corr. coefficient	0.5583
			Probability	0
	Total unemployment rate	UNEMP	Corr. coefficient	−0.6451
			Probability	0
	GDP per capita	GD	Corr. coefficient	0.6060
			Probability	0
	R&D expenditure	RD	Corr. coefficient	0.0998
			Probability	0.3042
Political	Business freedom	BF	Corr. coefficient	−0.0021
			Probability	0.9823
	Investment freedom	IF	Corr. coefficient	0.2028
			Probability	0.0353
	Regulatory quality	RQ	Corr. coefficient	0.0754
			Probability	0.4378

The formed regression model is presented below:

$$se_t = -3.0066 + 0.7484\ ane_t + 0.1153\ gd_t + 1.6871\ iuip_t + 0.2275\ iuis_t - 1.2826\ iuif_t - 0.7204\ unem_t$$

The correlation coefficient of the formed regression model is 0.40, and the adjusted R-squared is 0.37.

The p-value for all coefficients is less than the alpha level of 0.05, which indicates that it is statistically significant. The author conducted statistical validity tests. Probability t and probability χ^2 in the test statistics do not indicate significant autocorrelation and heteroskedasticity.

5. RESULTS AND DISCUSSION

The author delivered empirical research to identify the most essential variables for accelerating the sharing economy. The author attempt to assess whether economic, technological, social, and political environmental factors have an impact on the level of use of the sharing economy. To qualitatively assess what factors impact the usage of sharing economy platforms, the author perform a literature review and determine the technological, economic, social, and political variables for the research. The author constructed a regression model. The results of the equation formation show that the most fundamental variables in the usage of the sharing economy platform are annual net earnings, GDP, unemployment rate, and internet users. The present study corroborates earlier research findings, as demonstrated by Lingaitienė et al. (2022), who identified a robust association between the unemployment rate, internet penetration, and the utilisation of sharing economy platforms. Similarly, studies by Bergh et al. (2018) revealed a correlation between the usage of sharing economy services and GDP per capita. Additionally, the investigations conducted by Giovanini (2021) underscored a significant correlation between sharing economy adoption and income levels, highlighting the pivotal roles played by digital infrastructure and regulatory frameworks in fostering the utilisation of sharing economy platforms.

Nonetheless, the study exhibits additional constraints. The author's analysis is confined to a single sharing economy platform, Airbnb, and encompasses only 9 EU countries designated as CEE, utilising a limited set of 15 variables. Extending the study's scope to encompass a more extensive array of countries and sharing economy platforms would be advantageous. Furthermore, the inclusion of a broader spectrum of indicators is recommended, considering the ample availability of statistical data. This approach would enhance the comprehensiveness and generalisability of the findings, thereby contributing to a more robust understanding of the factors influencing sharing economy dynamics across diverse contexts.

While the research is based on a limited number of countries, the findings offer valuable insights for practitioners and policymakers seeking to encourage the adoption of sharing economy activities. This resonates with the long-standing observation that online platforms have facilitated increased accessibility to shared goods and services, fostering a more collaborative consumption landscape.

6. CONCLUSIONS

The unsustainable nature of the current linear consumption model, characterised by resource depletion and environmental degradation, necessitates a paradigm shift towards practices that promote environmental well-being. The concept of sustainable development, as outlined in key documents like the Brundtland Report and Agenda 21, offers a framework for achieving this goal. However, the urgency of the climate crisis demands more effective solutions. The sharing economy emerges as a promising avenue to decouple economic growth from resource consumption, potentially contributing to a more sustainable future. This study investigates the factors that can foster the expansion of the sharing economy, paving the way for a more comprehensive understanding of its potential for environmental sustainability.

The analysis of factors influencing the growth of the sharing economy underscores the interplay of technological, social, economic, and regulatory elements. The literature review reveals that technological advancements, particularly in digital infrastructure and mobile connectivity, play a pivotal role in facilitating the proliferation of sharing economy platforms. Furthermore, social factors contribute significantly to the sharing economy's growth. Researchers emphasise consumer acceptance, which is shaped by attitudes towards sustainable consumption and comfort with the sharing business model. Additionally, economic factors, along with policy and regulatory frameworks, also exert a profound influence on the development of the sharing economy. By comprehensively understanding the complex interplay of these factors, policymakers, businesses, and other stakeholders can create an environment that fosters the responsible and sustainable growth of the sharing economy, thereby maximising its potential to contribute to environmental well-being and social progress.

The study presents empirical research aimed at identifying key variables driving the growth of the sharing economy. Through a literature review and regression analysis, the author investigate the impact of economic, technological, social, and political factors on the utilisation of sharing economy platforms. The results highlight annual net earnings, GDP, unemployment rate, and internet users as fundamental variables influencing sharing economy usage. These findings align with previous studies indicating correlations between economic indicators and sharing economy adoption. Despite its focus on a limited number of countries and variables, the study offers valuable insights for practitioners and policymakers. It underscores the enduring role of online platforms in enhancing accessibility to shared goods and services, suggesting avenues for further research to broaden the scope and depth of understanding in this area.

REFERENCES

Apte, U. M., & Davis, M. M. (2019). Sharing economy services: Business model generation. *California Management Review*, 61(2), 104–131.

Atstaja, D., Koval, V., Grasis, J., Kalina, I., Kryshtal, H., & Mikhno, I. (2022). Sharing model in circular economy towards rational use in sustainable production. *Energies*, 15(3), 939. https://doi.org/10.3390/en15030939

Baller, S., Dutta, S., & Lanvin, B. (2016). *The Global Information Technology Report 2016 Innovating in the Digital Economy*. https://www3.weforum.org/docs/GITR2016/WEF_GITR_Full_Report.pdf

Bardhi, F., & Eckhardt, G. M. (2012). Access-based consumption: The case of car sharing. *Journal of Consumer Research*, 39, 881–889.

Belarmino, A., & Koh, Y. (2020). A critical review of research regarding peer-to-peer accommodations. *International Journal of Hospitality Management*, 84, 102315. https://doi.org/10.1016/j.ijhm.2019.05.011

Bergh, A., Funcke, A., & Wernberg, J. (2018). *Timbro sharing economy index*. https://timbro.se/ekonomi/timbro-sharing-economy-index/

Böcker, L., & Meelen, T. (2017). Sharing for people, planet or profit? Analysing motivations for intended sharing economy participation. *Environmental Innovation and Societal Transitions*, 23, 28–39. https://doi.org/10.1016/j.eist.2016.09.004

Botsman, R. (2013). *The sharing economy lacks a shared definition*. Fast Company.

Botsman, R., & Rogers, R. (2010). *What's mine is yours: How collaborative consumption is changing the way we live*. HarperCollins Business.

Brossart, D. F., Parker, R. I., & Castillo, L. G. (2011). Robust regression for single-case data analysis: How can it help? *Behavior Research Methods*, 43(3), 710–719. https://doi.org/10.3758/s13428-011-0079-7

Burinskienė, A., Grybaitė, V., & Lingaitienė, O. (2024). Sharing economy development: Empirical analysis of technological factors. *Sustainability (Switzerland)*, 16(4), 1702. https://doi.org/10.3390/su16041702

Chang, C. L., & Fang, M. (2023). Impact of a sharing economy and green energy on achieving sustainable economic development: Evidence from a novel NARDL model. *Journal of Innovation & Knowledge*, 8(1), 100297. https://doi.org/10.1016/J.JIK.2022.100297

Chiang, I. P., Lin, P. W., & Yang, W. L. (2021). Exploring the impacts of sharing economy drivers on consumers' usage intention. *Contemporary Management Research, 17*(1), 1–26. https://doi.org/10.7903/CMR.20075

Cohen, B., & Kietzmann, J. (2014). Ride on! Mobility business models for the sharing economy. *Organization and Environment, 27*(3), 279–296. https://doi.org/10.1177/1086026614546199

Cui, L., Hou, Y., Liu, Y., & Zhang, L. (2021). Text mining to explore the influencing factors of sharing economy driven digital platforms to promote social and economic development. *Information Technology for Development, 27*(4), 779–801. https://doi.org/10.1080/02681102.2020.1815636

Curtis, S. K., & Lehner, M. (2019). Defining the sharing economy for sustainability. *Sustainability, 11*(3), 567. https://doi.org/10.3390/su11030567

Curtis, S. K., & Mont, O. (2020). Sharing economy business models for sustainability. *Journal of Cleaner Production, 266*, 121519. https://doi.org/10.1016/J.JCLEPRO.2020.121519

Dabbous, A., & Tarhini, A. (2021). Does sharing economy promote sustainable economic development and energy efficiency? Evidence from OECD countries. *Journal of Innovation & Knowledge, 6*(1), 58–68. https://doi.org/10.1016/J.JIK.2020.11.001

Davis, M. M., Field, J., & Stavrulaki, E. (2015). Using digital service inventories to create customer value. *Service Science, 7*(2), 83–99. https://doi.org/10.1287/serv.2015.0098

Delina, R., & Tkáč, M. (2015). Role of e-business in the perception of ICT impact on revenue growth. *Journal of Business Economics and Management, 16*(6), 1140–1153. https://doi.org/10.3846/16111699.2013.797012

Dervojeda, K., Verzijl, D., Nagtegaal, N., Lengton, M., & Rouwmaat, E. (2013). *The sharing economy accessibility based business models for peer-to-peer markets case study 12 enterprise and industry*. https://ec.europa.eu/docsroom/documents/13413/attachments/2/translations/en/renditions/native

Dogan, A., & Pata, U. K. (2022). The role of ICT, R&D spending and renewable energy consumption on environmental quality: Testing the LCC hypothesis for G7 countries. *Journal of Cleaner Production, 380*, 135038. https://doi.org/10.1016/J.JCLEPRO.2022.135038

Etter, M., Fieseler, C., & Whelan, G. (2019). Sharing economy, sharing responsibility? Corporate social responsibility in the digital age. *Journal of Business Ethics, 159*, 159. https://doi.org/10.1007/s10551-019-04212-w

Garud, R., Kumaraswamy, A., Roberts, A., & Xu, L. (2022). Liminal movement by digital platform-based sharing economy ventures: The case of Uber technologies. *Strategic Management Journal, 43*(3), 447–475. https://doi.org/10.1002/smj.3148

Giovanini, A. (2021). Economia compartilhada e novas formas transnacionais de consumo na era dos unicórnios. *Revista Brasileira de Inovação, 20*, e021003. https://doi.org/10.20396/rbi.v20i00.8657844

Goudin, P. (2016). *The cost of non-Europe in the sharing economy: Economic, social and legal challenges and opportunities*. Publications Office.

Govindan, K., Shankar, K. M., & Kannan, D. (2020). Achieving sustainable development goals through identifying and analysing barriers to industrial sharing economy: A framework development. *International Journal of Production Economics, 227*, 107575. https://doi.org/10.1016/J.IJPE.2019.107575

Gyódi, K. (2017). *Airbnb and Booking.com: Sharing economy competing against traditional firms?* https://www.delab.uw.edu.pl/wp-content/uploads/2017/09/WP_3_2017_K.Gyodi_.pdf

Heinrichs, H. (2013). Sharing economy: A potential new pathway to sustainability. *GAIA – Ecological Perspectives for Science and Society, 22*(4), 228–231. https://doi.org/10.14512/gaia.22.4.5

Hong, S., & Lee, S. (2020). Sharing economy and government. *Journal of Open Innovation: Technology, Market, and Complexity, 6*(4), 177. https://doi.org/10.3390/JOITMC6040177

Hosu, I., & Iancu, I. (2016). *Digital entrepreneurship and global innovation*. https://www.igi-global.com/gateway/book/154306

Huckle, S., Bhattacharya, R., White, M., & Beloff, N. (2016). Internet of things, blockchain and shared economy applications. *Procedia Computer Science, 98*, 461–466. https://doi.org/10.1016/J.PROCS.2016.09.074

Issa Ismail, M., & Abdullah Rasheed, H. (2021). Robust regression methods/a comparison study. *Turkish Journal of Computer and Mathematics Education, 12*(14), 2939–2949.

Javed, B., Giang, A., He, P., Zou, Z., Zhang, Y., & Baiocchi, G. (2020). Boosting the eco-friendly sharing economy: The effect of gasoline prices on bikeshare ridership in three U.S. metropolises. *Environmental Research Letters, 15*, 114021. https://doi.org/10.1088/1748-9326/abbb52

Kathan, W., Matzler, K., & Veider, V. (2016). The sharing economy: Your business model's friend or foe? *Business Horizons, 59*(6), 663–672. https://doi.org/10.1016/j.bushor.2016.06.006

Kaushal, L. A. (2018). The sharing economy and sustainability: A case study of India. *Valahian Journal of Economic Studies*, *9*(2), 7–16. https://doi.org/10.2478/vjes-2018-0013

Lingaitienė, O., Grybaitė, V., & Burinskienė, A. (2022). Core elements affecting sharing evidence from the European Union. *Sustainability*, *14*(7), 3845. https://doi.org/10.3390/SU14073845

Mao, Y., Tian, X., & Ye, K. (2018). *The real effects of sharing economy: Evidence from Airbnb*. https://ecommons.cornell.edu/server/api/core/bitstreams/4f442886-1bd0-4734-8cea-8048a934c98b/content

Martin, E. W., & Shaheen, S. A. (2011). Greenhouse gas emission impacts of carsharing in North America. *IEEE Transactions on Intelligent Transportation Systems*, *12*(4), 1074–1086.

Möhlmann, M. (2015). Collaborative consumption: Determinants of satisfaction and the likelihood of using a sharing economy option again. https://doi.org/10.1002/cb.1512

Mont, O. (2004). *Institutionalisation of sustainable consumption patterns based on shared use*. https://doi.org/10.1016/j.ecolecon.2004.03.030

Moreno-Izquierdo, L., Rubia-Serrano, A., Perles-Ribes, J. F., Ramón-Rodríguez, A. B., & Such-Devesa, M. J. (2020). Determining factors in the choice of prices of tourist rental accommodation, 100632. New evidence using the quantile regression approach. *Tourism Management Perspectives*, *33*. https://doi.org/10.1016/j.tmp.2019.100632

Muñoz, P., & Cohen, B. (2017). Mapping out the sharing economy: A configurational approach to sharing business modeling. *Technological Forecasting and Social Change*, *125*, 21–37. https://doi.org/10.1016/J.TECHFORE.2017.03.035

Owyang, J. (2013). *The three market drivers: Causes for the collaborative economy*. https://web-strategist.com/blog/2013/05/09/the-three-market-drivers-causes-for-the-collaborative-economy/#:~:text=%5BThis%20rising%20behavior%20is%20being%20caused%20by%20three,iconic%20T%20...%20%202%20more%20rows%20

Pappas, N. (2018). *The complexity of consumer experience formulation in the sharing economy*. https://doi.org/10.1016/j.ijhm.2018.08.005

Parente, R. C., Geleilate, J. M. G., & Rong, K. (2018). The sharing economy globalization phenomenon: A research agenda. *Journal of International Management*, *24*(1), 52–64. https://doi.org/10.1016/j.intman.2017.10.001

Piscicelli, L., Ludden, G. D. S., & Cooper, T. (2018). What makes a sustainable business model successful? An empirical comparison of two peer-to-peer goods-sharing platforms. *Journal of Cleaner Production*, *172*, 4580–4591. https://doi.org/10.1016/J.JCLEPRO.2017.08.170

Rathnayake, I., Ochoa, J. J., Gu, N., Rameezdeen, R., Statsenko, L., & Sandhu, S. (2024). A critical review of the key aspects of sharing economy: A systematic literature review and research framework. *Journal of Cleaner Production*, *434*, 140378. https://doi.org/10.1016/j.jclepro.2023.140378

Roberts, H., Milios, L., Mont, O., & Dalhammar, C. (2023). Product destruction: Exploring unsustainable production-consumption systems and appropriate policy responses. *Sustainable Production and Consumption*, *35*, 300–312. https://doi.org/10.1016/j.spc.2022.11.009

Rojanakit, P., Torres De Oliveira, R., & Dulleck, U. (2022). The sharing economy: A critical review and research agenda. *Journal of Business Research*, *139*, 1317–1334. https://doi.org/10.1016/j.jbusres.2021.10.045

Schor, J. B. (2010). *Plenitude: The new economics of true wealth*. Penguin Press.

Schor, J. B., & Wengronowitz, R. (2017). The new sharing economy: Enacting the eco-habitus. In M. J. Cohen, H. Szejnwald Brown, & P. J. Vergragt (Eds.), *Social change and the coming of post-consumer society: Theoretical advances and policy implications* (Vol. 246, pp. 25–42). Routledge.

Singharat, W., Kraiwanit, T., Sonsuphap, R., & Shaengchart, Y. (2023). The sharing economy in a developing economy: The perspective of the leisure business. *Corporate Law and Governance Review*, *5*(2), 27–34. https://doi.org/10.22495/clgrv5i2p3

Skjelvik, J. M., Erlandse, A. M., & Haavardsholm, O. (2017). *Environmental impacts and potential of the sharing economy*. https://norden.diva-portal.org/smash/get/diva2:1145502/FULLTEXT01.pdf

Srovnalikova, P., Semionovaite, E., Baranskaite, E., & Labanauskaite, D. (2020). Evaluation of the impact of sharing economy on hotel business. *Journal of Tourism and Services*, *11*(20), 150–169. https://doi.org/10.29036/jots.v11i20.145

Strulak-Wójcikiewicz, R., & Wagner, N. (2021). Exploring opportunities of using the sharing economy in sustainable urban freight transport. *Sustainable Cities and Society*, *68*, 102778. https://doi.org/10.1016/J.SCS.2021.102778

Sundararajan, A. (2017). *The sharing economy: The end of employment and the rise of crowd-based capitalism*. The MIT Press.

Toni, M., Renzi, M. F., & Mattia, G. (2018). Understanding the link between collaborative economy and sustainable behaviour: An empirical investigation. *Journal of Cleaner Production*, *172*, 4467–4477. https://doi.org/10.1016/J.JCLEPRO.2017.11.110

Tu, Y. T., Aljumah, A. I., Van Nguyen, S., Cheng, C. F., Tai, T. D., & Qiu, R. (2023). Achieving sustainable development goals through a sharing economy: Empirical evidence from developing economies. *Journal of Innovation & Knowledge*, *8*(1), 100299. https://doi.org/10.1016/J.JIK.2022.100299

United Nations. (1987). *Report of the world commission on environment and development*. https://digitallibrary.un.org/record/139811?v=pdf

United Nations. (1992). *AGENDA 21*. http://www.un.org/esa/sustdev/agenda21.htm.

United Nations. (2002). *Report of the world summit on sustainable development: Johannesburg, South Africa, 26 August–4 September 2002*. United Nations. https://digitallibrary.un.org/record/478154?v=pdf

United Nations. (2012). *Outcome document of the United Nations conference on sustainable development*. https://sustainabledevelopment.un.org/futurewewant.html

United Nations. (2015). *Transforming our world: The 2030 agenda for sustainable development United Nations*. https://documents.un.org/doc/undoc/gen/n15/291/89/pdf/n1529189.pdf

United Nations. (2023). *The sustainable development goals report*. https://unstats.un.org/sdgs/report/2023/

United Nations, G. A. resolution 55/2. (2000). *United Nations millennium declaration*. https://www.ohchr.org/en/instruments-mechanisms/instruments/united-nations-millennium-declaration

Vitkovic, D. (2016). The sharing economy: Regulation and the EU competition law. *Global Antitrust Review*, *9*, 78–118.

Wang, D., & Nicolau, J. L. (2017). Price determinants of sharing economy based accommodation rental: A study of listings from 33 cities on Airbnb.com. *International Journal of Hospitality Management*, *62*, 120–131. https://doi.org/10.1016/j.ijhm.2016.12.007

Weng, J., Ying-Che Hsieh., Adnan, M. Z., & Li-Hsiang, Yi. (2020). The motivation for Muslim customers' participation in the sharing economy. *Resources, Conservation and Recycling*, 155. https://doi.org/10.1016/j.resconrec.2019.104554

Wu, J., Ma, P., & Xie, K. L. (2017). In sharing economy we trust: The effects of host attributes on short-term rental purchases. *International Journal of Contemporary Hospitality Management*, *29*(11), 2962–2976. https://doi.org/10.1108/IJCHM-08-2016-0480

Xu, F., Hu, M., La, L., Wang, J., & Huang, C. (2020). The influence of neighbourhood environment on Airbnb: A geographically weighed regression analysis. *Tourism Geographies*, *22*(1), 192–209. https://doi.org/10.1080/14616688.2019.1586987

Xu, J. (2024). Analysis of law-based administrative law governance in the context of the sharing economy. *Applied Mathematics and Nonlinear Sciences*, *9*(1), 1–16. https://doi.org/10.2478/amns-2024-0559

Yeganeh, H. (2021). An analysis of factors and conditions pertaining to the rise of the sharing economy. *World Journal of Entrepreneurship, Management and Sustainable Development*, *17*(3), 582–600. https://doi.org/10.1108/WJEMSD-06-2020-0054

Yildiz, M., & Altan, M. (2023). Exploring consumer motivation to participate in sharing economy. In A. Bexheti, H. Abazi-Alili, L. P. Dana, V. Ramadani, & A. Caputo (Eds.), *Economic recovery, consolidation, and sustainable growth*. ISCBE 2023. Springer Proceedings in Business and Economics.

Yin, W., Kirkulak-Uludag, B., & Chen, Z. (2021). Is the sharing economy green? Evidence from cross-country data. *Sustainability (Switzerland)*, *13*(21), 12023. https://doi.org/10.3390/su132112023

Zhu, J., Lin, N., Zhu, H., & Liu, X. (2023). Role of sharing economy in energy transition and sustainable economic development in China-NC-ND license (http://creativecommons.org/licenses/by-nc-nd/4.0/). *Journal of Innovation & Knowledge*, *8*(2), 100314. https://doi.org/10.1016/j.jik.2023.100314

Zhu, P., Ahmed, Z., Pata, U. K., Khan, S., & Abbas, S. (2023). Analysing economic growth, eco-innovation, and ecological quality nexus in E-7 countries: Accounting for non-linear impacts of urbanisation by using a new measure of ecological quality. *Environmental Science and Pollution Research*, *30*(41), 94242–94254. https://doi.org/10.1007/s11356-023-29017-3

Zhang, C., Tang, L., & Zhang, J. (2023). Identifying critical indicators in performance evaluation of green supply chains using hybrid multiple-criteria decision-making. *Sustainability (Switzerland)*, *15*(7), 6095. https://doi.org/10.3390/su15076095

INDEX

Actual service economy, 92–94
Additional payment for eco-friendly products, provision for, 297
Advanced manufacturing processes, 46
Advertising methods, 240
Aeolian Islands, 29
Agenda 21, 308
Agenda for Sustainable Development (2030), 309
Agricultural/agriculture, 35, 137
  products, 35
  sector, 147
Agriculture methane emissions (AME), 77, 82, 84
Air pollution, 67
Algebraic system, 99
Analysis techniques, 60
Anglo-Saxon model, 19
Anticipated green behaviour intention, 298
Anticipated intention of green behaviour, 298
Apple
  approach, 229
  labour practices, 226–229
  practices, 221
  profit-driven approach, 227
Application Programming Interface (API), 241
Artificial intelligence (AI), 49, 244, 247–248
Artificial neural networks (ANNs), 2, 275, 277
Asian Countries, previous research in, 68–71
Association of Southeast Asian Nations (ASEAN), 197
ASEAN-5, 197

bibliometric analysis of scientific literature, 199
case study and results, 199–205
centrality and clustering indices specific for GGM, 209
features and measures per variable of GGM, 210
literature review, 197
systematic review of scientific literature, 197–199
Attitude (A), 252
  of tourism, 248
Augmented reality (AR), 242, 246, 248
Automobiles, 310
Awareness, 299

Balanced scorecard (BSC), 274
Banco Português de Fomento (BPF), 14
Bank for International Settlements (BIS), 185
Banking system, 10
Bibliometric analysis, 197
Big data, 49
Biodiversity, 37
Bioeconomy, 132, 134, 140, 145
  contribution of bioeconomy to gross domestic product, 138–140
  strategy, 132
  TRN and value added from bioeconomy in GDP, 151–152
  TRN generated by, 154
  workforce NPE in, 155
Bitcoin, 190
Black money, 73
Blockchain, 49, 117–118
  blockchain-based smart contracts, 244
  technologies, 113–118, 182, 233, 240

Blue bonds market, 10
Blue economy, 2, 6–7, 11 (*see also* Shadow economy)
  financing case study, 15–18
  literature review of sustainable finance for blue economy state of art, 7–12
  principles and mechanisms of sustainable blue finance, 12–15
  recommendation, 18–19
BlueInvest model, 14
Breusch-Pagan test, 122
Bring Your Own Device (BYOD), 242
Business, 215
  model, 113
  processes, 55
  satisfaction in, 95
  sustainability, 48

Capacity-building initiatives, 16
Carbon emissions, 198, 310
Cashless transactions, 188–189
Central and Eastern Europe (CEE), 134, 316
Central and Eastern European Countries (CEECs), 137
Central bank digital currencies (CBDCs), 185
China's textile sector, 115
Circular economy (CE), 25, 134, 198 (*see also* Bioeconomy)
  adoption, 113, 117, 235
Clean energy transition, 117
Climate change, 6, 24, 30, 35, 49–50, 67, 134, 196, 200, 202
Cloud computing technology, 247
Cluster analysis, 60
Co-actions, 95–96
Co-occurrence map, 51
Co-production, 93, 95, 97
  mathematical model and stability analysis, 97–102
  numerical simulation, 103–104
  satisfaction and co-production in service economy, 94–97
  trajectories of system, 103–104

Cobalt, 222
  mining in DRC, 221, 232–234
Cobalt Blues, 232
Coefficients, 122
Common Agricultural Policy (CAP), 26
Community sectors, 139
Companies, 50, 242, 266
Comparative fit index (CFI), 302
Comparative regression models, 84
Competition market, 92
Conceptuality, 94
Confidence (Co), 252
Confirmatory factor analysis (CFA), 302
Consumers, 296
  acceptance, 312
  behaviour, 112, 315
  engagement, 117
Consumption patterns, 308
Control (C), 252
Convolutional neural networks (CNN), 278
Corporate financial performance (CFP), 277
Corporate governance (CG), 281
Corporate greenwashing, 213 (*see also* Greenwashing)
  application of ethical theories and greenwashing, 222–234
  case study analysis, 220
  case study selection, 220–222
  ethical theories, 213–218
  future directions, 235–236
  greenwashing, 218–219
  literature review, 213
  methodology, 219–220
Corporate practices, misleading eco-friendliness in, 218–219
Corporate responsibility (CR), 214–215, 226
Corporate Social Responsibility (CSR), 214, 260, 274
  actions influence of companies, 281
  case of ML methods, 288
  checking index reliability using ML techniques, 284–285
  construction of CSR index, 284

data description, 280–284
empirical results, 286–288
findings and empirical analysis, 285
literature review, 276–280
methodology and index framework, 284
preliminary analysis and descriptive statistics, 285–286
random forest method, 288–289
results, 289–290
Corporate sustainability, 212
Corporate Sustainability Reporting Directive (CSRD), 261
Correlation analysis, 303–304
Correlation coefficient, 317
Correlation coefficient value, 81
Corruption Index, 72
Cost savings, 310
Cost–benefit analysis (CBA), 274
COVID-19 pandemic, 17, 112, 182, 198, 203, 240–241
Creative destruction, 51
Credit data, 188
Cryptocurrency platforms, 186, 191
Cultural context, 312
Cultural identity, 34

Daily price volatility (DV), 191
Data, 162–166, 300
analysis, 139, 244, 249–254, 300
analytics, 244, 247
cleaning process, 162
collection, 60, 119, 219
description, 280
from financial statements, 282
influence CSR actions of companies, 281
and methods, 135–138
from non-financial statements, 282–284
sources, 162, 166
variables that determine corporate responsibility, 280–281
Debt security, 9
Decision tree, 276
Decision-making guidelines, 235

Deep learning, 276, 286
Dematerialisation, 244
Democratic Republic of Congo (DRC), 220
cobalt mining in, 221, 232–234
Deontological ethics, 213–214, 219, 222, 235
Dependent variable, 122
Descriptive analysis, 76–81
Development indicators, 123
Digital age, 244
Digital convergence, 244
Digital development, 243
Digital marketing, 242
Digital marketplaces, 186
Digital media, 254
Digital payments, 185, 189
Digital revolution, 243
Digital sharing platforms, 316
Digital technologies, 46, 242, 309–310
Digital tourism economy, 243
Digital transformation, 53
Digital trends, 243
Digitisation, 197, 240
Dirty money, 73
Disclosure theory, 161–162
Discrepancy approach, 71
Do No Significant Harm (DNSH), 160
Double materiality, 159
Durbin-Watson test, 122

E-banking, 183
E-commerce, 242
E-tourism, 246
Earth Summit, 308
Eco-friendly products, 299
anticipated intention of green behaviour, 298
environmentally conscious behaviours, 299
intention to purchase organic products, 298–299
literature review, 297
methodology, 300
participants, 300–301

provision for additional payment for, 297
relationships between concepts, 299–300
results, 303
Econometric methods, 277
Economics, 92, 94
   activity, 92, 94, 97
   contribution of bioeconomy to gross domestic product, 138–140
   crisis periods, 135
   development, 75
   downturns, 314
   entity, 92
   factors, 313
   growth, 196
   indicators, 138
   realism, 217–218, 234
   sustainability, 59
   TRN dynamics, 142–145
   value-added evolution, 140–142
Education system, 203
Efficiency, 112
Electronics sector, 198
Emerging Markets and Developing Economies (EMDEs), 161
Emerging technologies, 197
Emissions, 199
Energy costs, 112
Energy crisis, 111
Energy innovation, 2
Energy production and consumption, 2
Energy resources, 35
Energy sources, 116
Energy-efficient systems, 39
Entrepreneurs, 71
Envelope wages in Russia, 71
Environment, 50, 95, 183, 296
   shadow economy on, 67
   sharing economy benefits, 309–311
Environmental, social, and governance (ESG), 38, 159, 274, 276
   benefits and challenges of providing pro bono legal services in, 265–269
   case of ML methods, 288
   checking index reliability using ML techniques, 284–285
   construction of CSR index, 284
   data description, 280–284
   empirical results, 286–288
   factors, 280
   findings and empirical analysis, 285
   importance of pro bono legal services in, 263–265
   literature on ESG risk metrics, 161
   literature review, 276–280
   methodology and index framework, 284
   necessary legal support in, 260–262
   opportunities to develop and improve effectiveness of pro bono legal services, 269–270
   preliminary analysis and descriptive statistics, 285–286
   random forest method, 288–289
   results, 289–290
Environmental attitudes, 299
Environmental concerns, 314
Environmental issues, 68
Environmental Kuznets Curve, 70
Environmental performance, bibliometric analysis of relevant scientific literature on, 50–54
Environmental protection, 2
Environmental sustainability, 59, 214
Environmentally conscious behaviours, 299
Eora database, 111
Equilibrium point, 101
Estimates, 290
Ethical insights, combatting greenwashing with, 213–214
Ethical sourcing, 217–218, 234
Ethical theories, 213–214, 234
   Apple and Foxconn's labour practices, 226–229
   application of, 222
   cobalt mining in DRC, 232
   CR and global economic inequality, 214–215

Index 327

ethical sourcing *vs.* economic realism, 217–218
Nike and sweatshop allegations, 224–226
Rana plaza factory collapse, 222–224
short-term gains *vs.* long-term sustainability, 216–217
stakeholder *vs.* shareholder theories, 215–216
utilitarianism and deontological ethics, 213–214
Volkswagen emissions scandal, 229–231
European Bank for Reconstruction and Development (EBRD), 15
European Commission (EC), 7, 132
European Commission-Directorate General for Research and Innovation (EC-DGRI), 132
European Community, 137
European Countries, previous research in, 71–74
European energy
  crisis, 111, 118
  policies, 111
European industry, 112
European Investment Fund (EIF), 14
European Maritime and Fisheries Fund (EMFF), 14
European policy, 26
European textile brands, sustainability endeavours, 113–118
European textile waste landscape, 110
European Union (EU), 114, 132, 316
  analysing sustainable practices methodology in EU member states, 118–120
  data and methods, 135–138
  economic indicators, 138–145
  EU-27 Member States, 75, 138
  literature review, 134–135
  PCA on textile waste metrics, 120–121

regression analysis findings, 121–123
results, 138
social indicator, 145–147
studies on EU policies in sustainable finance, 159–161
Sustainable Finance Action Plan, 159
TRN and value added from bioeconomy in GDP, 151–152
TRN generated by bioeconomy, 154
VAFC, 153
workforce NPE in bioeconomy, 155
Excel software, 76
Exclusion problem, 264
External CSR, 281
External effects, 94–95

Fashion industry, 114, 117
  analysing sustainable practices methodology in EU member states, 118–123
  fashion indexes and blockchain technologies to improve sustainability, 113–118
  spatial analysis findings, 123–125
  sustainability endeavours of two top European textile brands, 113–118
  sustainability review in, 111–113
Fashion Revolution, 117
Fashion sector, 114
Fashion Transparency Index, 117
Fast fashion sector, 111
Financial data, 278
Financial inclusion, 182
Financial innovations, 183
  diagnosis of importance of financial innovations in modern economy, 188–192
  theoretical background, 183–188
Financial institutions, 188
Financial Market Participants (FMPs), 160
Financial materiality, 159
Financial outcomes, 275
Financial performance, 53

Financial services industry, 183, 190
Financial statements, data from, 282
Financial system, 7, 10
Financial technology (FinTech), 49, 182–183, 187, 189
Firm investments, 54
Fixed effect model (FE model), 82
Food, beverage, and tobacco manufacturing (FBT manufacturing), 139–140
Food and Agriculture Organisation (FAO), 135
Foreign direct investment (FDI), 198
Forestry sectors, 147
Foxconn Technology Group, 221
Foxconn's Labour practices, 221, 226–229
Free legal support, 266
Freeman's stakeholder theory, 214

GARCH-type models, 191
Gaussian graphic model, 205
Generalised linear model, 276
Generalised market economy, 95
Genuine CSR, 117
Geopolitical resilience, 117
Global business, 220
Global cobalt, 232
Global economic inequality, 214–215, 224
Global energy consumption, 113
Global fast fashion industry, 113
Global finance, 16
Global market, 115
Global supply chains, 213
Global trade tensions, 112
Global warming, 24
Globalisation, 196
Google Meet, 242
Gradient-boosted trees (GBTs), 288
Green behaviour, anticipated intention of, 298
Green bonds, 48–49
Green products, 297
Green wealth in motion
  methods and data, 314–317
  results, 317–318
  sharing for sustainable future, 309–311
  unveiling determinants of sharing economy development, 311–314
Green Wealth: Navigating Towards a Sustainable Future (book), 1–2
Greenhouse gas (GHG), 113, 309
Greenwashing, 111, 212–215, 218–219, 222, 226–227
  Apple and Foxconn's labour practices, 226–229
  application of, 222–234
  cobalt mining in DRC, 232–234
  combatting greenwashing with ethical insights, 213–214
  confronting, 217–218
  impacts, 236
  Nike and sweatshop allegations, 224–226
  Rana plaza factory collapse, 222–224
  strategies against, 216–217
  Volkswagen emissions scandal, 229–231
Gross domestic product (GDP), 136, 199
  contribution of bioeconomy to, 138–140
  TRN and value added from bioeconomy in, 151–152
Gross National Income (GNI), 161

H&M, 113
Hausman tests, 82, 84
Higg Index, 117
High-high clusters, 124
High-low clusters, 124
Hopf bifurcation, 93, 101
Human waste, 67
Humanity, 1
Hypothesis (H), 248–249
  verification, 253

Impact indicators, 160–161
Impact materiality, 159

Index

Independent variables, 122
India, 115
Inditex, 113
Individual actions, 92
Individual financial instruments, 12
Industrial chemicals, 67
Inflation rate (INFL), 199
Information technology (IT), 49
Innovation, 50, 197
  in technology, 46
Innovative business models, 235
Innovative digital technologies, 311
Intention for purchasing green
    products (IPGP), 298
Intention to purchase organic
    products, 298–299
Interdisciplinary field, 183
Intermediary funds, 14
Internal CSR, 281
International Labor Organization, 68
International tourism, 17
Internet access, 311
Internet economy, 247
Internet of Things (IoT), 49, 243–244,
    246, 248
Italian Gruppo di Azione Locale
    (GAL), 26

J.P. Morgan's ESG (JESG), 165
Judicare' model, 263

Knowledge society, 247

LABFRESH's waste index, 118–119
Labour workforce, 145
Law firms, 266
LEADER programme, 26
Least Developed Countries (LDCs), 8
Least Squares method, 316
Legal education, 264
Legal problem, 264
Legal services, 259
Legitimacy theory, 161
Lending institutions, 188
Linear consumption growth, 308
Linear regression models, 55, 82, 122

Local action group (LAGs), 26
  Tirreno-Eolie derives, 27
  Tirreno-Eolie district, 37
  Tirreno-Eolie framework, 37
Local autonomy, 74
Local development, 30
Logarithmic model, 188
Logistic regression, 276
Long-term sustainability, 213,
    216–217
Low-high clusters, 124
Low-low clusters, 124

M-estimators, 316
Machine learning (ML)
  case of, 288
  checking index reliability using,
    284–285
  techniques, 2, 275, 277
Market economy, 72
Market infrastructure, 187
Market interaction, 92
Market relations, 96
Market-based economy, 71
Mathematical model, 93, 97–102
Matrices, 33
Methane emissions for energy sector
    (MEES), 80, 82
Microsoft Team, 242
Mitigating pollution, 310
Mobile computing technology, 247
Mobile technologies, 312
Model assumptions verification, 122
Model error, 191
Modern economy, diagnosis of
    importance of financial
    innovations in, 188–192

Naive Bayes, 276
Nancial innovation, 187
National Institute of Statistics (NIS),
    136–137
Natural disasters, 38, 203
Natural resources, 24–25
Need for achievement (NA), 252
Neural network (NN), 279

Nike allegations, 221, 224–226
Nike's reform efforts, 224
Non-cooperative tax
  jurisdictions, 172
Non-financial data, 278
Non-financial outcomes, 275
Non-financial statements, data from, 282–284
Non-governmental organisations (NGOs), 259
Non-observed economy, 72
Non-profit legal support, 266
Non-renewable resources, 115
Number of persons employed (NPE), 136–137
  in bioeconomy, 137, 155
Numerical simulation, 103–104

Official Development Assistance (ODA), 16
Official economy, 68
Online banking, 183
Ordinary Least Square (OLS), 75, 82

Panel correlated standard error correction (PCSE), 203
Parallel economy, 72
Partial correlations (PCOR), 203
Particulate matter (PM2. 5), 54
Payment services, 187
Pearson correlation matrix, 56
Pearson's correlation coefficients, 81, 300, 303
Peer-to-peer (P2P), 186, 188
Perceived behavioural control (Cbp), 253
Personal data, 261
Policymakers, 243
Pollutants, 68, 70
Pollution, 38, 69
Pooled OLS method, 59
Portfolio PAI indicators, deterioration of, 169–170
Portfolio weights, 163, 167–169
Positive equilibrium point of system, 103

Post-Covid-19, 17
Potential consumers, 97
Predisposition to risk (RP), 252
Principal adverse impact indicators (PAI indicators), 159
  data, 162–166
  deterioration of portfolio, 169–170
  disclosure theory, 161–162
  exclusion effects, 166–167
  limitations of, 170–173
  literature on ESG risk metrics, 161
  literature review, 159
  methods, 162–166
  PAI portfolio metrics adding exclusion screens step, 178
  portfolio weight changes, 167–169
  results, 166
  studies on EU policies in sustainable finance, 159–161
Principal component (PC1), 120
Principal Component Analysis (PCA), 119
  on textile waste metrics, 120–121
Pro bono activities, 262
Pro bono beneficiaries, 266
Pro bono legal services, 261, 265
  benefits and challenges of providing pro bono legal services in ESG sector, 265–269
  importance in ESG Sector, 263–265
  necessary legal support in ESG sector, 260–262
  opportunities to develop and improve effectiveness, 269–270
Pro bono practice dates, 258
Pro bono service, 267
Pro bono work, 258–259
Pro deo, 258
Productivity-enhancing technologies, 242
Professional attorneys, 258
Promotion, 240
Provision for additional payment for eco-friendly products, 297

Index

Public financing, 16
Public sector services, 68
Public transportation, 37
Public–private partnerships (PPPs), 35

R-square value, 59, 82
Rana Plaza Factory Collapse, 221–224
Random effects model (RE model), 82
Random forest (RF), 275–276, 279, 288–289
Recovery and Resilience Facility (RRF), 14
Recurrent neural networks (RNN), 278
Recyclability, 110
Recycling
  methods, 110
  rates, 110
  waste, 134
Regional bioeconomy promotion strategies, 133
Regression analysis, 71, 314–315
  findings, 121–123
Regression coefficients, 84
Regression models, 59, 121, 205, 316
Regulatory Technical Standards (RTS), 162
Renewable electricity generation sector, 142
Renewable electricity production sector, 144
Renewable energy, 2, 53
  systems, 34
  technologies, 46
Resource efficiency, 117
Resources, 226
Return rate (Rt), 191
Reusable energy technologies, 198
Robo-advisors, 188
Robust least squares (RLS), 316
Romania's economy, 71–72
Routh–Hurwitz criterion, 101
Russia's shadow economy, 71

SARS-CoV-2 virus, 134
Satisfaction in service economy, 94–97
Scopus databases, 50
Scopus-indexed articles, 51
Sectoral analysis, 147
Selective disclosure, 218
Self-confidence (S-C), 252
Service, 94
Service economy, 93, 95
  satisfaction and co-production in, 94–97
Servicity, 95
SeyCCAT, 17
Shadow Economy (SE), 66–67, 71, 74, 76, 81, 82 (*see also* Blue economy)
  case study, 75–76
  descriptive analysis, 76–81
  literature review, 67–68
  previous research in Asian Countries, 68–71
  previous research in European Countries, 71–74
Shapiro-Wilk test, 123
Shareholder theories, 215–216, 226
Sharing economy
  benefits environment, 309–311
  platforms, 318
  services, 313
  unveiling determinants of, 311–314
Short-term gains, 216–217
Significant shift, 110
Simple econometric model, 82
Simple linear regression model, 82
Simple regression models, 55
Skill-building initiatives, 262
Slight emissions, 311
Slow fashion, 117
Small Island Developing States (SIDS), 8
Small-and medium sized enterprises (SMEs), 243
Smart communities, 240
Smart tourism, 246
Smartphone, 311
Social activity, 94
Social assistance system, 72
Social enterprises, 265–266

Social indicator, 145–147
Social innovations, 309
Social issues, 133
Social networks, 263
Social problem, 264
Social return on investment (SROI), 274
Social security, 68
Socio-cultural factors, 299
Socio-economic indicators, 134
South West Indian Ocean Fisheries Governance and Shared Growth Project (SWIOFISH3), 16
Sovereign bonds, 159
Spatial analysis findings, 123–125
Spearman correlation matrix, 56
Stability analysis, 97–102
Stakeholder, 215–216
Start-ups, 266
Stata software, 56
Statistical data, 141
Stock trading apps, 188
Strategy for financing, 14
Students, 241
Subjective norms (SN), 253
Supply chains, 218
Support vector machine, 276
Survey method, 71
Sustainability, 2–3, 7, 25, 31, 111–112, 135, 203, 215–217
    efforts, 214
    endeavours of top European textile brands, 113–118
    fashion indexes and blockchain technologies to improve, 113–118
    review in fashion, 111–113
    theoretical groundings of, 48–50
Sustainable activities, 14
Sustainable approach, 37
Sustainable blue economy, 6
Sustainable blue finance, principles and mechanisms of, 12–15
Sustainable consumption, 297
Sustainable corporate, 38

Sustainable development, 6, 25, 47–48, 132, 183, 308
    bibliometric analysis of relevant scientific literature on, 50–54
    brief literature review, 48
    methodology and research objectives, 54–55
    model, 196
    results, 56–62
    theoretical groundings of technological innovation and sustainability, 48–50
Sustainable economic models, 311
Sustainable economic stake
    mathematical model and stability analysis, 97–102
    numerical simulation, 103–104
    satisfaction and co-production in service economy, 94–97
    trajectories of system, 103–104
Sustainable energy, 114
Sustainable finance, 2
    combinations with most frequent co-occurrences, 10
    description of sample, 8
    literature review of sustainable finance for blue economy state of art, 7–12
    number of publications, 9
    studies on EU policies in, 159–161
Sustainable Finance Action Plan, 158
Sustainable Finance Disclosure Regulation (SFDR), 160
Sustainable futures
    circular economy framework for resource use, 26
    hierarchy AHP on three levels, 32
    LAG Tirreno-Eolie District, 29–30
    LAG Tirreno-Eolie municipalities, 29
    methodological framework, 28
    methods, 27–33
    results, 33–41
Sustainable government policies, 183
Sustainable growth and development, 118
Sustainable Ocean Economy, 12

Index 333

Sustainable practices, 30, 110, 124
Sustainable textile recycling, 110
Sustainable urban ecosystem, 25
Sweatshop allegations, 221, 224–226
Sweden's fiscal services, 74
SWOT framework, 33
Synegoros, 258
Systematic analysis, 197

Tax burden, 68
Tax evasion, 73
Tax on pollution (TP), 82
Technological innovation, 54
   bibliometric analysis of relevant scientific literature on, 50–54
   brief literature review, 48
   theoretical groundings of, 48–50
Technology, 46, 183, 241, 244
Temporal scope, 111–112
Territorial constraints, 34
Territorial development, 39
Textile business model, 115
Textile consumption, 115
Textile exports, 115
Textile industry in Europe, 116
Textile waste, 110, 119, 123
   metrics, 120
   non-impact, 122
   PCA on, 120–121
   production, 119
Tirreno-Eolie boasts, 33
Tourism
   data analysis, 249–254
   drivers of change in, 243
   hypothesis, 248–249
   industry, 76, 242
   research methodology and analysis, 248
   sector, 76
   stakeholders, 242
   theoretical and conceptual context, 243–248
Trade
   flows, 69
   positive and negative effects of, 70
Trading volume, 192

Traditional statistical methods, 276
Transformation, 242
Transparent supply chains, 117
Transport, 198
Transportation networks, 34
Travel agents, 240
Triple bottom line reporting (TBL reporting), 274
Tucker–Lewis index (TLI), 302
Turnover (TRN), 136
   from bioeconomy in GDP, 151–152
   dynamics, 142–145
   generated by bioeconomy, 154

Ukrainian War, 116
Unemployment rate (UR), 199
United Nations Conference on Environment and Development, 308
United Nations Sustainable Development Goals (SDGs), 7, 19, 25, 47, 111, 118, 121–123, 159, 269, 309
   SDG_2021 influence, 122
   SDGs14, 7, 9
Unofficial economy, 72, 74
Unsustainable practices, 38
Unsustainable resource extraction, 308
Urban sustainability, 25
Utilitarianism, 213–214, 219, 222, 235

Value Added at Factors Cost (VAFC), 153
Value co-creation, 95
Value-added (VA), 136
   from bioeconomy in GDP, 151–152
   evolution, 140–142
   products, 132
Value-in-interactional creation, 96
Virtual cryptocurrency system, 186
Virtual currency, 185
Virtual reality (VR), 243, 248
Vital bioeconomy sectors, 135

Volkswagen Emissions Scandal, 217, 221, 229–231
VOSviewer software, 9

Ward method, 60
Waste, 110
   crisis, 118
   management, 35, 119

Water pollution, 67
Wearable technology, 246
Web of Science (WoS), 8, 50, 53, 199
WhatsApp, 242
Worst-scoring issuers, 164–165

Zoom, 241

Printed and bound by CPI Group (UK) Ltd, Croydon, CR0 4YY
10/06/2025